Freedom of Navigation and Globalization

Center for Oceans Law and Policy

Series Editor

Myron H. Nordquist
John Norton Moore

VOLUME 18

The titles published in this series are listed at *brill.com/colp*

Freedom of Navigation and Globalization

Edited by

Myron H. Nordquist
John Norton Moore
Robert C. Beckman
Ronán Long

BRILL

NIJHOFF

LEIDEN | BOSTON

Library of Congress Cataloging-in-Publication Data

Freedom of navigation and globalization / edited by Myron H. Nordquist [and three others].
    pages cm.— (Center for oceans law and policy series ; v. 18)
    ISBN 978-90-04-28407-4 (hardback : alk. paper)—ISBN 978-90-04-28408-1 (e-book) 1. Freedom of the seas. 2. Law of the sea. 3. Piracy—Law and legislation. 4. Maritime terrorism—Law and legislation. 5. Maritime terrorism—Prevention. 6. Merchant marine—Security measures. 7. Security, International. I. Nordquist, Myron H., editor.

KZA1348.F74 2015
341.4'5—DC23

2014032532

This publication has been typeset in the multilingual 'Brill' typeface. With over 5,100 characters covering Latin, IPA, Greek, and Cyrillic, this typeface is especially suitable for use in the humanities. For more information, please see http://www.brill.com/brill-typeface.

ISBN 978-90-04-28407-4 (hardback)
ISBN 978-90-04-28408-1 (e-book)

Copyright 2015 by Koninklijke Brill NV, Leiden, The Netherlands.
Koninklijke Brill NV incorporates the imprints Brill, Brill Nijhoff and Hotei Publishing.
All rights reserved. No part of this publication may be reproduced, translated, stored in a retrieval system, or transmitted in any form or by any means, electronic, mechanical, photocopying, recording or otherwise, without prior written permission from the publisher.
Authorization to photocopy items for internal or personal use is granted by Koninklijke Brill NV provided that the appropriate fees are paid directly to The Copyright Clearance Center, 222 Rosewood Drive, Suite 910, Danvers, MA 01923, USA. Fees are subject to change.

This book is printed on acid-free paper.

Seoul Papers

Freedom of Navigation and Globalization is part of a series of publications on oceans law and policy associated with the Center for Oceans Law and Policy, University of Virginia School of Law. This volume is based on presentations made 2–3 May, 2013, at the Center's 37th Annual Conference which was held in Seoul, Republic of Korea. The primary organizers of the Conference were the Virginia Center and the Korea Maritime Institute. Sponsors were the Centre for International Law, National University of Singapore; the South China Sea Institute, Xiamen University; and the National University of Ireland, Galway. Associate Sponsors were the Ministry of Oceans and Fisheries (Korea); the Korea Institute of Ocean Science & Technology; the Korea Coast Guard; the Faculty of Law, University of Bergen, Norway; and the International Law Department, US Naval War College.

Contents

Introduction   1

Setting the Context: A Globalized World   4
Tommy Koh

PART 1
Counter Piracy Operations—Asia

1   Combating Piracy and Armed Robbery in Southeast Asia: An Evolution in Cooperation   9
Tara Davenport

2   The Small But Magnificent Counter-Piracy Operations of the Republic of Korea   51
Youngjoo CHO

PART 2
Transnational Threats

3   Counter Proliferation Activities and Freedom of Navigation   71
Douglas Guilfoyle

4   Slipping the Net: Why Is It So Difficult to Crack Down on IUU Fishing?   88
Seokwoo Lee, Anastasia Telesetsky, and Clive Schofield

5   Regulation of Private Maritime Security Companies in International Law   120
James Kraska

PART 3
Developments in Arctic Ocean

6 Arctic Council Update   139
   Ernst Nordtveit

7 Communications between the Arctic States and North Pacific Asian States on the Arctic Issues   150
   Jong Deog Kim and Anna Jane Choi

PART 4
Energy Security and Sealanes

8 Institutional Building for Maritime Security in Southeast Asia: The Role of ASEAN   163
   Hao Duy Phan

9 Freedom of Navigation and the Chinese Straight Baselines in the South China Sea   190
   Kuen-chen FU

10 The Cooperative Mechanism in the Straits of Malacca and Singapore   196
   Leonardo Bernard

PART 5
Balancing Marine Environment and Freedom of Navigation

11 European Law and Policy Review: Striking a Balance between Ecosystem Considerations and Navigation Rights under the Marine Strategy Framework Directive, the Law of the Sea Convention and the Draft Directive on Maritime Spatial Planning   221
   Ronán Long

12 Responsibility of Flag States for Pollution of the Marine Environment:
    The Relevance of the UNCLOS Dispute Settlement Regime   257
       Robert C. Beckman

13 Cooperative Environmental Mechanisms for the South
    China Sea   278
       Shichun WU

PART 6
Marine Data Collection

14 Marine Data Collection: US Perspectives   285
       J. Ashley Roach

15 Global Ocean Challenges   303
       Stephen A. Macko

Introduction

On May 2 and 3, 2013, the Center for Oceans Law and Policy (COLP) and the Korea Maritime Institute (KMI) were the primary co-organizers of a conference in Seoul, Republic of Korea, on the theme of Freedom of Navigation and Globalization. Sponsors of the program were the Centre for International Law, National University of Singapore (CIL); the National University of Ireland, Galway; and the South China Sea Institute, Xiamen University, China. Associate Sponsors were the Ministry of Oceans and Fisheries (Korea); the Korea Institute of Ocean Science & Technology; the Korea Coast Guard; the Faculty of Law, University of Bergen, Norway; and the International Law Department, US Naval War College.

We are pleased to present in this volume the papers which resulted from this conference. The opening address was delivered by Professor/Ambassador Tommy Koh, who, among many other things, was the President of the Third United Nations Conference on the Law of the Sea. Tommy emphasizes four pillars of globalization: world environment, international trade, freedom of navigation, and the 1982 Convention on the Law of the Sea (UNCLOS).

Part I focuses on counter piracy operations in Asia with a paper presented by Tara Davenport, at that time with CIL and now a post graduate student at Yale. Tara reports on the co-operative measures taken within the Southeast Asia region to combat piracy and armed robbery against ships. She explores the weaknesses in the international legal regime, examines contemporary practices and their limitations, and urges the need to generate political will to move regional cooperation forward. Next, RADM Youngjoo Cho highlights the historical activities of the Republic of Korea navy in countering piracy and outlines its counter piracy operations in Somalia. He concludes with a review of the lessons learned from the operations and suggests that the real solution is to rehabilitate Somalia as a strong maritime country.

In Part II, Professor Douglas Guilfoyle of University College London addresses counter proliferation activities and freedom of navigation. He notes that attempts to change the positive law dealing with maritime interdiction of Weapons of Mass Destruction (WMD) are limited and perhaps not practical given the difficulties of containing the proliferation of both WMD and conventional weapons by sea. In their paper, three authors—Seokwoo Lee, Anastasia Telesetsky and Clive Schofield—tackle the question of why it is so difficult to crack down on Illegal, Unreported and Unregulated (IUU) fishing throughout the world's oceans. They assess the impact and scale of IUU fishing, review its history and recent developments in detail, and suggest how to crack down on the problem with better incentive structures to protect marine fisheries globally. James Kraska in the next paper explores the regulation of private maritime security companies in dealing with transnational threats. The International Maritime Organization (IMO) mostly deferred to flag States on this issue as well as to ship-owners in authorizing the carriage and use of firearms for use in self-defense, a topic surrounded by legal ambiguity.

The discussion of developments in the Arctic Ocean in Part III includes an update on the activities of the Arctic Council by Professor Ernst Nordtveit of the University of Bergen, Faculty of Law. He describes the organization and work of the Council, the framework of its legal regime, new activities such as navigation in a changing environment, and recent decisions of the Council pertaining to permanent observer status. Jong Deog Kim and Anna Jane Choi of the Strategy Research Division, KMI, look at cooperative measures taken by China, Japan and Korea particularly with respect to science in the Arctic. They conclude with concrete suggestions for enhancing stronger communications between North Pacific Asian States.

The topic of energy security and sealanes is taken up in Part IV of this book. Hao Duy Phan, a Senior Research Fellow at CIL, begins with an examination of institutional building within ASEAN for maritime security in Southeast Asia. His paper's emphasis is on an overview of the activities and initiatives conducted pursuant to the ASEAN maritime security framework including its sectoral bodies. He concludes with recommendations for a stronger framework to strengthen regional cooperation for maritime security to better equip ASEAN to assist its Member States. Professor Kuen-chen Fu of Shanghai Jiao Tong University next compares freedom of navigation and the straight baseline system of China in the South China Sea. He believes there is actually no real issue of freedom of navigation in the South China Sea region today but that China could avoid theoretical obstacles to freedom of navigation in the future by unilaterally establishing internal waters and designating sea lanes to allow transit by foreign vessels and aircraft. Leonardo Bernard, a Research Fellow at CIL, covers the cooperative efforts of Indonesia, Malaysia, and Singapore to enhance navigational safety and environmental protection in the Straits of Malacca and Singapore. He analyzes the work achieved by the littoral States and identifies several challenges in improving the effectiveness of the present cooperative mechanisms.

Part V of this book is addressed to the seminal issue of balancing the protection of the marine environment and freedom of navigation. Professor Ronán Long of the National University of Ireland, Galway, reviews European law and policy which is designed to strike a balance between ecosystem considerations and navigation rights under European Union's (EU) Marine Strategy Framework Directive. The EU Directive applies the ecosystem approach, but given the importance of the interests, the author states that the European Parliament Committee tasked with giving a second reading ought to insert an express provision that provides that EU States are to preserve the freedom of navigation in UNCLOS as such States implement maritime spatial planning and coastal management strategies. The Director of CIL, Robert Beckman, then addresses the issue of whether the dispute settlement regime in UNCLOS and the 2001 International Law Commission (ILC) *Articles on the Responsibility of States for Internationally Wrongful Acts* can be used to hold flag States legally responsible for pollution violations. His thesis is that the provisions of UNCLOS establish clear obligations on flag States with respect to pollution of the marine environment and with the ILC Articles create effective mechanisms for holding errant States responsible for breaches of their international obligations. The last paper in Part IV is by the President of the National Institute for South China Sea Studies, China. Dr. WU evaluates the current mechanisms in the South China Sea marine environment, notes that disputes are an obstacle to cooperation and affirms that freedom of navigation and a healthy marine environment are in the common interest of all States.

Marine Data Collection is covered in Part VI, the final subject dealt with in this volume. Captain J. Ashley Roach, JAGC, USN (retired) discusses what marine scientific research is and identifies what marine scientific research is and is not subject to Part XIII of UNCLOS. Ash spent many years in the US Department of State dealing with his topic and this paper is one of the best reviews available of the various categories and subcategories and their attendant legal consequences. Given the lack of agreed definitions of the various methods for marine data collection, this paper provides important clarifications to promote further understanding. The last paper in the book is distinguished by its scientific focus. Professor Stephen A. Macko, Department of Environmental Studies, University of Virginia, outlines global challenges such as global warming, rising sea level and changes in the ice over in the Polar Regions. He discusses loss of coastal zones, decomposition of methane hydrates, and ocean acidification while deploring the limited base of scientific knowledge.

Conference PowerPoints are available at http://www.virginia.edu/colp/annual-conference.html

Setting the Context: A Globalized World

Tommy Koh

According to our good friend, Myron Nordquist, the theme of this conference is freedom of navigation and globalization. I would like to touch on three points: (i) how globalization has transformed the world we live in; (ii) the freedom of navigation as an enabler of globalization; and (iii) UNCLOS as the guarantor of the freedom of navigation.

Globalized World

A good friend, Kishore Mahbubani, has recently published his fourth book. It is titled, *The Great Convergence: Asia, the West and the Logic of One World*. In the second chapter of the book, Mahbubani argues convincingly that, for the first time in human history, we live in a single interdependent world. Although globalization has its detractors, I hold the view that, on balance, it has done more good than harm. The globalized world has four pillars, namely, the environmental pillar, the economic pillar, the technological pillar and the pillar of common human aspirations.

Four Pillars of Globalization

The fact that we live in one world environmentally is best demonstrated by the threat of global warming and climate change. The problem is real and it cannot be solved by any one country alone. It can only be solved by the collective

---

* Professor Tommy Koh is Ambassador-At-Large at the Ministry of Foreign Affairs, Chairman of the Centre for International Law and Rector of Tembusu College at the National University of Singapore. He is the Co-Chairman of the China-Singapore Forum, the India-Singapore Strategic Dialogue and the Japan-Singapore Symposium. He was Singapore's Permanent Representative to the United Nations in New York for 13 years. He was Ambassador to the United States of America for six years. He was also the President of the Third UN Conference on the Law of the Sea (1981–82). He chaired the Preparatory Committee for and the Main Committee at the Earth Summit. He has served as the UN Secretary General's Special Envoy to Russia, Estonia, Latvia and Lithuania. He was also Singapore's Chief Negotiator for the USA Singapore Free Trade Agreement. He has chaired two dispute panels for the WTO.

action of all the nations of the world. I regret to say that it is not clear whether we will have the political will to agree on a new legally binding agreement to replace the Kyoto Protocol, which expired in 2013. The fact that we live in one world economically was brought home vividly to us when the crisis on Wall Street in 2008 was quickly transmitted across the Atlantic and caused a crisis in Europe and, as a result, the world economy was in danger of going over the cliff. In this regard, the G20, of which South Korea is a member, has played a significant role. Nothing better demonstrates the fact that we live in one world technologically than the power of mobile telephony and the wonders of the information and communication industry. The Internet has made the Korean singer, Psy, into a global icon. We are also united by certain common aspirations, such as, to achieve a decent standard of living, to be treated with humanity and to live under the rule of law.

International Trade Drives Globalization

One of the drivers of the global economy is international trade. Trade has lifted more developing countries out of poverty than foreign aid. Trade has enabled the people of the world to access goods and services no matter where the producers are located. For example, it is because of trade that Samsung Galaxy is sought after by the young people all over the world. It is because of trade that Apple's iPhone and iPad are essentially produced, not in America but, at Foxcom's factories in southern China.

Freedom of Navigation Lifeblood of Shipping Industry

We often forget that over 90 per cent of international trade is sea-borne. It is ships, not aircraft, which carry most of our trade in goods. Shipping takes place within a framework of laws and rules. A fundamental value is freedom of navigation. A ship may safely navigate through the territorial area, contiguous zone and the Exclusive Economic Zone of any coastal State and the high sea in order to arrive at its destination. A ship may enter a port, discharge its cargo and leave. Freedom of navigation is the lifeblood of the shipping industry. It is a global public good. It is in the interests of all countries to uphold it. It is in the interests of no country to interfere with the freedom of navigation. Asian countries are highly dependent on trade for their prosperity. We are therefore a stakeholder in protecting the freedom of navigation.

UN Convention on the Law of the Sea

My third and final point is that the 1982 Convention on the Law of the Sea (UNCLOS) is the authoritative law on the law of the sea. The Convention represents a carefully negotiated package of balances between the rights and interests of the coastal State, on the one hand, and the rights and interests of the international community, on the world. In December 2012, I had the privilege of speaking to the UN General Assembly, on the occasion of the 30th anniversary of the opening for signature of the Convention. There was a consensus that the Convention has served the world well. We agreed that the Convention embodies the modern law of the sea. It has brought order and peace. We should faithfully abide by the Convention. We should refrain from under-mining it by deviating from it in our domestic laws and practices. We should also refrain from adopting a selective approach towards the Convention, i.e., choosing to abide by the provisions we like and ignore those we do not like. As the former President of UNCLOS III, I would like to appeal to all states and to scholars on the law of the sea, to comply faithfully with the Convention. I would also like to express the hope that when states disagree with one another, on the interpretation and application of the Convention, and if such disputes cannot be resolved by negotiation, they will refer such disputes to compulsory arbitration or adjudication under Part XV of the Convention. It is better to settle the disputes peacefully and in accordance with the law than to settle them by other means.

PART 1

Counter Piracy Operations—Asia

∴

CHAPTER 1

Combating Piracy and Armed Robbery in Southeast Asia: An Evolution in Cooperation

Tara Davenport

Over the past seven years, Southeast Asia[1] has managed to divest itself of the dubious honour of having the most pirate-infested waters in the world. This title has now been given to Africa, with reported[2] attacks against vessels in the Horn of Africa numbered at 150 in 2012, the majority of which were committed by Somali pirates.[3] In the same year, Southeast Asia came in a distant second, with 110 reported attacks.[4] This is a far cry from the situation in 2000

---

* Tara Davenport is a Global Associate at the Centre for International Law, National University of Singapore. She is presently pursuing her JSD at Yale Law School. The author's PowerPoint is available at http://www.virginia.edu/colp/pdf/Seoul-Davenport.pdf.

1 For present purposes, the definition of Southeast Asia adopted by the Information Sharing Centre of the Regional Cooperation Agreement on Combating Piracy and Armed Robbery Against Ships in Asia (ReCAAP ISC) will be used. It consists of the waters of the Gulf of Thailand, Indonesia, Malaysia, Myanmar, the Philippines, Singapore, the South China Sea, the Straits of Malacca and Singapore, Thailand and Vietnam.

2 It should be borne in mind that crew and ship owners tend to under-report attacks on vessels for various reasons, including concerns about the delay that investigations may cause and fear of undermining their commercial reputations: See D. Johnson and M. Valencia (eds.), *Piracy in Southeast Asia: Status, Issues and Responses* (Singapore: ISEAS, 2005), xii–xiii. There are two reporting organizations, namely the International Maritime Bureau (IMB) and the ReCAAP ISC. The IMB is a specialized arm of the International Chamber of Commerce and its Piracy Reporting Centre was established in 1992. Its reports cover all the geographical regions in the world and its membership is comprised primarily of private shipping companies. ReCAAP ISC, on the other hand, was established in 2006, and confines its reports to Asia and its members consist primarily of States.

3 International Maritime Bureau, *Piracy and Armed Robbery Against Ships Annual Report, 2012*, at 7.

4 Ibid., at 7. It should be noted that the IMB considers the South China Sea and Vietnam to be part of the Far East and not part of Southeast Asia. However, for the purposes of this article, Southeast Asia also includes the South China Sea and Vietnam. Accordingly, including the actual and attempted attacks that took place in the South China Sea and Vietnam, there were a total of 110 attacks in Southeast Asia.

when reported attacks against vessels in Southeast Asia reached its peak, numbering 257 (in the same year, there were only 61 attacks in Africa).[5]

This reversal in fortune has been primarily attributed to a series of co-operative measures taken by States within and outside the region. This cooperation is viewed as particularly remarkable as Southeast Asia has traditionally been perceived as a region averse to cooperative regimes, especially when it comes to maritime security. In this regard, this article will trace the development of regional cooperation in Southeast Asia to combat piracy and armed robbery against ships. It will examine the reasons why Southeast Asian States have historically been suspicious of cooperative regimes and the factors that motivated these States to cooperate. It will then explore the actual cooperative measures taken and examine the effectiveness of such measures in reducing piracy and armed robbery. Ultimately, this article will argue that while regional cooperation in Southeast Asia has made significant progress, there remains room for improvement.

Section I will discuss definitions of piracy and armed robbery under international law and explore the weaknesses in the international legal regime in dealing with the piracy/armed robbery threat. Section II will examine the development of piracy and armed robbery in Southeast Asia, from its roots to contemporary times. Section III will explore the various aspects of regional cooperation in Southeast Asia and Section IV will discuss current trends and the limitations of existing cooperative regimes. Section V will focus on how to generate sufficient political will so as to move regional cooperation forward.

1   Piracy and Armed Robbery against Ships under International Law

Merchants have been afflicted by pirates as long as ships have sailed the seas and indeed, it has been observed that "the Sumerians, Babylonians, Cretans and Egyptians have all mentioned piracy in their ancient records."[6] Not only has piracy existed for thousands of years, it has also historically plagued geographically diverse regions from Europe, the Americas, the Middle East, Africa and Asia.[7] The idea that pirates are *hostis humani generis*, i.e. enemies of all man-

---

5 International Maritime Bureau (IMB), *Piracy and Armed Robbery Against Ships Annual Report, 2000*, 6.
6 J.A. Wombwell, "The Long War Against Piracy: Historical Trends," Occasional Paper 32 (Combat Studies Institute Press, US Army Combined Arms Center, Fort Leavenworth, Kansas, 2010), 1.
7 Ibid., at 2.

kind, appears to have first emerged in the 14th century and gained traction in the 16th century.[8] Peirino Belli and Alberico Gentili planted the roots of this idea by suggesting that pirates were not entitled to a formal declaration of war before being attacked.[9]

It was the 17th century writings of the famous Dutch jurist Hugo Grotius and his conception of freedom of the seas that provided the most reasoned justification of why pirates were *hostis humani generis* (enemy of mankind).[10] Grotius' conception of freedom of the seas in *Mare Liberum* "was perhaps the most consequential in terms of how states were empowered to act against pirates under the classic law of nations."[11] As expressed by him, freedom of the high seas encompasses the idea that all States have the freedom to navigate the high seas specifically for the purpose of trade and commerce, an activity which benefited all of humanity. Accordingly, interference with free trade caused great suffering to humankind as a whole. Those who did interfere with such trade were *hostis humani generis* and were subject to enforcement through the waging of war. Further, because the high seas were under the jurisdiction of no State, all States had jurisdiction over acts of piracy on the high seas. In other words, "if no public authority exists or if it would fail to prosecute and punish pirates, the *ius gentium* guaranties every single person a private jurisdiction over pirates."[12] The notion that piracy was a threat to freedom of navigation and consequently trade, which rendered pirates *hostis humani generis* subject to the exercise of universal jurisdiction is widely accepted.[13] The definition of piracy, however, was an issue fraught with controversy, as will be explained below.

---

8   See H.D. Gould, "Cicero's Ghost: Rethinking the Social Construction of Piracy," in M.J. Struett, J.D. Carlson and M.T. Nance (eds.), *Maritime Piracy and the Construction of Global Governance* (New York: Routledge, 2013) at 24–30.

9   Ibid., at 30.

10 See generally, M. Kempe, "Beyond the Law: The Image of Piracy in the Legal Writings of Hugo Grotius," in H.W. Blom (ed.), *Property, Piracy and Punishment: Hugo Grotius on War and Booty in De Iure Praedae—Concepts and Contexts* (The Netherlands: Brill, 2009), 379–395.

11 Eric A. Heinze, "A Global War on Piracy? International Law and the Use of Force against Sea Pirates," in M.J. Struett, J.D. Carlson and M.T. Nance (eds.), *Maritime Piracy and the Construction of Global Governance* (New York: Routledge, 2013) at 48.

12 Kempe, *supra* note 10, 386.

13 Gould adopts a constructivist theory as to why pirates were *hostes humani generis*, namely that "calling pirates *hostis humani generis* is an essential part of what makes them *hostis humani generis*—to use the language of Constructivism, it is what constitutes them as enemies of humanity: See Gould, *supra* note 8, 35.

Definition of Piracy

Arguably, the definition of piracy under the 1982 United Nations Convention on the Law of the Sea (UNCLOS)[14] is the most widely accepted.[15] Piracy is defined as:

(a) any illegal acts of violence or detention, or any act of depredation, committed for private ends by the crew or the passengers of a private ship or a private aircraft, and directed:
  (i) on the high seas, against another ship or aircraft, or against persons or property on board such ship or aircraft;
  (ii) against a ship, aircraft, persons or property in a place outside the jurisdiction of any State;
(b) any act of voluntary participation in the operation of a ship or of an aircraft with knowledge of facts making it a pirate ship or aircraft;
(c) any act of inciting or of intentionally facilitating an act described in subparagraph (a) or (b).

If an act falls within the definition of piracy above, UNCLOS affords States certain rights of enforcement against acts of piracy. First, a warship of any flag or other ship in government service has the power to seize on the high seas a pirate ship[16] or a ship under the control of pirates and arrest the persons and seize the property on board.[17] Further, once seized, *"the courts of the State which carried out the seizure may decide upon the penalties imposed, and may also determine the action to be taken with regards to the ships ... or property, subject to third parties acting in good faith."*[18] Second, piracy also affords warships

---

14 United Nations Convention on the Law of the Sea, adopted 10 December 1982, UNTS 1833 (entered into force 16 November 1994).

15 UNCLOS has received widespread acceptance and presently has 166 Parties—see United Nations Treaty Collection at <http://treaties.un.org/Pages/ViewDetailsIII.aspx?&src=TREATY&mtdsg_no=XXI~6&chapter=21&Temp=mtdsg3&lang=en>. Further, the UNCLOS provisions on piracy are based on the provisions found in the 1958 High Seas Convention which codified existing customary international law (See R.R. Churchill and A.V. Lowe, *The Law of the Sea*, 3rd ed. (United Kingdom: Manchester University Press, 1999), 203). These provisions are consequently binding on non-parties.

16 Under Article 103 of UNCLOS, a ship is considered a pirate ship if it is intended by the persons in dominant control to be used for the purpose of committing one of the acts referred to in Article 101. The same applies if the ship has been used to commit any such act, so long as it remains under the control of the persons guilty of that act.

17 Article 105, UNCLOS.

18 Article 105, UNCLOS.

and ships on government service the right of visit. Under Article 110, a warship is entitled to board a foreign ship on the high seas if there are reasonable grounds for suspecting, *inter alia*, that the ship is engaged in piracy.

Even though the definition of piracy in Article 101 of UNCLOS stipulates that acts of piracy can only take place on the high seas, piracy and the associated enforcement rights can take place in the Exclusive Economic Zone (EEZ) as well.[19]

Definition of Armed Robbery against Ships

Piracy under UNCLOS and the accompanying enforcement powers only apply in the high seas and the EEZ, areas purportedly outside territorial jurisdiction. Attacks against vessels which take place in areas under territorial jurisdiction such as ports, internal waters, territorial seas, straits used for international navigation and archipelagic waters are not piracy. Instead, they are classified as "armed robbery at sea." The first official use of the term appears to be in 1983 (just a year after UNCLOS was adopted) when the Assembly of the International Maritime Organization (IMO) adopted Resolution A.545 (13) on "Measures to Prevent Acts of Piracy and Armed Robbery against Ships."[20] It appears, however, that the IMO only defined "armed robbery against ships" in 2001 in its Code of Practice for the Investigation of Crimes of Piracy and Armed Robbery against Ships:[21]

> Any illegal act of violence or detention, or any act of depredation, or threat thereof, other than an act of piracy, committed for private ends and directed against a ship, or against persons or property onboard such ship, within a State's internal waters, archipelagic waters and territorial sea.

These acts are governed solely by the national laws of the coastal State. Only the coastal State can exercise enforcement powers (such as the right to arrest and visit vessels) against vessels suspected of committing these acts in territorial waters. Unlike piracy, no other State has the right to exercise jurisdiction over acts that occur in territorial waters.

---

19 Article 58 (2), UNCLOS.
20 IMO, Assembly, Measures to Prevent Acts of Piracy and Armed Robbery against Ships, Resolution A 13/Res.545 (29 February 1984).
21 IMO Assembly, Annex, Code of Practice for the Investigation of the Crimes of Piracy and Armed Robbery against Ships, Resolution A 22/Res.922 (22 January 2002), paragraph 2.2.

Limitations of Definition of Piracy

While various aspects of the definition of piracy have been subject to scholarly criticism,[22] as will be explained below, the restriction of piracy to the high seas and EEZ is particularly relevant for Southeast Asia and will be the focus of discussion in this section.

The geographical restriction of acts of piracy to the high seas appears to have first been codified in 1926. The League of Nations Committee of Experts for the Progressive Codification of International Law[23] had produced draft Provisions for the Suppression of Piracy[24] in an attempt to codify the international law of piracy. The Draft Provisions had eight articles and assumed that there was a "single conception of what activities constitute the crime of piracy."[25] The provisions, *inter alia*, restricted piracy to the high seas, could only be committed for private (non-governmental) ends, gave every warship the right to interdict a suspected pirate vessel and allowed States to make certain determinations about the status of belligerents.[26] With regard to the restriction of piracy to the high seas, the Draft Provisions observed:

> Piracy has as its field of operation that vast domain which is termed 'the high seas.' It constitutes a crime against the security of commerce on the high seas, where alone it can be committed. The same acts committed in the territorial waters of a State do not come within the scope of international law, but fall within the competence of the local sovereign power.[27]

---

[22] See, for example, L. Azubuike, "International Legal Regime Against Piracy," 15 *Annual Survey of International and Comparative Law*, No. 1, (2009) 43; L. Bento, "Toward an International Law of Piracy Sui Generis: How the Dual Nature of Maritime Piracy Law Enables Piracy to Flourish," 29, *Berkeley Journal of International Law*, No. 2, (2011) 399; R. Collins and D. Hassan, "Applications and Shortcomings of the Law of the Sea in Combating Piracy: A Southeast Asian Perspective," 40 *Journal of Maritime Law and Commerce* (No. 1), (2009), 89.

[23] In 1924, the General Assembly of the League of Nations passed a resolution providing for the establishment of a 17-member committee to select and propose for the first conference on codification of a certain number of subjects within the field of international law. See generally H. Miller, "The Hague Codification Conference," 24 *American Journal of International Law*, No. 4, (1930), 674.

[24] A.P. Rubin, *The Law of Piracy*, 2nd Edition (Irvington-on-Hudson: Transnational Publishers Inc, 1999), 341.

[25] See J. Kraska, *Contemporary Maritime Piracy: International Law, Strategy and Diplomacy at Sea* (United States: ABC-CLIO, LLC, 2011), 117.

[26] Ibid.

[27] Report of the Sub-Committee of the League of Nations Committee of Experts for the Progressive Codification of International Law, League of Nations Document C.196.M.70.1927.V., p. 117.

The Draft Provisions were not put before the League of Nations Codification Conference of 1930 because it was "doubtful whether the question of piracy is of sufficient real interest in the present state of the world to justify its inclusion in the programme of the (proposed conference)" and because there were "difficulties in the way of concluding a universal agreement."[28]

However, the work of the Experts was picked up by a group of scholars who came together to produce the 1932 Harvard Research Draft Convention on Piracy, a proposed treaty consisting of 19 articles. In their commentary to the articles, the drafters of the Draft Convention noted that:

> It suffices here to give advance warning of the great variety in opinions as to the scope of the term and to emphasize the important difference between piracy in the sense of the law of nations and piracy under municipal law. Under the law of many states but not all, there is a crime called piracy. The crime is defined variously so as to include a narrower or a wider range of offences as compared with piracy under the law of nations. Furthermore, even where the range of the municipal crime is relatively narrow and covers categories of offences which in part parallel those of international law piracy, there will be found a lack of coincidence in some characteristics of the offences, e.g. in the place of their occurrence. International law piracy is committed beyond all territorial jurisdiction. Municipal law piracy may include offences committed in the territory of the state. *It is to be noted, then, that piracy under the law of nations and piracy under municipal law are entirely different subject maters and that there is no necessary coincidence of fact-categories covered by the term in any two systems of law* [emphasis added].[29]

Despite noting that there was "no authoritative definition" of piracy,[30] the drafters felt that it was still important to define it because it is "by the law of nations a special, common basis of jurisdiction."[31] Every State participates in a common jurisdiction to capture pirates and their ships on the high seas and to punish and prosecute for piracy persons who lawfully are seized.[32] The purpose of codifying international law on piracy was not to achieve uniformity of national laws but to establish "a limited jurisdiction to be conceded to each

---

28 Rubin, *supra* note 24, 334.
29 Harvard Research in International Law, "Draft Convention on Piracy," *American Journal of International Law*, Vol. 26, No. 1, Supplement: Research in International Law (1932), 741, 749.
30 Ibid., 749.
31 Ibid., 757.
32 Ibid., 782.

State on the basis of the nature of the events constituting piracy and of their non-territorial locality."[33] In other words, the objective of such codification efforts was to define the basis of state jurisdiction over offenses committed by foreign nationals against vessels outside of the territory of the prosecuting state.[34] Based on statutes, judicial opinions and the writings of prominent scholars,[35] Article 3 of the Harvard Draft defined piracy **as any act outside the territorial jurisdiction of a State** that was an:

> act of violence, or of depredation committed with intent to rob, rape, wound, enslave, imprison or kill a person or with intent to steal or destroy property, for private ends without bona fide purpose of asserting a claim of right, provided that the act is connected with an attack on or from the sea or in or from the air.[36]

The Harvard Draft Convention affirmed the geographical restriction of acts of piracy to the high seas on the basis that "the general current of professional opinion supports this limitation."[37] For acts that do not occur in the high seas, the State in whose territory the act is committed would have jurisdiction independently of the Draft Convention and in many cases, other states would have jurisdiction as "under the familiar principles of the law of nations."[38] The Harvard Draft Convention also acknowledged that there were some parts of the world where it was "peculiarly difficult to suppress violence and depredations against commerce in territorial waters" but that special agreements providing for concurrent police jurisdiction may be needed.[39]

This definition of piracy drafted in 1932 was to prove influential and in 1956, the essential elements with some modification[40] were adopted by the International Law Commission (ILC) in its 1956 Draft Articles on the Law of

---

[33] Ibid., 785.
[34] Kraska, *supra* note 25, 115.
[35] Ibid.
[36] Article 3, Harvard Research Draft Convention, *supra* note 29.
[37] Ibid., 788.
[38] Ibid., 789.
[39] Ibid., 790.
[40] For example, unlike the Harvard Research Draft Convention which included an 'intent to rob' as part of the definition of piracy, the ILC considered that the intention to rob is not required as acts of piracy may be prompted by feelings of hatred or revenge and not merely by the desire for gain. See 1956 Draft Articles on the Law of the Sea, Commentary to Article 39, *International Law Commission Yearbook, 1956, Volume II*, 282.

the Sea.[41] The ILC Draft Articles still maintained the high seas requirement on the basis that:

> [t]he Commission considers, despite certain dissenting opinion, that where the attack takes place within the territory of a State, including its territorial sea, the general rule should be applied that it is a matter for the State affected to take the necessary measures for the repression of the acts committed within its territory. In this, the Commission is also following the line taken by most writers on the subject.[42]

The eight provisions on piracy in the ILC Draft Articles[43] formed the basis for Articles 14–21 of the 1958 High Seas Convention, which is widely accepted to reflect customary international law on piracy.[44] In turn, these Articles were incorporated more or less *ad verbatim* into UNCLOS.

The question remains as to whether a definition adopted more than eighty years ago still remains effective today. Indeed, two developments have arguably challenged the wisdom of restricting the definition of piracy (and the accompanying enforcement powers) to the high seas. First, the definition was adopted at a time when piracy attacks on the high seas had significantly waned, as acknowledged by the drafters of both the 1926 Draft Provisions and the 1932 Harvard Research Convention.[45] Today, the increase in global trade has presented an unprecedented opportunity for "pirates" and since the early 1990s, attacks against vessels have been much more widespread than they were in the first half of the nineteenth century.

Second, at the time the definition was adopted, the high seas or "areas outside of territorial jurisdiction" were much larger than today, which meant

---

41 Ibid.
42 Ibid.
43 It should be noted, however, that the ILC did not adopt all the nineteen articles that were in the Harvard Research Draft Convention on Piracy and only eight articles on piracy were included in the ILC Draft Articles. This reportedly was because the ILC only adopted articles which they thought the 1958 Geneva Conference on the Law of the Sea would accept: See M. Murphy, "Piracy and UNCLOS: Does International Law Help Regional States Combat Piracy?" in P. Lehr (ed.), *Violence at Sea: Piracy in the Age of Global Terrorism* (New York: Routledge, 2007), 157.
44 See note 15.
45 For example, the Harvard Research Draft Convention stated "... large scale piracy disappeared long ago and that piracy of any sort on or over the high seas is sporadic except in limited areas bordered by States without the naval forces to combat it." See *supra* note 29, 764.

that universal jurisdiction over piratical acts could be exercised over a wider area. UNCLOS greatly expanded the amount of ocean space under territorial sovereignty by recognizing the rights of States to claim sovereignty over a 12 nautical mile territorial sea, straits used for international navigation as well as archipelagic waters.[46] The exact same act that would constitute piracy is not considered piracy if it occurs in these areas. Only the coastal State has powers of enforcement over these acts and while such a situation may work in States with strong maritime enforcement capacities and associated infrastructure, "weak states leave a fertile ground for pirates."[47] It is reported that between the years of 1989–1993, almost 62% of attacks by pirates occurred in waters under territorial sovereignty usually in territories with inadequate capabilities to control piracy.[48] A prime example of this is of course Somalia, where pirates would flee to Somalia territorial waters after attacking vessels on the high seas/EEZ to avoid arrest by naval forces. As will be explained below, the geographical restriction of piracy waters outside of territorial jurisdiction has also proved problematic for Southeast Asia.

2   The Development of Piracy and Armed Robbery in Southeast Asia

Southeast Asia: Geopolitics and Economic Importance

It has been said that only in the last three decades has the ambiguity over the territorial expanse of "Southeast Asia" been resolved.[49] Historically, Southeast Asia has been characterized by the absence of any unifying hegemonic power caused by different colonial regimes administering different parts of Southeast Asia.[50] After World War II and amidst the prevalent trend of self-determination and independence for colonies, Southeast Asian States achieved independence

---

46   See Parts II, III, and IV of UNCLOS.
47   Bento, *note 22*, 419.
48   B.H. Dubner, "Human Rights and Environmental Disaster—Two Problems that Defy the 'Norms' of International Law of Sea Piracy," 23 *Syracuse Journal of International Law and Commerce* No. 1 (2007), 25–26.
49   It has been suggested that the designation of Southeast Asia was first applied in 1943 to a region that included parts of modern-day South Asia (Sri Lanka and Northeast India) and which excluded the former Netherlands Indies and the Philippines: See L.S. Chia (ed.), *Southeast Asia Transformed: A Geography of Change* (Singapore: ISEAS, 2003), 1.
50   Ibid. The British ruled the former territories of Burma, Malaya, Singapore and Northern Borneo, the Dutch in Indonesia, the Portuguese in East Timor, the Spaniards and Americans in the Philippines, and the French in Laos, Cambodia, and Vietnam. Only Thailand escaped colonial occupation.

beginning with Indonesia in 1945. With the exit of colonial powers in the region, relations between the new governments of Southeast Asia were initially characterized by tension and discord. It was observed that these eight newly independent nations [Singapore was yet to be separated from Malaysia] and Thailand were "drifting into the grip of petty nationalisms and jealousies, complete with border disputes and rivalries among their leaders."[51] Regional relationships were further complicated by the continued dependence of regional countries on extra-regional powers and the super-power Cold War rivalry between the United States and the USSR.[52]

Ultimately, the unification of Southeast Asia and the ten States of Brunei, Cambodia, Indonesia, Malaysia, Myanmar, Laos, the Philippines, Singapore, Thailand, and Vietnam was accelerated by Cold War politics.[53] The creation of the Association of Southeast Asian Nations (ASEAN) in 1967[54] by Indonesia, Malaysia, the Philippines, Singapore, and Thailand[55] "reflected the desire of some of the nations in the region to institutionalize relations among the region's anti-communist states and to provide a forum to address anxieties about the actions of outside powers."[56] Since then, ASEAN has expanded its membership to ten, including Brunei, Vietnam, Laos, Myanmar, and Cambodia.[57] Timor Leste,[58] independent from Indonesia since 2002, and Papua New Guinea[59] have observer status at ASEAN, and both have expressed a desire to join ASEAN as full members.

---

51   A. Acharya, *The Making of Southeast Asia: International Relations of a Region* (Singapore: ISEAS, 2012) at 150, citing the statement of American scholar Albert Ravenholt.
52   Ibid.
53   D.A Desierto, "Postcolonial International Law Discourses on Regional Developments in South and Southeast Asia," 36 *International Journal of Legal Information* (2008), 388 at 418–19.
54   ASEAN was formed through constitutive instruments such as the 1967 ASEAN Bangkok Declaration, Bangkok, Thailand, 8 August 1967 and the 1976 Treaty of Amity and Cooperation in Southeast Asia, Indonesia, 24 February 1976.
55   Singapore, Indonesia, Malaysia, the Philippines, and Thailand became members of ASEAN on 8 August 1967.
56   Chia, *supra* note 12 at 1.
57   Brunei became a member of ASEAN on 8 January 1984, Vietnam on 28 July 1995, Laos and Myanmar on 23 July 1997, and Cambodia on 30 April 1999.
58   "Indonesia supports East Timor ASEAN Membership bid" *Jakarta Globe* (3 March 2011).
59   Luke Hunt, "Papua New Guinea Eyes ASEAN" *The Diplomat* (9 November 2011), online: The Diplomat <http://the-diplomat.com/asean-beat/2011/11/09/papua-new-guinea-eyes-asean/>.

Against this geopolitical backdrop, it is important to bear in mind that Southeast Asia has always been a distinctively maritime region.[60] Indeed, the maritime character of the region has been described as the "first and primary unifying factor of Southeast Asia."[61] Nine out of the ten Southeast Asian States (Brunei, Cambodia, Indonesia, Malaysia, Myanmar, the Philippines, Thailand, Vietnam, and Singapore) are coastal States, and two of these States (the Philippines and Indonesia) are the world's largest archipelagic States. Consequently, most of these States have extensive maritime interests. Further, due to the fact that the region sits astride key access routes between the Indian and Pacific Ocean, the region is also economically and strategically important to the economies of Northeast Asia, the United States, and other Western maritime powers.[62] All ASEAN States, with the exception of Cambodia, are parties to UNCLOS.[63] Both Papua New Guinea and Timor Leste are also parties.[64]

Southeast Asia also "sits astride key access routes between the Indian and Pacific Oceans that are economically and strategically important to the economies of Northeast Asia, the United States and the emerging maritime powers of Asia."[65] Key "chokepoints" which are critical for seabourne trade include the Straits of Malacca and Singapore, the Lombok/Makassar Straits, the Sunda Straits and the Philippine Straits.[66] For example, the most important waterway in Southeast Asia, the Straits of Malacca and Singapore sees more than 70,000 vessels passing through the Straits every year,[67] carrying about 40% of the world's trade.[68] It is has been estimated that this number will increase

---

60 As noted by Bateman, Ho, and Chan, *supra* note 10 at 4.
61 Chia, *supra* note 49, 5.
62 S. Bateman, J. Ho and J. Chan, "Good Order at Sea in Southeast Asia," *RSIS Policy Paper*, April 2009, 11. There are numerous straits used for international navigation in the region including the Straits of Malacca and Singapore, the Lombok/Makassar Straits/Sunda Straits/Philippines Straits. There are also major ports such as Singapore, Port Klang and Tanjung Pelapas in Malaysia and Tanjong Priok in Indonesia.
63 Cambodia signed UNCLOS on 1 July 1983 but has not ratified it.
64 Papua New Guinea ratified UNCLOS on 14 January 1997 and Timor Leste acceded to UNCLOS on 8 January 2013.
65 Bateman et al., *supra* note 62, 11.
66 Ibid., at 10–12.
67 S. Simon, "Safety and Security in the Malacca Strait: The Limits of Collaboration," in *Maritime Security in Southeast Asia: US, Japan, Regional and Industry Strategies*," National Bureau of Research Special Report No. 24, November 2010, 1, 3.
68 "Malacca Strait is a strategic 'chokepoint'," Reuters 4 March 2010 at <http://in.reuters.com/article/2010/03/04/idINIndia-46652220100304>.

to 114,000 ships by 2020.[69] The area is a critical energy route for Japan and China and it is estimated that 15 million barrels per day of oil flow through the Malacca Strait from the Middle East and West Africa, accounting for 90% of Japan's total crude oil imports and 80% of China's crude oil imports.[70] Similarly, approximately US $40 billion dollars' worth of cargo is carried through the Makassar Straits.[71]

Roots of Piracy in Southeast Asia

Scholarly literature has put the first mention of piracy in Southeast Asia in the 5th century based on the writings of Shi Fa-Hsien, a Buddhist Monk from Ceylon who travelled to China and described his fear of attacks from pirates in Straits of Malacca and the South China Sea.[72] However, it must be emphasized that "piracy" as it evolved in Southeast Asia was not "typically considered a rebellion against society and its law" and "was not outside civilization as *hostis humanis generis* but instead incorporated into the laws of society."[73] Instead, "raiding" as it was known, was authorized by local leaders as a way to control maritime trade traversing their waters by demanding taxes or patronage at their ports.[74] It was usually "the most respected warriors and leaders of traditional societies engaged in a competitive prestige system that participated in maritime raiding."[75] On the other hand, illegitimate raiding which was done without consent from local rulers, tended to be more violent and was punished accordingly.[76]

Organized raiding was prevalent during the mid-eighteenth century to the mid-nineteenth century but was significantly affected by the increase in the influence of the colonial powers in the region during that period.[77] The Dutch, British and Spanish colonial powers altered trading patterns and caused radical transformations to the socio-political make-up of the region causing fragmentations to Malay political control, and thus to control over organized raiding. Equally important was the fact that increased European control of the region brought with it a legal system which now defined "legitimate maritime activities,

---

69 Simon, *supra* note 67 at 3.
70 See note 68.
71 Bateman et al., *supra* note 62, 12.
72 A.J. Young, "Roots of Maritime Piracy in Southeast Asia" in D. Johnson and M. Valencia (eds.), *Piracy in Southeast Asia: Status, Issues and Responses* (Singapore: ISEAS, 2005), 7.
73 Ibid., 9.
74 Ibid., 8–11.
75 Ibid., 9–10.
76 Bateman et al., *supra* note 62, 9.
77 Ibid.

in contrast to the rather more flexible and fluid socio-cultural-political systems governing such relations and activities in local polities."[78] The idea that pirates were *hostis humani generis* and the accompanying legal consequences that flowed from that which had taken root in Europe was now being applied in Southeast Asia by the colonial powers. Acts of raiding against British trade was penalized as a criminal act of piracy.[79] Similarly, the Spanish also attacked raiding bases of the Sulu Sultanate and used enforcement against piracy as an excuse.[80] It has been said that "piracy provided an excuse or justification for foreign powers to extend their influence onto Southeast Asian territory."[81] As noted by Ong-Webb:

> [T]he label "pirate" was assigned by these foreign powers so as to render illegitimate what was generally accepted as legitimate activity by the indigenous societies in the same way that Europe during the sixteenth and seventeenth centuries gave such activities—called privateering—official sanction due to the hiring of private vessels by European States for hostile purposes.[82]

Thus began the criminalization or delegitimizing of attacks against vessels. This, accompanied by advanced technology, gunboats and new large steam driven vessels led to a dramatic reduction in acts of piracy/raiding against vessels by the end of the 19th century.[83] While attacks against vessels continued throughout the colonial period, they were much less frequent and of a smaller scale.[84]

1970s–1990s

The mid-twentieth century marked a new dawn for Southeast Asia. As mentioned above, Southeast Asian States were newly independent after World War II. However, the beginning of the Cold War meant that "the issue of piracy was essentially sidelined in importance by the wider East-West ideological

---

[78] Young, *supra* note 72, 14.
[79] Ibid.
[80] Ibid.
[81] Ibid.
[82] G.G. Ong-Webb, "Piracy in Maritime Asia: Current Trends," in P. Lehr, *Violence at Sea: Piracy in the Age of Global Terrorism* (New York: Routledge, 2007), 47.
[83] Robert Beckman, Carl Grundy-Warr and Vivian Forbes, "Acts of Piracy in the Malacca and Singapore Straits," 1 *IBRU Maritime Briefing* (1994), 4.
[84] Ibid.

struggle that was taking place between the super-powers and their respective blocs."[85] There were still attacks against vessels especially during the Malayan Emergency (1948–1960) and during Sukarno's policy of "Konfrantasi" against the newly established Malaysian Federation between 1963 and 1966. Such attacks were apparently "condoned" by the Indonesian government. In addition, in the 1970s, there were a significant number of attacks against the Vietnamese boat people fleeing the communist regime in Indochina reportedly by Malaysian and Thai pirates.[86] With the exception of attacks against the Vietnamese boat people, attacks against vessels during the 1970s were small-scale and did not involve physical injuries to crew.[87]

In the 1980s, attacks against vessels began to steadily increase, the majority in the Straits of Malacca and Singapore, and "concern was being expressed both by shipping interests and by governments."[88] However, the pirate attacks in the eighties were equated with petty thefts and housebreakings and:

> [t]heir perceived lack of both organization and sophistication reflected motivations that were impulsive and ad hoc in nature when compared to the "large gang" operations on container cargoes by West African pirates during the same time.[89]

1991–2004

However, the number and modus operandi of pirates were to soon change from the 1990s onwards. Near the end of the Cold War, there was a resurgence in attacks against vessels in Southeast Asia and from the 1990s, it "once again emerged as a prominent security problem in Southeast Asia."[90] For example, in 1989, the IMB reported that there were three attacks against vessels in the region.[91] This number rose to 60 in the 1990s,[92] and between 1998 and 2004 attacks against ships (piracy and armed robbery) in Southeast

---

85   Peter Chalk, "Contemporary Maritime Piracy in Southeast Asia," 21 *Studies in Conflict and Terrorism*, No. 1 (1998) 87, 88.
86   Ibid.
87   C. Liss, "Maritime Piracy in Southeast Asia" in *Southeast Asian Affairs 2003* (Singapore: Institute of Southeast Asian Studies, 2004), 55.
88   I.R. Hyslop, "Contemporary Piracy" in E. Ellen (ed.), *Piracy at Sea* (Paris: ICC Publishing, 1989), 3, 12.
89   Ong-Webb, *supra* note 82, 48.
90   Chalk, *supra* note 85, 88.
91   Ibid.
92   Ibid.

Asia were increasing at an alarming rate.[93] In the year 2000, the IMB Annual Report reported that the largest number of attacks in the world took place in Southeast Asia.[94] A total of 257 actual and attempted attacks were reported in Southeast Asia alone, out of 397 attacks worldwide. Indonesian waters were the most dangerous in the world with 117 attacks with the Straits of Malacca experiencing 75 attacks.[95] Between 1997 and 2004, Indonesia consistently saw the most attacks against vessels.[96]

Generally speaking, contemporary maritime piracy attacks in Southeast Asia during this time fall within three broad categories.[97] First, there are *opportunistic hit and run attacks*. Most of these can occur while the vessel is anchored or berthed but can also take place in territorial seas or outside territorial seas. Second, there is *kidnap for ransom* where the master and/or other members of the crew are taken off while the vessel is underway. The third category is *ship hijacking* usually to re-sell the ship or the cargo, the so-called phantom ship phenomenon that constitutes the most serious type of attack in Southeast Asia.[98]

Several trends have been noted during this time. First, there was a general increase in the use of small arms, automatic weapons and other paraphernalia such as knives and sticks.[99] Second, there was an increasing trend of violence towards crewmembers especially with regard to crewmembers being taken hostage.[100] Third, generally, tugboats, bulk carriers, general cargo vessels and container ships were increasingly targets of pirates in Southeast Asia.[101]

During this period, the profile of the pirates tended to be in four general categories:[102]

---

93 Ibid.
94 IMB Annual Report 2000, 4.
95 Ibid.
96 Ong-Webb, *supra* note 89, 54.
97 See Chalk, *supra* note 85, 88. James Kraska and Brian Wilson, "The Pirates of the Gulf of Aden: The Coalition is the Strategy," 43 *Stanford Journal of International Law* 241, 247.
98 "Decision Highlights 'Phantom Ship' Insurance Risk," 4 September 2002 at <http://www.internationallawoffice.com/newsletters/detail.aspx?g=306199f4-7b63-4745-ba6b-c6a5e31302cf>.
99 Ong-Webb, *supra* note 82, 52.
100 Ibid., 59–62.
101 Ibid.
102 Ibid., 76.

1. Hit and run robbers operating in small groups who boarded vessels to steal valuables belonging to the ship or crew and who rarely used violence;
2. Hit and run robbers operating in small groups who tend to employ violence in their attacks;
3. Organized pirate gangs who employ a much higher level of organization and sophistication and "where the use of overwhelming force and violence is expected."[103]
4. Pirates which are part of a secessionist or rebel group such as the Free Aceh Movement in Indonesia and the Abu Sayyaf Group in the Philippines who carry out pirate attacks to finance their insurgency against governments.[104]

Piracy or Armed Robbery?

The majority of attacks that take place in Southeast Asia occur in areas under territorial sovereignty and are therefore armed robbery against ships and not piracy under UNCLOS (see discussion above).[105] Congested coastal geography means that nearly all Southeast Asian waters are enclosed in territorial seas, archipelagic waters, Exclusive Economic Zones, and/or continental shelves.[106] The majority of attacks against vessels in Southeast Asia take place near the coast either when the ships are in port or at anchor, within straits used for international navigation or when they are transiting in the territorial sea.[107] The upper half of the Straits of Malacca and the South China Sea are the only areas in which attacks take place outside of territorial waters, in which case the UNCLOS piracy provisions will apply.[108]

---

103   Ibid.
104   Liss, *supra* note 87, 64.
105   It should be noted that the two reporting agencies the IMB and the ReCAAP ISC do not usually distinguish between piracy and armed robbery in their reports, therefore it is difficult to give statistical evidence that substantiates this statement. However, in 2012, RECAAP for the first time, distinguished between piracy and armed robbery. In 2012, out of 132 attacks against vessels, there were 7 incidents of piracy which occurred in the South China Sea and 125 incidents of armed robbery against ships, which is consistent with historical understandings of the nature of attacks in Southeast Asia.
106   Bateman et al., *supra* note 62, 8.
107   R. Beckman, "The 1988 SUA Convention and the 2005 SUA Protocol: Tools to Combat Piracy, Armed Robbery and Maritime Terrorism," 2 *Maritime Affairs*, No. 2, (2006), 1, 2.
108   R. Beckman, "Combating Piracy and Armed Robbery Against Ships in Southeast Asia: The Way Forward," 33 *Ocean Development and International Law* (2002) 317, 326.

General Drivers for Piracy and Armed Robbery against Ships in Southeast Asia

There were several reasons for the spike in attacks against vessels in the period 1998–2004. First and foremost, the 1997 Asian crisis and the overthrow of the Suharto regime in Indonesia "caused rampant unemployment, political instability, tight fiscal policy, and as a result exacerbated poverty throughout Southeast Asia."[109] Inevitably, people in coastal regions turned to piracy as a means to supplement their income.[110] For example, interviews with pirates in Batam revealed that they could make between $13,000–$16,000 Singapore dollars for a successful strike whereas with legal land-based jobs, they would earn $6 Singapore dollars per day.[111]

Second, it has also been said that the independence movement in the Indonesian province of Aceh also played a role in the escalation of attacks against vessels as the rebels in Aceh were reportedly responsible for some of the more serious attacks.[112]

Third, because the majority of attacks against vessels were committed within territorial waters, they were considered "armed robbery against ships" and responsibility for enforcement lay with the coastal States. However, this proved problematic for several reasons.

First, several of the Southeast Asian States had weak enforcement capabilities, which arguably allowed armed robbery against ships to flourish. In particular, the Philippines and Indonesia did not have adequate maritime resources to patrol the wide area under their jurisdiction.[113] In 2004 for example, the Indonesian Navy estimated that it would need 302 warships and 170 aircraft to monitor effectively the country's 17,000 islands.[114]

Second, there were also geographical restrictions which limited effective enforcement. States in the region were hindered by the fact that within their territorial and archipelagic waters, there exist "widely dispersed islands of greater or lesser size, some of which are inhabited, some of which are not" which "makes an ideal environment in which pirates can operate with relative

---

109 J. Dela Pena, "Maritime Crime in the Straits of Malacca: Balancing Regional and Extra-Regional Concerns," *Stanford Journal of International Relations* (Spring 2009), 1, 3.

110 C. Raymond, "Piracy in Southeast Asia: New Trends, Issues and Responses," Working Paper, Institute of Defence and Strategic Studies Singapore, October 2005, 13.

111 E. Freon, "Beyond the Sea: Fighting Piracy in Southeast Asia," RSIS Commentaries, 21 December 2009, 2.

112 IMB Annual Report 2004 at 16.

113 J. Bradford, "The Growing Prospects for Maritime Security Cooperation in Southeast Asia," 58 *Naval War College Review*, No. 3 (Summer 2005), 64, 78–79.

114 Simon, *supra* note 67, 5.

impunity."[115] The Philippines, for example, consists of more than 7,100 islands. Further, the close proximity of neighbouring territorial waters results in pirates using these waters as "de facto sanctuaries" since pirates can escape into a neighbouring State's territorial sea without fear of being pursued.[116]

Third, the myriad of overlapping claims in Southeast Asia, many of which have no maritime boundaries, has also made enforcement more difficult.[117] For example, in the Straits of Malacca and Singapore, while there are some boundaries agreed upon between the littoral States, sections remain undelimited.[118] Similarly, the South China Sea is also the scene of a complex sovereignty and jurisdictional dispute between Brunei, Malaysia, Vietnam, the Philippines, Taiwan and China.[119] Overlapping claims complicate the exercise of enforcement jurisdiction, as any unilateral action runs the risk of exacerbating the dispute and posing a threat to peace and security. At the same time, no enforcement results in a "de facto legal vacuum ... that may be conducive to proliferation of illegal activities."[120]

3   Regional Cooperation to Combat Piracy and Armed Robbery in Southeast Asia

Obligation to Cooperate in the Suppression of Piracy under UNCLOS
Article 100 of UNCLOS provides that "all States shall co-operate **to the fullest possible extent** in the repression of piracy on the high seas or in any other place outside the jurisdiction of any State (emphasis added)." It is interesting to note that the predecessor to this provision in the 1932 Harvard Research Draft Convention was a watered-down version of this obligation. It provided that "the parties to this Convention agree to make **every expedient use** of their powers to prevent piracy, separately and in co-operation."[121] The Commentary to this provision observes that pursuant to this Article, there is only a "general

---

115   S. Davidson, "Dangerous Waters: Combating Maritime Piracy in Asia," 9 *Asian Yearbook of International Law* 3 (2004) at 21.
116   Collins and Hassan, *supra* note 22, 103.
117   See generally T. Davenport, "Southeast Approaches to Maritime Boundaries," *Asian Journal of International Law* (2013), 1–49.
118   Ibid., 37–38.
119   Ibid., 38–39.
120   I. Papanicolopulu, "Enforcement Action in Contested Waters: The Legal Regime," at <http://www.gmat.unsw.edu.au/ablos/ABLOS10Folder/S7P2-P.pdf>.
121   Harvard Research Draft Convention, *supra* note 29, 741.

discretionary obligation to discourage piracy by exercising their rights of prevention and punishment as far as is expedient"[122]

In contrast, the equivalent article in the 1956 ILC Draft Articles which, as mentioned above, formed the basis of the 1958 High Seas Convention and UNCLOS, noted in its commentary that:

> Any State having an opportunity of taking measures against piracy, and neglecting to do so, would be failing in a duty laid upon it by international law. Obviously, the State must be allowed a certain latitude as to the measures it should take to this end in any individual case.[123]

Indeed, although UNCLOS does not address the specific obligations entailed in the duty to co-operate, it has been argued that Article 100 should be interpreted broadly due to the phrase "fullest extent possible."[124] Judge Wolfrum, for example, argues that Article 100 addresses three levels of cooperation: cooperation in general, cooperation in a particular region and cooperation to act against a particular incident of piracy.[125] With regard to the last point, Judge Wolfrum has argued that "a ship entitled to intervene in cases of piracy may not, without good justification, turn a blind eye to such acts," and went on to suggest that States permitting piracy activities may be subject to countermeasures and to an intervention by the Security Council.[126] Other scholars have argued that at the very minimum, compliance with Article 100 "would require sincere, concerted and proactive efforts to cooperate internationally in the repression of maritime piracy."[127]

It should be borne in mind that there is no equivalent duty to suppress armed robbery at sea in territorial waters.

---

122   Ibid., 867.
123   1956 ILC Draft Articles on the Law of the Sea, *supra* note 40, 282.
124   Y. Gottlieb, "Combating Maritime Piracy: Interdisciplinary Cooperation and Information-Sharing," 47 *Case Western Journal of International Law* 2014, forthcoming. Available at SSRN: <http://ssrn.com/abstract=2325279 or http://dx.doi.org/10.2139/ssrn.2325279>.
125   R. Wolfrum, "The Obligation to Cooperate in the Fight Against Piracy—Legal Considerations," 116 *Chuo Law Review* (2009) at 89.
126   R. Wolfrum, "Fighting Terrorism at Sea: Options and Limitations under International Law," 5 at <http://www.itlos.org/fileadmin/itlos/documents/statements_of_president/wolfrum/doherty_lectire_130406_eng.pdf>.
127   Gottlieb, *supra* note 124, 8.

Importance of Regional Co-operation in the Suppression of Piracy and Armed Robbery

Notwithstanding the ambiguity in the duty to cooperate under UNCLOS, the importance of regional cooperation to repress piracy is widely recognized. For example, the UN General Assembly in a 2009 Resolution recognized:

> the crucial role of international cooperation at the global, regional, subregional and bilateral levels in combating, in accordance with international law, threats to maritime security, including piracy, armed robbery at sea, terrorist acts against shipping, offshore installations and other maritime interests, through bilateral and multilateral instruments and mechanisms aimed at monitoring, preventing and responding to such threats, the enhanced sharing of information among States relevant to the detection, prevention and suppression of such threats, and the prosecution of offenders with due regard to national legislation, and the need for sustained capacity-building to support such objectives.[128]

It has also been argued that maritime security threats such as piracy and armed robbery require cooperation because such threats are "primarily transnational."[129] The planning and organization of these attacks often take place in one jurisdiction and are committed in another. Further, the victims of such attacks (both the ship and crew) and the perpetrators of such attacks may be from different countries.

In Southeast Asia, recourse to universal jurisdiction over acts of piracy is inherently limited, rendering UNCLOS "a very weak tool for preventing and suppressing attacks on ships in Southeast Asia."[130] This coupled with the weak enforcement capabilities of key Southeast Asian States, geographic restraints and sensitive maritime disputes would seem to underscore the need for operational, legal and capacity-building cooperation among States. However, as will be explained in the next section, Southeast Asian States have traditionally been reluctant to enter into co-operative regimes for a variety of reasons.

Obstacles to Regional Co-operation in Southeast Asia

There are several reasons behind the reluctance of Southeast Asian States to cooperate to suppress piracy and armed robbery against ships. First, as

---

128   United Nations General Assembly Resolution, A/Res/64/71 adopted by the General Assembly on 4 December 2009, at paragraph 69.
129   Bradford, *supra* note 113, 63.
130   Beckman, *supra* note 108, 328.

noted by Beckman, "the countries in Southeast Asia jealously guard their sovereignty and they oppose any suggestions for cooperative regimes which could undermine their sovereignty."[131] As noted by one scholar, "colonial rule, Cold War experiences and frequent attempts by China to export communism all reinforced internal conflict and led the Southeast Asian states to perceive sovereignty as a key element in ensuring regional as well as domestic stability."[132] As mentioned above, the founding aim of ASEAN was to prevent the region's involvement in the great power rivalry occurring during the Cold War. Accordingly, the principle of non-interference in each other's affairs has been a "cardinal principle, and characteristic of ASEAN concord since ASEAN's creation."[133] This sensitivity to sovereignty and the principle of non-interference "are undoubtedly the single most powerful inhibitor of maritime cooperation in Southeast Asia."[134] It has been said that:

> Even cooperative ventures that do not directly undermine sovereignty, such as joint exercises of voluntary information sharing, are viewed with caution lest they lead to creeping infringement. In some cases, reduction of sovereignty seems tantamount to decreased security; in other cases, leaders fear that cooperation might expose to their domestic constituencies problems that they desire to downplay. In yet other cases, national pride and the desire for prestige make governments reluctant to reveal inadequacies to their neighbors.[135]

Second (and linked to the first point), both Malaysia and Indonesia viewed the issue of piracy and armed robbery as a domestic concern to be addressed internally by each State as they deemed fit.[136] After all, the majority of attacks was committed in territorial waters in the Straits of Malacca and Singapore and was committed by Indonesians based in Indonesia.[137]

---

131   R. Beckman, "Piracy and Armed Robbery Against Ships in Southeast Asia" in D. Guilfoyle, *Modern Piracy: Legal Challenges and Responses* (United Kingdom: Edward Elgar, 2013), 15.
132   M. Molthof, "ASEAN and the Principle of Non-Interference," 8 February 2012, at <http://www.e-ir.info/2012/02/08/asean-and-the-principle-of-non-interference/>.
133   R. Ramcharan, "ASEAN and Non-Interference: A Principle Maintained," 22 *Contemporary Southeast Asia*, No. 1 (April 2000), 60, 60. The principle of non-interference has been expressed in a number of key ASEAN documents such as the 1967 Bangkok Declaration, ASEAN's founding document and the 1976 Treaty of Amity and Cooperation.
134   Bradford, *supra* note 113, 73.
135   Ibid.
136   Raymond, *supra* note 110, 35.
137   S. Eklof, "Piracy in Southeast Asia: Real Menace or Red Herring?" *Asia Pacific Journal: Japan Focus*, 5 August 2005, at <http://www.japanfocus.org/-Stefan-Eklof/2370>.

Third, for Indonesia in particular, the attacks against vessels within their waters were a low priority. In their eyes, they had more pressing concerns involving their land-based security including separatist movements and communal strife.[138] The Indonesian Navy was more concerned with illegal fishing on the eastern end of the archipelago than with piracy in the Malacca Strait.[139] Singapore, on the other hand, has always been somewhat of an outlier and has expressed a willingness to co-operate on a regional and extra-regional level.[140]

The Impetus for Regional Co-operation

Notwithstanding the above, from the year 2000 onwards when piracy and armed robbery reached its peak in Southeast Asia, the security situation was dire. From 2004 onwards, Southeast Asian States adopted a series of cooperative measures that were unprecedented in view of their traditional aversion to such co-operative regimes.

The first major factor that provided a significant impetus for regional co-operation in Southeast Asia was the fear of external influence or interference from extra-regional States. The threat to the freedom of navigation of international shipping inevitably sparked the concern of extra-regional States particularly Japan and the United States. As mentioned above, Japan imports 99% of its oil—80% of which travels through the Malacca Strait—and sea-lane security in Southeast Asia was a critical concern for Japan.[141] According to one scholar, "in mid-1990s, Japanese researchers had identified Southeast Asian piracy as a potential threat to Japan, and successfully politicized the issue by bringing it into the policy discourse."[142] There was an increasing perception that Japan was a victim of piracy and that it was one that "disproportionately affected Japanese shipping interests, and more importantly, Japanese people."[143] The 1999 hijacking of the Japanese-owned vessel the *Allondra Rainbow* after leaving Indonesia, and the Japanese crew who were cast overboard and left adrift, galvanized Japanese opinion on the security threat in Southeast Asian waters.[144] Similarly, the United States believed Southeast Asia was a "critical maritime region for commerce, for communication and for resources: three

---

138   Simon, *supra* note 67, 5.
139   Ibid.
140   Raymond, *supra* note 110, 35.
141   J. Manicom, "Japan's Role in Strengthening Maritime Security in Southeast Asia," The National Bureau of Asian Research, NBR Special Report No. 24, November 2010, 33–34.
142   J. Bradford, "Japanese Anti-Piracy Efforts Initiatives in Southeast Asia: Policy Formulation and the Coastal State Responses," 26 *Contemporary Southeast Asia*, No. 3 (2004), 488.
143   Manicom, *supra* note 141, 34.
144   Ibid., 33–34.

vital areas in which the oceans connect our nations.[145] Although the United States does not directly depend on these waterways for its energy needs (most Middle East oil bound for the United States crosses the Atlantic Ocean), other Southeast Asian exports such as manufactured goods and textiles are critical to the United States consumption-based economy.[146]

Coupled with the perception that piracy was a threat to freedom of navigation was the growing fear of maritime terrorism.[147] There was concern that vessels or fixed platforms could be used as targets for terrorists as was done by Al Qaeda in its attack against the *USS Cole* in Yemen in 2000 and the attack against the *Limburg* off Yemen in 2002, as well as the bombing of a Philippine domestic ferry in 2004 by the Abu Sayyaf group in the Philippines.[148] The September 11th attacks against the United States and the 2002 Bali bombings by Jemaah Islamiyah also enhanced concerns of maritime terrorism. In addition, there was an increasing conflation between maritime terrorism and piracy. For example, there was a widespread belief that the GAM who was fighting for the independence of Aceh from Indonesia was committing piratical attacks.[149] The purposes of such attacks were not only to use the revenues from piracy to help finance their insurgency but also to acquire maritime expertise in navigating a big vessel in preparation for an act of terrorism.[150] It was frequently reported, for example, that the attack against a chemical tanker off the coast of Sumatra by ten pirates armed with weapons and very high-frequency radios were actually "terrorists learning to drive a ship and the kidnapping (without any attempt to ransom the officers)" was an attempt to acquire expertise to help terrorists mount a maritime attack.[151] It warrants note that some commentators have argued that the conflation between piracy and maritime terrorism may be a political device "to persuade reluctant developing countries to let maritime powers pursue pirates and terrorists in their territorial and archipelagic waters."[152]

---

145 J. Bradford, "US Strategic Interests and Cooperative Activities in Maritime Southeast Asia," The National Bureau of Asian Research, NBR Special Report No. 24, November 2010, 20.
146 Ibid., at 21.
147 Ong-Webb, *supra* note 82, 83.
148 Ibid.
149 J. Chen, "The Emerging Nexus between Piracy and Maritime Terrorism in Southeast Asia Waters: A Case Study on the Gerekan Aceh Merdeka," in P. Lehr (ed.), *Violence at Sea: Piracy in the Age of Global Terrorism* (New York: Routledge, 2007), 139–140.
150 Ibid.
151 Ong-Webb, *supra* note 82, 86.
152 A.J. Young and M. Valencia, "Conflation of Piracy and Terrorism in Southeast Asia: Rectitude and Utility," 25 *Contemporary Southeast Asia*, No. 2 (August 2003), 269.

The concern about the twin threats of piracy and maritime terrorism prompted proposals of co-operative security initiatives by extra-regional States. For example, after the *Allondra Rainbow* incident, the Japanese proposed joint patrols between the Japanese Coast Guard and Southeast Asian coastal States with the aim of eventually forming a regional Coast Guard force.[153] This proposal was eventually rejected as States remain reluctant about foreign interference in their territorial waters.[154] Similarly, the Regional Maritime Security Initiative (RMSI) was a framework proposed by Admiral Thomas Fargo of the United States Pacific Command for neutral, multilateral security cooperation.[155] The RMSI was initially framed as a voluntary partnership of regional states that shared information and provided early warning to counter transnational threats.[156] However, the RMSI met with great opposition in Malaysia and Indonesia due to incorrect media portrayals that it would enable American forces to patrol the Malacca Straits.[157] Despite the failure of these two proposals, there is no doubt that they highlighted the possibility of extra regional interference with the objective of preserving maritime security if the Southeast Asian States did not do something first.

The second major impetus for cooperation within the region was the listing of the Straits of Malacca and adjacent ports in Indonesia (along with other areas such as Iraq, Lebanon, Somalia and Nigeria) as a 'war-risk area' in 2005 by the Joint War Committee (JWC) of Lloyd's Market Association.[158] These areas were deemed to be at risk from "war, strikes, terrorism and related perils." The decision by the JWC was based on a report by the security consultancy group Aegis Defence Services which reportedly "lumped together the various but distinct security concerns, such as piracy, robbery at sea, hijacking, kidnappings a ransom, civil war and the probability of maritime terrorism.[159] The result of this listing is that insurers raised premiums for vessels transiting through the Malacca Strait. Unsurprisingly, the JWC announcement was met with serious opposition from the shipping community, coastal States as well as the IMB.[160] However, it galvanized in particular the littoral States to take some action to

---

153   Ong-Webb, *supra* note 82, 83.
154   Manicom, *supra* note 141, 35.
155   Dela Pena, *supra* note 109, 5.
156   Ibid.
157   Manicom, *supra* note 141, 36.
158   Beckman, *supra* note 131, 19.
159   B. Thomas, "Malacca Strait a 'war-risk zone'? Lloyds should review its assessment," IDSS Commentaries, 19 August 2005, No. 57 of 2005 at <http://www.rsis.edu.sg/publications/Perspective/IDSS572005.pdf>.
160   Ibid.

reduce the incidences of piracy in Southeast Asia. This will be described in detail in the next section.

Cooperative Measures Adopted in Southeast Asia from 2004 Onwards

New Cooperative Mechanism for the Straits of Malacca

There had always been a limited level of cooperation in the Straits of Malacca and Singapore in relation to safety of navigation.[161] In the 1970s, three Ministerial Meetings between the littoral States were held,[162] whereby *inter alia*, it was agreed that the safety of navigation was the responsibility of the three littoral States; that there was a need for tripartite cooperation on the safety of navigation in the Straits and that a body should be established to coordinate such co-operation; that there should be consultation and cooperation on anti-pollution policy and on compensation for oil damage; and that a Council of Ministers should be established to discuss safety of navigation and marine pollution which should meet annually.[163] In 1975, a group of Experts, which came to be called the Trilateral Technical Experts Group (TTEG), was established. The TTEG met regularly to coordinate policies on the safety of navigation and environmental protection in the Straits.[164] However, the Council of Ministers was never established and after 1976, no ministerial level meetings expressly dealing with cooperation in the Straits were held until August 2005.[165]

After the September 11th attacks against the United States, as mentioned above, there was increasing concern about maritime terrorism and the IMO adopted a series of measures to address the security of ships and ports.[166] There was growing pressure on the littoral States to enhance co-operation particularly on maritime security. In 2004, the IMO Secretariat undertook a study

---

161　For a comprehensive description of this co-operation, please refer to R. Beckman, "The Establishment of a Cooperative Mechanism for the Straits of Malacca and Singapore under Article 43 of the United Nations Convention on the Law of the Sea," in A. Chircop et al., (eds.), *The Future of Ocean Regime-Building: Essays in Tribute to Douglas M. Johnston* (The Netherlands: Martinus Nijhoff, 2009), 233–260. Arguably, this cooperation is mandated by Article 43 of UNCLOS.

162　The first Ministerial Meeting was held in October 1972, the second in February 1975, and the third in February 1977. See Beckman, ibid., 235–236.

163　Ibid.

164　Ibid. For more information, see the Tripartite Technical Experts Group, at <http://www.cooperativemechanism.org.my/index.php?option=com_content&view=article&id=16&Itemid=10>.

165　Ibid.

166　Beckman, *supra* note 131, 17–19.

of vital shipping lanes and gave special attention to the Straits of Malacca and Singapore.[167] The IMO had also planned to sponsor a meeting to be hosted by Indonesia in September 2005 which was intended to provide a unique opportunity for the coastal States, user States and other stakeholders to work to enhance the safety of navigation, environmental protection and overall security in the straits.[168]

However, in August 2005, one month prior to the IMO-sponsored meeting in Jakarta, the foreign ministers of the three littoral States met in Batam to discuss these topics. The Batam Statement of 8th September 2005 issued by the Foreign Ministers of Indonesia Malaysia and Singapore set out the principles for cooperation with user states and other relevant stakeholders with regard to the Straits of Malacca and Singapore. The principles included, *inter alia*, (1) that the littoral States have sovereignty and sovereign rights in the Straits; (2) that the littoral States have primary responsibility over the safety, environmental protection and security of the Straits; and (3) that any measures adopted on these matters must be consistent with international law, including UNCLOS.[169] In addition, the 2005 Batam Statement stipulated that the ministers agreed to establish a TTEG on maritime security. Thereafter, the IMO convened three meetings on the Enhancement of Safety, Security and Environmental Protection in the Straits of Malacca. These meetings took place first in Jakarta, Indonesia in September 2005 followed by a meeting in Kuala Lumpur, Malaysia in September 2006, with the third taking place in Singapore in September 2007. The ultimate outcome of these meetings was the establishment of a new Cooperative Mechanism on the Safety of Navigation and Environmental Protection for the Straits of Malacca and Singapore. The Co-operative mechanism consists of three main components, namely:

1) *The Cooperation Forum* that serves as a platform for dialogue between the littoral States and the international maritime community on issues of common interest in the Straits;
2) *The Project Co-ordination Committee* that coordinated the implementation of Straits projects. These projects are identified and agreed upon through the Cooperation Forum to promote the safety of navigation and environmental protection in the Straits; and

---

167 Note by the Secretary-General, "Protection of Vital Shipping Lanes," IMO Document C93/15 (7 October 2004).
168 Beckman, *supra* note 131, 18.
169 Ibid.

3) *Aids to Navigation Fund* which receives direct financial contributions from the international maritime community to maintain marine navigational aids in the Straits.[170]

The establishment of a cooperative mechanism was described as a "historic breakthrough and landmark achievement in cooperation."[171] However, it is interesting to note that despite maritime security concerns providing an impetus for the mechanism, the cooperative mechanism is limited to measures to enhance safety and environmental protection in the Straits and does not cover maritime security.[172] As noted by Beckman, the littoral States appeared to have decided against using the cooperative mechanism to facilitate cooperation on maritime security,[173] although no explanation has been given for the omission. One can only speculate that there was some reluctance on the part of the States concerned to formalize co-operation on maritime security. Arguably, Article 43 of UNCLOS is only confined to navigational safety and the prevention, reduction and control of pollution from ships, and there is no obligation on Strait States and user States to cooperate on matters of maritime security.

Enforcement-Coordinated Patrols

Although the new cooperative mechanism was limited to safety and environmental protection, the three littoral States have cooperated in other ways to enhance the security of shipping in critical sea lines of communication in Southeast Asia. The Malacca Straits Patrols (MSP), established in 2005 as a direct response to maritime security issues in the region, is Southeast Asia's "only indigenous multilateral military arrangement that is ongoing involving the coast guards, navies, and air forces of the littoral states as well as Thailand (since 2008)".[174] A joint coordinating committee meets twice a year to oversee the MSP and also to facilitate the sharing of intelligence.[175] However, the MSP "is more coordinated than joint, with each country responsible for patrolling its own sector and each ship under national command."[176] Malacca Straits Standard Operating Procedures were agreed upon in 2006 whereby ships in

---

170 See Cooperative Mechanism at <http://www.cooperativemechanism.org.my/index.php?option=com_content&view=article&id=26&Itemid=7>.
171 Ibid.
172 Beckman, *supra* note 131, 19.
173 Ibid.
174 Simon, *supra* note 67, 10.
175 Ibid.
176 Ibid.

the MSP have the right of hot pursuit up to five nautical miles (nm) into the territorial sea of neighboring States.[177]

Another measure adopted under the rubric of the MSP is the "Eyes in the Sky" aerial patrols in the Straits which involve the three littoral States and Thailand.[178] Each flight carries personnel from the participating countries, and while each aircraft could enter each other's territory, the limit was set at 3 nm from the coast.[179] EIS was initially conceived as an open arrangement that may involve the participation of extra-regional countries on a voluntary basis if deemed necessary by the littoral States.[180] However, thus far, this has not been implemented.[181] It is said the EIS patrols do not provide sufficient coverage as it only occurs during the day when most attacks occur under the cover of night and further, the frequency of flights is not enough to patrol the large area needed to be effective.[182]

Regional Cooperation Agreement on Combating Piracy and Armed Robbery against Ships in Asia (ReCAAP)

Arguably, the most significant form of cooperation came when the Regional Cooperation Agreement on Combating Piracy and Armed Robbery against Ships in Asia (ReCAAP) was adopted in 2004.[183] The roots of ReCAAP can be found in Japan's attempt to address piracy in the early part of the 2000s. In January 2002, Prime Minister Koizumi Junichiro put forth "an ambitious multilateral plan to address regional maritime security."[184] The result was ReCAAP which was signed by 16 countries in November 2004 and came into force in September 2006. To date, there are 19 Contracting Parties to ReCAAP, namely Australia, Bangladesh, Brunei Darussalam, Cambodia, China, Denmark, India, Japan, the Republic of Korea, Laos, Myanmar, Netherlands, Norway, Philippines, Singapore, Sri Lanka, Thailand, the United Kingdom and Viet Nam. The European countries (Norway, the Netherlands, Denmark

---

177   Ibid.
178   Ibid.
179   I. Susanti, "Eyes in the Sky patrol over Malacca to start soon," *The Jakarta Post*, Jakarta, 9 September 2005, at <http://www.thejakartapost.com/news/2005/09/09/039eyes-sky039-patrol-over-malacca-start-soon.html>.
180   N. Khalid, "Security in the Straits of Malacca," *The Asia-Pacific Journal: Japan Focus*, 1 June 2006, at <http://www.japanfocus.org/-Nazery-Khalid/2042>.
181   Simon, *supra* note 67, 10.
182   Simon, *supra* note 67, 10.
183   2004 Regional Cooperation Agreement on Combating Piracy and Armed robbery against Ships in Asia, adopted 11 November 2004, entered into force 4 September 2006 (ReCAAP).
184   Manicom, *supra* note 141, 36.

and the United Kingdom) became parties to ReCAAP as they "have an interest in the safety of their substantial merchant fleet that traverse Asian waters on a daily basis."[185]

ReCAAP places a general obligation on Contracting Parties *"in accordance with its national laws and regulations and applicable rules of international law, to make every effort to take effective measures"* to prevent and suppress piracy and armed robbery against ships, to arrest pirates or persons who have committed armed robbery against ships, to seize ships or aircraft used for committing piracy or armed robbery against ships, to seize ships taken by and under the control of pirates/armed robbers and to seize property on board such ships and to rescue victim ships and victims of piracy or armed robbery against ships.[186]

The real objective of ReCAAP is to facilitate information sharing. ReCAAP establishes an Information Sharing Center (the ReCAAP ISC) to be located in Singapore.[187] The ReCAAP ISC consists of the Governing Council and the Secretariat.[188] The Governing Council is composed of one representative from each of the Contracting Parties, is responsible for making policies concerning all matters of the ISC and makes decision by consensus.[189] The expenses of the ISC are borne by the host State (Singapore), voluntary contributions from the Contracting Parties and voluntary contributions from international organizations and other entities in accordance with relevant criteria adopted by the Governing Council.[190]

The ISC has several functions, including *inter alia*:[191]

- To manage and maintain the expeditious flow of information relating to incidents of piracy and armed robbery against ships among the Contracting Parties;
- To collect and analyze the information transmitted by the Contracting Parties;

---

185   M. Hribernik, "Countering Maritime Piracy and Robbery in Southeast Asia: The Role of the ReCAAP Agreement," Briefing Paper 2013/2, European Institute for Asian Studies, March 2013.
186   Article 3, ReCAAP.
187   Article 4 (1) and (2), ReCAAP.
188   Article 4 (3), ReCAAP.
189   Article 4 (4), 4 (5) and 4 (6), ReCAAP.
190   Article 6, ReCAAP.
191   Article 7, ReCAAP.

- To circulate requests for cooperation and other relevant information on the measures that have been taken by Contracting Parties to accede to such requests;
- To provide appropriate alerts to the Contracting Parties in the event of an imminent threat of piracy or armed robbery against ships;
- To prepare statistics and reports on piracy and armed robbery attacks and to disseminate them to Contracting Parties; and
- To prepare non-classified statistics and reports on piracy and armed robbery attacks and to disseminate them to the shipping community and the IMO.

Contracting Parties are obliged to designate a focal point responsible for its communications with the ISC[192] and "make every effort" to require its ships, ship owners or ship operators to notify promptly relevant national authorities including focal points of incidents of piracy or armed robbery against ships.[193] Contracting Parties are also obliged to disseminate alerts sent by the ISC to ships within the area of the imminent threat.[194]

Apart from information sharing, ReCAAP also has provisions on co-operation between Contracting Parties to suppress acts of piracy and armed robbery. A Contracting Party may request any other Contracting Party through the ISC or directly in detecting pirates, armed robbers, ships used for piracy and armed robbery or under the control of pirates and armed robbers, victim ships and victims of piracy and armed robbery.[195] A Contracting Party may also request another Contracting Party (through the ISC or directly) to take appropriate measures, including arrest or seizure of ships/pirates/armed robbers as well as the rescue of victim ships and victims of piracy within the limits permitted by its national laws and regulations and applicable rules of international law.[196] The ISC must be notified of a direct request for co-operation.[197] The Contracting Parties which have received the request shall, in accordance with their respective national laws and regulations and subject to their available resources or capabilities, make every effort to take effective and practical measures for implementing such a request.[198] If a Contracting Party has taken

---

192   Article 9 (1), ReCAAP.
193   Article 9 (4), ReCAAP.
194   Article 9 (6), ReCAAP.
195   Article 10 (1), ReCAAP.
196   Article 10 (2) and 10 (3), ReCAAP.
197   Article 10 (4), ReCAAP.
198   Article 11 (1), ReCAAP.

any measures to implement the request, it must notify the ISC of the measures taken.[199] While ReCAAP does not strictly oblige Contracting Parties to comply with requests for co-operation, it does place considerable pressure on Contracting Parties to do so.

ReCAAP also obliges Contracting Parties to *endeavor* to extradite suspected pirates/armed robbers who are present in its territory to other Contracting Parties which has jurisdiction over them subject to its national laws and regulations. Similarly, a Contracting Party must also, subject to its national laws and regulations, endeavor to render mutual legal assistance in criminal matters, at the request of another Contracting Party. Again, it is not an outright obligation to extradite or provide mutual assistance and is limited by the standard "subject to its national laws and regulations."

Capacity-Building

ReCAAP also provides for capacity-building and the ISC is to endeavor to cooperate to the fullest extent in providing capacity building assistance, which can include technical assistance such as educational and training programs to share experiences and best practices.[200] In addition, ReCAAP recognizes that Contracting Parties may agree on cooperative arrangements such as joint exercises or other forms of cooperation.[201] ReCAAP ISC has undertaken capacity-building activities, including joint exercises, visits and exchange of personnel in different focal points, as well as capacity-building seminars which aim to enhance training of law enforcement officers through sharing of best practices.[202] In addition, Indonesia received aid and financial assistance from both the United States and Japan to help it defend its waters, including radar stations.[203]

Impact of Regional Co-operation in Piracy and Armed Robbery in Southeast Asia

Between 2005 and 2008, there was no doubt a decline in the incidents of piracy and armed robbery in Southeast Asia and the co-operative measures described above have largely been credited with the decline.[204] For example,

---

199   Article 11 (3), ReCAAP.
200   Article 14, ReCAAP.
201   Article 15, ReCAAP.
202   See generally, ReCAAP Executive Director's Report for 2012, at <http://www.recaap.org/Portals/0/docs/About%20ReCAAP%20ISC/ED%20Report%202012%204mb.pdf>.
203   Beckman, *supra* note 131, 21.
204   See Hribernik, *supra* note 185, 6–7.

the IMB observed that "this welcome reduction has been the cumulative effort of increased vigilance and patrolling by the littoral States." Similarly, the Secretary-General of the IMO noted in a 2012 speech that ReCAAP had been successful in helping "to almost eradicate piracy in what used to be the world's major piracy hotspot."[205]

However, it should be mentioned that other measures may have also contributed to the decline in numbers during this period. It is also suspected that the 2004 earthquake and tsunami and its effect on the population of Aceh where many pirates were based led to a reduction in attacks.[206] Raymond, for example, points to the fact that there was a 60% reduction in attacks in the Straits of Malacca in 2005 when compared to attacks in 2004.[207] However, she argues that this explanation cannot account for the continued decline in piracy from 2005–2007 as "four years on from the disaster, when life has certainly returned to some measure of normality in the affected areas, the frequency of pirate attacks has not returned to its 2004 levels."[208] Another factor which may have played a role in the decline is the 2005 peace agreement with the GAM in Aceh. After the tsunami, Indonesia and GAM were compelled to discuss disaster relief operations and this set the stage for a peace agreement in August 2005.[209] Part of the peace agreement was the surrender of hundreds of weapons and this may have contributed to less attacks being carried out.

The establishment of the Malaysian Maritime Enforcement Agency (MMEA) in 2004 has also arguably played a role in the reduction of attacks during this period. The aim of the MMEA was to "perform enforcement functions for ensuring the safety and security of the Malaysian Maritime Zone with a view to the protection of maritime and other national interests in such zones and for matters necessary thereto or connected therewith."[210] The Malaysian Maritime Zone is defined as "the internal waters, territorial sea, continental shelf, exclusive economic zone and the Malaysian fisheries waters and includes the air space over the Zone."[211] The establishment of the MMEA is said to be a

---

205 Speech by Koji Sekimizu on "Safeguarding Seafarers: A Shared Responsibility," at the ReCAAP ISC Piracy and Sea Robbery Conference 2012, 26 April 2012, at <http://www.imo.org/MediaCentre/SecretaryGeneral/SpeechesByTheSecretaryGeneral/Pages/ReCAAP-ISC-PIRACY.aspx>.
206 See Raymond, *supra* note 110, 37.
207 Ibid.
208 Ibid.
209 Ibid.
210 Preamble, Malaysian Enforcement Agency Act 2004, Act 633, entered into force 1 July 2004 (MMEA Act).
211 Section 2, MMEA Act.

direct response to the terrorism threat after the 9/11 attacks as well as the rising piracy incidents in the Straits of Malacca and the prospective involvement of the United States through the RMSI.[212] Malaysia previously had no coast guard and responsibility for protecting Malaysia's coastline was divided among several agencies.[213]

It is for obvious reasons impossible to determine the extent to which each of the above factors played in reducing piracy and armed robbery attacks in Southeast Asia. It is near impossible to provide empirical evidence that regional co-operation measures played a role in reducing attacks in Southeast Asia. Yet this does not diminish the importance of the role of regional cooperation in the suppression of piracy and armed robbery. Indeed, the fact that there has been regional co-operation on an issue that has been traditionally the prerogative of individual coastal States is remarkable given the aversion of such States to cooperation However, as will be explained below, the question is whether the present level of regional cooperation is sufficient to withstand current trends in piracy and armed robbery attacks in Southeast Asia and this will be dealt with below.

4 Current Trends and Continuing Challenges

Current Trends

Between 2009 and 2011, there appeared to be a general upswing in the number of total attacks (both attempted and actual) against vessels in Southeast Asia, which came down slightly in 2012. There were 72 attacks in 2009, 120 attacks in 2010, 128 attacks in 2011 and 111 attacks in 2012.[214] While final statistics are not yet out for 2013, there are reports which indicate that compared to other regions in the world, Southeast Asia may be the region with the highest number of attacks against vessels.[215] It is true that the number of attacks against vessels have not reverted back to the days in the early 2000s when attacks in Southeast Asia were at its zenith. Further, it is also true that the majority of

---

212 I. Ooi, "The Malaysian Maritime Enforcement Agency Act 2004: Malaysia's Legal Response to the Threat of Maritime Terrorism," 21 *Australian and New Zealand Maritime Law Journal* (2007), 70, 71.

213 Ibid., 74.

214 See ReCAAP Annual Report 2012.

215 See "Southeast Asia still worst for pirates despite high-profile Somali attacks," Australian News, 28 October 2013, <http://www.news.com.au/world/southeast-asia-still-worst-for-pirates-despite-highprofile-somali-attacks/story-fndir2ev-1226746660014>.

attacks in Southeast Asia remain opportunistic petty theft at anchorage or underway usually of ship's spares, cash and equipment.[216] However, there are three discernible trends in attacks in Southeast Asia which remain a cause for concern.

First, maritime security analysts have described a phenomenon known as "cluster piracy."[217] Cluster piracy "entails a group of pirates operating within a specific maritime area in a short time period and systematically attacking a number of vessels."[218] It has been said that there were 57 reported incidents involving cluster piracy within the Anambas/Natuna/Tembalan corridor in the Indonesian EEZ.[219] It is believed that organized criminal syndicates are responsible for such cluster piracy, which commonly occurs during the transitional monsoon period between March and October.[220]

Second, another issue which has always been a problem in Southeast Asia, but which appears to have increased in recent years is the hijacking of tugboats for re-sale. Between 2009 and 2012, there were altogether 12 reported incidents of hijacking: 1 in 2009, 3 in 2010, 5 in 2011 and 3 in 2012.[221] As noted by Beckman:

> Tugboats are being hijacked, renamed and supplied to a pre-arranged buyer. They are usually hijacked off the coast of Malaysia, near the northern entrance to the Singapore Strait. The modus operandi in the tug hijackings is the same. The tugboats aborted by a well-organized group of hijackers who immediately assume control of the vessel and detained the crew. The crew are not injured or mistreated. They are tied up and then released in a life raft, usually within the central South China Sea. The tugboats then proceed to their final destinations while undergoing repainting and renaming to prevent identification.[222]

---

216 Beckman, *supra* note 131, 23.
217 K. Hoesslin, "International Maritime Crimes in the ASEAN Region: Incidents and Trends," in R. Beckman and J.A Roach, *Piracy and International Maritime Crimes in ASEAN: Prospects for Co-operation* (United Kingdom: Edward Elgar, 2012), 121–122.
218 Beckman, *supra* note 131, 24.
219 Ibid.
220 Ibid.
221 See ReCAAP Information Sharing Centre, "Special Report on Hijacked Missing Tug Boats and Barges in Asia," March–June 2011, paragraph 5, at <http://www.recaap.org/AlertsReports/IncidentReports.aspx?EntryId=291>.
222 Beckman, *supra* note 131, 24–25.

It is believed that organized criminal syndicates are responsible for such hijackings.[223]

Third, pirates are increasingly attacking vessels in order to siphon and re-sell valuable cargoes of marine gas oil stored in the vessels. While there were no incidents reported in 2009 and 2010, there was one incident reported in 2011 and three reported in 2012.[224] In 2013, there have also been three incidents of illegal siphoning of marine gas oil to date.[225] The attackers will usually board the vessel, tie up the crew and bring another vessel alongside to transfer the marine gas oil.[226] In some instances, the vessel is boarded, the crew left adrift on life rafts and the vessel is hijacked for purposes of selling both the vessel and the marine gas oil/fuel oil on board the vessel.[227] The ReCAAP ISC has opined that the high oil price is the motivation for such attacks:

> It is a lucrative business believed to involve syndicates who target specific tankers with MGO onboard. It is believed that the culprits have access to insider information on the route taken by the tanker and possible location where the siphoning process could be carried out.[228]

Continuing Challenges for Regional Co-operation
As is evident from above, while piracy and armed robbery are nowhere near as serious as before, there will always be increasing challenges as perpetrators change tactics and technology improves. While Southeast Asian States have made progress in co-operating to address piracy, there still remain significant limitations, which will be discussed below.

---

223   See K. Hoesslin, "Tankers, Tugs, Territorial Disputes, and Those on the Take: Southeast Asia's 2013 Maritime Security Outlook," *Strategic Insights* No. 44, January 2013, 16, 17.
224   See ReCAAP Annual Report 2012, 28–31.
225   See ReCAAP Report for November 2013, 4, at <http://www.recaap.org/DesktopModules/Bring2mind/DMX/Download.aspx?Command=Core_Download&EntryId=318&PortalId=0&TabId=78>.
226   See for example, the incident onboard the vessel *Scorpio* on 13 September 2012 which was boarded by six masked robbers who tied the crew, brought the vessel to another location where another tanker came alongside to transfer the marine gas oil/fuel oil from *Scorpio* to the other ship. See ReCAAP Annual Report 2012, at 29.
227   For example, the attack on the chemical tanker *Zafirah* was suspected to be a hijacking for purposes of selling marine gas oil in Vietnam ports. See ReCAAP Annual Report 2012 at 30.
228   ReCAAP Annual Report 2012, at 31.

Enforcement Cooperation

Enforcement cooperation remains limited due to the traditional reluctance of States to cooperate on enforcement, which is viewed as a direct intrusion into sovereignty. While the trilateral patrols by Singapore, Malaysia and Indonesia in the Straits of Malacca are a welcome development as it is the first "significantly operationalized multilateral cooperation in Southeast Asia to develop without an extraregional partner,"[229] there have been reports that the trilateral patrols are more for "show" than of real utility.[230] This does not seem likely to change any time soon, but confidence and mutual trust can be fostered through increased joint exercises.

Information Sharing

First, there remain impediments to effective information sharing. The major challenge is the fact that Malaysia and Indonesia, key littoral States which border the Straits of Malacca, have not ratified ReCAAP. While attacks in Malaysia's waters have more or less remained steady in the last three years, attacks in Indonesian waters have steadily increased from 19 in 2009 to 71 in 2012.[231]

With regard to Malaysia, it is said that its reluctance to ratify the agreement is due to "its objection to the location of the ISC in Singapore and views ReCAAP as an unnecessary competitor to the IMB's Piracy Reporting Center, located in the Malaysian capital Kuala Lumpur."[232] For Indonesia, it has the usual concerns that ratifying the Agreement would undermine the country's sovereignty.[233] The Foreign Minister of Indonesia stated that one of the concerns was that the ISC may publish reports unfairly critical to member States as had been done by the IMB which had misrepresented incidents that had occurred in Malaysian waters as having occurred in the Indonesian side of the Straits of Malacca.[234] Further, as mentioned above, it views the issue of piracy as a domestic concern and does not see the need for outside interference. Arguably, the burgeoning number of extra-regional States joining ReCAAP has enhanced the perception that ReCAAP is an excuse for other States to get involved in regional issues.

---

229 Bradford, *supra* note 113, 68.
230 Ibid.
231 Hribenik, *supra* note 185, 9.
232 Ibid., 8.
233 Ibid.
234 Bradford, *supra* note 113, 69.

While it is said that both Malaysia and Indonesia cooperate with the ReCAAP ISC to some degree at an operational level,[235] undoubtedly the ratification of ReCAAP by both these countries will no doubt strengthen anti-piracy efforts in the region. It will allow Indonesia and Malaysia to gain access to a regional maritime security network comprising national authorities who are also responsible for managing the threat of piracy and armed robbery in the region.[236] It will also allow them to interact and build closer ties with enforcement officials from other States, thereby increasing mutual confidence which will inevitably strengthen anti-piracy efforts. Equally as important, it will allow both Indonesia and Malaysia to be viewed as responsible maritime nations and reinforce their commitment to anti-piracy initiatives in the region.[237]

It should also be reiterated that ReCAAP does not provide for any enforcement powers beyond what is already provided for in international law, nor does it envisage joint law enforcement operations. Indeed, ReCAAP expressly states that nothing in the Agreement entitles a Contracting Party to exercise any jurisdiction or performance of functions which are exclusively reserved for the authorities of that Contracting Party by its national law.[238] ReCAAP also recognizes that the obligations undertaken under the Agreement can only be implemented in accordance with the respective national laws and regulations and subject to their available resources or capabilities of contracting parties. While these qualifications have rendered ReCAAP open to criticisms that it "lacks teeth,"[239] they were arguably a necessary compromise given the sovereignty concerns of States in the region.

Legal Cooperation

To date, regional co-operation in Southeast Asia has been for the most part limited to operational cooperation. A critical element has been omitted, namely legal cooperation through extradition and mutual legal assistance mechanisms. UNCLOS does not provide for such mechanisms and as men-

---

235   Beckman, *supra* note 131, 21.
236   See National Interest Analysis of Australia, Chapter 2 Regional Cooperation Agreement on Combating Piracy and Armed Robbery against Ships in Asia, House of Representatives Committees, at <http://www.aph.gov.au/parliamentary_business/committees/house_of_representatives_committees?url=jsct/11september2012/report/chapter2.htm>, paragraph 2.11.
237   Ibid., paragraph 2.13. Also see Hribenik, *supra* note 185, 9.
238   Article 2 (5), ReCAAP.
239   R. Geib and A. Petrig, *Piracy and Armed Robbery at Sea: The Legal Framework for Counter-Piracy Operations in Somalia and the Gulf of Aden*, (United States: Oxford University Press, 2011), 75.

tioned above, ReCAAP only obliges States to *endeavor* to extradite suspected pirates/armed robbers who are present in their territory and *endeavor* to render mutual legal assistance. Undoubtedly, what happens to perpetrators after they are captured can provide a considerable deterrent to future perpetrators.

Southeast Asian States can use existing international frameworks such as the 1988 Suppression of Unlawful Acts Against the Safety of Maritime Navigation (SUA Convention),[240] the 1979 Convention against the Taking of Hostages (Hostages Convention)[241] and the 2000 UN Convention against Transnational Organized Crime (UNTOC).[242] This has been addressed comprehensively elsewhere[243] and for present purposes, it suffices to mention a few brief points.

Essentially, these Conventions adopt a common scheme. First, the Conventions oblige States to establish specific offences in their national legislation with appropriate penalties. For example, if attacks involve either taking control of a ship or the use of violence against crew members which endanger the safety of navigation, these would be offences under the SUA Convention.[244] Similarly, if crew members are taken hostage and held for ransom at sea, these would also be offences under the Hostages Convention.[245] Second, they oblige States to take into custody alleged offenders which are present in their territory and to either extradite them to another State Party with jurisdiction or prosecute the alleged offenders for offences. Third, these Conventions provide for several mechanisms for extradition (even in the absence of an extradition treaty) and mutual legal assistance. For example, with regard to extradition under the SUA Convention:[246]

a) the offences are deemed to be extraditable offences under any extradition treaty in force between any of the State Parties;

---

240 *Convention for the Suppression of Unlawful Acts against the Safety of Maritime Navigation*, adopted 10 March 1988, 1678 UNTS 222 (entered into force 1 March 1992) (SUA Convention).
241 *International Convention against the Taking of Hostages*, adopted 17 December 1979, 1316 UNTS 206 (entered into force 17 December 1979) (Hostages Convention).
242 *United Nations Convention against Transnational Organized Crime*, adopted 15 November 2000, 40 ILM 335 (entered into force 29 September 2003).
243 See for example, Beckman, *supra* note 131, 28–32; Also see generally R. Beckman and J.A. Roach, *Piracy and International Maritime Crimes in ASEAN: Prospects for Co-operation* (United Kingdom: Edward Elgar, 2012).
244 Article 3, SUA Convention.
245 Articles 1–2, Hostages Convention.
246 Article 11, SUA Convention.

b) State Parties shall include these offences among the extraditable offences in any future extradition treaty; and
c) State parties that do not make extradition conditional upon the presence of a treaty shall consider the offences set out in the Convention as extraditable between themselves, while those which make extradition conditional upon the existence of a treaty may at their option consider the Conventions as a basis for extradition.

If all the States in a region are parties to one of the Conventions, a person who commits an offense under that Convention will have no place of refuge. However, the effectiveness of these conventions will depend upon their ratification and proper implementation. Within ASEAN, Indonesia and Vietnam are not parties to the 1979 Hostages Convention; Indonesia, Malaysia and Thailand are not parties to the SUA Convention; whereas all ASEAN member states are parties to UNTOC. Further, even States which have ratified these Conventions have not implemented them properly, thereby undermining their effectiveness.[247]

5   Conclusions: Generating Sufficient Political Will

Regional cooperation in Southeast Asia has certainly progressed from the time that cooperation did not seem possible. While it is impossible to determine empirically the extent to which regional cooperation has reduced piracy and armed robbery in Southeast Asia, there is no doubt that it has had an impact. However, it has been a gradual evolution in cooperation done incrementally with sovereignty concerns still posing a major barrier. Limitations remain and there is always room for improvement. The previous section has outlined some suggestions on how States in Southeast Asia can enhance regional cooperation. The question remains, however, whether such States will have sufficient political will to move forward on regional cooperation.

Previous experience demonstrates that the economic impact of piracy appears to be the major factor galvanizing States to take action. There are countless examples where the perceived threat to international trade posed by piratical attacks has been a catalyst for States to cooperate, the most recent example being Somalia. The pirate attacks in the Horn of Africa by Somali pirates have consistently been portrayed in the media and other forums as

---

247   For example, the Philippines has ratified the SUA Convention but has not passed implementing legislation: See Beckman, *supra* note 131, 31.

a "threat to global trade" or a "threat to international shipping."[248] This has been a significant impetus behind the unprecedented cooperation between a large number of States to suppress piracy in the Horn of Africa.[249] Similarly, in Southeast Asia, the economic impact of the attacks against vessels played a direct and indirect role in motivating States to take action. It was the perceived threat to freedom of international navigation and the consequent possibility of external interference coupled with the raising of the insurance premiums that jump-started cooperation in Southeast Asia. The same confluence of factors that existed in the early 2000s do not presently exist and one could even ask whether piracy and armed robbery in Southeast Asia still pose a threat to freedom of navigation. After all, the number of incidents has reduced dramatically, the majority of attacks in Southeast Asia appear to be petty theft and take place while vessels are berthed in harbours or at anchor.

Notwithstanding this, piracy and armed robbery in Southeast Asia still remain a cause for concern. First, there is evidence that suggests that organized criminal syndicates that carry out piracy and armed robbery attacks are also engaging in other illegal activities such as smuggling of narcotics and other contraband items, and trafficking of guns and people.[250] Piracy/armed robbery is just one activity, and the revenue streams from each illegal activity are used to mutually reinforce each other. In other words, piracy/armed robbery is not just a threat to freedom of navigation (and hence a problem for extra-regional States), it is a transnational law and order problem that requires concerted action from regional States.

Second, an aspect that is often overlooked due to the overemphasis placed on piracy as an economic concern is the threat to the safety of the lives of the crew. Even petty thefts at anchorage put the crew at risk of violence (not to mention the emotional trauma). This is an issue that should be of utmost concern to States in the region as many of their nationals are in fact seafarers. In a 2012 study, it was reported that both the Philippines and Indonesia are the top

---

248 For example, Victoria Collins reports that between 2004 and 2010, the majority of media reports on Somali piracy framed it as a threat to trade. See V. Collins, "Dangerous Seas: Moral Panic and the Somali Pirate," 45 *Australian and New Zealand Journal of Criminology* No. 1 (2012) 106, 116.

249 For a description of the co-operative measures, please refer to Kraska and Wilson, *supra* note 97.

250 See for example, K. Hoesslin, "The Piracy Umbrella: Time to Re-examine the Various Tactics of Piracy," *Strategic Insights* No. 20 December 2009.

two suppliers of seafarers, with the Philippines supplying 21.86% of seafarers, and Indonesia supplying 8.26%.[251]

In this writer's view, the above reasons, more than the perceived economic impact of piracy/armed robbery, should be more than enough to generate the political will necessary to enhance regional cooperation.

---

[251] S. Galic, Z. Lusic, D. Pusic, "Seafarers Market," 1 *International Journal of New Trends in Arts, Sports & Science Education* No. 3 (2012) 33, 34.

CHAPTER 2

The Small But Magnificent Counter-Piracy Operations of the Republic of Korea

RADM Youngjoo CHO

1   Introduction

Upon learning the modern histories of the Republic of Korea (ROK) and Somalia, which are both maritime countries, several similarities can be found between the two countries. They were colonial countries in the 20th century and became independent states after the Second World War. Unfortunately, they experienced devastating wars after their independence, had a military junta in the 1960s, and remained under the quasi-military government for over three decades.[1] However, as it stands in 2013, the ROK has become a wealthy maritime country with the sea being a critical factor in its national security and prosperity. On the other hand, since 1991, Somalia has been the archetypal failed state suffering from civil war and insecurity leading to poverty, unemployment, poor health, and terrorism.

All the more, in absence of the rule of law, war-torn Somalia provides freedom of action for pirates. Consequently, piracy off the Somali coast and in the Gulf of Aden is a threat to international shipping and remains the single greatest challenge to regional and global maritime security. In this context, the UN Security Council has issued a series of resolutions since 2008 to facilitate an international response and authorizes international navies to counter piracy both in Somali territorial waters and ashore with the consent of Somalia's Transitional Federal Government (TFG).[2] The striking contrast of the modern

---

*   Rear Admiral Youngjoo CHO, Ph.D., is Deputy Commander, Republic of Korea Navy 1st Fleet.
1   For more details, see https://www.cia.gov/library/publications/the-world-factbook/geos/so.html and https://www.cia.gov/library/publications/the-world-factbook/geos/ks.html.
2   In terms of the Somalia situation, the UN Security Council has issued total 46 resolutions since 1991 such as S/RES/1356/1407/1425/1474/1519/1558/1587/1630/1676/1724/1725/1744/1766/1772/1801/1811/1814/1816/1831/1838/1844/1846/1851/1853/1863/1872/1897/1910/1916/1918/1950/1964/1976/2002/2010/2015/2020/2036/2060/2067/2072/2073/2077/2093/2102/2111. See http://www.un.org/en/sc/documents/Resolutions.

history between the ROK and Somalia vividly teaches us how important the sea is in the security and prosperity of states.

The importance of the maritime environment is demonstrated in the following statistics: (1) 70% of the Earth is covered in water; (2) 80% of the world's population lives within 100 miles of the coast; (3) 90% of the world's commerce is seaborne; and (4) 75% of that trade passes through a few, vulnerable, international straits. In particular, the Gulf of Aden is of strategic importance because it connects trade between the East and the West through the neighboring strait of Bab el Mandeb and the Suez Canal, with approximately 23,000 ships (500 Korean flagged ships) crossing the area annually.[3] In addition, more than 55% of the world's crude oil and 40% of its natural gas are located in Gulf states making the Strait of Hormuz where some 40,000 ships making transit every year, a core maritime commerce route. To sum up, 21% of global oil production and 43% of oil exportation shipping derive from the Indian Ocean with 30% of world maritime trade as well as 50% of world container shipping taking place. Consequently, the Indian Ocean is a major artery for the economy not only of the ROK but also of the entire world.

The sea, a common heritage of mankind, produces prosperity when peace and freedom prevail, while it is an arena for disputes and aggression when lawless and ungoverned. In a globalized world, the act of piracy in one area ripples across the globe because countries depend on secure and reliable shipping lanes for their food, energy, and consumer goods brought by cargo ships and tankers. In truth, peace is not a given. Peace has to be established and maintained by power. Peace and stability of the international system is guaranteed only when it is supported by sufficient military power and the will to use it.[4]

In this context, the National Assembly of the ROK approved the foreign deployment of naval forces in response to international calls and its own necessity for counter-piracy operation in March of 2009, allowing the ROK Navy to join the Combined Task Force 151. Since then, the ROK Navy has been engaging audaciously in counter-piracy operations and has contributed to the remarkable progress in the region. In light of this success it is worthwhile to discuss

---

3 For more details about merchant shipping statistics of the ROK, see http://www.kmi.re.kr/kmi/kr.

4 There are many debates on the relationship between arms and war. This opinion is based on the age-old maxim of Roman philosopher Vegetius, "*Si vis pacem, para bellum*" (If you want peace then prepare for war), and the function of military power as an ultimate method for preventing war. For more details and a balanced view of military force, see James L. Payne, *Why Nations Arm*, Oxford: Basil Blackwell, 1989.

ROK naval counter-piracy operations and to draw some lessons in combating piracy off Somalia.

2 Small but Capable and Ready Navy of the Republic of Korea

The ROK Navy named the first overseas deploying forces as the "Cheong Hae (blue water) Unit" after the naval base established by Admiral Bogo Jang who exercised maritime dominance of the Korean peninsula in the era of Unified Silla. Drawing inspiration from this revered historical figure, ROK Navy Cheong Hae Unit showed the advanced combat capability in counter-piracy operations as soon as it arrived in the region in 2009. Notable achievements of the Unit include not only disrupting pirate attacks on merchant vessels but also successful military rescue operations of pirated merchant vessels and crews.

It is natural for large naval powers to deploy combat ships overseas to maintain global peace and security and secure their national interest. However, it is extraordinary for Korea because in our 5000 year history, the sea was seldom a matter of importance. As Korea neglected the sea, we suffered from the invasion of foreign countries over 900 times.[5] Particularly, in modern history, the price has been severe. Due to the absence of proper naval power, Korea was colonized by Japan for 36 years. Even after liberation from Japan, the Korean peninsula was torn down by the tragic fratricidal war of three years and still remains divided by the 38th parallel suffering from the agony of division. It is fortunate that after liberation there were maritime pioneers to lay the foundation of the ROK Navy and dedicate their lives to development of a modern and capable navy. In the end, Korea made a historic decision to deploy a state-of-the-art combat ship to the Gulf of Aden in 2009. In light of this, it is necessary to understand the maritime history of Korea and the development of the ROK Navy to grasp the true meaning of the foreign deployment of the ROK Navy.

2.1 *Background Maritime History of Korea*
Korea is a peninsular country that has traditionally disregarded maritime activities and even considered them taboo in their socio-political culture. The Korean Government did not exploit the geographical opportunity offered by the sea nor did it exert the potential maritime talents of the Koreans. As a result, throughout history, Koreans suffered countless invasions from neighboring

---

5   For more details, see Military Academy of the ROK, *Hankuk Cheonjaengsa* [*The War History of Korea*], Seoul: 88 Ilsinsa, 1987; Naval College of the ROK, *Hankuk Haejeonsa* [*The History of Naval Warfare of Korea*], Taejon: The ROK Navy, 1999.

countries such as China, Russia, and Japan by both land and sea. In modern times Korea was a colony of Japan from 1910 to 1945 and during this time the Japanese prevented the Koreans from developing any maritime activities.[6]

However, the maritime history of Korea demonstrates that the Koreans possessed sufficient talents to manage maritime enterprises and to command the local sea line of communications as required by Korea's geographical condition as a peninsular state. For example, during the period of 828 to 846, Admiral Bogo Jang established Silla (the first unified nation of Korea) as a strong maritime state, secured command of the seas in Northeast Asia and took a leading position in maritime trade between Korea, China and Japan.[7]

When the Mongols (the Won Dynasty of China) invaded Koryo (the Second unified nation of Korea) in 1231 and crushed the Koryo Army, the Mongols could not completely conquer Koryo for 39 long years and had to settle for an amicable alliance because the naval power of Koryo was strong enough to protect its nation. In addition, when the Japanese embarked on their first Korean campaign in 1592 and ravaged the Korean Peninsula for seven years, Admiral Soonshin Yi's victory at sea saved Choson (the third unified nation of Korea) with a newly designed "Turtle Ship" which was the first "iron clad fighting ship" in the world.[8]

Then, after the liberation of 1945, as historical heroes such as Admiral Bogo Jang and Soonshin Yi led the maritime activities of Korea, another maritime pioneer emerged. His name was Admiral Wonil Shon. Admiral Shon founded

---

6 The Koreans lost their sovereignty, and suffered from Japanese colonial oppression because they forgot the importance of the sea. For more details, see Namsun Choi, "Bada rul izeo burin kukmin [People who forgot the sea]", Naval Headquarters of the ROK, *Hankuk Haeyangsa [Maritime History of Korea]*, Seoul: Naval Headquarters of the ROK, 1954. Namsun Choi was a leading Korean intellectual during the era of Japanese control. His activities include publishing Korea's first popular modern magazine, pioneering modern poetry in Korean, drafting the Declaration of Independence for the 1919 March First Independence Movement, and publishing numerous articles on Korean culture.
7 Admiral Chang is called "the trade prince of the maritime commercial empire". He was a former general of the Chinese Tang dynasty. After returning to Korea he served under King Heungdoc as a commissioner for the seas with 10,000 sailors and soldiers. He established a major naval base at Wando, the southwestern island of Korea, and an advanced base in the Shantong peninsular of China. Under his control the maritime trade between Korea, China and Japan was well protected and flourished for eighteen years. For more details, see the ROK Navy, *Commissioner Chang Bogo's Maritime Dominance and Maritime Security facing the ROK Navy in the 21st Century*, Proceedings of the 8th On-Board Workshop, Taejeon: the ROK Navy, 2000; Naval College of the ROK, op cit.
8 For more details about the naval warfare of Admiral Yi, see Sungdo Cho, *Yi Sun-Shin: a National Hero of Korea*, Chinhae: Choongmoo-Kong Society, 1970.

the ROK Navy with a few like-minded people soon after the liberation on 11th November 1945. The maritime pioneers led by Admiral Shon laid the foundation of the ROK Navy and its development to the present date.

2.2 Naval Development of the Republic of Korea

The birth of the modern ROK Navy was unique in comparison with the history of other navies. It was founded not by a government but by an individual, Admiral Wonil Shon, with like-minded people on 11 November 1945, and was only integrated into the ROK armed forces with the establishment of the ROK government on 15 August 1948.[9]

Since its birth, the development of the ROK Navy can be seen as transitioning through four major phases: (1) establishment and development through the Korean War (1945–1953); (2) development derived by the ROK-US combined defense policy (1953–1973); (3) independent development focused on the North Korean threat (1974–1992); and (4) development towards "a bluewater" navy (1993-present).

The first phase (1945–1953) was the period of laying the cornerstone of the ROK Navy. Due to the lack of national capability, the Navy's development was heavily affected by US policy toward Korea. Before the Korean War, the Americans did not regard Korea as a major national interest in the post-war political and strategic context.[10] They did not provide any combatants and relied mainly on ex-US and ex-Japanese minesweepers which enabled a very limited coastal defense against the North.[11] Then, as invasion by North Korea was imminent after the US withdrawal from Korea, Admiral Shon launched a campaign and purchased four small combatants from the United States by a

---

9   Admiral Wonil Shon was born on 5 May 1909 as a son of Jungdo Shon who was a minister and one of the thirty three National Representatives of Independence Movement of 1 March 1919 against the Japanese colony. He graduated in navigation at National Central University of China. He devoted himself entirely to establishing the ROK Navy so he is called the Father of the ROK Navy. He was a Chief of Naval Operations, a Minister of National Defense, and an Ambassador to West Germany. For more details, see Navy Headquarters of the ROK, *Haegun Munhwa [The Culture of ROK Navy]*, Taejeon: The ROK Navy, 1985.

10 Though Korea was liberated on 15 August 1945, it was again the victim of power politics, because of its lack of national power and its geo-political situation as a small country among great powers. For more details, see Soon-sung Cho, *Korea in World Politics 1940–1950*, Berkeley and Los Angeles: University of California Press, 1967; Shannon McCune, "The Thirty-Eight Parallel in Korea", *World Politics*, 1949.

11 Navy Headquarters of the ROK, *Daehanminkuk Haegunsa Je Iljip [The History of ROK Navy, Vol. I]*, Seoul: Gaemoonsa, 1954.

subscription obtained from all members of the ROK Navy.[12] Fortunately, one of the vessels arrived in Korea just before the outbreak of the Korean War and it saved the Pusan Perimeter, the last bastion on the peninsula and later a base of operations for the UN counter-attack, by sinking a 1,000-ton enemy armed steamer with 600 troops 26th June 1950, the second day of the Korean War.[13]

All of a sudden, the Korean War changed the US policy towards Korea. Americans interpreted the North Korean invasion as part of the Soviet communist expansion policy as well as an attack on the authority of the United Nations.[14] During the Korean War, the ROK Navy was able to make considerable progress in size and rapidly acquired more modern naval knowledge, skill, and tactics as a limited coastal defense navy.

The second phase (1953–1973) of the development of the ROK Navy was the total dependency on the military aid of the United States.[15] During the second phase, the aim of the ROK Navy was to develop its fleet strength and combat

---

12 For more details, see Eunhae Hong, *Wooridelleun Ibadaweehae: Shon Wonil Jedok Hwoekorok* [*We for the Sea: The Memoir of Admiral Wonil Shon*], Seoul: Inshekongup Hyupdongjohap, 1998.

13 It is called "Daehan Haehyup Haejeon [Korean Strait Naval Warfare]". For more details, see ROK Naval War College, *Hankuk Haejeonsa* [*Naval Warfare History of the ROK*], Daejeon: Naval War College of the ROK, 2000.

14 President Truman remembered Hitler moving into the Rhineland and recalled the axiom that aggression must be resisted everywhere. See Joseph S. Nye, Jr., *Understanding International Conflicts*, New York: Longman, 1997. For information about US reaction against the Korean War, UN resolution, and the Korean situation see Committee on Foreign Affairs, *Background Information on Korea: Report of the Committee on Foreign Affairs Pursuant to H. Res. 206*, Washington: US Government Printing Office, 1950.

15 The United States accepted making a defense treaty with South Korea to block the future communist invasion rather than carrying out another war. During the Summit talk with President Eisenhower in 1954, President Rhee stressed that there were an additional million communist Chinese forces besides North Korea Armed Forces. In this context, President Rhee requested ROK military expansion as a military spearhead against China such as Army 565,000, Navy 16,600, Air force 22,400, and Marine Corps 26,000. Until the 1960s, South Korea channeled a relatively small amount, 4% of the GNP, into military outlays. Under the circumstances, South Korea could not afford much investment for national defense and had to depend on the United States for a considerable part of the maintenance cost of its armed forces. The share of US military aid in the total defense outlays was 99.8% in 1961 and about 70% in 1968. See US Department of State, *Foreign Relation of the United States*, 1952–1954, Washington, DC: US Government Printing Office, 1984; The Institute of National Defense and Military History, *Kukbang Jungchaek Byuncheonsa 1945–1994* [*The Changing History of National Defense Policy of the ROK 1945–1994*], Seoul: Kunin Kongjaehwoe, 1995.

capability to guarantee independently the maritime security of South Korea against the North. To this end, the assistance of the US Navy was vital as the ROK Navy was only able to carry out force development through American military aid. With the assistance of the US Navy, the ROK Navy strengthened its capability focusing first on amphibious warfare (1953–1957), next on anti-submarine warfare (1958–1966), and lastly on anti-infiltration warfare capability (1967–1973) against the North Korean Navy.

Then in the early 1970s, the Americans suddenly changed their policy and withdrew a US division from Korea although the North Korean military threat was greatly increasing at that time. In response the South Koreans, under President Junghee Park, started to develop a self-reliant national defense capability against the North. The ROK Navy took its first steps towards fulfilling its long-cherished dream, independent naval development, with the construction of two domestically designed fast attack craft called *Student-one and Student-two* funded by a patriotic subscription of students from all over the country in 1972.[16]

The third phase (1974–1992) was the transitional period for the ROK Navy, during which it converted its force development from total dependence on the US Navy to independent naval development. In 1972, US President Nixon suddenly withdrew the US 7th Division from Korea due to the aftermath of the Vietnam War and the opening of diplomatic relationship with China.[17] Upon this change in US policy towards Korea, the ROK realized that no two nations have precisely the same objectives and in a given set of circumstances each will react according to its needs. In response to the increasing North Korean military threat, President Park launched the Yulgok Project in 1974.[18] Through the Yulgok Project force development of the ROK Armed Forces finally could escape from dependence on US military aid and carry out independent defense planning.

The ROK Navy did not forget the dream that its founders possessed of being an independent naval power for the maritime security of Korea. During the third phase, the ROK Navy built various domestic naval ships: PK in 1974, PKM

---

16 See The ROK Navy Headquarters, *To the Sea To the World: Fifty Years History of the ROK Navy with Photography*, Seoul: Sugyung Munhwasa, 1995.

17 As the Nixon Administration reduced the US troop level in Korea by about one-third, from 63,000 to 43,000 in 1971, the US 7th division withdrew from Korea. See Institute of National Defense and Military History, *Keonkun Osipnyunsa* [*The Fifty Years History of the ROK Armed Forces*], Seoul: Inshekongup Hyupdongjohap, 1998.

18 For more details, see the Ministry of National Defense of the ROK, *The Past, Present and Future of Yulgok Project*, Seoul: Ministry of National Defense, 1994.

in 1979, FF in 1981, PCC in 1982, MHC in 1987, and AOE in 1990.[19] The ROK Navy greatly improved its fleet strength and combat capability by the domestic construction of modernized Korean combat ships for use against the North. As a result, it was able to successfully support two very important events—the Asian Games in 1986 and the Seoul Olympic Games in 1988—and continuous national development through the sea. In this context, the success of independent naval shipbuilding projects was a paramount achievement of the ROK Navy and a dramatic turning point in ROK naval development.

The fourth phase (1993-Present) is the period that the ROK Navy turned the direction of its force development towards a "blue-water navy" to meet strategic requirements in the post-Cold War era against both North Korea and other regional countries.[20] The ROK Navy stopped building inferior naval combatants—FF, PCC and PKM—in the early 1990s and started to build modernized Korean destroyers (DDH-I, II and III) and amphibious ships (LST and LPH) in addition to mine warfare and fleet support ships.

The ROK Navy also acquired 209-class and 214-class diesel submarines and is currently constructing 3,000 ton-class submarines domestically. In addition, it introduced P-3C maritime patrol aircraft from the United States and Lynx helicopters from the United Kingdom. As a result, the ROK Navy has become a competent three-dimensional coastal defense navy and is converting to a blue-water navy, although still inferior to regional naval powers.[21]

Since 1945 Korean history has demonstrated a remarkable geo-political difference between the South and the North. North Korea (Democratic People's Republic of Korea), which is adjacent to continental Asia, continues to follow the pro-continental history of old Korea. By contrast, South Korea (the Republic of Korea) has completely converted to a maritime country because of the barrier to the north. The difference between two countries is remarkable. North Korea, on the one hand, is suffering from severe economic difficulties, political instability and isolation in the international community due to its closed culture and political despotism. South Korea, on the other hand, has developed into an open and advanced industrial society with its wealth dependent on maritime trade. The sea is a critical factor for South Korea for its survival, security and prosperity.

---

19   See The ROK Navy Headquarters, *To the Sea to the World: Fifty Years History of the ROK Navy with Photography.*
20   For more details about blue-water navy development, see the ROK Navy Internet site http://www.navy.go.kr/main-1.html.
21   For more details, *supra*, note 19.

2.3 Counter-Piracy Operations and the Republic of Korea Navy

On March 13 of 2009, the ROK Government deployed a destroyer as part of the Escort Unit for counter-piracy operations in Gulf of Aden. This might sound insignificant to most, but for Korea it was of great significance as it was the first-ever overseas dispatch of a combat ship, surmounting the difficulties originating from the continental history of the ROK. It is not a stretch to say that deploying a state-of-the-art destroyer overseas is a milestone for the ROK in only several decades after liberation and going through the tragic Korean War.

The ROK Navy is equipped with actual war-fighting capability which is a prerequisite for an overseas deployment. Ironically through the disastrous Korean War the ROK Navy made huge progress and learned modern naval knowledge, skills and tactics very quickly. In addition it has improved its combat potential under the serious and incessant North Korean threats such as infiltration of armed espionage ships, naval engagements between surface combatants, and even a torpedo attack on a ROK combatant. The ROK Navy is pushing forward with realistic multilateral combined and joint exercises in order to generate maximum combat power during contingencies.[22]

These are the reasons why the ROK Navy Escort Unit is the most capable and powerful conducting counter-piracy operations off Somalia despite its small size. It is also considered a remarkable feat for the ROK to dispatch a core combat ship overseas for global maritime security all the while under the existing serious North Korean threat.

3 Magnificent Achievements of the ROK Navy

Pirate attacks off the coast of Somalia have occurred since the beginning of Somalia's civil war in the early 1990s. From 2007 the attacks escalated dramatically and peaked in 2011 with attacks against 544 ships. However in 2012, figures show roughly a 75% decline in pirate attacks compared with 2011 according to the US Navy which expects a further drop in 2013. For the counter-piracy operations in the Gulf of Aden and off the coast of Somalia, there are three multinational naval forces (CTF-151, EU, and NATO) and individual participants from China, Russia, India, and Japan (see figure 1).

Increased patrols and proactive efforts by naval ships have reduced pirate attacks in the Gulf of Aden and off the coast of Somalia. Since commencing counter-piracy operations in March 2009, the ROK Navy has maintained a

---

22 For more details, see the Ministry of National Defense of the ROK, *Defense White Paper 2012*, Seoul: Ministry of National Defense, 2013.

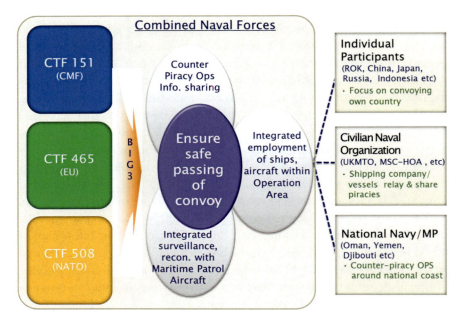

FIGURE 1   *Counter piracy operations system.*

capable, willing, and competent force on station against piracy. As of 17th of April 2013, the ROK Navy has completed 11 escort missions in the Gulf of Aden and the 12th unit continues to carry out the mission. As a result of this tremendous effort there have been several significant achievements of the ROK Navy against piracy.

First, the ROK Navy has contributed in improving security and safety of the region by successfully accomplishing multi-national maritime security operations. The ROK Navy has joined maritime security operations periodically under the command of CTF-151 operating in the Gulf of Aden and in the waters off the Somali coast in the Indian Ocean. To conduct more effective deterrent operations and to lower the success rate of Somali pirates, CTF-151 established a Maritime Security Patrol Area (MSPA) and Internationally Recommended Transit Corridors (IRTC) in the Gulf of Aden. The operational area of CMF is shown in figure 2.

Under the tactical control of CTF-151, the ROK Navy conducts counter-piracy patrols in a designated area of the IRTC. Particularly, the Cheong Hae Unit successfully conducted a series of rescue operations immediately after arriving off the coast of Somalia. On the 4th of May, the North Korean merchant vessel *Dabaksol* made a distress call that it was under pirate attack in IRTC. The Cheong Hae Unit was just 52NM away from her and within minutes after receiving the

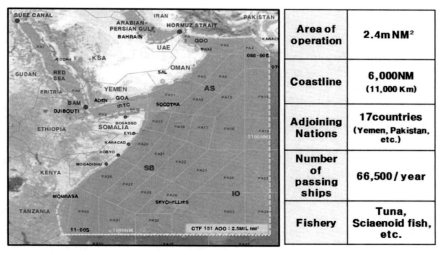

FIGURE 2   Operation area.

distress call, a Lynx of the ROK Navy launched with snipers onboard and was sent to the scene. This action was enough to disrupt the pirate attack against the North Korean merchant vessel. Within the first months of deployment of the Cheong Hae Unit, similar rescue operations were accomplished six times and gained a reputation from coalition forces for robust and ready combat capability. As of April 2013, the Cheong Hae Unit accomplished 17 very similar outstanding rescue operations including three combined operations in cooperation with US, Japanese, and Turkish Navies. The operations are shown in the table below.

TABLE 1   Rescue Operation against Pirate Attacks

BT	Date	Ship Name (Nationality)	Means
The 1st Unit	17th Apr '09	MV Puma (Denmark)	Lynx
	4th May '09	MV Dabaksol (North Korea)	Lynx
	6th May '09	MV Nepheli (Panama)	Lynx
	13th May '09	FV Aurora 9 (South Korea)	Combined Operation
	13th May '09	MV Amira (Egypt)	Combined Operation
	31st May '09	MV Al Mircap (Kuwait)	Lynx
	4th Aug '09	MV Notosscan (Bahamas)	Lynx/RIB/VBSS

TABLE 1 (*cont.*)

The 2nd Unit	26th Aug '09	MV Southern Cross (Italy)	Lynx
	19th Sep '09	MV Alexandria (Cyprus)	Combined Operation
The 3rd Unit	6th Feb '09	MV Oriental Wisteria (South Korea)	Lynx
The 4th Unit	2nd Jun '10	MV Hyundai 203 (South Korea)	Lynx/RIB/VBSS
	6th Sep '10	MV Atlantic Grace (Hong Kong)	Lynx/RIB/VBSS
The 5th Unit	15th Sep '10	MV Jag Prerana (India)	Lynx/RIB/VBSS
The 7th Unit	2nd Jul '10	MV STX Azelia (South Korea)	Lynx
	6th May '11	MV D & K (UAE)	Lynx
The 8th Unit	22nd Nov '11	MV Duckling (Panama)	Lynx
The 9th Unit	15th Feb '12	MV Emirate Peace (Seychelles)	Lynx

In addition to ship deployments, the ROK Navy assumed command of CTF–151 twice, led by ROK Rear Admirals in April 2010 and June 2012. By carrying out the mission successfully, the ROK Navy has greatly contributed to the remarkable progress in stopping pirate attacks in the region. The ROK Navy also significantly contributed in enhancing military cooperation between the coalition forces (CMF/EU/NATO) and independent participating navies such as China, Russia, India, and Malaysia. The concept of counter-piracy operations for coalition forces is shown in figure 3.

Second, the ROK Navy has escorted over 7,600 vessels and not a single one has come to any harm from pirates under its protection. In general, one destroyer of the ROK Navy escorts civilian vessels back and forth across the Gulf of Aden. The escort method primarily involves forming a convoy at the assembly point (there are two assembly points for escorting vessels designated at the eastern and western ends of the Gulf). Since civilian vessels differ in their capabilities, the ROK Navy organizes the most appropriate convoy formation to effectively protect the vessels. When the convoy sails across the Gulf of

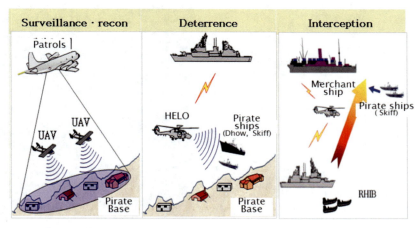

FIGURE 3   *Counter piracy operations concept.*

Aden the destroyer guards the group and a helicopter carried on the destroyer watches the surrounding area from the sky.

Through this procedure, the ROK Navy makes one round trip of the IRTC a week sailing across the Gulf of Aden, making absolutely certain that the convoy is safe and secure, day and night. Through these escort activities, the ROK Navy provides a tremendous sense of security in the Gulf of Aden and off the coast of Somalia. The concept of the counter-piracy patrol is shown in figure 4.

Lastly, the Cheong Hae Unit carried out three tremendous military rescue operations on merchant vessels with pirates onboard. Among them, the most famous rescue operation was "Operation Dawn of the Gulf of Aden" which originated when South Korean chemical tanker *Samho Jewelry* was hijacked by a group of Somali pirates 600km southeast of Muscat, Oman on 15 January 2011. The twenty-one crew members were held hostage, among them were eight South Koreans, eleven Burmese, and two Indonesians. At that time the ROK Government was very careful planning a rescue operation since the hostages' safety was the priority. Accepting this risk, the ROK Government boldly ordered the Cheong Hae Unit to conduct a military rescue operation for *Samho Jewelry* in light of the previous case of the South Korean merchant vessel *Samho Dream* which had been captured for seven months and released after paying a ransom of 9.5 million US dollars just nine months previous. Moreover, after releasing the merchant vessel *Samho Dream*, South Korean

■ Individual countries
  : Convoy within GOA IRTC

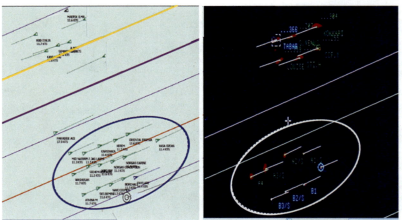

FIGURE 4   *Counter piracy patrol concept.*

flagged vessels were targeted by Somali pirates as the most attractive target. For this reason the ROK Government desperately wanted to conduct the rescue operation despite the high risk to the ship and crew.

To digress briefly and describe the environment surrounding the area prior to the operation, the presence of naval forces in the Gulf of Aden and the Somali Basin saw little success in deterring pirates. In the Somali Basin, naval counter-piracy measures have been far less successful. What seemed to have the most success against pirates in the Gulf of Aden was the joint effort of industry and navies. Captains and ship-owners preferred naval vessels to keep their distance after a hijacking in order to mitigate the situation, thereby protecting the crew.

Resuming to the rescue operation, a destroyer of the Republic of Korea called *Choi-young* was dispatched to the scene and caught up with the *Samho Jewelry*. Amid rising tensions, the ROK national authorities finally gave the green light to initiate a boarding operation, as intelligence reports suggested that a pirate "mother ship" was being dispatched from Somalia to provide reinforcement. The rescue operation of the *Samho Jewelry* began on the 21st of January at 04:46 local time and its daring execution led to five hours of chilling drama on the high seas. When it was over, the ROK Navy had rescued twenty-one sailors, killed eight pirates and captured five others. Although the captain of the tanker was wounded during the rescue operation, he survived his injury and no other

COUNTER-PIRACY OPERATIONS OF THE REPUBLIC OF KOREA 65

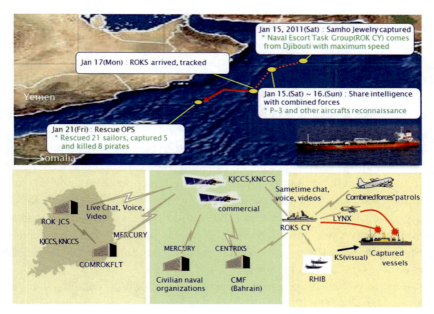

FIGURE 5   Operation Dawn of the Gulf of Aden.

crew members were hurt.[23] The ROK Navy named the historic rescue, Operation Dawn of the Gulf of Aden. A brief outline of the operation is shown in figure 5. In the aftermath of hostage rescue operations on the *Samho Jewelry*, eight dead bodies of pirates were delivered to Somalia through Oman. The five arrested pirates were sent to Republic of Korea where one was sentenced to life imprisonment, one for fifteen years, and three for thirteen years in prison in accordance with Korean law. All five are currently serving their respective sentences.

The above measure's legality is deemed legitimate according to international and domestic law. In particular, the sending of the dead bodies of eight pirates was all done under humanitarian conditions. The punishments imposed on the five arrested pirates have legal ground according to international laws such as the UN Convention on the Law of the Sea, the Convention for the Suppression of Unlawful Acts against the Safety of Maritime Navigation (SUA Convention), domestic criminal law, and the ROK Punishment of Damaging Ships and Sea Structures Act.

However, complementary legal issues were identified in the judiciary procedure. They became issues at hand because the ROK Navy did not possess

---

23   For more details, see http://en.wikipedia.org/siki/operation_Dawn_of_Gulf_of_Aden and http://www.youtube.com/watch?=VrfvHWUCr.0.

any authority regarding arrests and investigations of civilians as do the police. Confusion arose on whether or not the ROK Navy can arrest the captured pirates, who were civilians. In response, the ROK government swiftly sent police officers to the field and legally took delivery of the respective captured personnel. In order to supplement the above mentioned procedural issues, the ROK National Assembly is currently pushing for a special law to vest judicial police authority to ROK Navy ship officers as well.

It is said that Operation Dawn of the Gulf of Aden draws comparison to Operation Entebbe, a hostage rescue mission Israeli commandos carried out at Entebbe Airport in Uganda in 1976. The bold military operation showed resolve and ROK's stance on any illegal activities by pirates targeting South Korean vessels. Considering the fact that pirates and hostages were mixed together and information was limited, the ROK Navy can be said to have conducted a perfect operation. The operation is all the more extraordinary as the mission was a success far away from home.

There were two other rescue operations successfully conducted by the Cheong Hae Unit. On 20 April 2011, the South Korean merchant vessel *Hanjin Tienjin* was under threat of hijacking by Somali pirates who had already climbed aboard. As soon as receiving a distress call from *Hanjin Tienjin*, the ROK Government dispatched ROKS *Choi-young* again to the scene and ordered another rescue operation. ROKS *Choi-young* successfully rescued the vessel and the crew of twenty who escaped into the shelter safely. Second, four Koreans of the hijacked Singapore merchant vessel *Gemini* in 2010 were declared released from Haradera after paying a ransom on 30 April 2011. The Cheong Hae Unit (ROK ship *Kang-gamchan*) was dispatched to the scene and rescued four Korean hostages using the organic helicopter "Lynx" from a pirate camp in Haradera returning them to the ship without any harm.

The above three rescue operations showed the well-equipped and trained combat capability of the ROK Navy leaving a great impression with coalition forces. These operations demonstrate the excellent operational capabilities of the ROK Navy in spite of its first ever overseas combat operation. In particular, Operation Dawn of the Gulf of Aden is worthy of praise as the pivotal point of counter-piracy operations making the number of severe pirate attacks decline rapidly.

4 Lessons from the Operations and Suggestions

What we can draw upon in summary is that the risk of attack in the waters off Somalia is unlikely to disappear completely in the near term. The US National Intelligence Council classified Somalia as a highly vulnerable country up to

2030. Although the unprecedented level of naval patrols by more than twenty nations has deterred numerous attacks, the area is simply too vast to prevent all incidents. Although the collective effort of multi-national navies made a dramatic 75% decline in pirate attacks last year compared with 2011, Somali pirates have adapted to these efforts and are improving their capabilities as well as expanding their operations to farther and farther off shore.

From the experience of counter-piracy operations around Somalia, the ROK Navy drew the conclusion that convoys are most successful when they contain a number of merchant vessels fewer than 12, sail at high speeds, and position the warship in front of the convoy. In addition, to protect merchant vessels effectively there must be coordination naval forces operating in the region, a vigilant watch against the approach of pirates, and proper measures to prevent and disrupt pirates' boarding. As naval forces achieve the early detection of distant pirates they increase the chance of preventing pirates from getting on board. Also, increased speed along an evasive course increases the chance that pirates will break off a chase because of the consumption of time and fuel. Rough seas can also slow down pirate skiffs. In addition, merchant vessels' appliance of "Best Management Plan (BMP)" and embarkation of "Private Armed Security Teams (PAST)" have contributed greatly to reduce the rate of success of pirates.

Another worthwhile mention is that coordination between naval forces is vital to cover a vast and remote area of operations quickly, efficiently, and in absence of host nation support. With separate command structures, duplications and even contradictions are unavoidable, likely at the expense of an efficient, cohesive counter-piracy effort. Due to the lack of unity of command these precious military resources are not achieving maximum effectiveness. All the more, some naval ships do not give assistance to vessels flying particular flags from certain countries. A few individual states have deployed naval units to the region, mainly for the protection of their own merchant ships. For these reasons, defense experts point to a need for a central authority to coordinate piracy patrols. In line with this, SHADE (Shared Awareness of Deconfliction) conferences and concerted counter-piracy efforts among CTF 151 (CMF), CTF 465 (EU), and CTF 508 (NATO) are encouraged to draw deeper collaboration among the various counter-piracy forces.

Naval patrols are a required component of an effective counter-piracy strategy but cannot succeed if not done in unison. One of the solutions should be establishing an effective legal mechanism for prosecution of pirates since there are no clear policies in dealing with the captured pirates. Nine out of ten Somali pirates apprehended by naval patrols are released because there is no jurisdiction to prosecute them. Consider Korea as an example. The Korean Constitution states that it will follow approved international laws and enforcement effects.

The UN Convention on the Law of the Sea states that the act of piracy is an act of violation against the world and therefore any nation may apprehend those responsible. However due to the absence of domestic law that entrusts legal authority of prosecution, countries cannot prosecute those responsible. As such, Korea is working arduously to guarantee a special law to resolve this issue.

In addition, captured pirates have convinced themselves that there is little to fear from the naval forces. First, pirates are likely to regard prisons in the developed countries as luxury hotels where accommodation and food are far better than they can expect at home. Second, pirates will invoke their statutory human rights and many end up as asylum seekers and apply for family reunification. Third, those found guilty will most likely face short sentences and also apply for asylum status. The cost of all this, of course, is high considering the meager results. Consequently, legal problems significantly hinder efforts to deal with Somali pirates.

In sum, through the counter-piracy operations off the Somalia and the Gulf of Aden, the ROK Navy drew some valuable lessons, such as effectiveness of convoys, a need for enhanced coordination and unity of command, and the necessity for a more effective legal mechanism to prosecute the pirates. Military action alone cannot resolve the problem of piracy off Somalia although the collective effort of multi-national navies has resulted in a dramatic decline in pirate attacks in 2012 compared with 2011. Somali pirates have adapted to these efforts and are improving their capabilities as well as expanding their operations farther away from the shore. The problem of piracy off the coast of Somalia cannot be resolved by military operations alone. In fact, the main causes of piracy are predominantly political, economic, and social. Somalia needs leadership and institutions that can guide and lead the country in the right direction. These issues require time and money and the willingness of both the Somali government and the international community. A long-term solution can be found only if the international community and regional governments make concerted efforts to solve the root causes of piracy. Only by working together whether on the high seas or on the ground in Somalia, can those affected by piracy hope to bring about its end.

The fundamental solution of piracy in the region is to rehabilitate Somalia as a strong maritime country on the basis of the sea. It is supported by the striking polarity of the 68-year history of South and North Korea since 1945. Maritime South Korea, completely battered and torn by the tragic Korean War after the Liberation from Japan, has completely transformed itself into a wealthy, democratic and industrialized country while the continental North Korea is now on the verge of collapse due to its devastating economic difficulties, diplomatic isolation, and political instability.

PART 2

Transnational Threats

∴

CHAPTER 3

Counter Proliferation Activities and Freedom of Navigation

Douglas Guilfoyle

Abstract

The threat of the proliferation by sea of weapons of mass destruction (WMD) and related precursor technologies (WMD materiel), especially to terrorist groups, is one which has attracted significant attention. The issue became particularly topical following the So San interdiction of 2002 and the launch of the Proliferation Security Initiative in 2003. Though the PSI has facilitated inter-governmental co-operation, the true extent of its achievements is at best unclear. Attempts to change the positive law dealing with maritime interdiction of WMD materiel have been notably limited in scope and, perhaps, of questionable practical value. While some feared the erosion of freedom of navigation in the name of counter-proliferation, such developments have not come to pass. If anything, developments have reinforced the primacy of freedom of navigation and the exclusive jurisdiction of the flag State on the high seas as fundamental tenets of the law of the sea. A further question, however, is why WMD proliferation has absorbed such attention when trafficking in small arms by sea is likely far more destabilising. The paper reflects upon the difficulties of containing the proliferation of both WMD and conventional weapons by sea.

1 Introduction

The threat of the proliferation by sea of weapons of mass destruction (WMD) and associated precursor or dual use technologies (WMD materiel), especially

---

*   Douglas Guilfoyle, Reader in Law, University College London, Faculty of Laws. Dr. Guilfoyle joined the UCL Faculty of Laws in 2007, after submitting his doctoral dissertation at the University of Cambridge. During his graduate studies Douglas held a British Council Chevening Scholarship and a Gates Cambridge Trust Scholarship. Prior to undertaking graduate study Douglas worked as a judge's associate in the Federal Court of Australia and as associate to the President of the Australian Administrative Appeals Tribunal. He has also worked as a litigator in Sydney. The author's PowerPoint is available at http://www.virginia .edu/colp/pdf/Seoul-Guilfoyle.pdf.

to terrorist groups, is one which has attracted significant attention.[1] The issue was particularly topical following the *So San* interdiction of 2002 and the launch of the Proliferation Security Initiative (PSI) in 2003.[2] Though the PSI brought about significant developments in inter-governmental co-operation to counter maritime proliferation,[3] the extent of its achievements is at best unclear. Attempts to change the positive law dealing with maritime interdiction of WMD materiel have been notably limited in scope and, perhaps, of debateable practical value. While some feared the erosion of freedom of navigation, or that norm-entrepreneurs would push for a new customary international rule permitting high seas WMD interdiction, this has not eventuated. If anything, developments have simply reinforced the status of freedom of navigation and the exclusive jurisdiction of the flag State on the high seas as fundamental tenets of the law of the sea. A further question, however, is why WMD proliferation has absorbed such attention when trafficking in small arms by sea is likely far more destabilising. The present chapter will thus reflect upon the difficulties of containing the proliferation of both WMD and conventional weapons by sea.

1 See especially: N. Klein, *Maritime Security and the Law of the Sea* (Oxford, Oxford University Press, 2011), Chapter 4; D. Guilfoyle, *Shipping Interdiction and the Law of the Sea* (Cambridge, Cambridge University Press, 2009), Chapter 9; C.H. Allen, *Maritime Counterproliferation Operations and the Rule of Law* (Westport, Praeger Security International, 2007); Y.-H. Song, 'The US-led Proliferation Security Initiative and UNCLOS: legality, implementation, and an assessment', 38 O.D.I.L., 2007, 101; M. Malirsch and F. Prill, 'The Proliferation Security Initiative and the 2005 Protocol to the SUA Convention', 67 *Zeitschrift für ausländisches öffentliches Recht und Völkerrecht*, 2007, 229; D.H. Joyner, 'The Proliferation Security Initiative: Nonproliferation, Counterproliferation and International Law', 30 *Yale Journal of International Law*, 2005, 507; W. Heintschel von Heinegg, 'The Proliferation Security Initiative: security vs freedom of navigation?', 35 *Israel Yearbook on Human Rights*, 2005, 181–203; M. Byers, 'Policing the High Seas: The Proliferation Security Initiative', 98 A.J.I.L., 2004, 526. It remains on the UN agenda, largely at the level of technical assistance: Report of the Secretary-General, 'United Nations Global Counter-Terrorism Strategy: Activities of the United Nations system in implementing the Strategy', UN Doc. A/66/762 (4 April 2012), paras 60–66.
2 Academic interest, however, peaked in 2005–7 and has been limited since. (Based on a survey of articles, books or book chapters catalogued by the Peace Palace Library with 'Proliferation Security Initiative' in the title.)
3 E. Belcher, 'The Proliferation Security Initiative: Lessons for Using Nonbinding Agreements', Council on Foreign Relations, 2011 <http://www.cfr.org/proliferation/proliferation-security-initiative/p25394>.

2 Maritime Proliferation of WMD and the Rise of the PSI

2.1 *Introduction*

In 2002, and following the events of 11 September 2001, concern about the possibility of terrorist organisations gaining WMD was widespread. On 27 June 2002 the leaders of the Group of Eight (G8) most highly industrialised States declared:

> The attacks of September 11 demonstrated that terrorists are prepared to use any means to... inflict appalling casualties on innocent people. We commit ourselves to prevent terrorists... from acquiring or developing nuclear, chemical, radiological and biological weapons;... and related materials, equipment and technology.[4]

An accompanying statement of principles referred to the need for "international cooperation to detect, deter and interdict... illicit trafficking in such items". The first high-profile incident of such cooperation was the high seas interdiction of the *So San* by the Spanish Navy acting on US intelligence in late 2002.[5] The *So San*, a vessel of uncertain nationality,[6] had left North Korea with a concealed cargo of Scud missiles and dual-use chemicals. When Yemen publically claimed to have legally purchased these weapons, both vessel and cargo were released.

The incident was widely credited with the establishment of the US-led Proliferation Security Initiative (PSI), announced by President George W. Bush in May 2003; PSI participant States agreeing a non-binding Statement of Interdiction Principles (PSI Principles) later that year.[7] The ostensible purpose of the PSI was to work *within* existing international law to interdict shipments

---

4 Statement by G8 Leaders, 'The G8 Global Partnership Against the Spread of Weapons and Materials of Mass Destruction', Kananaskis, 27 June 2002, <http://www.g7.utoronto.ca/summit/2002kananaskis/arms.html>. Compare: 'Non Proliferation of Weapons of Mass Destruction: A G8 Declaration', 2 June 2003, <http://www.g8.fr/evian/english/navigation/2003_g8_summit/summit_documents/non_proliferation_of_weapons_of_mass_destruction_-_a_g8_declaration.html> (terrorism and WMD proliferation as 'the pre-eminent threat[s] to international security').
5 See generally: Byers, 'Policing the High Seas'; Guilfoyle, *Shipping Interdiction*, pp. 234–5 and 244–5.
6 It eventually claimed Cambodian nationality: Byers, 'Policing the High Seas', 526 n. 5.
7 'Proliferation Security Initiative: Statement of Interdiction Principles', 4 September 2003, <http://www.state.gov/t/isn/c27726.htm> (hereafter, PSI Interdiction Principles).

of WMD or precursor technologies to "States or non-state actors of proliferation concern" through coordinated action.[8] Thus the PSI expresses political commitments by PSI participants:

> ... to seriously consider providing consent ... to the boarding and searching of its own flag vessels by other states, and to the seizure of [any] WMD-related cargoes [discovered]; and

> ... to take appropriate actions to (1) stop and/or search in their internal waters, territorial seas, or contiguous zones ... vessels ... reasonably suspected of carrying ... cargoes [of WMD materiel] to or from states or non-state actors of proliferation concern and to seize such cargoes ...; and (2) to enforce conditions on vessels entering or leaving their ... internal waters ... reasonably suspected of carrying such cargoes, such as requiring ... boarding, search, and seizure of such cargoes ...

Obviously, such actions should have no impact on high-seas freedoms of navigation without flag State consent. As at November 2012, the PSI was listed as having 102 participants.[9]

The usual example given of a PSI interdiction is the *BBC China* episode.[10] The *BBC China* was a vessel suspected by the United Kingdom and United States of carrying uranium centrifuge components to Libya in 2003. The vessel was flagged in Antigua and Barbuda but was German-owned. The German government, a PSI participant, requested the owner direct it into an Italian port where customs officials removed the components. The operation ultimately relied on Italian customs law rather than international law. It also illustrates the common characterisation of the PSI as an "activity, not an organization"[11] or an "informal coalition" addressing practical problems.[12] (Although some have suggested the *BBC China* was a "separate operation" which does not represent a PSI success story.)[13] Beyond *ad hoc* cooperation, a principal feature

---

8 Ibid., Principle 1.
9 See: <http://www.state.gov/t/isn/c27732.htm>; note, however, the requirements of being a "participant" may be "fairly weak": M.B. Nikitin, 'Proliferation Security Initiative (PSI)', CRS Report for Congress, RL34327, 15 June 2012, 2.
10 Guilfoyle, *Shipping Interdiction*, p. 245; Klein, *Maritime Security*, pp. 202–3.
11 Guilfoyle, *Shipping Interdiction*, p. 236.
12 Malirsch and Prill, 'Proliferation Security Initiative', 240.
13 Nikitin, 'Proliferation Security Initiative', 5; Song, 'US-led Proliferation Security Initiative', 128.

of the PSI has been its policy-level meetings, Operational Expert Group meetings and joint training exercises aimed at fostering closer cooperation and inter-operability.[14]

The PSI's successes are hard to measure. By their nature, intelligence-led interdiction operations are unlikely to be publicized and the benefits of closer cooperation are hard to quantify. In 2006 the PSI was said to have played a "key role" in intercepting "more than 30 shipments".[15] This appears consistent with other US government reports of 11 interdictions in 2004–2005 and "roughly two dozen" interdictions in 2005–6.[16] More recent claims appear lacking. It has thus been observed that: "the need to attribute an operation to PSI appears to have receded. Recent PSI meetings have emphasised capacity-building, best practices and cooperation across agencies and governments."[17]

A more readily measurable PSI aim was to "work to strengthen... relevant international law and frameworks" to prevent WMD proliferation.[18] To what extent has this law-making or law-changing objective been achieved? Certainly the aim to "strengthen" international law was behind the US-led push to conclude: the 2005 Protocol to the SUA Convention (the SUA Protocol)[19] and an allied series of bilateral counter-proliferation agreements; and relevant UN Security Council resolutions on counter-proliferation.[20] Each of these measures is assessed in turn.

2.2 *The PSI, Treaty Law and Customary Law*

The 2005 SUA Protocol, largely negotiated through meetings of the IMO Legal Committee, was "the first [multilateral] international instrument creating crimes of transporting WMD materiel by sea and providing for the suppression of such crimes through high-seas interdictions."[21] In 2004–2010 the

---

14   Song, 'US-led Proliferation Security Initiative', 107–9; Malirsch and Prill, 'Proliferation Security Initiative', 234.
15   Nikitin, 'Proliferation Security Initiative', 3.
16   Ibid.
17   Ibid.
18   PSI Interdiction Principles, Principle 3.
19   Protocol to the Convention for the Suppression of Unlawful Acts against the Safety of Maritime Navigation, 1 November 2005, IMO Doc. LEG/CONF.15/21 (SUA Protocol 2005). Entered force 28 July 2010. A consolidated text is available in A.V. Lowe and S.A.G. Talmon (eds.), *Legal Order of the Oceans: Basic Documents on the Law of the Sea* (Oxford, Hart, 2009).
20   See SC Res. 1540 (28 April 2004) (on counter-proliferation generally); SC Res. 1718 (14 October 2006) and 1874 (12 June 2009) (North Korea); and SC Res. 1747 (24 March 2007), 1803 (3 March 2008) and 1929 (9 June 2010) (Iran).
21   Guilfoyle, *Shipping Interdiction*, p. 254.

United States also concluded a widely-discussed series of eleven bilateral PSI ship-boarding agreements with major flag States under which it could board partner-State vessels suspected of involvement in WMD proliferation.[22] The pace of this bilateral treaty-making practice has slowed with no new agreements since 2010, perhaps reflecting a shift in US priorities.[23] Generally, both the SUA Protocol and the US bilateral agreements require flag State consent to a high-seas interdiction of a suspect vessel, though (at the flag-State's election) such consent may be presumed in certain cases. For example, some of the bilateral treaties allow boarding and inspection if within a specified period—usually two or four hours following an *acknowledged* request to board—a flag State has made *no* reply ("four-hour deemed consent").[24] Some others simply provide comprehensive permission in advance to boarding and inspection. The SUA Protocol generally requires flag State consent to boarding and inspection, but parties may opt into a provision allowing either four-hour deemed consent or granting comprehensive permission in advance (discussed further below).[25]

For the 2005 SUA Protocol to be regarded as a success, two requirements must be met. First, it must be sufficiently widely ratified. Second, it is ultimately reliant upon national legislation for its enforcement: the crimes it creates can only be prosecuted under national law.[26] On this basis the SUA Protocol is, at present, a qualified success at best. Despite the diplomatic effort made by the United States, United Kingdom and like-minded States to secure its conclusion, as at 31 March 2013 it has gained only 23 ratifications.[27] None of these are from the United States, United Kingdom or other G8 States. Certainly two

---

22   Ibid., pp. 246–54; Klein, *Maritime Security*, pp. 184–7. The agreements are formally reciprocal, allowing boarding of US vessels.
23   Belcher, 'The Proliferation Security Initiative', 11. Agreements were concluded in: 2004 with Liberia, Marshall Islands, Panama; 2005 with Belize, Croatia, Cyprus; 2007 with Malta, Mongolia; 2008 with The Bahamas; and 2010 with Antigua and Barbuda, St. Vincent and the Grenadines. See: <http://www.state.gov/t/isn/c27733.htm>.
24   Guilfoyle, *Shipping Interdiction*, pp. 249–51.
25   Art. 8 *bis*(5)(d) and (e), SUA Protocol 2005.
26   Compare: M.D. Fink, 'The Right of Visit for Warships: Some Challenges in Applying the Law of Maritime Interdiction on the High Seas', 49 *Military Law and Law of War Review*, 2010, 19.
27   Algeria, Austria, Bulgaria, Cook Islands, Côte d'Ivoire, Dominican Republic, Estonia, Fiji, Latvia, Liechtenstein, Marshall Islands, Netherlands, Nauru, Palau, Panama, Saint Kitts and Nevis, Saint Lucia, Saint Vincent and the Grenadines, Serbia, Spain, Switzerland, Turkey, Vanuatu. See: <http://www.imo.org/About/Conventions/StatusOfConventions/Documents/Status%20-%202012.pdf> (as at 30 November 2012).

of the world's three largest flag States by registered tonnage, Panama and the Marshall Islands, have ratified the Protocol and have relevant laws prohibiting WMD transfers.[28] While this might allow suspect cargoes aboard such vessels to be interdicted at sea by a third State under the Protocol, this could only occur if a significant naval power ratified it.[29] None has.

It might be thought that, in the event of non-parties like the United States or United Kingdom wishing to interdict a shipment aboard the vessel of a SUA Protocol party, they could simply enter into an *ad hoc* arrangement permitting them to do so and, with flag State consent, assume jurisdiction to prosecute any offences discovered aboard. Nonetheless, the interdicting State would—if it intended to prosecute—need an applicable national law. An obstacle to the United Kingdom ratifying the SUA Protocol is, presumably, its failure to pass any such law applicable to proliferation aboard foreign vessels.[30] The United States is in a better position to conduct such *ad hoc* prosecutions. Relevant US law is broad enough to capture the acts of foreigners outside the United States conspiring to use WMD against a US citizen abroad or any person or property within the United States.[31] US law also criminalises transport of WMD materiel by "any vessel ... on the high seas" with knowledge it is intended for use in a terrorist offence "transcending national boundaries".[32] Relying on such *ad hoc* arrangements to found prosecutions can, in some jurisdictions, encounter human rights difficulties. For example, the question may arise whether the defendants had notice that they could be subjected to the criminal law

---

[28] See relevant 1540 Committee Reports: UN Doc S/AC.44/2004/(02)/82 (Marshall Islands, 10 December 2004); S/AC.44/2004/(02)/120/Add.1 (Panama, 8 March 2006).

[29] The US could seek to interdict suspect WMD shipments aboard Panamanian or the Marshall Islands flag vessels under its bilateral agreements with them. See the treaties listed at: <http://www.state.gov/t/isn/c27733.htm>.

[30] See, e.g., ss 44 and 47(7) Anti-terrorism, Crime and Security Act 2001 c. 24 (nuclear and biological weapons offences only extend extra-territorially to acts done by a "United Kingdom person"). There have been no amendments to the Aviation and Maritime Security Act 1990 c. 31 implementing the SUA Convention.

[31] See: 18 USC § 2332a and b.

[32] 18 USC § 2283; however, the offence must also constitute a federal offence listed in 18 USC § 2332b(g)(5)(B) all of which require some nexus to the US or must be committed "within the jurisdiction of the United States". One candidate might be 18 USC § 956(a)(1) (conspiracy to kill, kidnap, main or injure in a foreign country)—on the theory that a vessel on the high seas surrendered to US jurisdiction becomes a place within US jurisdiction. See discussion in: *US v Bellaizac-Hurtado*, 700 F.3d 1245 (2012) (US constitutional authority to prescribe "felonies committed on the high seas" noted).

of the interdicting State.[33] However, a key achievement of the PSI may simply be that it has changed the terms of debate and made *ad hoc* consent more likely. The idea of (consensual) WMD interdiction is no longer as controversial as it was in 2002.

Some feared that the PSI and treaty-law initiatives like the SUA Protocol could give rise to (or were designed to create) a customary international law rule permitting interdiction of vessels suspected of WMD proliferation. A *widely-ratified* SUA Protocol might have contributed to the crystallisation of customary prohibition on WMD proliferation binding on third States; however, that precondition remains elusive. Further, as noted, the SUA Protocol does not contain any right to unilaterally board suspect vessels without flag State consent—which further limits any norm its text might be capable of generating. Indeed, the United States had strongly advocated for the inclusion of an *automatic* "authorization to board" and search a suspect vessel if "there is no response from the [flag State] within four hours of acknowledgement of receipt of a request to confirm [a suspect vessel's] nationality".[34] As noted, under the Protocol as concluded, such four-hour deemed consent only operates if a party "opts in". While there are examples of such boarding rights in bilateral agreements, they are limited in number.[35] In the absence of widespread treaty practice, a new customary international law rule permitting unilateral WMD interdiction on the high seas is unlikely to crystallize.[36] The treaty practice in this area has not, therefore, disturbed the status of freedom of navigation and the exclusive jurisdiction of the flag State on the high seas as fundamental tenets of the law of the sea. Indeed, a potential weakness of the SUA Protocol may be its very reliance on flag State jurisdiction. States engaged

---

33   *Medvedyev and Others v. France*, Application no. 3394/03, European Court of Human Rights (Grand Chamber), 29 March 2010, <http://www.unhcr.org/refworld/docid/502d45dc2.html>.

34   Art. 8 *bis*(5)(d).

35   Of the treaties at <http://www.state.gov/t/isn/c27733.htm>, see: Art. 4(3)(b), US-Liberia PSI Agreement; Article 4(3)(b), US-Marshall Islands PSI Agreement; Article 4(3)(d), US-Mongolia PSI Agreement; Article 4(3), US-Belize PSI Agreement; Article 4(3)(b) and (c), US-Cyprus PSI Agreement; Art. 5(3)(b) and (c), US-Malta PSI Agreement. Similar arrangements apply between the United States and Panama. On similar drug interdiction treaties see: Guilfoyle, *Shipping Interdiction*, p. 89.

36   Contra J. Doolin, 'The Proliferation Security Initiative: Cornerstone of a New International Norm', 59 *Naval War College Review*, 2006, 50.

in proliferation are, perhaps, unlikely to do so under the flags of PSI participants or of parties to the Protocol.[37]

2.3 UN Security Council Resolutions and WMD Counter-Proliferation

Security Council Chapter VII resolutions dealing with WMD proliferation may be seen as aligned with PSI efforts to "strengthen... relevant international law", in particular UNSCR 1540. At its core UNSCR 1540 obliges all states to "adopt and enforce... effective laws" prohibiting non-state actors from, *inter alia*, acquiring, possessing or transporting WMD materiel.[38] At China's request, any reference to "interdiction" was omitted from the resolution.[39] Some commentators see in this a reluctance to "legally validate" PSI activities.[40] However, the *obligation* upon States under UNSCR 1540 to "adopt and enforce" counter-proliferation laws may permit States to interdict vessels passing through their territorial sea transporting WMD materiel destined for non-State actors.[41] (The most convincing argument being that States enjoy a plenary criminal law enforcement jurisdiction over offences occurring within the territorial sea which is normally restrained out of comity; a jurisdiction which UNSCR 1540 obliges them to use.)[42] However, there remains "room for differing interpretations" regarding whether such territorial sea interdictions would be a violation of innocent passage rights.[43] It is also unclear that any such interdictions have occurred in practice.[44]

---

[37] R. Pedrozo, 'The Impending Nuclear Disaster: Flaws in the International Counter-Proliferation Regime at Sea', 9 *Loyola University Chicago International Law Review*, 2011–12, 127; Song, 'US-led Proliferation Security Initiative', 119.

[38] SC Res. 1540 (28 April 2004), para 2.

[39] UN Doc. S/PV.4950 (22 April 2004), 6.

[40] Klein, *Maritime Security*, p. 282.

[41] Heintschel von Heinegg, 195; Joyner, 'The Proliferation Security Initiative', 535–6.

[42] Guilfoyle, *Shipping Interdiction*, pp. 240–43; compare Allen, *Maritime Counterproliferation*, p. 165. Note Art. 27(1), United Nations Convention on the Law of the Sea 1982, 1833 U.N.T.S. 397 (UNCLOS) (using "should not" rather than "shall not" in describing limits on coastal State jurisdiction in the territorial sea). Note J. Kraska, 'Broken Taillight at Sea: The Peacetime International Law of Visit, Board, Search, and Seizure', 16 *Ocean & Coastal Law Journal*, 2010, 19–20 (US position that Art. 19(2), UNCLOS is an exhaustive list of activities rendering passage non-innocent).

[43] Klein, *Maritime Security*, pp. 207–8.

[44] No examples are reported in relevant UN documents: e.g. 'Report of the Secretary-General: Measures to prevent terrorists from acquiring weapons of mass destruction,' UN Doc A/67/135 (10 July 2012).

Other than transfers of WMD materiel to non-State actors, the PSI was founded to prevent such transfers to States of "proliferation concern". Only two States were ever publically referred to as such by PSI participants: North Korea and Iran.[45] While the Security Council's failure to approve a general mandate for high-seas WMD interdiction was perhaps readily understandable, one might have expected fewer objections to interdiction as a targeted sanction. This has not proven the case regarding North Korea. UNSCR 1718 required States to "prevent the direct or indirect supply, sale or transfer to [North Korea], through their territories or by their nationals, or using their flag vessels or aircraft" of certain listed WMD materiel and large weapon systems as well as prohibiting North Korean export of such materiel.[46] UNSCR 1718 makes no reference to interdiction. In UNSCR 1874 the Security Council went further: first, by calling on "Member States to inspect vessels, *with the consent of the flag State*, on the high seas" (emphasis added) suspected of trafficking in WMD materiel covered by UNSCR 1718; and second, by deciding that where "the flag State does not consent to [such] inspection" it must "direct the vessel to ... an appropriate ... port" for inspection.[47] UNSCR 1874 also expanded the North Korean weapons embargo (and export prohibitions) to cover conventional weapons and to prohibit refuelling ("bunkering") of North Korean vessels engaged in prohibited export activity. Thus these measures made *no* formal inroads into the principle of the exclusive jurisdiction of flag States on the high seas.[48] (Though the provisions on diversion to port do clearly involve some interference with freedom of navigation.) Ultimately, Pedrozo sees the prohibition on bunkering as having been more successful in curtailing North Korea's ability to use its own flag vessels in proliferation activity that the (weak) high seas boarding and inspection provisions.[49]

Security Council Resolution 1929 dealing with non-proliferation and Iran can only be treated briefly here. In any event, UNSCR 1929 contains a similar high seas inspection provision to UNSCR 1874, once again based on flag State consent.[50] Such provisions are of largely symbolic or political value as flag

---

45 'Chairman's Statement', Proliferation Security Initiative, Brisbane Meeting, 9–10 July 2003, <http://2001-2009.state.gov/t/isn/rls/other/25377.htm>.
46 SC Res. 1718 (14 October 2006), para. 8(a)(ii) and (b).
47 SC Res. 1874 (12 June 2009), paras 12 and 13.
48 Pedrozo, 'The Impending Nuclear Disaster', 127.
49 Ibid., 113 (discussing the 2009 *Kang Nam 1* episode).
50 SC Res. 1929 (9 June 2010), para. 15 which must be read in light of SC Res. 1747 (24 March 2007) and SC Res. 1803 (3 March 2008); Pedrozo, 'The Impending Nuclear Disaster', 112–118, 127; Kraska, 'Broken Taillight at Sea', 34–39.

States could already authorise such boardings,[51] although the diversion to port provisions perhaps add something to the substantive law.

2.4 Assessment

How should we assess the impact of counter-proliferation efforts on the law of the sea? Quite exaggerated claims were once made about the PSI's possible consequences. Perry posited that "the PSI Principles, in practice, will represent a Potemkin Village behind whose facades the United States will undertake a broad campaign of interdiction" and that the PSI would inevitably undermine customary law by "blurring" jurisdictional boundaries.[52] Others suggested the PSI would undermine freedom of innocent passage in the territorial sea and threatened freedom of navigation on the high seas.[53] Such concerns do not appear to have materialised. The clandestine nature of much PSI activity means it is unlikely to have an impact on customary law formation, which requires public knowledge of State practice.[54] PSI-related efforts to create new multilateral treaty law or generally binding Security Council resolutions have also created no new high-seas interdiction rights absent flag State consent.[55] Simply put, none of these developments could support a new norm allowing counter-proliferation interdiction *without* flag State consent. This should not surprise us. The United States and its allies have powerful incentives to uphold freedom of navigation. Any generally accepted new grounds for interference with foreign vessels on the high seas could be used to justify interference with their own shipping.[56] As regards other maritime zones, the impact of the relevant Security Council Resolutions on territorial sea enforcement measures remains ambiguous. For all the discussion it has generated, it would appear counter-proliferation has done little to change the law of navigation under UNCLOS.

---

51   Kraska, 'Broken Taillight at Sea', 36; compare Pedrozo, 'The Impending Nuclear Disaster', 113 and 127.
52   T. Perry, 'Blurring the ocean zones: the effect of the Proliferation Security Initiative on the customary international law of the sea', 37 O.D.I.L., 2006, 33, 40 and 47.
53   T.V. Thomas, 'The Proliferation Security Initiative: Towards Relegation of Navigational Freedoms in UNCLOS: An Indian Perspective', 8 *Chinese Journal of International Law*, 2009, 657 *passim*.
54   Klein, *Maritime Security*, p. 206; compare: Song, 'The US-led Proliferation Security Initiative', 101–2.
55   On arguments that breach of UNSCRs could justify interdiction as a countermeasure see: D Guilfoyle, 'Interdicting Vessels to Enforce the Common Interest: Maritime Countermeasures and the Use of Force on the High Seas', 56 I.C.L.Q., 2007, 69–82.
56   Klein, *Maritime Security*, p. 206; M. Byers, 'Policing the High Seas', 542–3 and 545.

3 Proliferation of Small Arms

Armed violence using small arms and light weapons (SALW) kills as many as 526,000 persons annually.[57] Easy access to SALW in many parts of the world undermines human security[58] by "creating and sustaining a culture of violence".[59] SALW are "also the weapons of choice in most present-day conflicts and are responsible for the vast majority of conflict deaths" particularly in sub-Saharan Africa.[60] There is a general consensus that SALW proliferation intensifies and protracts internal conflicts;[61] indeed, even when such conflicts end peace may simply displace surplus SALW into neighbouring countries, promoting regional instability. SALW therefore clearly "pose a far more real threat to more people than" WMD.[62] SALW, along with other "destabilising commodity flows", are often delivered by sea; indeed, maritime transport "is the primary means of delivering shipments of conventional arms to actors involved in conflicts in Africa".[63]

This obvious problem has lead to numerous international instruments addressing the issue. These are typically framed as soft law but include a number of treaties, most notably the 2013 Arms Trade Treaty [see Table 1].

Given the scourge of SALW, this proliferation of universal and regional instruments is unsurprising. More surprising is their weakness. Measured against the standard of the Nuclear Non-Proliferation Treaty, for example, all these instruments are obviously deficient: most are not legally binding, and those that are lack the compulsory "monitoring and verification arrangements"

---

57   See: <http://www.smallarmssurvey.org/armed-violence.html>.
58   "Human security" involves paying attention to the security needs of human individuals, rather than just those of the State alone: Klein, *Maritime Security*, p. 6.
59   S.R. Grillot, 'Global Gun Control: Examining the Consequences of Competing International Norms', 17 *Global Governance*, 2011, 530.
60   A. Efrat, 'Toward Internationally Regulated Goods: Controlling the Trade in Small Arms and Light Weapons', 64 *International Organization*, 2010, 98.
61   Grillot, 'Global Gun Control', 540; Programme of Action to Prevent, Combat and Eradicate the Illicit Trade in Small Arms and Light Weapons in All Its Aspects, UN Doc. A/CONF.192/15 (2001), para. 5.
62   C. Carr, 'Combating the International Proliferation of Small Arms and Light Weapons' in J. Forest, *Countering Terrorism and Insurgency in the 21st Century: International Perspectives*, vol. 2 (Wesport, Praeger Security International, 2007), 127.
63   H. Griffiths and M. Jenks, 'Maritime Transport and Destabilizing Commodity Flows', Stockholm International Peace Research Institute, Policy Paper 32 (January 2012), vi.

COUNTER PROLIFERATION ACTIVITIES AND FREEDOM OF NAVIGATION   83

which are generally "a cornerstone of arms control agreements".[64] Space precludes detailed discussion of the applicable instruments but one may note that the long-anticipated Arms Trade Treaty (ATT):

- has no inspection or compliance mechanism beyond a reporting requirement,[65] a mechanism which has proved weak and essentially voluntary in the human rights context;[66]
- its cornerstone is a risk assessment obligation for arms exporting States, such that a weapons transfer must not proceed if there is an "overriding risk" the transfer "would contribute to or undermine peace and security" or facilitate certain violations of international law (though risks can be mitigated, *inter alia*, by "confidence-building measures");[67]
- it does not apply "to the international movement of conventional arms by, or on behalf of, a State Party for its [own] use" thus potentially exempting all weapons transfers to State actors which are ATT parties;[68]

and in particular it does not contain any:

- provision on weapons marking or tracing (making arms diversion and smuggling easier to indentify, counter and prosecute);
- inspection regime or post-shipment follow-up provisions (thus requiring arms exporters to take some responsibility for the final use of weapons);[69]
- any requirement that arms smuggling, arms diversion or arms export document fraud be made serious criminal offences in national law;
- any detailed provisions on mutual assistance in criminal matters, only general provisions encourage cooperation and information sharing;[70] or

---

64 Efrat, 'Toward Internationally Regulated Goods', 99.
65 Art. 13, ATT.
66 Report of the Human Rights Committee (2012), UN Doc. A/67/40, Vol. I, iii (deploring the fact that "a large number of States parties do not comply with their reporting obligations", 46 State parties being at least five years overdue).
67 Art. 7 and compare Art. 6, ATT.
68 Art 2(3), ATT. Although this may mean the risk assessment procedure must be applied to States which are not parties.
69 As commonly suggested by civil society: *Small Arms Survey 2011* (Cambridge, Cambridge University Press, 2011), 53.
70 Compare Arts. 11(3) and (5), 13(2) and 15 ATT with Art 18, The United Nations Convention Against Transnational Organized Crime 2000, 2225 U.N.T.S. 209.

- provisions allowing the visit, boarding, search and seizure (with flag state consent) of vessels suspected of arms smuggling and their cargoes as contemplated in numerous other treaties.[71]

Like most other instruments dealing with conventional arms, the ATT is thus relatively weak. The possible causes of this situation are complex. One may certainly analyse the failure to achieve any substantive international regulation of SALW as one of normative conflict: proponents of greater control have been unable to overcome the difficulties for regulation created by the "legitimate" uses of SALW in the international order.[72] Norms such as "sovereignty, self defence, self-determination and territorial integrity" may also suggest the right of State and non-State actors to "acquire weapons to defend themselves, [or] battle tyrannical authorities".[73] Such a narrative has proved difficult to counter through arguments based on human rights, the suffering of civilians in conflict, etc. Powerful SALW exporting States (and SALW manufacturing lobbyists) may also seek to frame the debate as one about free trade in a product with legitimate uses (e.g. law enforcement).[74] However, such a normative analysis falls short of a full explanation.

Efrat posits a useful model of State behaviour in relation to trade in goods with significant negative externalities.[75] He conceptualises the pressures upon States along two axes: the influence of exporters/consumers on decision making; and the influence of negative externalities on decision making. The former may be highest in cases including: States that are significant exporters of SALW and States which are significant consumers of SALW (including repressive States). The latter may be highest in cases where: States experience significant levels of harm from SALW (e.g. through violent crime or armed conflict) or where States have a strongly humanitarian foreign policy (which may reflect the influence of pressure groups, public opinion or the values of policymakers). States subject to high levels of exporter/consumer influence and low levels of negative externality influence will clearly favour weak or no inter-

---

[71] E.g. Art. 17, United Nations Convention against Illicit Traffic in Narcotic Drugs and Psychotropic Substances 1988, 1582 U.N.T.S. 95; Art. 8, The Protocol against the Smuggling of Migrants by Land, Sea and Air, Supplementing the United Nations Convention against Transnational Organized Crime 2000, 2241 U.N.T.S. 507; Art. 8 *bis*, SUA Protocol 2005.

[72] See generally: Grillot, 'Global Gun Control'.

[73] Ibid., 540. Note the highly state-centric list of "principles" in the preamble to the ATT and contrast the diverse set of sovereigntist, free-trade and human rights concerns expressed alongside it.

[74] Ibid., 540.

[75] Efrat, 'Toward Internationally Regulated Goods'.

national regulation. States subject to low levels of exporter/consumer influence and high levels of negative externality influence will clearly favour strong international regulation (especially in the case of weak States experiencing significant armed violence which they cannot curb alone). States subject to weak pressure on both axes will generally favour moderate regulation; States subject to strong pressure on both axes are obviously caught in conflicting currents and may adopt a variety of positions. This "heterogeneity of preferences" results in a "lack of shared interest in cooperation".[76] In the absence of a shared interest in cooperation, several consequences follow:

- arms-exporting countries will enjoy "superior bargaining power" as without their participation any system of international regulation "would be nearly futile";
- consensus-based negotiation procedures (such as those used in negotiating the ATT) will strengthen this advantage and drive the result towards the "lowest common denominator"; and
- most crucially, in the absence of common interests, the existing distribution of power among States will heavily influence the outcome of negotiations.[77]

As most of the world's largest arms exporters are also great powers[78] a relatively weak ATT was perhaps to be expected.

That said, there has been some Security Council willingness to target small arms transfers as part of sanction regimes or responses to particular armed conflicts. UN maritime arms embargoes were imposed by the Security Council in respect of conflicts in:[79] Iraq in 1990;[80] Yugoslavia in 1991–2;[81] Haiti in 1993;[82] and Sierra Leone in 1997.[83] This, however, only draws attention to the absence of a UNSCR of general application such as UNSCR 1540 targeting transfers

---

76 Efrat, 'Toward Internationally Regulated Goods', 108.
77 Efrat, 'Toward Internationally Regulated Goods', 125–6.
78 The Stockholm International Peace Institute listed the top seven arms exporters for 2012 as (export values in million USD): the US (8,760), Russia (8,003), China (1,783), the Ukraine (1,344), Germany (1,193), France (1,139) and the UK (863). See: <http://armstrade.sipri.org/armstrade/page/toplist.php>.
79 See generally: R. McLaughlin, 'United Nations mandated naval interdiction operations in the territorial sea?', 51 I.C.L.Q., 2002, 249–278.
80 SC Res. 661 (6 August 1990) and 665 (25 August 1990).
81 SC Res. 713 (25 September 1991) and 787 (16 November 1992).
82 SC Res. 875 (16 October 1993).
83 SC Res. 1132 (8 October 1997).

of WMD and WMD materiel to non-State actors. Arguably, given the scale of casualties caused by non-State actors in some conflicts using SALW, a similar resolution targeting SALW transfers would be warranted. Any effort to achieve such a resolution, of course, would run up against the same forces preventing the conclusion of a strong ATT regulatory framework. It would thus appear that maritime interdiction of SALW is something that the great powers can only reach agreement on in a case-by-case manner, as evidenced by the various Security Council measures discussed above.

4   Conclusions

A powerful criticism of efforts to counter proliferation of WMD by sea, at least to the extent that such efforts concern non-State actors acquiring such weapons, is that the threats involved are remote. Terrorist groups are methodologically conservative: they typically avoid tactics with a high risk of failure, innovate only incrementally, and are reluctant to engage "external" technical expertise of the type WMD attacks may require.[84] Further, the more complex the procurement of components for a weapon, the greater the chance of detection and the less likely terrorists are to use it.[85] SALW, by contrast, pose a much more certain, present and measurable danger to human life globally. Both WMD materiel and SALW proliferation may occur by sea; indeed, at least in the case of Africa, the majority of SALW imports occur by sea.[86] In this context, it is remarkable that by far the more high-profile effort has gone into making the idea of maritime interdiction of WMD materiel. Further, it is also superficially surprising that so little inroad has been made into the exclusive jurisdiction of the flag State or the principle of freedom of navigation. The sad reality is, great powers probably have the least to fear from SALW proliferation and are the more likely targets of WMD attacks by non-State actors (no matter how relatively small that risk). They also have strong incentives to uphold the principles of freedom of navigation and of flag State jurisdiction to protect their own trade and shipping from interference. The present maritime counter-proliferation regime simply reflects these interests.

---

[84]   M. Murphy, *Small Boats, Weak States, Dirty Money: Piracy and Maritime Terrorism in the Modern World* (London, Hurst, 2009), p. 262.
[85]   Ibid.
[86]   Griffiths and Jenks, 'Maritime Transport and Destabilizing Commodity Flows', vi.

TABLE 1   *Instruments dealing with trade in and proliferation of SALW*

Universal instruments	Regional instruments
UNTOC Firearms Protocol (2001)[87] UN Program of Action (2001–)[88] International Tracing Instrument (2005)[89] Arms Trade Treaty (2013)[90]	Inter-American Convention (1997)[91] ECOWAS Moratorium (1998) and Code of Conduct (1999)[92] Nairobi Declaration (2000)[93] Bamako Declaration (2000)[94] OSCE Document (2000)[95] SADC Protocol (2001)[96]

---

87   Protocol against the Illicit Manufacturing of and Trafficking in Firearms, their Parts and Components and Ammunition Supplementing the United Nations Convention against Transnational Organized Crime 2001, 2326 U.N.T.S. 208.

88   United Nations Program of Action to Prevent, Combat and Eradicate the Illicit Trade in Small Arms and Light Weapons in All Its Aspects: <http://www.poa-iss.org/poa/poahtml.aspx>.

89   International Instrument to Enable States to Identify and Trace, in a Timely and Reliable Manner, Illicit Small Arms and Light Weapons, UN Doc. A/CONF.192/15 (8 December 2005).

90   Arms Trade Treaty, text annexed to UN Doc. A/CONF.217/2013/L.3 (27 March 2013) ('ATT').

91   Organization of American States Inter-American Convention Against the Illicit Manufacturing of and Trafficking in Firearms, Ammunition, Explosives, and other Related Materials (14 November 1997), <http://www.oas.org/juridico/english/sigs/a-63.html>.

92   Declaration of a Moratorium on Importation, Exportation and Manufacture of Light Weapons in West Africa (31 October 1998), <http://www.fas.org/nuke/control/pcased/text/ecowas.htm> and subsequent Code of Conduct (10 December 1999), <http://www.poa-iss.org/RegionalOrganizations/ECOWAS/Moratorium%20and%20Code%20of%20Conduct.pdf>.

93   Nairobi Declaration on the Problem of the Proliferation of Illicit Small Arms and Light Weapons in the Great Lakes Region and the Horn of Africa (15 March 2000), <http://www.recsasec.org/publications/Nairobi_Declaration.pdf>.

94   Bamako Declaration on an African Common Position on the Illicit Proliferation, Circulation and Trafficking of Small Arms and Light Weapons (30 November 2000), <http://2001-2009.state.gov/t/ac/csbm/rd/6691.htm>.

95   Organization for Security and Co-operation in Europe Document on Small Arms and Light Weapons (24 November 2000), <http://www.osce.org/fsc/20783>.

96   Southern African Development Community Protocol on the Control of firearms Ammunition and other Related Materials (14 August 2001), entered force on 8 November 2004, <http://www.sadc.int/documents-publications/show/796>.

CHAPTER 4

Slipping the Net: Why Is It So Difficult to Crack Down on IUU Fishing?

Seokwoo Lee, Anastasia Telesetsky, and Clive Schofield

1   Introduction

Illegal, unreported and unregulated (IUU) fishing is now well recognized as a key threat to the management and sustainability of fisheries and therefore a pressing matter of global concern. Due to the illicit, shadowy nature of such activities, estimating the precise scale of IUU fishing is inherently difficult. Despite uncertainties it is clear that the scale of this activity is enormous with estimates of the total annual catch for 2011, for example, ranging from 11 to 26 million tonnes, equating to 14–33% of the world's total legal catch.[1] IUU fishing has been described as "one of the most severe problems affecting world fisheries"[2] and the "main obstacle in achieving sustainable fisheries in both areas under national jurisdiction and the high seas,"[3] with "far-reaching consequences for the long-term sustainable management of fishery resources."[4] IUU fishing has critical implications for long-term food security since it is estimated that fisheries provide at least 15% of the average per capita protein intake for at least 4.2 billion people in the

---

[*] Seokwoo Lee is Professor of Law at Inha University, Incheon, Korea; Anastasia Telesetsky is Associate Professor of International Law, University of Idaho College of Law, USA; Clive Schofield is Professor and Director of Research at the Australian National Centre for Ocean Resources and Security (ANCORS) and Global Challenge Lead, Sustaining Coastal and Marine Zones, University of Wollongong, Australia. Professor Schofield is the recipient of an Australian Research Council Future Fellowship (FT100100990).

[1]   *See*, "The Future of Fish—The Fisheries of the Future", *World Ocean Review* 2013, Maribus, 2013, p. 70.

[2]   UNGA Report of the Secretary-General, A/54/429, para. 249, Sep. 30, 1999, available at http://www.un.org/Docs/journal/asp/ws.asp?m=A/54/429.

[3]   UNGA Report of the Secretary-General, A/59/298, para. 36, Aug. 26, 2004, available at http://www.un.org/Docs/journal/asp/ws.asp?m=A/59/298.

[4]   UN A/AC.259/1, para. 1, May 15, 2000), available at http://www.un.org/Docs/journal/asp/ws.asp?m=A/AC.259/1.

world.[5] It likewise has multiple and significant implications for job security particularly for artisanal fishing communities since 8% of the global population are either involved directly or indirectly in the fishing industry.[6] IUU fishers have lasting direct impacts on legal fishers who follow the conservation and management rules by drawing down stocks resulting in informational gaps about the state of fishing stocks. In some fisheries, the IUU fishing activities have exceeded the legal fishing activities.[7]

The main driver of IUU fishing is generally understood to be greed and the desire to realize quick profits. IUU fishers can lower administrative and operating costs, avoid paperwork, ignore quotas, and still charge premiums from unknowing buyers (or, indeed, those who do not care to know).[8] In performing a cost-benefit analysis, IUU fishers understand that the chance of being detected in the act of either IUU fishing or offloading IUU fishing products is low since the seas are vast and there are approximately 4,764 ports in 153 coastal States with at least some of these ports having no restrictive port measures.[9] In many if not most cases, the profits for those involved in IUU fishing and especially the beneficial owners of the vessel will far exceed any possible sanction, including forfeiture of the entire vessel. Indeed, it has been observed that the value of fish that can be caught in a matter of weeks from one vessel can exceed the vessel's capital value.[10] Such lucrative pickings make for a powerful incentive to pursue IUU fishing activities. A fishing vessel that is only concerned with revenues will pursue IUU fishing strategies because there is no price discrimination between IUU caught fish and legally captured fish, operating and crew costs are reduced for IUU vessels, and IUU vessels have the opportunity to catch more fish because they are not limited by a catch quota.[11]

---

5   Food and Agriculture Organization, FAO Status of World Fisheries and Aquaculture for 2010: 3; and, *Rio Ocean Declaration*, UNESCO 6 (2012), *available at* http://www.unesco.org/new/fileadmin/MULTIMEDIA/HQ/SC/pdf/pdf_Rio_Ocean_Declaration_2012.pdf.

6   Id. at 6.

7   IUU estimates of the value of toothfish landings in the region managed by the Commission for the Conservation of Antarctic Marine Living Resources during the 1996–2000 fishing season are $518 million. The legitimate landings were worth $486 million. Carl-Christian Schmidt, "Economic Drivers of Illegal, Unreported, and Unregulated Fishing", 20 *International Journal of Marine and Coastal Law* 479, 483 (2005).

8   Seafish, *Seafish Guide to Illegal, Unreported and Unregulated Fishing*, November 2012, p. 3, available at http://www.seafish.org/media/publications/SeafishGuidetoIUU_201211.pdf.

9   World Port Source, available at www.worldportsource.com.

10 *The "Volga" Case (Russian Federation v. Australia) (Prompt Release) (Oral proceedings)* (2002) ITLOS Case No 11, ITLOS/PV.02/02 (12 December 2002), para. 22.

11 Schmidt *supra* note 7 at pp. 484–485.

Ineffective management regimes coupled with poor governance also permit IUU fishing to take place.[12] Poor fisheries governance has many aspects: inadequate fisheries regulations, lack of implementation or enforcement of measures, (including ineffective, or lack of, monitoring, control and surveillance (MCS) systems),[13] lack of transparency and traceability of fish products, failure to follow scientific advice, failing to restrict or rigorously inspect flag of convenience (FOC) vessels, and the lack of enough "no-go" areas for fishing.[14] Other causes exacerbating IUU fishing include overcapacity of vessels, overfished stocks,[15] the practice of "trans-shipping" catches between vessels,[16] ports of convenience,[17] inadequate penalties for IUU fishing,[18] and the granting of government subsidies that encourage overfishing.[19] Cumulatively, these fishing practices are impoverishing States and communities and unjustly enriching a few vessel owners and operators.

An effective solution to ending IUU fishing practices to a large extent continues to elude world bodies, national governments, and NGOs. This chapter examines the existing legal and policy framework, taking a close look at recent developments, and analyzes why it has proven so difficult to crack down on IUU fishing. Section 2 of this chapter explains the scope and impact of IUU fishing. Section 3 takes a brief look at the history of "IUU fishing"

---

12 See D.J. Agnew, J. Pearce, G. Pramod, T. Peatman, R. Watson, et al. (2009), *Estimating the Worldwide Extent of Illegal Fishing*, PLoS ONE, 4(2): e4570, available at http://www.plosone.org/article/info%3Adoi%2F10.1371%2Fjournal.pone.0004570 (showing relationship between governance indices and the level of illegal and unreported fishing).

13 See *Monitoring, Control and Surveillance*, Fisheries and Aquaculture Department, FAO, available at http://www.fao.org/fishery/topic/3021/en.

14 "Fishing problems: poor fisheries management", WWF Global, available at http://wwf.panda.org/about_our_earth/blue_planet/problems/problems_fishing/fisheries_management/.

15 *Fishing capacity*, Fisheries and Aquaculture Department, FAO, available at http://www.fao.org/fishery/topic/2898/en.

16 Margot L. Stiles, Ariel Kagan, Emily Shaftel, Beth Lowell, *Stolen Seafood: The Impact of Pirate Fishing on Our Oceans*, OCEANA, 2013, p. 18, available at http://oceana.org/sites/default/files/reports/Oceana_StolenSeafood.pdf.

17 Darren Calley, Market Denial and International Fisheries Regulation, Martinus Nijhoff Publishers (2012): 143.

18 *High Seas Task Force. 2006. Closing the net: Stopping Illegal Fishing on the High Seas.* Governments of Australia, Canada, Chile, Namibia, New Zealand, and the United Kingdom, WWF, IUCN and the Earth Institute at Columbia University, pp. 32–34, available at http://www.imcsnet.org/imcs/docs/hstf_final_report.pdf.

19 See OCEANA, *Pirates and Plunder: Fisheries subsidies support illegal or rogue fishing*, Feb. 20, 2007, available at http://oceana.org/sites/default/files/reports/Pirates_and_Plunder_FINAL_011.pdf.

terminology and the challenge of restricting IUU activities. Section 4 analyzes the three primary instruments negotiated on IUU fishing: the International Plan of Action to Prevent, Deter and Eliminate Illegal, Unreported and Unregulated Fishing (IPOA-IUU); the 2009 Agreement on Port State Measures to Prevent, Deter and Eliminate IUU fishing and the 2013 Voluntary Guidelines for Flag State Performance. Section 5 examines recent developments, such as the definition of IUU fishing and enforcement efforts among regional organizations and States, the relationship between IUU fishing and transnational crimes, and a pending request for an advisory opinion from the International Tribunal for the Law of the Sea (ITLOS). Section 6 analyzes the issues surrounding implementation and enforcement efforts and proposes the adoption of novel technological developments by port and coastal States to reduce IUU fishing effort.

2   Impact and Scale of IUU Fishing

The impact of IUU fishing is difficult to overstate. First, IUU fishing impacts the environment, undermining the sustainability of fish stocks and affecting marine biodiversity. Overfishing, which IUU fishing significantly amplifies, can cause the collapse of fish populations, threatening the extinction of certain fish species in severe cases. In particular, endangered, protected species are at greater risk of poaching by IUU fishers.[20] In addition, due to the fishing methods employed by many IUU fishers, even non-target species are affected through bycatch.

Second, IUU fishing has significant economic impacts. According to one recent estimate that suggested that IUU vessels "steal" approximately 25% of the world's fish resources, the value attached to this catch was $23.5 billion.[21] Consequently, law-abiding fishermen face a loss of revenue.[22] For example, researchers have estimated that 50% of the Russian king crab harvest is the product of IUU fishing and a large influx of this crab has entered into the US market resulting in the prices of crab slipping from around $22 per crab in 2012 to around $16.90 per crab in 2013.[23] IUU fishing also contributes to overfishing, which in turn affects the economy when profits fall and commercial fisheries struggle.

---

20   Id. at 9.
21   Fiona Macleod, "Illegal Fishing on High Seas Leaves Poor Countries Floundering", *Mail & Guardian* (July 19, 2013).
22   Id. at 10.
23   Jeanine Stewart and Eva Tallaksen, "King Crab Prices Keep Dropping on Suspected IUU Fishing", March 17, 2013 available at http://www.undercurrentnews.com/2013/05/17/king-crab-prices-keep-dropping-on-suspected-iuu-fishing/#.UhV4uJXGlcw.

Third, IUU fishing hurts society, giving rise to a range of socio-economic and developmental impacts. Frequently, IUU fishing vessels engage in IUU fishing in the waters belonging to developing countries, harming local economies and societies.[24] The loss of revenue to law-abiding fishermen caused by IUU fishing places many jobs in the industry at risk.[25] Coastal communities and developing countries are especially and disproportionately at risk. As noted above, fisheries resources play an important role in providing for a significant portion of the primary protein requirements of billions of people globally. This is accentuated in the context of coastal fishing communities in the developing world, giving rise to major food security concerns as a result of IUU fishing. In addition, IUU fishing has been connected to other transnational criminal activities such as human trafficking and other abuses.[26]

The scale of IUU fishing is also recognized as extremely significant. The very nature of "IUU" fishing, however, means that statistics are not readily available, making it difficult for researchers to quantify the scale of IUU fishing. Nevertheless, there are a number of credible estimates which serve to underscore the extraordinary and highly concerning scale of IUU fishing. The economic losses caused by IUU fishing are estimated to be between US $9 to 24 billion and 11 to 25 million metric tons of fish per year.[27] West Africa alone loses approximately $1.5 billion to IUU fishers.[28] Some estimates suggest that as much as 20% of seafood is derived from IUU fishing.[29]

At the regional and national scales, IUU Fishing is an increasingly critical and pressing concern. The illegal activities of many Chinese fishing vessels are well known. For example, Chinese fishing fleets operating in African waters have apparently reported only 9% of their catch.[30] Further, in 2011, the

---

24 Stiles et al., *supra* note 16 at 11.
25 Id. at 6.
26 See United Nations Office on Drugs and Crime (2011), Transnational Organized Crime in the Fishing Industry, A UNODC Study, available at http://www.unodc.org/unodc/en/human-trafficking/2011/issue-paper-transnational-organized-crime-in-the-fishing-industry.html.
27 See Agnew et al. *supra* note 12. See also NOAA and European Commission. Joint Statement between the European Commission and the United States Government on Efforts to Combat Illegal, Unreported, and Unregulated (IUU) Fishing. 7 Sept. 2011.
28 Richard Valdmanis and Simon Akam, "Illegal Fishing Plunders and Strains West Africa", *Reuters* (March 15, 2012).
29 Stiles et al. *supra* note 16 at 3.
30 Daniel Pauly et al. (2013), *China's distant-water fisheries in the 21st century*, Fish and Fisheries. doi: 10.1111/faf.12032, available at http://onlinelibrary.wiley.com/doi/10.1111/faf.12032/abstract.

Republic of Congo banned 69 Chinese fishing vessels from its waters due to IUU fishing activities.[31] This trend is perhaps not surprising since the number of fishery workers in China has increased by six million individuals since 1985 in part because fishery workers make double the wages of a farmer.[32]

Vessels from the Republic of Korea also have a poor reputation. In a recent report produced by international non-governmental organization (NGO) Greenpeace, there were at least 34 cases where Korean fishing companies engaged in IUU fishing and human rights abuses within their fleets, giving the country a bad reputation and potentially harming its fish trade with the United States and the European Union.[33] In addition, on April 19, 2013, a major Korean tuna vessel with a hold full of tuna was denied port landing in Mauritius due to evidence of IUU fishing.[34] However, in July 2013, South Korea amended its fisheries law (Water Fisheries Act) to more severely penalize IUU fishing, so there may be future improvements.[35] This can be regarded as a positive step and may yield improved practice in the future if well implemented and adequately enforced.

In the East China Sea, there are frequent IUU fishing issues in Exclusive Economic Zones (EEZs). Fishery disputes between the Koreas and China are frequent.[36] Recently, however, efforts have been made by both sides to crack

---

31 "Congo bans 69 Chinese fishing boats", Dec. 30, 2011, *News24*, available at http://www.news24.com/Africa/News/Congo-bans-69-Chinese-fishing-boats-20111230.

32 Huiguo Yu and Yunjun Yu, "Fishing Capacity Management in China: Theoretic and Practical Perspectives", 32 *Marine Policy* 351, 357 (2008).

33 The Greenpeace East Asia Report, *Korea's Distant Water Fisheries: IUU Fishing, International Violations and Human Rights Scandals* (April 11, 2013), available at http://www.greenpeace.org/international/Global/international/briefings/oceans/2013/Korea-fisheries-scandal-briefing.pdf.

34 John Briley, *Major Tuna Vessel Is Denied Port Landing Because of Evidence of Illegal Fishing*, The PEW Charitable Trusts, Environmental Initiatives, April 19, 2013, available at http://www.pewenvironment.org/news-room/other-resources/major-tuna-vessel-is-denied-port-landing-because-of-evidence-of-illegal-fishing-85899469998.

35 Distant-Water Industry Development Act, Act No. 12486, amended on March 18, 2014; Distant-Water Industry Development Enforcement Ordinance, Presidential Decree No. 25130, amended on January 28, 2014; Distant-Water Industry Development Enforcement Regulation, Ministry of Oceans and Fisheries Decree No. 67, amended on January 29, 2014. See also, Greenpeace, *New South Korean fisheries law a good first step to curb illegal fishing*, July 2, 2013, http://www.greenpeace.org/international/en/press/releases/New-South-Korean-fisheries-law-a-good-first-step-to-curb-illegal-fishing-/.

36 "Illegal Chinese Fishing in Korean Waters Gets Worse", *Chosun Ilbo* (Nov. 12, 2011), available at http://english.chosun.com/site/data/html_dir/2011/11/12/2011111200513.html.

down on illegal fishing.[37] Similarly, illegal fishing also occurs in Japan's EEZ, in turn leading to incidents, friction and disputes.[38] Existing bilateral fisheries agreements between East China Sea States have not alleviated pressure on limited fishery resources.

3   A Brief History of "IUU Fishing" Terminology

IUU fishing has been known by a variety of other names and descriptions, among them "pirate fishing," "rogue fishing," and the "plundering of ocean stocks." In fact, the term "IUU" fishing is relatively new.

The genesis of the term IUU fishing was the UN Conference on Environment and Development (otherwise known as the 'Earth Summit') in 1992, which resulted in the Agenda 21 document.[39] In Chapter 17 of Agenda 21, the document denounces unregulated fishing, and calls for sustainable fishing practices and improved management of high seas fisheries.[40] Subsequently, in a 1994 UN General Assembly Resolution, the Assembly used the term "unauthorized fishing" and called for greater enforcement efforts.[41]

In the Fifteenth Meeting of the Commission for the Conservation of Antarctic Marine Living Resources (CCAMLR) in 1996, the terms "illegal fishing" and "unreported fishing" were frequently used.[42] The following year saw the first formal use of the term "IUU fishing" at the Sixteenth Meeting of CCAMLR.[43]

Subsequently, the use of the term spread quickly. In 1999, "IUU fishing" appeared in the meeting reports for the FAO Sessions and the 7th Session on the UN Commission on Sustainable Development, and in 2000, the IMO

---

37   "Korea, China to Crack Down on Illegal Fishing", *Chosun Ilbo* (Jun. 27, 2013), available at http://english.chosun.com/site/data/html_dir/2013/06/27/2013062701387.html.
38   Shelley Clarke, *Illegal Fishing in the Exclusive Economic Zone of Japan*, MRAG Ltd., August 27, 2007, available at http://www.mrag.co.uk/Documents/IUU_Japan.pdf.
39   See http://www.un.org/geninfo/bp/enviro.html.
40   Agenda 21, UNEP, available at http://www.unep.org/Documents.Multilingual/Default.asp?documentid=52.
41   UN General Assembly (Dec. 19, 1994), A/RES/49/116, available at http://www.un.org/depts/los/general_assembly/general_assembly_resolutions.htm.
42   CCAMLR, Report of the Fifteenth Meeting of the Commission (Nov. 1996), available at http://www.ccamlr.org/en/system/files/e-cc-xv.pdf.
43   CCAMLR, Report of the Sixteenth Meeting of the Commission (Nov. 1997), available at http://www.ccamlr.org/en/system/files/e-cc-xvi.pdf.

Session meeting report also employed the same terminology. Regional fishery management bodies also began adopting the term.

Despite widespread use now, "IUU fishing" does not have a universally accepted legal definition. Generally speaking, IUU fishing refers broadly to any unauthorized fishing activities that violate national, regional, or international rules and regulations.[44] Perhaps the most widely adopted description of IUU fishing comes from paragraph 3 of the 2001 International Plan of Action to Prevent, Deter and Eliminate Illegal, Unreported and Unregulated Fishing (IPOA-IUU), a voluntary instrument.[45]

Under this definition "illegal fishing" refers to activities:

- conducted by national or foreign vessels in waters under the jurisdiction of a State, without the permission of that State, or in contravention of its laws and regulations;
- conducted by vessels flying the flag of States that are parties to a relevant regional fisheries management organization but operate in contravention of the conservation and management measures adopted by that organization and by which the States are bound, or relevant provisions of the applicable international law; or
- in violation of national laws or international obligations, including those undertaken by cooperating States to a relevant regional fisheries management organization.

In contrast, "unreported fishing" refers to fishing activities:

- which have not been reported, or have been misreported, to the relevant national authority, in contravention of national laws and regulations; or
- undertaken in the area of competence of a relevant regional fisheries management organization which have not been reported or have been misreported, in contravention of the reporting procedures of that organization.

While "unregulated fishing" refers to fishing activities:

- in the area of application of a relevant regional fisheries management organization that are conducted by vessels without nationality, or by those flying

---

44 See *supra* note 4, at 2.
45 FAO, *International Plan of Action to Prevent, Deter and Eliminate Illegal, Unreported and Unregulated Fishing* (IPOA-IUU), Rome, 2001, available at http://www.fao.org/docrep/003/y1224e/y1224e00.HTM.

the flag of a State not party to that organization, or by a fishing entity, in a manner that is not consistent with or contravenes the conservation and management measures of that organization; or
- in areas or for fish stocks in relation to which there are no applicable conservation or management measures and where such fishing activities are conducted in a manner inconsistent with State responsibilities for the conservation of living marine resources under international law.

While IPOA-IUU paragraph 3 is more detailed than previous explanations, this description of IUU Fishing is not a "strict definition," let alone a legal definition.[46] The heading of the section under which the provisions fall under reads "Nature and Scope of IUU Fishing." This can be interpreted as indicating that the contents of the provision were intended to be descriptive or explanatory in character, rather than definitive.[47] The language used in paragraph 3 is not intended to apply beyond the IPOA-IUU document and does not reflect language normally used in formal legal definitions.[48]

So what does the IPOA-IUU tells us about "IUU fishing"? While it does not provide a legal definition, it separates and describes each aspect of IUU fishing, giving a broad description of their respective scope and nature. Rather than proving to be necessarily problematic, this broad classification actually has the benefit of giving implementing States and RFMOs the flexibility to adapt a definition of IUU fishing that suits their particular needs.[49] To date, the IPOA-IUU's version of IUU fishing has been widely adopted in subsequent instruments and publications.[50] At this time, the IPOA-IUU explanation of IUU fishing has gained acceptance as an authoritative description of the types of activities that States want to legally constrain.

While IPOA-IUU paragraph 3 may be an acceptable starting place for developing a shared operational definition of what constitutes IUU fishing, relying on the contents of paragraph 3 may prove problematic in shaping long-term State responses to what has become a chronic and devastating problem for

---

[46] Mary Ann Palma, Martin Tsamenyi, William Edeson, *Promoting Sustainable Fisheries: The International Legal and Policy Framework to Combat Illegal, Unreported and Unregulated Fishing*, Martinus Nijhoff Publishers 2010, p. 37.
[47] Id.
[48] Id.
[49] Id.
[50] For example, the FAO Port State Measures Agreement refers to paragraph 3 of the IPOA-IUU for its legal definition of IUU Fishing. Also, many countries follow the IPOA-IUU provision in their national plans of action. See, e.g., National Plans of Action, IPOA-IUU, FAO, available at http://www.fao.org/fishery/ipoa-iuu/npoa/en.

marine fishing. First, the current definition does not contemplate that IUU fishing is only one part of the problem. As Davor Vidas argues, States should focus their attention not just on IUU fishing but "IUU operations" which includes fishing vessel purchases, vessel registration, actual fishing, possible transshipments of catch, reprocessing of IUU catch, possible exportation, and delivery to consumers.[51] Addressing IUU operations in a comprehensive manner, encompassing all the stages involved, is critical if legal interventions are to be effective. It is not clear that the paragraph 3 explanation contemplates a whole-of-chain approach. It may be possible to read "illegal fishing" as encompassing a broader set of undesirable activities since the term refers to the more general classification of "activities" and not, as is the case with unreported and unregulated fishing, to "fishing activities." It would be preferable to have a greater degree of specificity and harmonization regarding what activities or fishing activities qualify as IUU activities. Second, IPOA-IUU paragraph 3 fails to provide any legal guidance about the legality of IUU fishing. No mention is made that illegal fishing, unreported fishing, and unregulated fishing are all activities that must be universally prohibited.

In practice, what States have ended up with is legal 'eutrophication' of what constitutes the concept of IUU fishing. There is a proliferation of laws that is arguably choking the ability of concerned States to be effective in preventing, deterring, or eliminating harmful capture fishery practices. Every State and every region is entitled to approach the topic of what constitutes IUU activities independently. However, this fragmented approach has the potential for detrimental ecological results when different standards apply to the management of shared stocks, migratory stocks, and straddling fish stocks in different areas of maritime jurisdiction. A diversity of legal approaches is not necessarily advantageous for biodiversity. What qualifies as a reasonable non-discriminatory conservation and management measure for one State or RFMO should reasonably apply as an international standard across the globe. Otherwise, fishing interests in order to ply their trade 'legally' will seek spaces to fish, transship, and land cargoes where there are legal lacunae because either relevant law does not exist or the law that does exist is vague or incomplete in character, whether unintentionally or otherwise.

It might be argued that IPOA-IUU paragraph 3 contemplates this problem in the guise of "unregulated fishing" as a reference to all the:

---

51 Davor Vidas, "IUU Fishing or IUU Operations" in *Bringing New Law to Ocean Waters*, D.D. Caron and H.N. Scheiber (eds.), (2004):128–129.

fishing activities.... in areas ... [for] which there are no applicable conservation or management measures and where such fishing activities are conducted in a manner inconsistent with State responsibilities for the conservation of living marine resources under international law.

The language on "State responsibilities... under international law" serves as a catch-all to include a mosaic of international instruments, such as the UN Convention on the Law of the Sea,[52] the UN Fish Stocks Agreement, the FAO Code of Conduct for Responsible Fisheries, the FAO Compliance Agreement, FAO Port State Measures Agreement, and the WTO Agreements, among others. However, this does not provide for a legitimate approach to determine whether any given activity must be prohibited to protect living marine resources. This becomes problematic for both State actors and fishing vessel owners and operators. Individual States may fail to prosecute activities that other States consider to be IUU activities (for example, failure of distant water fishing nations to prosecute activities in West Africa). At the same time, some fishing vessel owners and operators may be confronted with a welter of conflicting rules that may lead to an exit strategy from better managed fisheries resulting in greater harvesting impacts on the least well managed fisheries.

The lack of a commonly or generally accepted definition of IUU fishing is then part of what makes it so difficult to crack down on IUU fishing. Until there is some uniform agreement on what constitutes IUU fishing, individual parties will continue to find ways to interpret their activities as either legal or consistent with *de minimis* State responsibilities.

4 IUU Fishing and the Evolution of Law and Policy over the Last Decade

The issue of IUU fishing has been on the agenda of international organizations for over two decades. Some progress has been made to create a multilateral response to the challenges that are posed by enforcement on the part of flag States and the need for legal disincentives that outweigh the economic incentives for IUU activities. Three negotiated documents are of particularly significance: the International Plan of Action to Prevent, Deter and Eliminate IUU Fishing (IPOA-IUU); the Agreement on Port State Measures to Prevent,

---

52   United Nations, *United Nations Conventions on the Law of the Sea*, U.N. Sales No E.97.V.10 (1983). *See* 1833 UNTS 3, entered into force 16 Nov. 1994, *available at* <http://www.un.org/Depts/los/convention_agreements/convention_overview_convention.htm>.

Deter and Eliminate IUU Fishing; and the Voluntary Guidelines for Flag State Performance. This section examines the contributions of these documents to the objective of combating IUU fishing and suggests that these documents represent a progressive evolution towards a more effective regime that, in our view, can be enhanced further by taking into consideration the recent developments discussed in Section 5.

4.1 *International Plan of Action to Prevent, Deter and Eliminate IUU Fishing*

In March 2001, the FAO Committee on Fisheries (COFI) approved the IPOA-IUU. While the IPOA-IUU is a voluntary instrument,[53] it is based on the rules of international law, adopting or incorporating by reference provisions from multiple fisheries and non-fisheries specific instruments. The stated purpose of the IPOA-IUU is:

> to prevent, deter and eliminate IUU fishing by providing all States with comprehensive, effective and transparent measures by which to act, including through appropriate regional fisheries management organizations established in accordance with international law.[54]

To this end, the document presents a fairly comprehensive 'toolbox' of measures that States and regional organizations can adopt, either individually or collectively,[55] in order to combat IUU fishing. This toolbox includes provisions addressing the responsibilities of all States, coastal State and port State measures, as well as internationally-agreed market measures and regional mechanisms through Regional Fisheries Management Organizations (RFMOs).

In addition, the IPOA-IUU encourages States to create their own National Plan of Action (NPOA), adapting as appropriate to their situation the measures available in the IPOA-IUU's toolbox.[56] RFMOs are also encouraged to form Regional Plans of Action. The IPOA-IUU also contains various provisions calling for the adoption of the measures at both the domestic and regional level.

However, the IPOA-IUU is not without its weaknesses. In addition to not providing a sufficient legal definition of IUU fishing, it does *not* tell us a number of important things, such as how to address unregulated fishing, what IUU fishing

---

53 Id., para. 4.
54 Id., para. 8.
55 FAO, Fisheries Department, IPOA-IUU, *Technical Guidelines for Responsible Fisheries* No. 9, para. 16, Rome 2002.
56 IPOA-IUU, para. 25–27.

activities each country should focus on, the specific measures that are required to address each component of IUU fishing, how to develop a strategy to combat IUU fishing, and the legal implications of some of the measures included.

Nonetheless, the IPOA-IUU represents an important initiative to address the dearth of "political will, priority, capacity, and resources" that had been assigned to the IUU issue.[57] Simply negotiating the IPOA-IUU constituted an indication of some political will to address IUU impacts. The concept of the National Plans of Action and Regional Plans of Action were intended to narrow the gap in capacity and resources for both developed and developing nations. It is uncertain to what extent this has happened. Presently, only ten states (Argentina,[58] Australia,[59] Belize,[60] Canada,[61] Chile,[62] Ghana,[63] Japan,[64] Korea,[65] New Zealand,[66] United States[67]) and two intergovern-

---

57 IPOA-IUU *supra* note 45 at para. 1 Introduction.
58 República Argentina, *Plan de acción nacional para prevenir, desalentar y eliminar la pesca ilegal, no declarada y no reglamentada* available at ftp://ftp.fao.org/FI/DOCUMENT/IPOAS/national/argentina/PAN-INDNR.pdf.
59 *Australian National Plan of Action to Prevent, Deter and Eliminate Illegal, Unreported and Unregulated Fishing* available at http://www.daff.gov.au/__data/assets/pdf_file/0006/33963/npoa_iuu_fishing.pdf.
60 *National Plan of Action to Prevent, Deter and Eliminate Illegal, Unreported and Unregulated (IUU) Fishing on the High Seas*, ftp://ftp.fao.org/fi/DOCUMENT/IPOAS/national/belize/NPOA_IUU.pdf.
61 *Canada's National Plan of Action on Illegal, Unreported and Unregulated Fishing* available at http://www.dfo-mpo.gc.ca/npoa-pan/npoa-iuu-eng.htm#2.5.
62 Chile, *National Plan of Action to Prevent, Deter and Eliminate Illegal, Unreported and Unregulated Fishing* available at ftp://ftp.fao.org/Fi/DOCUMENT/IPOAS/national/chile/iuu.pdf.
63 *Republic of Ghana National Plan of Action to Prevent, Deter and Eliminate Illegal, Unreported and Unregulated Fishing* ftp://ftp.fao.org/fi/DOCUMENT/IPOAS/national/Ghana/NPOA_IUU.pdf.
64 *Implementation of the National Plan of Action to Prevent, Deter, and Eliminate Illegal, Unreported and Unregulated Fishing* available at ftp://ftp.fao.org/Fi/DOCUMENT/IPOAS/national/japan/NPOA-iuu.pdf.
65 *Korea National Plan of Action to Prevent, Deter and Eliminate Illegal, Unreported and Unregulated Fishing* (on file with author).
66 *New Zealand Plan of Action to Prevent, Deter and Eliminate Illegal, Unreported and Unregulated Fishing* available at http://www.fish.govt.nz/NR/rdonlyres/A7043588-9001-4B8C-A69C-BAD7CD0C3356/0/iuufishing.pdf.
67 *National Plan of Action of the United States of America to Prevent, Deter and Eliminate Illegal, Unreported and Unregulated Fishing* available at http://www.nmfs.noaa.gov/ia/iuu/iuu_nationalplan.pdf.

mental entities (European Commission[68] and the Lake Victoria Fisheries Organization[69]) have formulated Plans of Action and distributed them to the FAO. There are other countries and regions and regional organizations that have subsequently developed IUU policies in response to the IPOA-IUU including Gambia, Mexico, Namibia, Seychelles, Spain, Tonga, Tuvalu, and CCAMLR.[70] The National Plans and Regional Plans if implemented have the potential to make significant changes in practices by flagged vessels and port officials. For example, the European Commission called for several specific action items including organizing an international diplomatic conference to establish objective legal criteria for ensuring that the right to fly the flag of a State is based on the existence of a substantive link between that State and a given fishing vessel.[71] The key weakness evident to date is that so few National or Regional Plans have been implemented particularly by States associated with flags of convenience. A recurring problem for controlling IUU fishing is the inadequate oversight of vessels by numerous flag States. States have attempted to address this most recently with the 2013 Voluntary Guidelines for Flag State Performance.

4.2 The Agreement on Port State Measures to Prevent, Deter and Eliminate IUU Fishing

Over the past couple of decades, States have recognized that not all flag States will assert effective control over vessels flagged under their registry to end IUU fishing. As a result, States are intervening at a different strategic point in the IUU fishing chain, that is, in port, by imposing port restrictions on vessels known to be engaged in or suspected of IUU fishing. Under the Fish Stocks Agreement, port States are expected to enforce conservation and management

---

[68] *European Commission Community action plan for the eradication of illegal, unreported and unregulated fishing* available at http://eur-lex.europa.eu/LexUriServ/site/en/com/2002/com2002_0180en01.pdf.

[69] *Regional Plan of Action to Prevent, Deter an Eliminate Illegal, Unreported and Unregulated Fishing on Lake Victoria and its Basin.*

[70] Food and Agriculture Organization, Review of National and Regional Plans of Action Already Prepared and Disseminated in Report of the FAO Regional Workshop on the Elaboration of National Plans of Action to Prevent, Deter and Eliminate Illegal, Unreported and Unregulated Fishing—Caribbean Subregion. Port of Spain, Trinidad and Tobago, 22–26 November 2004, para. 41 available at http://www.fao.org/docrep/008/y5921e/y5921e09.htm.

[71] European Commission *supra* note 65 p. 10.

measures by prohibiting landings and transshipments that may have been procured through IUU fishing.[72]

The Food and Agriculture Organization's Committee on Fisheries understood that port State measures required more than just a few conservation leaders. Otherwise, IUU vessels would simply steam to a neighboring port and offload its catch into the stream of commerce. In order to end IUU fishing, there would need to be a global commitment. In 2005, the FAO drafted a Model Scheme on Port State Measures to Combat IUU fishing which marked a starting point for the negotiations of the binding 2009 Agreement on Port State Measures. Under the Port State Agreement, Parties are expected to integrate port fishery measures to combat IUU fishing with other port controls.[73] Vessels that expect to enter a port that is subject to the Agreement are required to give advance notice of their intent to enter a port and provide documentation of total catch on board as well as fishing authorizations and transshipment authorizations.[74] Each State Party has the right to authorize or deny entry to its ports of vessels known or suspected to be engaged in IUU fishing but must give notice to the flag States.[75] Port States are encouraged to inspect vessels particularly when the vessels have already been denied entrance into a port under the Agreement, when other parties request an inspection, or when there are clear grounds to suspect a vessel of IUU fishing.[76] To enhance accountability, the flag State of an alleged IUU vessel is expected to immediately launch an investigation of the vessel and if there is sufficient evidence of IUU fishing, the flag State must take enforcement action based on the flag State's laws and regulations.[77]

Even though the Agreement represents a distinct and welcome evolution towards adopting a broader view of the challenges of preventing, deterring and eliminating IUU operations, the current status of the Agreement as an operational document to combat IUU fishing remains ambiguous. For example, even though the Agreement took a tougher stance on IUU vessels by empowering port States to refuse landings, the Agreement did not evolve the definition of

---

72 Agreement for the Implementation of the Provisions of the UNCLOS relating to the Conservation and Management of Straddling Fish Stocks and Highly Migratory Fish Stocks, UN Doc. A/CONF.164/37, adopted 4 December 1995, entered into force 11 December 2001 at Article 23.
73 Agreement on Port State Measures to Prevent, Deter and Eliminate Illegal, Unreported and Unregulated Fishing available at http://www.fao.org/fileadmin/user_upload/legal/docs/1_037t-e.pdf.
74 Id. at Article 8(1) referencing Annex A.
75 Id. at Article 9 and Article 18.
76 Id. at Article 12(3).
77 Id. at Article 20.

IUU fishing but simply referred back to the paragraph 3 IPOA-IUU definition discussed above. Second, there has been a lack of commitment to adopting the agreement. Even though there have been a number of coastal States who have signed the agreement, there have been only a handful of ratifications[78] and 25 ratifications are necessary for the agreement to enter into force. Very few traditional "ports of convenience" have ratified.

4.3 Flag State Guidelines

The most recent international development to combat IUU fishing is the adoption of the Voluntary Guidelines for Flag State Performance.[79] The guidelines focus on the chronically weak link of poor flag State response and call for "effective flag State responsibility."[80] While there is nothing surprising or particularly new in the list of shared principles for the guidelines,[81] the guidelines make explicit certain useful developments in thinking about the contemporary nature of IUU fishing as a widespread activity that may be exacerbated when States fail to implement restricted fishing regimes. First, the guidelines apply to both "fishing and fishing related activities" which seems to acknowledge and address the nature of IUU operations and might include transshipments and landings.[82] Second, the guidelines are expected to apply broadly in areas beyond national jurisdiction as well as within EEZs.[83] Third, the guidelines apply to all ships regardless of size.[84] Fourth, in response to the IPOA-IUU, the flag State should have a national framework to combat IUU fishing.[85] Finally, the flag State is expected to have in place a licensing regime for its ships which will include conditions for protecting marine ecosystems and be based in part on a vessel's history of compliance.[86]

---

78 As of June 2014, Chile, the European Union, Gabon, Norway, Myanmar, Oman, Seychelles, Sri Lanka, the United States and Uruguay had ratified, accepted, approved, or acceded to the Agreement.

79 Food and Agriculture Organization, Voluntary Guidelines for Flag State Performance (February 8, 2013) available at ftp://ftp.fao.org/FI/DOCUMENT/tc-fsp/2013/VolGuidelines_adopted.pdf.

80 Id. at para. 2.

81 Id. The emphasis on flag States coordinating activities internally among the various national agencies may be considered a newer principle of "effectiveness".

82 Id. at para. 3.

83 Id.

84 Id. at para. 4.

85 Id. at para. 18(b).

86 Id. at para. 19(a) and (b).

The intent of the guidelines appears to be, in part at least, to prevent indiscriminate flag hopping. Only the future will tell the value of these guidelines in enhancing flag State responsibility. There is some question about how useful the guidelines will be in light of their somewhat complex framing. The guidelines are largely organized into two sections on performance assessment measures and performance assessment actions. It is not clear what the rationale was in dividing the document into these sections since most of the measures also appear to be actions. When the document is read as a whole, it seems readily apparent that it is the product of a committee with little effort to harmonize the text as a norm-shaping document. Instead of using the 11 principles in Paragraph 2 of the guidelines as a structure for the document, the remainder of the document is a somewhat disconnected laundry list of suggestions. As a result of this format, the document may prove to be less useful for governments in terms of its practical application than a more tightly negotiated set of guidelines.

Because the content of the guidelines derives in part from the Law of the Sea, these guidelines will likely be a topic of at least brief discussion by the ITLOS in their deliberations over an advisory opinion on State responsibility for IUU fishing. Since so much of the guidelines is derivative of existing international law and there has been growing frustration among some international actors regarding the use of flag hopping, it is somewhat surprising that the parties who contributed to these guidelines were not willing to seek a firmer binding commitment on improving particular aspects of flag State performance that are exacerbating IUU fishing. Without a binding commitment, it arguably might have served the parties better to have focused on negotiating for funding mechanisms for specific capacity building projects to combat IUU fishing rather than deriving somewhat vague standards to govern performance assessment. This perhaps reflects political considerations and limitations.

5   Recent Developments

The evolution of policy reactions to IUU fishing continues to contemplate a broader conception of "IUU operations" with particular recent emphasis on port State measures and renewed interest in flag State responsibility. The expansive efforts to intervene in a more broadly defined set of IUU activities are apparent in a number of recent developments. For example, after the IPOA-IUU was published in 2001, a number of States and RFMOs went on to adopt legal definitions more restrictive than the IPOA-IUU's description and these definitions are now governing RFMO member enforcement activities. In addition, in recent years the relationship between IUU fishing and transnational crimes has been increasingly identified and analyzed. Finally, the ongoing IUU fishing issue may be directly addressed by an authoritative international judicial body. That is, at the time of this writing, there is a pending request for an advisory opinion before the International Tribunal for the Law of the Sea (ITLOS) dealing with the issue of IUU fishing.[87] In this section of the chapter these developments that seem to suggest an even more concerted effort to rein in IUU operations are examined.

5.1 Developments in the Definition of IUU Fishing and Enforcement Efforts

Many factors come into play when ascertaining the scope and nature of IUU fishing including existing regulations and instruments; the definitions of fish, fishing vessels, and fishing activity; the location where the activity takes place; and the identity of the actors. IUU fishing can also be seen from four perspectives: fisheries development as an industry, fisheries management, the environment, and maritime security. These must be considered when a State or RFMO creates a legal definition of IUU fishing, whether it adopts paragraph 3 of the IPOA-IUU or tries to create its own definition. Definitions matter because a number of vessel and fish processing activities that are impacting the long-term health of the fishery resources are not considered universally to qualify as IUU fishing activities and therefore fall outside the ambit of regulated activities. Unsurprisingly, IUU operations reside within these loopholes.

Although many States have adopted paragraph 3 of the IPOA-IUU as their definition for IUU fishing in their national plans of action,[88] some States have adopted more stringent and specific definitions. Moreover, while many RFMOs use the IPOA-IUU definition, a number of RFMOs have extended their jurisdictional net beyond the activities of their member States.

5.1.1 RFMO Trends

An RFMO is "an intergovernmental fisheries organization or arrangement... that has the competence to establish fishery conservation and management measures."[89] They are established by international fishery agreements between States with a common interest in fishing a certain fish species or area of the high seas.

---

87   Case No. 21: Request for an advisory opinion submitted by the Sub-Regional Fisheries Commission (SRFC) (March 27, 2013), available at http://www.itlos.org/index.php?id=252.
88   See *supra* note 43.
89   IPOA-IUU, para. 6(c).

In recent years, RFMOs have begun creating "black lists" of IUU fishing vessels. Most of these RFMOs blacklist vessels that fly the flags of non-contracting parties, although some RFMOs also blacklist vessels flying the flags of contracting parties. Many RFMOs now maintain IUU vessel lists, such as ICCAT,[90] IOTC,[91] IATTC,[92] NEAFC,[93] NAFO,[94] CCAMLR,[95] WCPFC,[96] and SEAFO.[97] An increasing number of RFMOs also permit, or are moving towards, the reciprocal listing or recognition of IUU vessels found on other RFMOs' lists.[98] In addition, the major tuna RFMOs (CCBST, IATTC, ICCAT, IOTC, and WCPFC) have combined their efforts to create a joint list of tuna authorized vessels with the presumption that an unlisted vessel is an IUU vessel.[99]

Further, many RFMOs now apply a 'presumption' of IUU fishing against vessels that meet, or fail to meet, certain criteria, placing the burden of demonstrating that the vessel did not engage in IUU fishing on to the vessel. For example, the WCPFC in its Conservation and Management Measures have extended the IUU presumption to all vessels operating within the WCPFC region regardless of whether they are members of the WCPFC or not who fail to comply with the Conservation and Management Measures. Significantly, the WCPFC measures innovatively address the reality of larger IUU operations since a vessel is presumed to be an IUU vessel if it is under the control of any owner who has been connected to another IUU vessel.[100]

In terms of enforcement against IUU fishing practices, greater emphasis is being placed on flag registration, assistance from authorized fishing vessels,

---

90 International Commission for the Conservation of Atlantic Tuna, available at http://www.iccat.int/en/IUU.asp.
91 Indian Ocean Tuna Commission, available at http://www.iotc.org/English/iuu/search.php.
92 Inter-American Tropical Tuna Commission, available at http://www.iattc.org/VesselRegister/IUU.aspx?Lang=en.
93 Northeast Atlantic Fisheries Organisation, available at http://www.neafc.org/mcs/iuu.
94 North Atlantic Fisheries Organisation, available at http://www.nafo.int/fisheries/frames/fishery.html.
95 Commission on the Conservation of Antarctic Marine Living Resources, available at http://www.ccamlr.org/en/compliance/illegal-unreported-and-unregulated-iuu-fishing.
96 Western and Central Pacific Fisheries Commission, available at http://www.wcpfc.int/vessels#IUU.
97 Southeast Atlantic Fisheries Organization, available at http://www.seafo.org/VesselList.html.
98 See, for example, "List of Vessels Presumed to Have Carried Out IUU Fishing Activities in the ICCAT Convention Area and Other areas" available at http://www.iccat.int/en/IUU.asp.
99 See "Tuna-org" available at http://www.tuna-org.org/GlobalTVR.htm.
100 WCPFC, Conservation and Management Measures 2010–06.

and port State measures. For example, SEAFO and WCPFC consider any unregistered vessel to be conducting IUU fishing.

5.1.2   State Trends—United States

On July 10, 2012, the US National Oceanic and Atmospheric Administration (NOAA) proposed a rule that would, among other things, revise the definition of IUU fishing in the High Seas Driftnet Fishing Moratorium Protection Act.[101] This proposed rule addressed matters such as flagrant reflagging, beneficial ownership, lack of registration, and illegal incursions of a nation's vessel into the waters of another nation.[102] On January 16, 2013, the final version of the proposed rule came into effect.[103] The new definition of IUU fishing reads as follows:[104]

> For the purposes of the Moratorium Protection Act:
> ...
> *Illegal, unreported, or unregulated (IUU) fishing* means:
> (1) In the case of parties to an international fishery management agreement to which the United States is a party, fishing activities that violate conservation and management measures required under an international fishery management agreement to which the United States is a party, including but not limited to catch limits or quotas, capacity restrictions, bycatch reduction requirements, shark conservation measures, and data reporting;
> (2) In the case of non-parties to an international fishery management agreement to which the United States is a party, fishing activities that would undermine the conservation of the resources managed under that agreement;
> (3) Overfishing of fish stocks shared by the United States, for which there are no applicable international conservation or management measures, or in areas with no applicable international fishery

---

101   High Seas Driftnet Fishing Moratorium Protection Act (Moratorium Protection Act) (50 CFR 300.200 et seq.), as codified in 16 U.S.C. 1826h–k, as amended by the Magnuson-Stevens Fishery Conservation and Management Reauthorization Act (2006) and the Shark Conservation Act (Pub. L. 111–348) (2011).
102   77 FR 40553, available at https://federalregister.gov/a/2012-16838.
103   78 FR 3338, available at https://federalregister.gov/a/2013-00703.
104   § 300.201, e-CFR, available at http://www.ecfr.gov/cgi-bin/retrieveECFR?gp=1&SID=7978 b4e24b5600d27feedd41a6c060d7&ty=HTML&h=L&r=PART&n=50y11.0.2.11.1#50:11.0 .2.11.1.14.21.2.

management organization or agreement, that has adverse impacts on such stocks; or,

(4) Fishing activity that has a significant adverse impact on seamounts, hydrothermal vents, cold water corals and other vulnerable marine ecosystems located beyond any national jurisdiction, for which there are no applicable conservation or management measures or in areas with no applicable international fishery management organization or agreement.

(5) Fishing activities by foreign flagged vessels in U.S. waters without authorization of the United States.

Other measures combating IUU fishing include: (1) listing of States whose vessels have been involved in IUU fishing; (2) listing of States whose vessels engaged in protected living marine resource (PLMR) bycatch, and the adoption of a PLMR list; (3) certification procedures where a negative certification could mean denial of port privileges, prohibition of imports, and application of other economic sanctions for a vessel; (4) and alternative procedures, for example, whereby the Secretary of Commerce may allow entry of fish or fish products on a shipment-by-shipment, shipper-by-shipper, or other basis subject to certain conditions.

In addition, under Section 403(a) of the Magnuson-Stevens Fishery Conservation and Management Reauthorization Act (2006), NOAA Fisheries are required to produce a biennial report to the US Congress. The reports list States that have been identified for engaging in IUU fishing, or the bycatch of protected species (including shark catches) on the high seas and who lack comparable conservation and management measures as the United States. Those nations that have been so identified enter into consultations with NOAA Fisheries who then determine whether to positively or negatively certify the State in question. Negative certifications may result in US port access denials and import restrictions on fish products from that nation.

These measures appear to have yielded at least some results. In 2009, six States—France, Italy, Libya, Panama, China and Tunisia—were identified in the biennial report and consultations were conducted.[105] After consultations, the United States was convinced that all six States had taken satisfactory measures to address the violations of the vessels involved. In 2011, another six

---

[105] Biennial Report to Congress—January 2009, available at http://www.nmfs.noaa.gov/ia/iuu/msra_page/2009_report.pdf.

States were listed: Colombia, Ecuador, Italy, Panama, Portugal, and Venezuela.[106] After consultations, the United States eventually gave each State a positive certification.[107] Moreover, in January 2013, the NOAA identified 10 more States: Colombia, Ecuador, Ghana, Italy, Mexico, Panama, the Republic of Korea, Spain, Tanzania, and Venezuela,[108] and consultations are currently underway. NOAA will be issuing a new set of identification of States that are facilitating IUU fishing in January 2015 and will indicate the outcome of the January 2013 consultations. These consultations are significant because, in theory at least, they put direct diplomatic pressure on flag States and remind flag States of their responsibility. Yet questions remain about the efficacy of these consultations since certain flag States including Italy and Panama continue to be cited in all three of the most recent reports for IUU vessel activity under their flag. Apparently, repeat listings do not trigger conditions such as trade restrictions between the United States and States found to have inadequate regulatory frameworks including oversight of fishing fleets. The sanction of a negative certification therefore seems to carry minimal bite for repeat offenders.

5.1.3   Regional Trends—European Union

The European Union is the world's largest importer of fish product, making it an attractive target as a market for IUU fishers.[109] Estimates place illegal fish imports into the EU at around €1.1 billion. For over a decade, the European Union has been working hard to combat this situation, by passing numerous regulations dealing with IUU fishing.[110]

Some major features of the European Union's IUU regulations can be summarized as follows. The European Union has port State control over third country

---

106   Biennial Report to Congress—January 2011, available at http://www.nmfs.noaa.gov/ia/iuu/msra_page/2011_report.pdf.
107   Biennial Report to Congress—January 2013, available at http://www.nmfs.noaa.gov/ia/slider_stories/2013/01/msra_2013_report.html.
108   Id.
109   Seafish, *IUU Fishing*, available at http://www.seafish.org/retailers/responsible-sourcing/protecting-fish-stocks/iuu-fishing.
110   The legal basis for the European Union's IUU regulations is Council regulation (EC) No 1005/2008, and the implementing regulation is Commission regulation (EC) No 1010/2009. There have been numerous subsequent amendments since then: for example, Commission regulation (EU) No 86/2010 (29 January 2010), Commission Regulation (EU) No 395/2010 (7 May 2010), Commission regulation (EU) No 468/2010 (28 May 2010), Commission Regulation no. 202/2011 (Mar. 1, 2011), Commission Implementing Regulation (EU) No 724/2011 (25 July 2011). All EU regulations can be easily searched at: http://eur-lex.europa.eu/en/index.htm.

fishing vessels. A catch certification scheme for third country fisheries products imported to the EU also exists. Moreover, the EU has adopted an IUU vessels list.

In addition, the European Union maintains a list of non-cooperating third States. Factors that are considered when adding a third State to the list include the following: (1) failure to discharge duties as flag, port, coastal, or market States; (2) measures taken by the State against IUU fishing or access to IUU fish; (3) cooperation with the EU to respond to its queries; (4) whether the State concerned has taken effective measures against IUU operators; (5) history, nature, extent and gravity of the IUU fishing; (6) existing capacity of the competent authorities; (7) ratification of international agreements; (8) status of the State as party to RFMOs; and (9) any acts or omissions by the States concerned that may have diminished the effectiveness of applicable laws.

Under its regulations, the European Union is authorized to take strong action against non-cooperating States. Possible measures include: (1) prohibition of importation from the IUU vessel; (2) prohibition on reflagging an IUU vessel to European Union; (3) prohibition on chartering arrangements with IUU vessels; (4) prohibition of private trade agreements between European Union nationals and non-cooperating State; (5) prohibition of joint fishing operations; (6) the European Union shall propose the denunciation of any standing bilateral fisheries agreement or fisheries partnership agreements with non-cooperating States; and (7) the European Union shall not enter into negotiations to conclude a bilateral fisheries agreement or fisheries partnership agreements with such States.

On September 7, 2011, the European Union and the United States signed a Joint Statement, pledging bilateral cooperation to combat IUU fishing.[111] The Joint Statement promotes cooperation between the European Union and the United States to achieve the sustainable use of fisheries resources while preserving marine biodiversity. It also creates a system to exchange information on IUU activities. In addition, it calls for active participation in RFMOs to strengthen control, monitoring and enforcement of vessels, and encourage other countries to ratify and implement the port State measures (PSM) Agreement.

5.2 *IUU Fishing and Transnational Crimes*

The link between IUU fishing and transnational crime was identified at a United Nations Office on Drugs and Crime (UNODC) Expert Group Meeting

---

111   Joint Statement: Between the European Commission and the United States Government on Efforts to Combat Illegal, Unreported and Unregulated (IUU) Fishing, Sep. 7, 2011, available at http://ec.europa.eu/commission_2010–2014/damanaki/headlines/press-releases/2011/09/20110907_jointstatement_eu-us_iuu_en.pdf.

on 8–9 March, 2011.[112] During the meeting, government representatives discussed the involvement of organized criminal groups in IUU fishing, and the relationship between IUU fishing and crimes such as money laundering, drug trafficking, and smuggling of people.

A UNODC study arising from the meeting addressed recent trends in IUU fishing and transnational crimes.[113] Some of the topics discussed included: (1) the abuse that fishers who were trafficked for the purpose of forced labour faced on board fishing vessels; (2) the frequency of child trafficking in the fishing industry; (3) transnational organised criminal groups engaged in marine living resource crimes in relation to high value, low volume species such as abalone; and (4) the high degree of logistical coordination and legal sophistication displayed by some transnational fishing operators engaged in marine living resource crimes.

In addition to the UNODC meeting, a UNICPOLOS meeting also examined the relationship between IUU fishing and transnational crime, including international environmental crime.[114] What becomes apparent from a review of these international efforts is that there has been little existing effort to end IUU fishing as a human rights violation. Most of the attention in the IUU policy arena has been on ecological resources and ecological sustainability. It may prove to be a more fruitful and immediate international intervention strategy to focus State attention on the human victim aspect of IUU fishing.

In this context, INTERPOL has for the first time in 2013 become publicly engaged as an organization in combatting illegal fishing and its associated crimes. In September 2013, INTERPOL provided notification of a fishing vessel currently named "Snake" which is alleged to be illegally fishing in the South Atlantic Ocean and has already been blacklisted by CCAMLR and SEAFO and is unable to enter a number of global ports.[115] This represents a new and exciting trend of States cooperatively pursuing IUU fishing as a transnational crime.

---

112 UNODC, "Experts meet in Vienna to discuss the involvement of Transnational Organized Crime in the Fishing Industry", Mar 9, 2011, available at http://www.unodc.org/unodc/en/human-trafficking/2011/experts-meet-in-vienna-to-discuss-the-involvement-of-transnational-organized-crime-in-the-fishing-industry.html.
113 United Nations Office on Drugs and Crime (2011), "Transnational Organized Crime in the Fishing Industry: A UNODC Study", available at http://www.unodc.org/unodc/en/human-trafficking/2011/issue-paper-transnational-organized-crime-in-the-fishing-industry.html.
114 Ninth Meeting of the UN Open-ended Informal Consultative Process on Oceans and the Law of the Sea (UNICPOLOS) in 2008.
115 Gabriela Raffaele, Fish Information and Services, "INTERPOL requested for the first time to detect illegal fishing activities" (September 9, 2013). www.FIS.com

5.3 Pending Case before the ITLOS

In addition to the national and regional legislative changes and the introduction of IUU fishing as a prominent transnational crime issue, there are potentially significant developments in international adjudication regarding IUU fishing. West Africa has been the target of illegal fishing for decades as a result of a combination of overfishing by both foreign trawlers and coastal fishing communities coupled with lack of indigenous capacity to monitor and undertake enforcement action particularly against industrial trawlers. Large-scale IUU fishing especially on the part of European and Asian fleets has exacerbated the losses of artisanal fishing communities. On March 28, 2013, the Sub-Regional Fisheries Commission (SRFC)[116] requested the ITLOS to provide an advisory opinion regarding several issues related to IUU fishing.[117] The issues raised were:

1. What are the obligations of the flag State in cases where illegal, unreported and unregulated (IUU) fishing activities are conducted within the Exclusive Economic Zones of third party States?
2. To what extent shall the flag State be held liable for IUU fishing activities conducted by vessels sailing under its flag?
3. Where a fishing license is issued to a vessel within the framework of an international agreement with the flag State or with an international agency, shall the State or international agency be held liable for the violation of the fisheries legislation of the coastal State by the vessel in question?
4. What are the rights and obligations of the coastal State in ensuring the sustainable management of shared stocks and stocks of common interest, especially the small pelagic species and tuna?

On March 24, 2013, the Tribunal gave Order 2013/2, inviting the SRFC States and a number of other regional organizations to "present written statements on the questions submitted to the Tribunal for an advisory opinion" no later than November 29, 2013.[118]

---

116 The SRFC consists of seven member states (Cape Verde, the Gambia, Guinea, Guinea-Bissau, Mauritania, Senegal and Sierra Leone) and is located in Dakar, Senegal.
117 Case No.21: Request for an advisory opinion submitted by the Sub-Regional Fisheries Commission (SRFC) (March 28, 2013), available at http://www.itlos.org/index.php?id=252.
118 Order 2013/2. ITLOS (Mar. 24, 2013), available at http://www.itlos.org/fileadmin/itlos/documents/cases/case_no.21/C21_Ord_2013-2_24.05_E.pdf.

This request for an advisory opinion is a significant and exciting development. Procedurally, it is the first time that the *full* Tribunal has been requested to render an advisory opinion. Substantively, the issues presented focus on the link between State responsibility, IUU fishing, and the Law of the Sea. While the outcome of this case is, at the time of writing, still pending such that definitive conclusions cannot be drawn, one thing is clear: the outcome of the case will affect the development of international law in this area.[119] In particular this case has the long-term potential to stimulate greater oversight by distant-water fishing nations over their fishing fleets.

6 Implementation and Enforcement Issues: How Can We Crack Down on IUU Fishing?

There are a number of obstacles and challenges facing governments and regional organizations in their efforts to crack down on IUU fishing. It is suggested that these related and interconnected issues need to be addressed through a multi-pronged approach. First, there remains the problem of defining IUU fishing. There is no globally accepted legal definition of IUU fishing. Part of this problem stems from disagreement over which fishing activities should qualify as prohibited IUU fishing activities. In addition, there is the question of whether to follow the description provided in paragraph 3 of the IPOA-IUU or to create a different definition or list of IUU fishing activities. As noted above, different States and regional fishing organizations use variable definitions as to what constitutes IUU fishing. Unless, there is one shared definition among States, IUU operations will seek to register within jurisdictions where their activities are not deemed to be illegal. Continuity between international agreements for an IUU fishing definition and national definitions is essential.

Second, IUU fishing often involves weak flag States exercising little to no governance over registered vessels either because of a lack of capacity to govern or because of willful interest in attracting revenue without assuming international responsibilities for managing ocean resources. In 2005, the Lloyd's Register of Ships listed 1,200 large-scale fishing vessels who were either flying flags of convenience or whose flag was unknown. Some of these 1,200 vessels are new vessels that may have been constructed to participate in

---

119 One of the key issues in the case will be to what extent the ITLOS will be willing to exercise its jurisdiction to issue an advisory opinion.

IUU operations.[120] The lack of flag State enforcement is a recurring problem. As the lack of flag State enforcement stems from different sources depending on the State, there are different policy interventions that may be appropriate. For States that are attempting in good faith to monitor their flagged vessels but simply lack patrol vessels or a monitoring network, there may be opportunities to build on existing interdiction programs.

An example of this type of initiative, albeit with a focus on countering the proliferation of weapons of mass destruction (WMDs) and terrorism, is the Proliferation Security Initiative (PSI). In 2003, partially in response to the tragedy of September 11, 2001, eleven States including the United States agreed to interdict, board, and search any vessel with their flag suspected of carrying cargos of weapons of mass destruction as well as "seriously consider providing consent" to the boarding of ships flying their flag by other States.[121] The initiative currently has over 70 members and is considered to be an important tool in combatting black markets.[122] The United States has eleven shipboarding agreements that permit it to board ships suspected of carrying illicit shipments of weapons of mass destruction, their delivery systems, or related materials.[123] For States that are attempting to combat IUU fishing but are unable to perform interdictions of their own ships, these consensual shipboarding agreements offer an untapped opportunity to improve enforcement by extending the enforcement network.

The limitation of course is that these agreements will only really be effective for States that are attempting to enforce IUU measures but failing to do so because of constraints on human and financial resources. Moreover, the harsh reality is that even developed States struggle to deliver adequate monitoring control and surveillance (MCS) for their own waters in light of the broad spatial scope of maritime jurisdiction and limitations on the assets available to devote to the task. That said, there are some notable examples of international cooperation aimed at maximizing the impact of scarce surveillance and

---

120 Australian Government Department of Agriculture, Forestry, and Fisheries et al., *The Changing Nature of High Seas Fishing* (October 2005) at pp. 3–4 available at http://www.daff.gov.au/__data/assets/pdf_file/0008/5858/iuu_flags_of_convenience.pdf.
121 Proliferation Security Initiative Statement of Interdiction Principles (September 4, 2003) available at http://www.state.gov/t/isn/c27726.htm.
122 Proliferation Security Initiative available at http://www.state.gov/t/isn/c10390.htm.
123 Shipboarding Agreements available at http://www.state.gov/t/isn/c27733.htm (Covering agreements between the United States and Antigua Barbuda (2010), Bahamas (2008), Belize (2005), Croatia (2005), Cyprus (2005), Liberia (2005), Malta (2007), Marshall Island (2004), Mongolia (2007), Panama (2004), and St. Vincent and the Grenadines (2010)).

enforcement resources. Attention can be drawn to the innovative practice of the small island States of the Western and Central Pacific Ocean, particularly under the terms of the Nauru Agreement[124] as well as the bilateral measures that Australia and France have initiated in order to combat IUU fishing in the Southern Ocean.[125]

There are also States that are willfully ignoring IUU fishing practices by failing to enforce licensing schemes for high seas fishing and other responsibilities. These states are arguably failing to "effectively exercise" their "jurisdiction and control in administrative, technical and social matters over" their flagged ships.[126] One arguably radical option in this regard is to adopt the view that, because sovereignty comes with responsibilities, States that fail in "good faith" to meet their responsibilities to exercise jurisdiction and control should be considered by the international community as having illegitimate registries. A State that chronically flags to vessels conducting IUU fishing without systematically prosecuting such fishing vessels might be considered a State that willfully refuses to "effectively exercise" its jurisdiction and control. Vessels flagged from such a State might be considered by the international community not as "flagged" vessels but as "stateless" vessels capable of boarding and interdiction because the State has failed to exercise its jurisdiction and control such that the vessel can be considered linked to a State. This could act as an important incentive for vessel owners not to flag with States that intentionally frustrate international conservation and management programs because the States have no intention of enforcing conservation and management measures. The possibility of being boarded by any other State's enforcement vessels may prove to be a credible threat that would reduce the attractiveness of

---

[124] The 1982 Nauru Agreement Concerning Cooperation in the Management of Fisheries of Common Interest (Nauru Agreement, 1982) was negotiated by the equatorial Pacific island States whose waters include the most significant fisheries: Papua New Guinea, Federated States of Micronesia, Kiribati, Marshall Islands, Nauru, Palau, Solomon Islands were all original signatories. Tuvalu subsequently became a party in 1991. See, for example, Hanich, Q., Schofield, C.H. and Cozens, P. (2009) "Oceans of Opportunity?: The Limits of Maritime Claims in the South Pacific", pp. 17–46 in Hanich, Q. and Tsamenyi, M. (eds), *Navigating Pacific Fisheries: Legal and Policy Trends in the Implementation of International Fisheries Instruments in the Western and Central Pacific Region*, (Wollongong: Ocean Publications).

[125] Gullett, W. and Schofield, C.H. (2007) "Pushing the Limits of the Law of the Sea Convention: Australian and French Cooperative Surveillance and Enforcement in the Southern Ocean", *International Journal of Marine and Coastal Law*, Volume 22, No. 4: 545–583.

[126] Law of the Sea Convention, Article 94.

registering a fishing vessel with a flag of convenience State. It remains to be seen whether this suggestion would prove to be politically palatable to many States, especially given the way in which it challenges flag State authority and thus touches on the sovereignty of flag States.

Third, it is clear that enhanced MCS is crucial to addressing IUU fishing. The scale of both IUU fishing activities and the geographical scope of operations is a daunting challenge in combating IUU fishing. In this context, enhancements to existing monitoring and surveillance approaches and technologies are worthy of consideration. There have been efforts led by the FAO to require all fishing vessels to have an International Maritime Organisation number for tracking purposes and to install Vessel Monitoring Systems on every fishing vessel.[127] Each of these requirements would improve tracking for vessels but must be required of all ships involved in the IUU fishing operation including refueling and transshipment vessels. Requiring VMS and an IMO number is part of an enforcement strategy but is not sufficient on its own since it is not impossible to tamper with and turn off VMS systems.

Additionally, challenges arise concerning the processing of VMS data. While enormous volumes of data are now routinely collected globally, this has largely been limited to ship identity, position, and speed which do not necessarily reveal actual activities at sea. The more vessels there are operating within a fishery, the more complicated it may be to analyze the VMS data to determine who is legally and illegally fishing unless the VMS data can be easily correlated with fishing allocations based on geography (open fishery/restricted or prohibited access) or time (open season/closed season). Interpretation of the data therefore becomes critical and can be significantly enhanced when married to other intelligence on vessel movements and activities, including in respect of vessels not tracked. Significant recent progress has been made and convictions achieved through the use of vessel tracking information and relating this to illegal fishing activity. Nonetheless, VMS is of limited use for monitoring whether a ship is using appropriate gear, fishing for targeted species, exceeding quota, or discarding excess bycatch. One of the abiding challenges remains capacity to undertake maritime surveillance and enforcement activities. Many States, particularly those with weak governance, do not have the financial or operational capacity to purchase patrol boats and train enforcement officials to address enforcement. In some areas, this has been addressed by shiprider

---

[127] Food and Agriculture Organization, *Report of the Joint FAO/IMO Ad Hoc Working Group on Illegal, Unreported, and Unregulated Fishing and Related Matters*, FAO Fisheries Report No. 637, (October 9–12, 2000): 4–5.

agreements,[128] but more attention needs to be given to outfitting coastal States that are victims of IUU fishing activities to ensure that the coastal State can provide a credible threat of enforcement.

Attention can be drawn to novel developments including deploying new technologies at both the surveillance and enforcement as well as at the landing stages. Two possibly fruitful areas of investment would be in drones and in genetic testing. Drones could assist in surveillance. Palau in early 2013 explored the use of drones for fishing surveillance to enforce a potential ban on commercial fishing.[129] Drones which were initially developed to collect atmospheric data are being relied upon for marine scientific monitoring in the Pacific Northwest.[130] With a military quality drone costing about $20,000, drones may prove far less expensive than having a fleet of patrol boats and may make it possible for capacity poor states to more strategically utilize the one or two patrol boats in their fleets.[131]

At the landing stage, port States may also wish to explore innovative, cutting-edge options such as the possibility of using DNA barcoding in order to genetically identify the species of fish being landed to determine whether vessel log books are accurate. This proposal is inspired by the widespread mislabeling of fish in order to circumvent restrictions on the fishing of certain vulnerable stocks. In the United States, mislabeling of fish has become a chronic problem with one-third of the fish in an approximately 1,200 sample analysis being mislabeled.[132] While it may not be easy to translate a mislabeled fish into an illegal, unreported, or unregulated catch, there may be linkages between companies that regularly mislabel products either by species or geographical region and companies that participate in IUU activities. Testing at the landing site might identify some of the more suspicious practices. For example, in the US study, researchers discovered that endangered IUCN Red List species such as the overfished Atlantic halibut were being fraudulently labeled as Pacific halibut, a fish that still has sustainable stocks.[133]

---

128 Andrew Norris, "Bilateral Agreements" (Summer 2009) at www.uscg.mil/proceedings (Describing bilateral shiprider agreements between the United States and the Palau, the Federated States of Micronesia, the Marshall Islands, and Kiribati).

129 Sean Dorney, "Palau looks to drones to monitor fishing ban", *ABC Radio Australia*, (March 25, 2013).

130 Sandi Doughton, "Northwest Scientists Using Drones to Spy on Nature", *Seattle Times* (July 16, 2013).

131 Id.

132 Kimberly Warner, Walker Timme, Beth Lowell and Michael Hirshfield, "Oceana Study Reveals Seafood Fraud Nationwide" (February 2013).

133 Id. at p. 26.

Fourth, the corporate dimensions of IUU fishing have been repeatedly ignored. IUU fishing is often committed by a multinational corporate enterprise.[134] There is a desperate need for greater transparency of the beneficial owners of vessels so that there can be a chain of accountability and the parent company will not be "protected from the liability caused by the acts and activities of the subsidiaries."[135] Current domestic law does not make it easy to ascertain beneficial ownership because of the complex laws surrounding corporate entities. Working within this context of low accountability, the creation of incentives to promote good corporate governance may offer some scope for development.

Fifth, the listing of vessels flagged to non-members presents a problem for RFMOs and governments that largely remains to be addressed. Not all RFMOs have equivalent IUU lists making consistent enforcement difficult since an IUU vessel may exit one fishery and gain entrance to another fishery without having to disclose its IUU activities. Additionally, RFMOs may be hesitant to list vessels from States that are currently applying for cooperating non-member status for fear of creating a reason for the non-member not to cooperate.

7 Conclusion

Why is it so hard to crack down on IUU fishing? In part it is because existing technology is insufficient for detection of IUU fishing and fleets have little to no legal incentive, not to take extra fish or fish in an area in which they not entitled to fish.

One route towards addressing this large-scale and complex issue is for States to create better incentive structures for the detection of IUU fishing in order to discourage vessels from overfishing. In order to better combat IUU fishing States must invest in drafting a clear list of what specific activities constitute IUU fishing, increase multilateral enforcement efforts against transnational criminal fishing (which might include the option of offering bounties for information leading to detection), and significantly increase the criminal penalties for IUU fishing activities in national fishing codes. In addition, greater attention must be given to assisting States that in good faith are attempting to combat IUU fishing. Finally, States must devise approaches that tackle the IUU

---

134 L. Griggs and G. Lugten, "Veil over the nets (unraveling corporate liability for IUU fishing offences", 31 *Marine Policy* (2007): 159–168.
135 Id. at 162.

operation as a whole with a specific emphasis on creating incentives or disincentives that trigger behavioral changes from corporate actors.

This chapter has outlined a number of problematic issues and challenges as well as a range of options to enhance efforts to crack down on IUU fishing so that fewer IUU fishers will end up "slipping the net". Despite some progress and innovative options identified for the future, it remains abundantly clear that more has to be done to protect the marine fisheries particularly for communities that do not have alternatives for food security. Cracking down on IUU fishing is crucial to ensuring sustainable fisheries for both existing and future generations.

CHAPTER 5

Regulation of Private Maritime Security Companies in International Law

James Kraska

Abstract

By 2014, maritime piracy worldwide has plummeted to its lowest levels in six years; only 15 incidents were reported off the coast of Somalia in 2013, down from 75 in 2012, and 237 in 2011. The greatest reason for the drop in piracy worldwide is the decrease in Somali piracy off the coast of East Africa, and the most important factor in the decrease in Somali piracy is the prevalence of private maritime security companies. As privately contracted security guards on ships in the India Ocean become ubiquitous, however, flag states, coastal states, and the International Maritime Organization have scrambled to develop regulations for their use. In particular, there are no uniform standards for the carriage of firearms by foreign-flagged vessels transiting in the territorial sea of a coastal state. States also disagree on the appropriate rules for the use of force that may be employed by armed security guards. This chapter explores the evolution and trajectory of norms governing these two issues. It concludes that flag states may carry firearms while in innocent passage in the territorial sea, although state practice is moving in the other direction, and that states may set variable rules for the use of force by private security personnel so long as they are consistent with international human rights law.

This chapter explores new regulation of private maritime security contractors (PMSC) and Privately Contracted Armed Security Personnel (PCASP) on board international shipping vessels to defend the ships against attack by armed pirates. Since the widespread introduction of armed guards on commercial ships beginning in 2010, flag States, coastal States, and port States have worked to develop international rules concerning carriage of weapons on board commercial ships and the use of force in self-defense.

---

* Dr. James Kraska is Professor in the Stockton Center for the Study of International Law at the U.S. Naval War College and Senior Fellow, Center for Oceans Law and Policy, University of Virginia School of Law. The author's PowerPoint is available at http://www.virginia.edu/colp/pdf/Seoul-Kraska.pdf.

International shipping carriers and protection and indemnity associations (P&I clubs) scrambled to work with states to develop new rules and implement them. The Security Association for the Maritime Industry (SAMI) emerged from efforts in 2008 by a consortium of maritime security providers to develop best practices. After several years in which resistance to private security kept the issue off the agenda, the International Maritime Organization (IMO) finally included some basic recommendations on PCASP and PMSC in 2009, and these are contained in Maritime Safety Committee circular 1333.[1] At the time, countering maritime piracy was regarded as a task that will "generally fall to the security forces of the States involved."[2] Circular 1333 advised

> For legal and safety reasons, flag States should strongly discourage the carrying and use of firearms by seafarers for personal protection or for the protection of a ship. Seafarers are civilians and the use of firearms requires special training and aptitudes and the risk of accidents with firearms carried on board ship is great. Carriage of arms on board ships may encourage attackers to carry firearms or even more dangerous weapons, thereby escalating an already dangerous situation. Any firearm on board may itself become an attractive target for an attacker.[3]

The IMO believed that the use of privately contracted armed security on ships may lead to an escalation of violence, and it deferred to flag States on the issue of whether their ships should carry military teams or law enforcement.[4] Similarly, IMO guidance to ship-owners that was released in conjunction with the recommendations to governments, cautioned that ships "entering the territorial sea and/or ports of a State are subject to that State's legislation." In further discouragement of private security, the IMO guidance stated, "carrying firearms may pose an even greater danger if the ship is carrying flammable cargo or similar types of dangerous goods."[5]

---

1 IMO Doc. MSC.1/Circ. 1333, Recommendation to Governments for preventing and suppressing piracy and armed robbery against ships, June 26, 2009.
2 Id., Annex, ¶ 2.
3 Id., Annex, ¶ 5.
4 Id., Annex, paras. 7 and 8.
5 IMO Doc. MSC.1/Circ. 1334, Guidance to shipowners and ship operators, shipmasters and crews on preventing and suppressing acts of piracy and armed robbery against ships, June 23, 2009, Annex, ¶ 59.

Background

Over the past four years, the international shipping industry has turned toward the use of PMSCs to provide shipboard security against Somali pirate action groups (PAGs) operating in the "High Risk Area" of the Indian Ocean (Figure 1).[6] PAGs operate from dhow mother ships, using fast skiffs powered by outboard motors to track and board commercial ships. Shipowners and ship operators reluctantly turned toward the use of PMSCs to deter attack from PAGs after other responses—namely, coalition warship patrols and adoption of passive security shipping industry "Best Management Practices"—were insufficient to protect their ships and crews.[7] Importantly, the deployment of warships from some twenty states, loosely organized around task forces led by the North Atlantic Treaty Organization, the U.S. Commander, Maritime Force in Bahrain, and the European Union, did little to stem attacks. In the end, the desperation of commercial shipping to halt hostage taking and ship hijacking created the maritime security industry virtually overnight. As the use of PMSCs rapidly expanded throughout 2011–12, the number of successful piracy attacks on international shipping in the Indian Ocean plummeted.[8] Consequently, private security has become an important and permanent feature of regional counter-piracy in East Africa.

---

6 The HRA is set forth in the Best Management Practices as an area bounded by Suez, the Strait of Hormuz to the North (26°N), 10°S and 78°E. Best Management Practices 4th ed., August 2011 (BMP4), *reprinted in* IMO Doc. MSC.1/Circ. 1339, Best Management Practices for Protection Against Somali Based Piracy, Sept. 14, 2011, Annex, Ch. 2. The UK Maritime Trade Operations (UKMTO) voluntary Reporting Area is slightly larger, as it includes the Arabian Gulf. Somali pirate attacks have occurred at the farthest extremities of the HRA, including 78° E.

7 Naval forces have disrupted more than 100 attacks, but tyranny of time, distance, and space means that there are insufficient warships and aircraft to monitor the entire High Risk Area. Naval destruction of PAG caches and cantonments on the beach helped reduce the capability of pirates to launch attacks against shipping.

8 In 2009, Somali pirates operating in Somali waters, as well as in the Gulf of Aden, off the coast of Oman, in the Red Sea, and in the Indian Ocean, conducted 214 actual and attempted attacks of maritime piracy. By 2011, there were 237 such incidents, but then, with the introduction of armed security on board ships, attacks virtually evaporated. In 2013, there were only 15 such incidents—and not one ship successfully hijacked by Somali pirates. International Chamber of Commerce, International Maritime Bureau, PIRACY AND ARMED ROBBER AGAINST SHIPS: REPORT FOR THE PERIOD 1 JANUARY–31 DECEMBER 2013 (January 2014), pp. 5–8. *See also*, Alaric Nightingale and Michelle Wiese Bockmann, *Somalia Piracy Falls to Six-Year Low as Guards Defend Ships*, BLOOMBERG BUSINESS WEEK, Oct. 22, 2012.

As the incidence of piracy in the Gulf of Guinea region of West Africa rose, PMSCs have been deployed in that area as well, to protect shipping, and in particular, vessels servicing the large number of offshore oil and gas platforms. The coast of Togo, Benin, and Nigeria, and specifically, the territorial waters of Benin and Nigeria, and the Nigerian and Benin Exclusive Economic Zones (EEZs) north of 3° North are deemed at particular risk.[9] The horizontal expansion of armed security at sea to the East and West coast of Africa, and the legal questions arising from employment of PCASP on board ships has generated a considerable body of regulation by flag States,[10] guidance and recommendations by the International Maritime Organization, the shipping industry, and the International Standardization Organization, as well as no small amount of academic scholarship.[11]

The use of PMSCs, however, raises numerous issues in international law, two of which are addressed in this chapter: the authority of privately contracted maritime security guards on board commercial ships to carry weapons, and the authority of PCASP to use deadly force in self-defense or defense of the crew. Generally, international regulations merely state that PMSCs and PCASP should comply with "applicable flag, coastal and port State legislation and relationships governing the transport, carriage, storage, provision and use of

---

9   IMO Doc. Circ. Ltr. No. 3394, Interim Guidelines for Owners, Operators, and Masters for Protection against piracy in the Gulf of Guinea Region, Aug. 15, 2013, Attachment, ¶ 2.
10 See, e.g. Information on Port and Coastal State Requirements Related to Privately Contracted Armed Security Personnel on board ships, Maritime Transport Sector, Government of Egypt.(undated), Guidelines on Deployment of Armed Security Guards on Merchant Ships, Government of India (undated), Interim Guidance to UK Flagged Shipping on the Use of Armed Guards to Defend Against the Threat of Piracy in Exceptional Circumstances, Department for Transport, United Kingdom, November 2011 (Updated June 2012), Version 1.1, and Interim IMO Guidelines on the use of Privately Contracted Armed Security Personnel on Board Ships in the High Risk Area, Maritime Security Advisory 03/2011, Bureau of Maritime Affairs, The Republic of Liberia, May 24, 2011.
11 See, e.g., Anna Petrig, *The Use of Force and Firearms by Private Maritime Security Companies against Suspected Pirates*, 62 INTERNATIONAL AND COMPARATIVE LAW QUARTERLY 667 (July 2013); LIFTING THE VEIL ON PRIVATE MARITIME SECURITY (Claude Berube and Patrick Cullen, eds., 2012); Alice Priddy and Stuart Casey-Maslen, *Counter-piracy Operations by Private Maritime Security Contractors*, 10 JOURNAL OF INTERNATIONAL CRIMINAL LAW 839 (2012); James Kraska, *International and Comparative Regulation of Private Maritime Security Companies Employed in Counter-piracy*, in Douglas Guilfoyle, ed., MODERN PIRACY: LEGAL CHALLENGES AND RESPONSES (2013), 219–249; and John J., Jr. Pitney and John-Clark Levin, PRIVATE ANTI-PIRACY NAVIES: HOW WARSHIPS FOR HIRE ARE CHANGING MARITIME SECURITY (2013).

firearms, ammunition and security equipment...."[12] Given that the rules are often inconsistent, nonexistent, and in a state of flux, however, the guidelines typically raise more questions than they answer. Addressing and resolving questions on the carriage and use of firearms, therefore, often is case-specific and fact-dependent. References to generalized rules that evoke adherence to international law merely beg the question.

The use of PMSCs by the shipping industry to protect merchant ships at sea is governed by civil and criminal law of self-defense, even when it is conducted simultaneously in areas patrolled by warships. Since piracy is a maritime crime, methods to address it are governed by the peacetime law of international human rights. The use of contractors during periods of armed conflict raises separate and distinct issues that arise from the law of war, and are not relevant in the context of maritime piracy.

General Authority

The international law of the sea, as reflected in United Nations Convention on the Law of the Sea (UNCLOS), is silent on whether ships may carry weapons or use force in self-defense. Under Articles 92 and 94 of UNCLOS, flag States are presumed to exercise plenary authority over ships flying their flag. Article 92 recognizes "exclusive flag State jurisdiction" over a vessel on the high seas, and Article 94 enumerates "duties of the flag State." The master of the ship retains, at all times "ultimate responsibility for the safe navigation and overall command of the vessel."[13] International guidelines developed specifically for the division of authority between the master and the private security team stipulate that the "Master remains in command and is the overriding authority

---

12 Revised Interim Guidance to Shipowners, Ship Operators, and Shipmasters on the Use of Privately Contracted Armed Security Personnel on Board Ships in the High Risk Area, IMO Doc. MSC.1/Circ. 1405/Rev. 2, May 25, 2012, ¶ 5.12.1.

13 Baltic and International Maritime Council (BIMCO), Standard Contract for the Employment of Security Guards on Vessels (GUARDCON) (2012). BIMCO is the world's largest shipping industry association. The master's authority is defined in SOLAS XI-2 Reg. 8(1), which states: "The master shall not be constrained by the Company, the charterer or any other person from taking or executing any decision which, in the professional judgment of the master, is necessary to maintain the safety and security of the ship. This includes denial of access to persons (except those identified as duly authorized by a Contracting Government) or their effects or refusal to load cargo, including containers or other closed cargo transport unit." *See also* Annex I, European Regulation (EC) No. 725/2004.

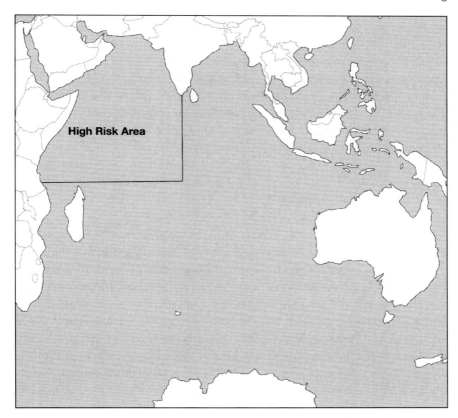

FIGURE 1   The high risk area in the Indian Ocean.

on board" the ship.[14] In short, generally the master's authority covers how private security is employed on the ship, and the conditions under which they may exercise the use of force.

The United States has long had rules pertaining to the use of PMSCs and PCASP on board ships that fly its flag.[15] Similarly, the United Kingdom issued

---

14 Int'l Org. for Standardization Publicly Available Specification (ISO/PAS) 28007, Ships and Marine Technology—Guidelines for Private Maritime Security Companies Providing Privately Contracted Armed Security Personnel (PCASP) on Board Ships, 2012-12-15, ¶ 5.2.1(a) (ISO/PAS 28007:2012(E)).

15 33 CFR Part 104 and MARSEC Directive 104–6. Armed civilian security personnel who are U.S. citizens must meet requirements for licensure and bonding, certification, and training set forth in 18 U.S.C. § 922(g). Foreign citizens must meet a substantially equivalent standard and the requirements of all port States visited while the armed security remains

guidelines in November 2011.[16] Other flag States, such as India, as well as the large open registries or "flags of convenience," are disseminating guidelines.

The Member States of the International Maritime Organization have issued guidance to ship operators and shipowners and recommendations to governments on the employment of private security at sea.[17] The International Standardization Organization (ISO) has also issued interim guidelines, which are adopted by IMO. Although these sets of regulations provide a broad basis for State action, they are relatively general and ambiguous.

Carriage of Weapons

Generally, carriage of PCASP, firearms and security-related equipment is subject to flag State legislation and policy.[18] International guidelines state that ships carrying firearms and PCASP should comply with "applicable national laws relating to the procurement, carriage including export and import licensing, storage, use and disposal of firearms and security related equipment."[19] This rule, however, tends to beg the question, as flag States, coastal States, and port States have adopted a kaleidoscope of inconsistent national legislations and policies, which sometimes differ as much from one part of a state to another as they do among nations.[20] The fourth edition of the shipping industry "Best Management Practices" or BMP4 states that the carriage of firearms

---

onboard. The contracted security company must be appropriately licensed and bonded in a state and meet any requirements imposed by all foreign countries visited. Id.

16   DEP'T FOR TRANSPORT, UNITED KINGDOM OF GREAT BRITAIN AND NORTHERN IRELAND, INTERIM GUIDANCE TO UK FLAGGED SHIPPING ON THE USE OF ARMED GUARDS TO DEFENSE AGAINST THE THREAT OF PIRACY IN EXCEPTIONAL CIRCUMSTANCES, VERSION 1.1 (November 2011; Updated June 2012) [UK Guidance].

17   See Revised Interim Guidance to Shipowners, Ship Operators, and Shipmasters on the Use of Privately Contracted Armed Security Personnel on Board Ships in the High Risk Area, IMO Doc. MSC.1/Circ. 1405/Rev. 2, May 25, 2012 and Revised Interim Recommendations for Flag States Regarding the Use of Privately Contracted Armed Security Personnel on Board Ships in the High Risk Area, IMO Doc. MSC.1/Circ. 1406/Rev.1, Sept. 16, 2011.

18   Revised Interim Recommendations for Flag States Regarding the Use of Privately Contracted Armed Security Personnel on Board Ships in the High Risk Area, MSC.1/Circ. 1406/Rev. 1, Sept. 16, 2011, Annex, ¶ 2.

19   ISO/PAS 28007, ¶ 4.2.4(b)(3).

20   IMO Doc. MSC.1/Circ. 1405/Rev. 2, May 25, 2012, ¶ 1.2 (The absence of applicable regulation and industry self-regulation coupled with complex legal requirements governing the legitimate transport, carriage and use of firearms gives cause for concern). See also Revised Interim Recommendations for Port and Coastal States Regarding the Use

and PCASP are a matter for ship operators, in accordance with their voyage risk assessment and approval of the flag State. Guidance by the Government of the UK, for example, states that armed guards should only be used on board a ship while transiting in the High Risk Area, although they may be embarked and disembarked at the "soonest safe, convenient, and lawful opportunity" outside the HRA.[21]

After a significant increase in the number of ship operators employing PCASP in the High Risk Area, in May 2012, the member States of the IMO released supplementary guidance to the private maritime security companies that employ private security personnel on board ships in the High Risk Area.[22] The 2012 guidance states that PMSC "should acknowledge the possible existence of legal responsibilities" promulgated by flag States, the nations where the PMSC are registered, and countries through which PCASP may transit.[23] In particular, PMSC should "have awareness and understanding" of national laws concerning the transport, carriage, storage, and use of firearms, and therefore, have "access to competent maritime legal advice on a 24/7 basis...."[24]

Carriage of Firearms in Foreign Territorial Seas

The trajectory of state practice suggests that it is unclear whether mere carriage of weapons and PCASP are inconsistent with the right of innocent passage. Some coastal States may assert authority or jurisdiction over PCASP on

---

of Privately Contracted Armed Security Personnel on Board Ships in the High Risk Area, IMO Doc. MSC.1/Circ. 1408/Rev. 1, May 25, 2012.

21 UK Guidance, ¶ 6.7.
22 IMO Doc. MSC.1/Circ. 1443, Interim Guidance to Private Maritime Security Companies Providing Privately Contracted Armed Security Personnel on Board Ships in the High Risk Area, May 25, 2012, Annex. Circular 1443 supplements and should be read in conjunction with earlier guidance, including, interim guidance set out in IMO Doc. MSC.1/Circ. 1405/Rev. 2 on Revised interim guidance to shipowners, ship operators and shipmasters on the use of privately contracted armed security personnel on board ships in the High Risk Area; IMO Doc. MSC.1/Circ. 1406/Rev. 2 on Revised interim recommendations for flag States regarding the use of privately contracted armed security personnel on board ships in the High Risk Area; and IMO Doc. MSC. 1/Circ. 1408/Rev. 1 on Revised interim recommendations for port and coastal States regarding the use of privately contracted armed security personnel on board ships in the High Risk Area.
23 IMO Doc. MSC.1/Circ. 1443, Annex, ¶ 1.3.
24 Id., ¶ 3.3.1 and 3.3.2.

board ships conducting innocent passage in the territorial sea. India, for example, has issued Guidelines that state:

> Deployment of armed security guards on merchant ships does change the very paradigm of a merchant ship, which is granted a liberty to transit the territorial waters of any state under the concept of "innocent passage." Further, a merchant ship arriving with weapons on board, in a commercial port of a coastal state, would also invoke concern for customs, police and other security agencies tasked with law enforcement and coastal security.[25]

The UK Guidance states that when ships are carrying firearms while in foreign territorial seas, "it is essential that the laws of [the] coastal State are respected and complied with."[26] Although the United Kingdom references the right of innocent passage in accordance with UNCLOS in cases in which passage is "not prejudicial to the peace, good order or security" of the coastal State, it also acknowledges that any "exercise or practice with weapons" during innocent passage may not be consistent with the regime. Therefore, shipping companies are directed to "take legal advice on the legal requirements" of coastal States whose territorial seas they transit, "even if firearms on board are security stored and comply with any requirements put in place by that State."[27]

This chapter suggests that carriage of firearms by PCASP indeed is wholly consistent with innocent passage, and that it does not violate any prohibition set forth in Article 19 of UNCLOS so long as weapons and personnel are used solely for the purpose of self-defense against maritime threats. Article 27 of UNCLOS specifies that coastal States should not assert criminal jurisdiction over ships in innocent passage except, *inter alia*, if the actions on the ship constitute a crime, the consequences of which "extend to the coastal State," or "if the crime is of a kind to disturb the peace of the country or the good order of the territorial sea." Presupposing that even if simple carriage of firearms constitutes a crime in the coastal State, mere innocent passage does not "extend to" the coastal State or "disturb the peace" or good order in the territorial sea. This view, however, appears to be a minority perspective, as states assert authority over the transit of firearms on board ships in innocent passage.

---

25 Ministry of Shipping, Government of India, Guidelines on Deployment of Armed Security Guards on Merchant Ships, ¶ 4 (August 2011).
26 UK Guidance, ¶ 6.8.
27 UK Guidance, ¶ 6.9.

In 2011, an IMO circular contained a questionnaire on port and coastal State requirements related to PCASP on board ships transiting near the State or entering port.[28] In particular, the IMO's Facilitation Committee (FAL) recommended that coastal States bordering the Indian Ocean, Arabian Sea, Gulf of Aden, and Red Sea distribute information on their national legislation, procedures and best practices relating to the carriage, embarkation and disembarkation of firearms and security-related equipment through their territory and, as appropriate, rules concerning the movement of privately contracted armed security personnel:[29]

> The use of privately contracted armed security personnel on board ships may lead to an escalation of violence. The carriage of such personnel and their weapons is subject to flag State legislation and policies and is a matter for flag States to determine in consultation with ship owners, companies, and ship operators, if and under which conditions this will be allowed. Flag States should take into account the possible escalation of violence, which could result from carriage of armed personnel on board merchant ships, when deciding on its policy.[30]

Similarly, IMO Resolution 1044(27) urged coastal States to: "decide on their policy on the embarkation, disembarkation and *carriage* of privately contracted armed security personnel and of the firearms, ammunition and security-related equipment [author's italics]."[31] The 90th Session of the IMO's Maritime Safety Committee also concluded that "ships entering the territorial sea and/or ports of a State are subject to that State's legislation."[32] India has gone even further, proposing at IMO that both private maritime security contractors and members of the armed forces providing security or protection on board

---

28 IMO Doc. MSC/MSPWG 1/4/3, Development of Guidance on the Use of Privately Contracted Security Personnel on Board Ships, Sept. 12, 2011, Annex, IMO Doc. MSC-FAL/Circ.[2], Draft Questionnaire on Information on Port and Coastal State Requirements related to PCASP on Board Ships.

29 Id., Annex, ¶ 5.

30 IMO Doc. MSC.1/Circ. 1333, Recommendation to Governments for preventing and suppressing piracy and armed robbery against ships, June 26, 2009, Annex, ¶ 7.

31 Id., at ¶ 8(c)–(d).

32 IMO Doc. MSC 90, Report of the Maritime Safety Committee on its Ninetieth Session May 31, 2012, ¶ 20.11.

merchant ships transiting in a coastal State's EEZ be required to report "details" of their presence on the ship.[33]

In order to determine the direction of coastal State practice on the regulation of the carriage of firearms by foreign commercial ships during innocent passage, the Facilitation Committee (FAL) of the IMO solicited information from a range of states. The responses to the FAL Questionnaire illustrate a range of practices among States on the issue of regulation of firearms in innocent passage. States were asked to report:

> What requirements, if any, do you have in place for ships carrying firearms and/or the security-related equipment for use by the PCASP or of PCASP when transiting through your territorial seas and/or contiguous zones before arrival in or after departure from your ports, anchorages, roadstead or offshore terminals?[34]

While every state surveyed had some requirement for providing notification by ships of the presence of defensive armaments to be made upon entry into port or while getting underway from port, there was a more mixed set of rules pertaining to innocent passage.

Australia was somewhat circumspect in its reply, stating: "Obligations (for example, for notification, authorization or storage) may be imposed by a number of Australian Government agencies, including the Australian Customs and Border Protection Service and the Defense Export Control Office. Notification is often required in advance, and should be provided directly to the relevant agency."[35] The United States dodged the question entirely, reporting only that "This authority falls within the responsibility of the U.S. Coast Guard, the Department of State, the Department of Homeland Security, Coast Guard [sic], Customs and Border Protection, Department of Justice, Bureau of Alcohol, Tobacco, Firearms, and Explosives, and Other U.S. Government Agencies."[36]

---

33   IMO Doc. MSC 90/20/16, Piracy and Armed Robbery against Ships: Armed Security Personnel on Board Ships, Submitted by India, Mar. 27, 2012.

34   IMO Doc. MSC-FAL/Circ. 2, Questionnaire on information on port and coastal State requirements related to privately contracted armed security personnel on board ships, Nov. 17, 2011, ¶ 1.6.

35   IMO Doc. MSC-FAL/Circ. 2 (Australia), ¶ 1.6.

36   IMO Doc. MSC-FAL/Circ. 2 (United States), ¶ 1.6.

Brazil was more straightforward, and indicated that ships in innocent passage that carry firearms for use by PCASP must alert public authorities before arrival in the territorial sea.[37] Likewise, Denmark considers a transit of the territorial sea to be an "import" under the Weapons and Explosives Act. A license of authorization is required from the Ministry of Justice.[38] Egypt has similar rules.

For passage through the Suez Canal, shipping agencies are required only to present a report from the merchant vessel detailing the armaments and ammunition on board, which is to remain inside a locked box under authority of the shipmaster until the vessel is clear of Egyptian territory. The locked box is to be presented to Port Security to be inspected, and then delivered back to the vessel as it departs the port. Failure to declare or present the weapons, even if a ship is exercising innocent passage, may result in criminal prosecution under law no. 394 of 1954.[39]

India claims that the very deployment of armed security guards on merchant ships "does change the very paradigm of a merchant ship which is granted a liberty to transit the territorial waters of any state under the concept of 'innocent passage'."[40] India's law regulation recognizes that armed security is perhaps the only effective deterrent against maritime piracy. As Somali piracy has pushed eastward into the Arabian Sea, traffic routes have shifted to escape danger, resulting in a "quantum jump" in the number of merchant vessels transiting Indian territorial seas and EEZ.[41] All foreign ships visiting Indian ports are required to secure their firearms and ammunition in a locked space prior to arrival in the territorial sea.[42] The regulations also states that the right of innocent passage cannot be "summarily withdrawn," so it is imperative that ships are notified about standards for carriage of weapons in the territorial sea, EEZ, and the Indian Search and Rescue Region.[43] Transit through any of these areas with armed personnel or ammunition on board requires compliance with the same rules for entry into port: ships must provide the regional coast

---

37 IMO Doc. MSC-FAL/Circ. 2 (Brazil), ¶ 1.6.
38 IMO Doc. MSC-FAL/Circ. 2 (Denmark), ¶ 1.2 and 1.6.
39 Information on Port and Coastal Requirements Related to Privately Contracted Armed Security Personnel on board ships, Maritime Transport Sector, Government of Egypt, Nov. 1, 2012.
40 See, IMO Doc. MSC-FAL/Circ. 2 (India), ¶ 1.2 and Government of India, Ministry of Shipping, Notification No. vide F. SR-13020/6/2009-MG(pt.), Aug. 29, 2011.
41 Ministry of Shipping, Notification No. vide F. SR-13020/6/2009-MG(pt.), ¶ 1.7.
42 Id. ¶ 7.5.
43 Id. ¶ 7.2.

guard (and the port authority and customs, if applicable), a 96-hour pre-arrival notification for security (PANS) that includes the names, addresses, and details of identification of the security personnel, information on the number and type of weapons (including make, model, bore, caliber, serial number etc.), and information on the licenses and registration of the PMSC.[44]

Jordan permits weapons to be carried on board a ship in innocent passage if the voyage through the territorial sea is less than 24 hours in length. If the transit exceeds 24 hours, the ship is required to transfer all weapons and ammunition to the Royal Jordanian Naval force Base during the period of the transit.[45]

Liberia is a special case. The country maintains a strict embargo on armaments aboard ships entering Liberian territorial waters pursuant to the total arms embargo imposed upon the nation by United Nations Security Council Resolution 788.[46]

France has adopted a more liberal view of the carriage of firearms in innocent passage. Ships transiting French territorial waters are accorded the benefit of Article L.5211-1 of the Transport Code of France, which recognizes the right of innocent passage, provided that "no armed person is visible and that no weapon, individual or collective, is handled or is visible on the exterior of the ship."[47] The ship must keep weapons and ammunition in separate lockers or locked spaces, or in the alternative, hand them over to a government service for the duration of the transit. The latter option is chargeable at a market cost. Finally, once the ship departs the territorial sea, it must notify French authorities by VHF.

Similarly, the United Kingdom does not prohibit the carriage of firearms by foreign ships conducting innocent passage. The U.K. responded to the inquiry from FAL by stating:

> It is considered that the UK is not within or neighboring a Piracy High Threat Area. The presence of firearms on board shipping transiting UK waters should be considered a highly exceptional circumstance. In those exceptional circumstances whereby firearms cannot be removed from the vessel prior to arrival in UK waters, all firearms and ammunition should be secured and stowed in a safe condition under direct control of the Master. All such firearms and ammunition will be subject to declaration upon arrival in UK Port or, in the case of boarding by UK enforcement authorities in territorial waters, will be declared to those proper

---

44 Id. ¶ 7.3, 7.5.3 and 7.2.
45 IMO Doc. MSC-FAL/Circ. 2 (Jordan), ¶ 1.6.
46 IMO Doc. MSC-FAL/Circ. 2 (Liberia), ¶ 1.6 and S/RES/788 (1992) (Nov. 19, 1992), ¶ 8.
47 IMO Doc. MSC-FAL/Circ. 2 (France), ¶ 1.6.

agencies. It should be noted that UK flag vessels are further subject to the full provisions of the UK Firearms Acts 1968–97.[48]

Spanish law does not impose any special requirement on vessels in innocent passage that carry armed security personnel, weapons, or ammunition.[49] Hong Kong also has no regulation of firearms aboard ships exercising innocent passage, although vessels entering port must declare the presence of firearms to the Customs and Excise Department 24 hours in advance of arrival.[50] Israel also does not have any requirement for ship reporting of PCASP or the presence of weapons on board a vessel conducting innocent passage.[51]

Mauritius requires that weapons and ammunition be properly stowed under lock while a ship is conducting innocent passage, in accordance with the Ship Security Plan. If the vessel is boarded by Mauritius Police Forces, all armed security guards are to be mustered unarmed at a designated location on the ship.[52]

Use of Force

Generally, private security on board ships should take "reasonable steps to avoid and deter the use of lethal force."[53] PCASP should implement a "graduated approach," taking steps that are reasonable and proportionate, and that include non-lethal options, such as warning shots. Lethal forces should be used only in self-defense and be necessary and proportionate to the perceived threat.[54] In particular, the "decisions [made by the Master concerning the use of force] will be binding, without derogating from the inherent right of self-defense."[55] Furthermore, if the Master "judges that there is a risk to the safety of the ship, crew and or environment, he has the authority to order the security personnel to cease firing."[56] If the Master is not available, the senior officer in command on the ship assumes the Master's authority.

---

48   IMO Doc. MSC-FAL/Circ. 2 (United Kingdom), ¶ 1.6.
49   IMO Doc. MSC-FAL/Circ. 2 (Spain), ¶ 1.6.
50   IMO Doc. MSC-FAL/Circ. 2 (Hong Kong), ¶ 1.6.
51   IMO Doc. MSC-FAL/Circ. 2 (Israel), ¶ 1.6.
52   IMO Doc. MSC-FAL/Circ. 2 (Mauritius), ¶ 1.6.
53   ISO/PAS 28007, ¶ 5.3(b).
54   ISO/PAS 28007, ¶ 5.3(e).
55   ISO/PAS 28007, ¶ 5.3(e).
56   ISO/PAS 28007, ¶ 5.3(f).

The IMO Guidance to the shipping industry states that PCASP should not use firearms except in self-defense or defense of others.[57] Furthermore, armed security should "take all reasonable steps to avoid the use of force. If force is used, it should be in a manner consistent with applicable law. In no case should the use of force exceed what is strictly necessary and reasonable in the circumstances. Care should be taken to minimize damage and injury and preserve human life."[58]

In 2012, the IMO provided guidance directly to PMSC that employ PCASP, and the relevant Maritime Safety Committee circular, cautioned that the industry was affected by a protean body of law governing the use of force.[59] Recognizing that the principal applicable law is the law of the flag State, the IMO also indicated that the use of force could be governed by coastal State and port State regulations, depending upon the location of an incident, or the nationalities of the ship, the companies, and the individuals involved.[60]

Under the guidelines, IMO suggests that PCASP take "all reasonable steps" to avoid the use of force, and that force should be used only as part of a graduated response plan.[61] Furthermore, force should not "exceed what is strictly necessary and reasonable in the circumstances."[62] The use of force should be reserved for situations of self-defense or defense of others, and "care should be taken to minimize damage and injury," and to "respect and preserve human life."[63]

A plan for graduated response should set forth the roles and division of authority between the Master and the PCASP team leader. These two individuals must share the same understanding of the rules for the use of force.[64] A log of each incidence of the discharge of a weapon, such as in training or self-defense, should be maintained. The logbook may include:

1. The time and location of the incident;
2. The details of events leading up to the incident;
3. Written statements by those involved in the incident from the PCASP team;

---

57   IMO Doc. MSC.1/Circ. 1405/Rev. 2, May 25, 2012, ¶ 5.15.
58   IMO Doc. MSC.1/Circ. 1405/Rev. 2, May 25, 2012, ¶ 5.14.
59   IMO Doc. MSC.1/Circ. 1443, Annex, ¶ 5.13.
60   Id.
61   Id., para 5.15.2.
62   Id., ¶ 5.15.3.
63   Id., ¶ 5.15, paras 3 and 4.
64   Id., ¶ 5.17.

4. Any injuries and/or material damage sustained;
5. Applicable lessons learned from the incident;
6. Recommended procedures to prevent recurrence, if applicable; and
7. Documentation, including video or photography, of any tests, including drug or alcohol tests, taken during the investigation of the incident.[65]

Under U.S. law, seafarers have the right to use force, up to and including deadly force, in self-defense and defense of others. The ship's master and crew have authority to actively "oppose and defend against any aggression, search, restraint, depredation, or seizure, which shall be attempted," pursuant to a piratical attack.[66] Self-defense is recognized by the US Coast Guard from common law and historical usage as "the act of thwarting an attack upon oneself, another person, or both by using force, up to and including deadly force."[67] Force may be used if the seafarers are in imminent danger—which is present in cases where there is a reasonable belief that the attackers have the means and opportunity to inflict great bodily harm or death on the individual or others in the vicinity.[68] Non-deadly force may be used to prevent theft or intentional damage to or destruction of property, including a U.S.-flagged vessel.[69] Warning shots are a signal under U.S. law and not considered a use of force.[70]

The United Kingdom also authorizes the use of force to repel pirates. Deadly force may be used in self-defense or defense of another, but the force must be proportionate and reasonable under the circumstances."[71] Force also may be used for the prevention of a crime, such as piracy.[72] The United Kingdom has a graduated response to the use of force. Each stage of the response ladder should be "reasonable, proportionate and necessary to the threat."[73] Furthermore, measures to display capability to use force, such as making firearms visible or issuing verbal warnings or warning shots, should be "implemented in such

---

65   Id., ¶ 5.19–20.
66   33 U.S.C. § 383.
67   United States Coast Guard, Dep't of Homeland Security, Port Security Advisory (3-09), Guidance on Self-defense or Defense of Others by U.S.-Flagged Commercial Vessels Operating in High Risk Waters, June 18, 2009, ¶ 2.
68   USCG Advisory 3-09, ¶ 2.d.
69   Non-deadly force may include maneuvers by the vessels, deployment of sonic blasts, use of fire hoses, or the use of disabling fire. USCG Advisory 3-09, ¶ 3.c.
70   Id., 3-09, ¶ 3.g.
71   UK Guidance, ¶ 8.10.
72   Id., ¶ 8.13.
73   Id., ¶ 8.5.

a way so as not to be taken as acts of aggression."[74] The law in England and Wales stipulates that a "person may use force which is reasonable in the circumstances as they genuinely believed them to be...."[75]

Conclusion

Flag States may authorize the carriage and use of firearms for use in self-defense. Within the territorial sea of a foreign state, however, some coastal States may assert jurisdiction over commercial vessels that transit in innocent passage while carrying weapons or PCASP on board. The text of UNCLOS suggests that coastal States may exercise civil jurisdiction over such ships if such carriage constitutes a crime, the consequences of which "extend to the coastal State," or "is of a kind to disturb the peace of the country or the good order of the territorial sea"[76] The meaning of these provisions, however, lack clarity, and leave uncertain the right to carry weapons while in innocent passage. Among those states surveyed by the IMO Facilitation Committee, only France and the United Kingdom had affirmative law that protected innocent passage. Hong Kong and Spanish laws are silent on the issue, and presumably those nations permit ships to conduct innocent passage with PCASP and armaments on board.

Similarly, the use of firearms in self-defense is surrounded by ambiguity. Presumably, the law of self-defense of the flag State of the vessel controls the application of armed force. Other States, however, may also claim jurisdiction over cases involving the discharge of weapons or the application of deadly force. The state of persons injured or killed may claim passive personality jurisdiction over PCASP who use deadly force. Likewise, coastal States and port States also may claim jurisdiction in cases involving the use of force.

---

74   Id., ¶ 8.5.
75   Id., ¶ 8.9. There are variations in the law of self-defense among the three jurisdictions of the United Kingdom (i.e., England & Wales, Northern Ireland, and Scotland). "In England & Wales (and Northern Ireland) the decision about whether a person used reasonable force will be assessed in the context of the circumstances as the accused genuinely believed them to be (even if he or she was mistaken as to the true circumstances). Under Scots law, a person will only be able to claim self-defense (which includes defense of another) if that person believed that he/she (or a third party) was in imminent danger and had reasonable grounds for that belief." Id., ¶ 8.7.
76   UNCLOS, Article 27 1(a) and (b).

PART 3

Developments in Arctic Ocean

∴

CHAPTER 6

Arctic Council Update

Ernst Nordtveit

Introduction

This chapter is based on my paper delivered at the conference held by the Center for Oceans Law and Policy in Seoul in May 2013, but is updated in order to include the decisions made at the ministerial meeting in Kiruna on 15 May 2013 (the Kiruna meeting). The chapter provides an update on the development of the Arctic Council as an organization, and on the recent activities and policies of the Council. The most central issue is the relation between the countries of the Arctic Council and countries outside the region, with expressed interests in the development in the Arctic, especially the question of observer status for countries outside the Arctic region. The chapter will also present recent initiatives of the Arctic Council on shipping, petroleum activity and on the changes in the Arctic as a result of climate change and development of the organization in order to meet these changes.

A short presentation of the Arctic Council and its historical background and development is given, but this will be limited to the most central issues. For further information on the background and development of the Arctic Council, please refer to other existing sources.[1] The challenges the Arctic Council and the Arctic States face as a result of the changes in the Arctic due to global warming and the possible influence this might have on the development of the Arctic Council are also discussed.

---

* Ernst Nordtveit, University of Bergen, Faculty of Law. The author's PowerPoint is available at http://www.virginia.edu/colp/pdf/Seoul-Nordtveit.pdf.

1 More information on the Arctic Council and Arctic issues can be found at http://www.arctic-council.org/index.php/en/ and http://www.arcticportal.org/arctic-council. See also Tennberg, Monica. *The Arctic Council: a study in governmentality*. University of Lapland, 1998; Evan T. Bloom. "Establishment of the Arctic Council" *American Journal of International Law*, Vol. 93, No. 3 (Jul., 1999), pp. 712–722; Koivurova, Timo, Erik Jaap Molenaar, and D.L. VanderZwaag. "Canada, the EU, and Arctic Ocean governance: a tangled and shifting seascape and future directions." *J. Transnat'l L. & Pol'y* 18 (2008): 247; and Molenaar, Erik J. "Current and Prospective Roles of the Arctic Council System within the Context of the Law of the Sea." *International Journal of Marine and Coastal Law* 27.3 (2012): 553–595.

Organisation and Work of the Arctic Council

The Arctic Council was established by The Ottawa Declaration 1996. The Council is a high-level inter-governmental forum to provide a means for promoting cooperation, coordination and interaction among the Arctic States, with the involvement of the Arctic indigenous communities and other Arctic inhabitants on common Arctic issues, in particular to address issues of sustainable development and environmental protection in the Arctic.

Member States are the eight States with territories in the Arctic area: Canada, Denmark (including the Faroe Islands and Greenland), Finland, Iceland, Norway, Russia, Sweden and the United States. In addition, organizations representing indigenous peoples in the Arctic are permanent members of the Council. These organisations are Aleut International Association (AIA), Arctic Athabaskan Council (AAC), Gwich'in Council International (GCI), Inuit Circumpolar Council (ICC), Russian Association of Indigenous Peoples of the North (RAIPON) and the Saami Council in Norway.

It follows from the Declaration on the Establishment of the Arctic Council that status as observer is open to non-Arctic states, inter-governmental and inter-parliamentary organizations, global and regional non-governmental organizations. We now return to the process and discussion prior to and at the Kiruna meeting on observer status as indicated below.[2]

The council is organised with a rotation of chairmanship between the eight member States, decided by a ministerial meeting every second year. The change of chairmanship from Sweden to Canada at the Kiruna meeting in May 2013 concluded the first cycle of chairmanships.

A meeting of deputy ministers between the ministerial meetings has also been established. The Council has not had any permanent administration. However, in 2013 a permanent Secretariat for the Arctic Council was established in Tromsø in Norway. The Secretariat was operational from the start of the Canadian chairmanship in May 2013.

The Council does not have the authority to make binding decisions for the member States, and is thus not a supra-national organization.[3] The Arctic Council has been a consensus-based organisation, and has not made decisions by vote. Agreements on several projects and issues have been reached as a

---

[2] See list of observers: http://www.arctic-council.org/index.php/en/about-us/arctic-council/observers.

[3] For further analysis of the Arctic Council see Koivurova, Timo, and Erik J. Molenaar. "International governance and regulation of the marine Arctic." *Oslo: WWF International Arctic Programme* (2009) 12–14.

result of the work of the Council. We shall return to consider these agreements below. The work of the Council has also been project-driven, in the sense that the work has been concentrated on various concrete projects agreed upon by the parties. Several studies on issues relevant to the Arctic have been carried out by working groups established by the Council.[4] Implementation of the policy decided by the Arctic Council is left to the discretion of member States within their jurisdiction.

Since the Arctic Council was established, the situation in the Arctic has changed dramatically. The Council faces new challenges, which are likely to influence its role and function. The Council's main challenge is the effect of climate change on ice cover,[5] ecosystems and livelihood in the Arctic. The Arctic is believed to be in an initial phase of a transformation that is expected to fundamentally change the character of the area within a few decades, as a result of climate change and increased human activity. Decrease in the coverage of sea ice, snow cover and permafrost as well as changes in biodiversity and ecosystems, e.g. migration patterns and distribution of fish and distributional shifts in other species, will create challenges as well as opportunities for exploitation of the Arctic area. Formerly remote and mostly inaccessible areas of the Arctic will be transformed to an open sea area of high geopolitical interest, with increased possibilities for extensive ship traffic, petroleum and mineral exploration, fisheries and tourism. This development will of course have the strongest effects on the states in and around the Arctic, but the effects of the changes in the Arctic influence the interests of a large number of states outside the Arctic area. The development in the Arctic area has attracted strong global interest. The uncertainty of future development makes decisions difficult, and creates a need for preparedness for action as the development unravels.

The Legal Regime of the Arctic as Framework for the Arctic Council

The function of the Arctic Council should be viewed against the background of the legal regime in the region, as the cooperation in the Arctic Council must

---

4   See the webpage of the Arctic Council for more information.
5   The ice cover in the Arctic was at its smallest extent ever recorded in September 2012. Also in 2013 it was well below average but larger than in 2012. Levels of multiyear ice remain extremely low also in 2013. The ice is thinner, and satellite data suggests that first-year ice may now cover the North Pole area for the first time since winter 2008. The predictions are that much of the Arctic Ocean will be free from ice in the summer in a few decades.

take place within the framework established by the general international public law applied to the Arctic area.[6]

Unlike Antarctica, the Arctic is not regulated by a general treaty, and there is no central institution with legislative power. The Arctic area consists of the land and sea territories of the adjacent states, and of sea areas which fall in part under EEZ jurisdiction and are in part high seas international waters. No special international rules apply to the territories, EEZs or continental shelves of the Arctic States. The UN Convention on the Law of the Sea (UNCLOS) is the basis for divisions of rights, and regulates the activity in the Arctic Ocean. Since 2008 the states of the Arctic Ocean have in the Ilulissat Declaration confirmed their commitment to solving any issues on the basis of the international law of the sea. The Declaration was made by the Arctic Ocean's five coastal States. The commitment was repeated in the Arctic Council Tromsø Declaration in 2009.

The legal regime for the Arctic is thus a complicated relationship between national law, international law and indigenous customary law. The national legal systems in the eight countries in the Arctic are applicable in the land and sea territories, and with certain limitations in the Exclusive Economic Zones (EEZs) or continental shelves of each country. The ecosystem management and biodiversity protection in large areas is consequently under the jurisdiction of the Arctic States. Ocean areas outside the EEZs are legally open to access, which will be a growing problem as the ice cover decreases and eventually disappears. Natural resources on and in the seabed beyond the outer limits of the continental shelves would be controlled through the International Seabed Authority (ISA).

The Arctic Council does not have any influence on the borders of the continental shelf or the EEZs in the Arctic, as these questions are regulated by and follow the procedures set out in the UNCLOS. The outcome of such processes and the resolution of border conflicts are, however, of importance for the Council's function.

The five coastal States in the Arctic—Canada, Denmark (Greenland), Iceland, Norway, Russia and the United States—either have or are in the process of presenting their claims regarding the extent of their continental shelves in the Arctic. The Commission on the Limits of the Continental Shelf set up under Annex II to UNCLOS (UNCLOS article 76 (8)) has given its recommendation for Norway, but for the other countries the question is still pending. Depending on the outcome of the decision process on the continental shelf

---

6 See Molenaar, Erik J. "Current and Prospective Roles of the Arctic Council System within the Context of the Law of the Sea," *supra* note 1.

claims, the Arctic might contain an international seabed area. If this is the case, the International Seabed Authority will also have a position in the Arctic.

Division lines between the EEZs and the continental shelves are to be solved by negotiation, according to UNCLOS article 83. Norway and Russia reached an agreement on the division of the continental shelf in the Barents Sea in 2010, and a provisional agreement between Canada and Denmark on the border in the Lincoln Sea was reached in 2012.

Navigation

One area of new activity in the Arctic as a result of decreasing ice cover in the summer season is the growth in ship traffic in the area. The interest in using the route through the Arctic between East Asia and Europe and North America is strong also among states outside the Arctic, and the traffic in the Arctic is expected to grow. Increased ship traffic will create challenges for the Arctic States, both due to the danger of pollution from ship accidents and the need for search and rescue operations in a large and not easily-accessible area. Such operations can in practice only can be carried out by the coastal States in the Arctic, and often only by the nearest coastal State to the incident.

The coastal States can regulate navigation within their territorial seas and the EEZs as far as international law allows.[7] The Arctic Council does not have the competence to enact binding regulations for the Arctic for member States or other states, but can of course work to establish agreements between the member States on how they shall exercise their jurisdiction in the territorial sea areas or in the EEZs. Standard setting of safety regulations is left to the International Maritime Organization (IMO) under the UNCLOS. The strategy of the Arctic Council in this respect has been to encourage the establishment of active cooperation within the IMO on development of relevant measures to reduce the environmental impact of shipping in Arctic waters. The Arctic Council has encouraged continuous work in the IMO to update the Guidelines for Ships Operating in Arctic Ice-covered Waters.[8] IMO has begun work on an international code of safety for ships operating in polar waters (Polar Code).[9]

---

7 Skodvin, K.E., *Freedom of Navigation in the Exclusive Economic Zone under the LOS convention*, (Dissertation for the degree of philosphiae doctor (PhD), 2013.
8 See 2009: A.1024(26) on Guidelines for ships operating in polar waters.
9 More information is found here: http://www.imo.org/mediacentre/hottopics/polar/Pages/default.aspx.

As a response to the increase in aeronautical and maritime traffic and other human activity in the Arctic, the Arctic Council has developed an agreement among the eight member States of the Arctic Council on cooperation on aeronautical and maritime search and rescue in the Arctic. The agreement was concluded in Nuuk in May 2011, and put into force on 19 January 2013. This was the first binding agreement under the Arctic Council cooperation.

The agreement is linked to international agreements on search and rescue operations. The SAR Convention and the Chicago Convention shall be used as the basis for conducting search and rescue operations under the agreement. Each country will be responsible for regions defined in Annex 1 to the agreement, and has the obligation to build necessary capacity and competence, exchange of information, joint training and evaluation of operations and like matters.

Offshore Petroleum Activity

The Arctic is believed to harbour huge deposits of oil and gas, and the Arctic states are interested in the possibility of exploring for offshore petroleum resources on their continental shelves in the Arctic area. The risk related to petroleum activity in the Arctic is great due to weather conditions and ice. The impact of oil spills on ecosystems and biodiversity is also believed to be far more serious in the Arctic than in warmer areas, as the breakdown of hydrocarbons will be very slow. As each State has the jurisdiction on petroleum and other natural resources in and on the continental shelf, national regulation of safety and other issues linked to petroleum exploration will apply. Joint standards and regulations must be based on agreements.

Development of joint standards for petroleum activity was an early priority for the Arctic Council. The Arctic Council Offshore Oil and Gas Guidelines were last revised in 2009. These guidelines are not binding for the states in the area, but the Council has urged all states to apply these guidelines throughout the Arctic as minimum standards in national regulations. The discussion of development of safety standards after the Macondo accident in the Mexican Gulf will also influence the discussion of safety standards in the Arctic, but has not yet led to any change in the Arctic Council Offshore Oil and Gas Guidelines. The European Union and the United States have enacted new regulations, which will also apply in the Arctic for countries bound by the EU-regulation.[10]

---

10   See Directive 2013/30/EU of the European Parliament and of the Council of 12 June 2013 on safety of offshore oil and gas operations and amending Directive 2004/35/EC.

A task force to make a proposal for the agreement that came to be called Cooperation on Marine Oil Pollution Preparedness and Response in the Arctic was established in Nuuk in 2011. The task force was co-chaired by the United States, Russia and Norway. The agreement was signed at the Kiruna meeting on 15 May 2013, as the second binding agreement negotiated under the Arctic Council.

The agreement imposes an obligation on each party to the agreement to "maintain a national system for responding promptly and effectively to oil pollution incidents" adapted to the risk, and to establish a minimum level of pre-positioned oil spill combating equipment, program for training etc. in cooperation with the oil and shipping industries. The agreement applies to any oil spill incident, regardless of the cause of the incident. The States shall monitor the areas under their jurisdiction, and as far as feasible, the adjacent international areas. Each party might request assistance from the other States when an oil spill occurs (article 8). The agreement also contains a provision on reimbursement of costs and the establishment of operational guidelines for the cooperation.

Adaptation of Actions for a Changing Arctic (AACA)

Global warming is expected to lead to great changes in climate, physical conditions, biodiversity, and related aspects in the Arctic. The development is however not expected to be linear, but rather will vary, and might be difficult to predict—at least in detail. In order to meet the climate variability, change and the effects of the development, it is necessary to obtain better predictions and information about the development. At the meeting of deputy ministers on 15 May 2012, a proposed work plan was approved as an Arctic Council project, in order to create a better foundation for development of more informed, timely and responsive policy and decision-making related to adaptation in a rapidly changing Arctic. The goal is to improve predictions of climate change and other causes of changes in the Arctic, and to inform the development and implementation of adaption actions by Arctic Council members and permanent participants. The work was reported at the Kiruna meeting,[11]

---

[11] See DMM02-15 May 2012-Stockholm, Sweden Item 4-Adaptation of Actions for a Changing Arctic. More information on the program can be found on the Arctic Council's website.

and is planned to be completed by 2017.[12] In a longer perspective, this initiative might influence future development of the organisation and function of the Arctic Council.

Permanent Observer Status for Non-Arctic States and Organisations

The development in the Arctic influences the climate in large regions outside the Arctic region, and processes that are taking place in the Arctic influence the global marine environment. The opening of the Arctic for shipping influences transport and marketing possibilities for many countries in East Asia, Europe and North America. Countries outside the Arctic thus have strong interests in the development of navigation and other activity in the Arctic. For example, the prospects of fisheries in a future ice-free international sea area in the Arctic attract the interest of countries outside the region. The special conditions in the Arctic also make the area interesting from a purely scientific point of view.

Against this background, many states are interested in the proceedings and activity of the Arctic Council. A great number of states and organisations have shown considerable interest in obtaining permanent observer status on the Arctic Council. Prior to the Kiruna meeting, status as a permanent observer had been granted to France, Germany, the Netherlands, Poland, Spain and the United Kingdom.

At the Kiruna meeting, applications for permanent observer status from the following countries and organisations were up for decision: China, Italy, Japan, South Korea, Singapore, India, European Union, Oceana, the Association of Oil and Gas Producers (OGP), the OSPAR Commission, Greenpeace, the International Hydrographic Organisation (IHO), the World Meteorological Organization (WMO) and the Association of Polar Early Career Scientists (APECS).

It is fair to say that the question of how the Arctic Council would handle this issue attracted great international interest, and also was debated in the meeting. The member States felt the need to establish a common policy for how applications for observer status should be processed and what role the observers should have. In the Kiruna meeting, the member States agreed on an "observer manual to guide the Council's subsidiary bodies in relation to meeting logistics and the role played by observers".

---

12 See Proposed Work Plan Adaptation Actions for a Changing Arctic (AACA) Section C: AMAP proposed Work Plan for completion by 2017 AACA, for the SAO meeting Haparanda Nov. 2012 AACA Part c AMAP.

The outcome of the discussion in the Kiruna meeting was that Italy and the five Asian States China, India, Japan, South Korea and Singapore were accepted as permanent observers. None of the organisations that had applied were accepted. The question of observer status for the European Union has been prevented by the EU Regulation 1007/2009 on trade in seal products, which influences the relations between Canada and the European Union. The final decision of the application from the European Union was deferred until this issue has been resolved.

The issue of representation for Greenland in the Arctic Council was a special problem at the Kiruna meeting, as a result of the relations between Greenland and Denmark. Greenland and the Faroe Islands are represented by Denmark in the Arctic Council. At the previous ministerial meeting in Nuuk in 2011, Greenland and the Faroe Islands were allowed to make statements. The Prime Minister of Greenland, Aleqa Hammond, decided not to attend the Kiruna meeting as a protest against the lack of a seat and a vote in the Arctic Council for the government of Greenland. The question of representation for Greenland and the Faroe Islands must be expected to be raised again.

Policy for Future Development

The Arctic Council and the Arctic States are aware of the need to develop a policy in order to meet the rapid and far-reaching changes in the Arctic. In the declaration from the 2013 Kiruna meeting,[13] the Council focused on the need to improve the economic and social conditions in the region, the need to act on climate change, protecting the Arctic environment and strengthening of the Arctic Council.[14]

The declaration announces the establishment of a task force to facilitate the creation of a circumpolar business forum. The Council is opening up for a more "central role of business" in the development of the Arctic region, and emphasizes the need for infrastructure, such as seaports and airports as a basis for more business activity.

---

13 KIRUNA DECLARATION On the occasion of the Eighth Ministerial Meeting of the Arctic Council. http://www.mfa.is/media/nordurslodir/Final_Kiruna_declaration.pdf.

14 The outcome of the Kiruna meeting is discussed further in an article by Dr. Cécile Pelaudeix, which is published on the website of the Arctic Council: <http://eu-arctic-forum.org/publications/arctic-council-kiruna-ministerial-meeting-strengthened-role-of-the-arctic-council-in-a-globalized-arctic-china-in-the-eu-on-hold/>.

The rapid physical and ecological changes in the Arctic lead to changes in the living conditions for the peoples in the Arctic. These changes also influence the livelihood and traditional life in a manner that is a threat to the physical and mental health of the area's inhabitants. The Council "... **decide** to undertake further work to improve and develop mental wellness promotion strategies". The Council also "acknowledge the importance of the indigenous peoples' traditional ways of life to their economic well-being, culture and health and **request** Senior Arctic Officials to recommend ways to increase awareness regionally and globally on traditional ways of life of the Arctic indigenous peoples and to **present** a report on this work at the next Ministerial meeting in 2015."

On climate change, the declaration states that "substantial cuts in emissions of carbon dioxide and other long-lived greenhouse gases are necessary for any meaningful global climate change mitigation efforts...", and the countries "commit to strengthen our efforts to find solutions." The countries of the Arctic Council also confirm their commitment to work to conclude a protocol under the United Framework Convention on Climate Change (UNFCCC), to conclude a protocol or other legal instruments or agreed outcomes with legal force no later than 2015, aimed at limiting the increase in global average temperature to below two degrees Celsius above pre-industrial levels.

Because the Kiruna meeting concluded the first round of chairmanships in the Arctic Council, the Swedish Government had proposed a special political statement, "Vision for the Arctic", in addition to the general declaration. In this document, the Arctic Council ministries confirm that the Arctic member States will remain the prime governing actors in the Arctic, and underlines that "[m]embership of the Arctic Council is and will remain for the Arctic States with the active participation and full consultation of the Arctic Indigenous Peoples Organizations. Decisions at all levels in the Arctic Council are the exclusive right and responsibility of the eight signatories to the Ottawa Declaration."

It is further stated that as the "Arctic is changing and attracting global attention", the members of the Arctic Council will "build on our achievements and will continue to cooperate to ensure that Arctic voices are heard and taken into account in the world". The vision thus must be said to confirm and strengthen the Ilulissat Declaration in making it clear that the member States of the Arctic Council assume leadership in future development of the Arctic region, and view development in the Arctic as their main responsibility.

The statement that the position of observer is open to countries and organisations "who can contribute to the work of the Arctic Council and share the commitment of the Arctic States to the peaceful resolution of disputes and abide by the criteria for observers established by the Arctic Council" is also an emphasis of the position of the Arctic States.

The vision also expresses an ambition to "pursue opportunities to expand the Arctic Council's roles from policy-shaping into policy-making". What this will mean remains to be seen.

CHAPTER 7

Communications between the Arctic States and North Pacific Asian States on the Arctic Issues

Jong Deog Kim and Anna Jane Choi

Abstract

Due to the transformative state the Arctic is in, the North Pacific region has been affected greatly. China, Japan, and Korea have been showing interest in the Arctic Council since 2008 and in 2013, they were accepted as Observer States in the Arctic Council. Also, during the last two decades, the North Pacific Asian States have worked closely to promote cooperation with the relevant international parties, particularly in the area of science, in the Arctic. However, as the Arctic is becoming more complex, China, Japan, and Korea are finding ways to produce a stronger level of communication in order to face the issues and challenges surrounding the Arctic.

Introduction

Once thought of as a largely inaccessible part of the Earth, the Arctic is experiencing transformative changes on environmental, geopolitical, economic and social fronts. These changes have no doubt caused the Arctic Council to be recognized as the preeminent forum for the Arctic agendas. For the last 17 years, the Arctic Council showed significant performance in Arctic environmental protection, sustainable development, and indigenous people's welfare. On the other hand, some agendas confronting the future of the Arctic are deeply connected with not only Arctic States, but non-Arctic States and organizations including international society and business. Many non-Arctic States want an opportunity to contribute to reducing uncertainty and bridging the gap with their own capacity. Among them, North East Asian states such as China, Japan, and Korea are eager to cooperate on Arctic issues within their capacity and as market related.

---

* Jong Deog Kim, Director General of Strategy Research Division, Korea Maritime Institute. Note: The views expressed are the sole responsibility of the authors and do not reflect the views of KMI or the Korean government. The author's PowerPoint is available at http://www.virginia.edu/colp/pdf/Seoul-Kim.pdf.

** Anna Jane Choi, Researcher, Strategy Research Division, Korea Maritime Institute.

Even though the North Pacific region may not take part in the direct decision-making process of the Arctic Council, their roles as permanent observers have established a communicative and cooperative platform between Arctic and non-Arctic States. This paper will briefly introduce the needs and communicative situation between the Arctic and non-Arctic States as well as future perspectives from Asian experts.

Arctic in the Global Society

For the last decade, the Arctic has become a new global agenda for Arctic as well as non-Arctic States and now faces several major challenges. First is the transformation in the Arctic causing new global environmental, geopolitical, economic, and social agendas to emerge. As stated by UN Secretary General Ban Ki-moon, "This Arctic is the place where this global warming is happening much faster than any other region in the world. It looks like it's seemingly moving in slow motion but it is moving faster and faster, much faster than expected."[1] Now the international community is looking for other alternatives to protect and preserve the unique and sensitive environment of the Arctic Ocean. With these changes, Iceland President Olafur Ragnar Grimsson explained: "We live in an ice-dependent world. It is a wrong scenario to think that this will only be of concern to those living in the Arctic."[2] Along with its importance to the lives of the indigenous people in the Arctic, Arctic issues have and will affect the Arctic and non-Arctic States.

Second is the insufficient governance surrounding the Arctic Ocean. It is true that creating a complete governance to accommodate every Arctic and non-Arctic State is difficult. After the Arctic Council was created, it established a very successful mechanism for sustainable and peaceful cooperation by developing binding frameworks such as the "Agreement on the Cooperation on Aeronautical and Maritime Search and Rescue in the Arctic". However, a lot of discussions on the Arctic have raised concerns on the gaps and uncertainty on limited information, knowledge, and infrastructure. Moreover, economic activities like the Northern Sea Route (NSR) usage need concrete and agreed guidelines for a sustainable development in the Arctic.

Third is whether the Arctic will be an area of cooperation or conflict. On one hand, the Arctic Council has strengthened its capacity and cooperation through meaningful and binding agreements, promoting working groups, and

---

1   *The Telegraph*, 1 Sep. 2009.
2   *Our Ice-dependent World*, 7 Feb. 2013.

accepting six new Observer states. On the other, conflicts have already become a challenge in the areas of: (1) the high sea and continental shelf, (2) international navigation rules, and (3) States' different navigation standards. However, the Arctic is still considered to be a zone of peace and new Observer States such as China, Japan, and Korea are becoming more active and promoting cooperation through the fields of science, technology, shipping, resources, and culture. As former U.S. Secretary of State, Hillary Rodham Clinton eloquently stated, "The world increasingly looks to the North. Our goal is certainly to promote peaceful cooperation."[3]

Lastly is the alternative regional connectivity between the North Atlantic and North Pacific. Although the changing Arctic has brought several challenges, Arctic States and non-Arctic States have established connecting links for cooperation. For example, the melting sea ice has allowed many to use the NSR and studies have shown that the NSR can cut costs compared to the Suez Canal route. There has been focus on the NSR since Russian President Vladimir Putin reported "It is our intention to turn the Northern Sea Route into a key transport route of global importance. We believe that NSR has a bright future as an international transport artery capable of being a competitor to more traditional routes, both when it comes to price, safety and quality."[4] In the long term, the NSR will provide new economic, business, and trade opportunities across the Arctic, to the North Atlantic and to the North Pacific.

Why Communication

Communication between the Arctic States and non-Arctic States has always been one of the challenges when tackling Arctic issues. Through communication, the international community has been able to promote the activity of conveying information by the exchange of thoughts, messages, or information through speeches, visuals, signals, writing, and behavior.[5] The Arctic has shifted to an area of interest and communication and is currently playing an active role, particularly in the Arctic Council's working groups and with other parties that may share the same interests surrounding the Arctic. Therefore, the Arctic Council has developed a communication strategy as a framework for all of its communication work. The main objective for this strategy is for the Arctic Council to be perceived as the pre-eminent forum for international

---

3   *USA TODAY*, 2 Jun. 2012.
4   *Barents Observer*, 25 Sep. 2011.
5   http://en.wikipedia.org/wiki/Communication.

cooperation in the Arctic[6] and contribute to collaborative partnerships on Arctic issues.

Issues surrounding the Arctic have been the focal point for Arctic States and non-Arctic States. As table 1 represents, some issues in the Arctic Ocean can be categorized into Arctic-based and Arctic-related. Arctic-based issues directly affect the Arctic such as how the change in the environment may impact the indigenous communities. On the other hand, Arctic-related issues not only affect the Arctic but also the interested States and organizations that are involved. For example, the use of commercial ships may have many stakeholders from the non-Arctic States.

Issues in the Arctic Ocean

TABLE 1   *Arctic-based and Arctic-related issues in the Arctic*

	Arctic-based	**Arctic-related**
Environment	land-based pollution, ecosystem, monitoring in territorial sea, indigenous people, MPA	climate change of the Arctic and its impact to outside, ship-based pollution, invasive species, scientific monitoring
Shipping	marine environment, setting shipping route in territorial sea, SAR	freedom of navigation, shipping service ship/plant guideline
Resource Dev.	resource management, marine pollution	resource logistics, high sea resources
Fisheries	resource management, indegenous people	high sea fisheries, migratory species, regional fisheries org.
Tourism	SAR, tourism related services	tourist supply, ship building, international regulation
Infrastructure	sea/air port, hinterland, water/power, labours	Research/monitoring station, meteorological facility, investment
Governance	AC, UNCLOS, IMO, International rules	UNCLOS, IMO, International rules

North Pacific States in the Global Economy

China, Japan, and Korea are neighboring States in East Asia with export-oriented economies. The similarities between the North Pacific States show that they are interlinked with the global economy and the Arctic.

---

6   Communication Strategy Final Draft, March 2012.

The North Pacific Asian States' global GDP is 20.5 percent as figure 1 shows; oil consumption is 19 percent as seen in table 2; and import of fish and fisheries product is 21.8 percent, as table 3 demonstrates. The three countries heavily

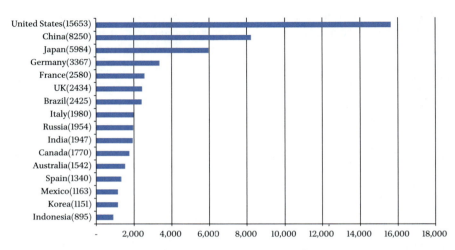

FIGURE 1   *Global GDP. Source: http://knoema.com/nwnfkne/gdp-ranking*

TABLE 2   *Oil consumption. Source: http://www.eia.gov*

	Oli Consump., Mil.tons		% of Total World	
	2011	2010	2011	2010
Total	4059.07	4031.91	100.00	100.00
US	833.56	849.94	20.54	21.08
China	461.83	437.75	11.38	10.86
Japan	201.40	200.31	4.96	4.97
India	162.25	156.18	4.00	3.87
Russia	136.01	128.94	3.35	3.20
Saudi	127.81	123.21	3.15	3.06
Brazil	120.73	118.05	2.97	2.93
Germany	111.55	115.39	2.75	2.86
RO Korea	105.96	106.02	2.61	2.63
Canada	103.10	102.67	2.54	2.55

TABLE 3 *Import of fish and fisheries products. Source: The State of the World Fisheries and Aquaculture 2012, FAO.*

Top ten exporters and importers of fish and fishery products

	2000	2010	APR
	(US$ millions)		(Percentage)
IMPORTERS			
United States of America	10 451	15 496	4.0
Japan	15 513	14 973	−0.4
Spain	3 352	6 637	7.1
China	1 796	6 162	13.1
France	2 984	5 983	7.2
Italy	2 535	5 449	8.0
Germany	2 262	5 037	8.3
United Kingdom	2 184	3 702	5.4
Sweden	709	3 316	16.7
Republic of Korea	1 385	3 193	8.7
Top Ten SUBTOTAL	26 349	69 949	10.3
REST OF WORLD TOTAL	33 740	41 837	2.2
WORLD TOTAL	**60 089**	**111 786**	**6.4**

Note: APR refers to the average annual percentage growth rate for 2000–2010.

TABLE 4 *Shipbuilding. Source: Clarkson Research Service 2011.*

Shipbuilding Country / Region	Value of Vessels on order at 1st Oct 2011 ($bn)														
	Tankers					Bulkers				Specialised Vessels					
	VLCC> 200,000dwt	Suezmax 120-200,000dwt	Aframax 80-120,000dwt	Panamax 60-80,000dwt	Handy 10-60,000dwt	Capesize> 100,000 dwt	Panamax 60-100,000 dwt	Handymax 40-60,000 dwt	Handysize 10-40,000 dwt	LNG Carriers	LPG Carriers	Container >3,000teu	Container <3,000teu	Offshore	Other	Total
Japan	1.5	0.1	1.5	0.1	3.1	10.9	9.2	4.2	5.4	0.5	1.1	1.1	0.2	1.2	5.0	45.1
South Korea	8.6	6.0	4.2	1.4	6.7	6.3	5.2	3.5	4.5	9.7	1.0	35.6	0.5	1.8	42.5	137.5
Taiwan	-	-	-	-	-	0.1	0.0	-	-	-	-	2.6	0.4	-	0.0	3.1
china P.R.	7.0	1.7	0.5	0.5	3.7	19.6	18.1	14.3	7.5	1.1	0.7	10.6	2.9	7.4	16.7	112.3
Other Asia	0.3	0.2	0.2	-	0.4	3.1	0.8	3.4	1.9	-	0.0	1.7	0.1	8.3	4.1	24.5
TOTAL ASIA	17.4	8.0	6.4	2.0	13.9	40.0	33.3	25.4	19.3	11.3	2.8	51.6	4.1	18.7	68.3	322.5
Germany	-	-	-	-	0.1	-	-	-	-	0.0	-	-	0.0	0.6	6.0	6.7
Denmark	-	-	-	-	-	-	-	-	-	-	-	-	-	-	0.1	0.1
France	-	-	-	-	-	-	-	-	-	-	-	-	-	-	1.6	1.6
Italy	-	-	-	-	0.0	-	-	-	-	-	-	-	-	0.1	5.8	5.9
netherlands	-	-	-	-	-	-	-	-	0.0	-	-	-	0.1	0.2	2.1	2.4
Spain	-	-	-	-	0.0	-	-	-	-	-	-	-	-	1.3	0.8	2.1
Finland	-	-	-	-	-	-	-	-	-	-	-	-	-	0.3	1.3	1.6
Norway	-	-	-	-	-	-	-	-	-	-	-	-	-	3.7	0.2	3.9
Turkey	-	-	-	-	0.4	-	-	-	0.0	-	-	0.0	-	0.2	1.2	1.8
Poland	-	-	-	-	-	-	-	-	-	-	-	0.0	0.0	0.5	0.2	0.7
Ukraina	-	-	-	-	-	-	-	-	-	-	-	-	-	0.0	0.1	0.1
Croatia	-	-	-	-	0.3	-	-	0.1	-	-	-	-	-	-	0.5	0.9
Other Europe	-	0.1	0.1	-	1.1	-	0.2	0.3	0.1	-	-	0.7	0.0	0.1	1.2	3.9
TOTAL EUROPE	0.0	0.1	0.1	0.0	1.9	0.0	0.2	0.4	0.1	0.0	0.0	0.7	0.3	6.8	21.1	31.7
Brasil	-	1.2	0.9	0.9	0.7	-	0.1	-	-	-	0.3	-	0.3	1.3	8.4	14.1
United States	-	-	-	-	0.3	-	-	-	-	-	-	-	-	1.7	0.5	2.5
Others	-	-	-	-	0.2	0.0	-	0.0	0.0	-	-	-	-	3.5	0.3	4.0
TOTAL OTHERS	0.0	1.2	0.9	0.9	1.2	0.0	0.1	0.0	0.0	0.0	0.3	0.0	0.3	6.5	9.2	20.6
GLOBAL TOTAL	17.4	9.3	7.4	2.9	17.0	40.0	33.6	25.8	19.4	11.3	3.1	52.3	4.7	32.0	98.6	374.8

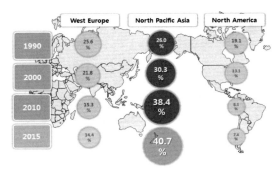

FIGURE 2   *Global logistics market.*

rely on trade with the Middle East and Africa and exchange major fisheries products with their neighboring countries. However, recent trade with South America, Africa, and Europe has increased. Lastly, in the shipbuilding area, the North Pacific States are dominating the global market with a market share of almost 80 percent as represented in table 4.

Moreover, the three Asian States are currently the major providers and consumers in the global logistics market. For the case of container throughput, China, Japan, and Korea account for 40 percent of the total global service as represented by figure 2. The North Pacific region has become the center for the global shipping industry and will continue to hold this position as resource providers and consumers in ocean development equipment.

Approaches by North Pacific Asian States

Climate changes in the Arctic have been directly and indirectly affecting the North Pacific region. With the Arctic transforming, China, Japan, and Korea have a deep interest in the Arctic on the various agendas. As seen in table 5, these three countries have been working closely with the Arctic States to promote scientific, economic, and social cooperation. For example, all three Asian states have established scientific research stations and built research ice-breakers, useful implementation for UNCLOS and the IMO for Arctic related issues.

TABLE 5   *Approaches by China, Japan, and Korea in the Arctic*

China	Japan	Korea
· Huanghe station	· Ny Alesund station	· Dasan station
· Arctic Expedition	· Scientific Cooperation	· Ice Breaker- Araon
· Scientific Cooperation	· Polar Research Institute	· Scientific Cooperation
· Polar Research Institute	· Ice Breaker- Shirase	· Polar Research Institute
· Ice Breaker- Xuelong	· Arctic Research Consortium	· NPAC Series
· China-Nordic Arctic Sym.	· INSROP, JANSROP	· Test/Commercial Shipping
· Test/Commercial Shipping	· Test/Commercial Shipping	· Energy Cooperation
· Energy/Resources Cooperation	· Energy Cooperation	· Summit Talks
· Summit Talks	· Arctic TF in MFA	· Setting as a National agenda
· Direct Investments	· NSR Review Team in MLIT	· FTA w/ EU(DEN, FIN, SWE), EFTA(NOR, ICE), US
· Joint Research Centers	· Arctic Security Parl. Union	· Shipping Agreement w/ US, NOR, RUS
· FTA w/ICELAND	· Arctic Ambassador	· Establishment of MOF
· Enhancement of SOA	· Establishment of HQ of OA	· Ad hoc Observer in AC
· Ad hoc Observer in AC	· Ad hoc Observer in AC	· UNCLOS, IMO
· UNCLOS, IMO	· UNCLOS, IMO	

Awareness of Communication

In 2013, 38 experts from China, Japan, and Korea were asked to take a survey on the communication between Arctic and non-Arctic States. On a scale of one to seven, one being the lowest and seven being the highest, participants were asked three questions.

The first question asked what they thought about the communication level on the major Arctic issues between Arctic and non-Arctic States.

Results showed that the communication level was not very high, as represented in figure 3. Issues such as climate change, marine environmental protection, and scientific research were the highest at about level four. Shipping/logistics, oil/gas resources, and Arctic governance issues were only around level three and issues on minerals development, fisheries, and indigenous and local communities were about level 2.

The second question from the survey asked what participants thought about the communication level on the Arctic issues at major international organizations or forums between Arctic and non-Arctic States. As shown on Figure 4, the results were fairly higher than the first question, but still ranged between level three and level four.

Finally, the last question asked about the expectation level on the overall cooperation in the Arctic Ocean between Arctic and non-Arctic States in the future. The results showed that the average level of expectation was 4.66.

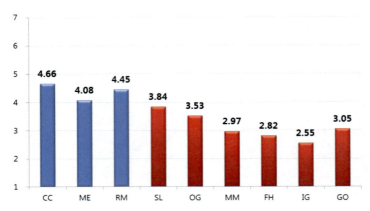

FIGURE 3   *Communication level between Arctic and non-Arctic States.*

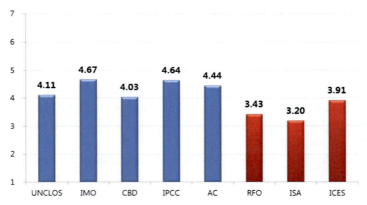

FIGURE 4   *Communication level at international organizations or forums between Arctic and non-Arctic States.*

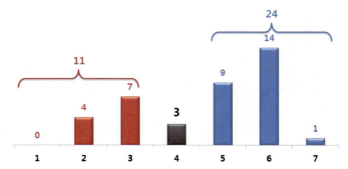

FIGURE 5   *Expectation level on cooperation between Arctic and non-Arctic States.*

Possibility of Communication Expansion

The Arctic Council has strengthened its capacity and communication through establishing guidelines and agreements, promoting working groups, and accepting new Observer States. And as represented on table 6, many international, regional, bilateral, academic and business societies can provide opportunities to enhance communication between Arctic and non-Arctic States.

TABLE 6 *Possible communication expansion mechanism*

AC	International	Regional	Bilateral	Aca./Biz
Observer group	UNCLOS	WCPFC	FTA	IASC
Working Groups	IMO	NAFO	Energt Agreement	IASSA
Expert Groups	UNFCCC	NEAFC	Resource Agreement	ICES
Task Forces	ISA	NASCO	Shipping Agreement	Arctic Frontiers
Standing Secretariat	FAO	NPAFC		FARO
	CBD	CCBSP		PAG
	CITES	ICCT		ASF
	CMS	APEC		Uarctic
	Spitsbergen Treaty			NPAC
	WTO			Other Academic networks

Findings

In conclusion, evaluation of communication between the Arctic States and non-Arctic States, in particular North Pacific Asian States results in the following findings:

1. Transformative change in the Arctic calls for concerted global efforts to address issues surrounding the Arctic, such as climate change, the environment and ecosystem, and shipping routes.
2. Formal and informal communication is one of the most crucial elements for a better and sustainable Arctic development (e.g., through Arctic Council, academic networks and business forums).
3. Arctic States and non-Arctic States, including indigenous peoples, should be encouraged to share their knowledge and benefit from one another through research, training and education.
4. In the long-term, region to region approaches through shipping routes may provide innovative and alternative opportunities from the Arctic.
5. Finding the proper solution among various stakeholders through communication may be one of the challenges during the second round of the Arctic Council for a sustainable Arctic development.

Overall, the North Pacific Asian States have acknowledged the important issues and challenges that are surrounding the Arctic. Both Arctic States and non-Arctic States must take a careful approach and lay a communicative groundwork to respond to every Arctic issue. In addition, China, Japan, and Korea will have to establish cooperation on Arctic affairs through joint measures with all partners in the Arctic.

PART 4

Energy Security and Sealanes

∴

CHAPTER 8

Institutional Building for Maritime Security in Southeast Asia: The Role of ASEAN

Hao Duy Phan

Abstract

Southeast Asia lays aside major sea lanes between the Indian Ocean and the Pacific Ocean. It is estimated by the United States Energy Information Administration that over half of the world's merchant fleet tonnage transits the Straits of Malacca and Singapore, the Strait of Sunda and the Strait of Lombok annually. More than half of global liquefied natural gas (LNG) trade is transported via the South China Sea. Given the high volumes of oil, gas and cargo transported through regional waters and growing energy demands regionally and worldwide, sea lanes in Southeast Asia have become increasingly critical to international trade and energy security. The importance of these sea lanes, however, has been growing in tandem with concerns over issues of maritime security.

As an important regional organization that includes littoral States adjacent to these sea lanes, the Association of Southeast Asian Nations (ASEAN) has a potentially central role to play in promoting and facilitating regional maritime security. This paper highlights the significance of regional cooperation for that very purpose, offering a stocktaking overview of the activities and initiatives conducted under the framework of ASEAN maritime security cooperation. The first section traces the growing salience of maritime security issues on the ASEAN agenda and examines major ASEAN instruments on maritime security. The second section then visits various sectoral bodies of ASEAN that aim to address maritime security issues in the region. The next section provides a detailed account of recent efforts by ASEAN and its dialogue partners to deal with maritime security issues, particularly efforts undertaken within the framework of the ASEAN Regional Forum (ARF). In the concluding section, the paper offers various suggestions to increase the efficacy of ASEAN cooperation in this area. It makes the case for a stronger legal framework and more institutionalized ASEAN mechanisms that are instrumental to strengthening regional cooperation for maritime security. This stronger framework and enhanced mechanisms should be

---

* Hao Duy Phan, Senior Research Fellow, Centre for International Law, National University of Singapore. The author's PowerPoint is available at http://www.virginia.edu/colp/pdf/Seoul-Phan.pdf.

able to serve coordinating functions as well as monitor the implementation of existing and future regional instruments, plans and programs on maritime security. The end result would be an ASEAN better equipped and enabled to follow up on member States' commitments and thereby contribute to further enhancing sea lanes security in Southeast Asia.

1   Introduction: Regional Cooperation to Enhance Maritime Security

Southeast Asia lays aside major sea lanes between the Indian Ocean and the Pacific Ocean. Ships from the Indian Ocean pass through either the Straits of Malacca and Singapore or the Strait of Sunda and traverse the South China Sea, usually on the west of the Spratly Islands towards their destinations.[1] Deep draught ships may pass through the Strait of Lombok and cross the Celebes Sea before proceeding east of the Philippines to their destination or tracking across the Sulu Sea and exiting the Philippine archipelago through Mindoro Strait.[2]

It is estimated that more than half of the world's merchant fleet tonnage passes through these straits annually, with the majority continuing on to the South China Sea.[3] Almost a third of global crude oil and over half of global liquefied natural gas (LNG) trade is transported via the South China Sea.[4] The volume of trade that goes through the South China Sea each year is worth more than USD5 trillion, making it one of the most important trade routes in the world.[5] In 2011, the amount of oil transported through the Straits of Malacca and Singapore was 15.2 million barrels per day (MMbbl/d), compared to 13.8 MMbbl/d in 2007. Of this amount, 1.4 MMbbl/d was delivered to terminals in Singapore and Malaysia and the rest moved through the South China Sea to their destinations.[6] Due to the high volume of oil, gas and cargo transported

---

1   *See* Robert Beckman, "The UN Convention on the Law of the Sea and the Maritime Disputes in the South China Sea", 106 *American Journal of International Law* (2013), 142 at 143; John H. Noer, *Chokepoints: Maritime Economic Concerns in Southeast Asia* (National Defense University Press, 1996), 7.
2   Sam Bateman, "Sea Lane Security", *Maritime Studies* (2003), 17 at 21.
3   US Energy Information Administration, *South China Sea* (Analysis Briefs, 2013) 8, available at http://www.eia.gov/countries/analysisbriefs/South_China_Sea/south_china_sea.pdf (last accessed 15 October 2013).
4   Id.
5   Michael A. Mc Devitt, M. Taylor Fravel, and Lewis M. Stern, *The Long Littoral Project: the South China Sea, A Maritime Perspective on Indo-Pacific Security* (Center for Naval Analyses, 2013) 3.
6   US Energy Information Administration, *World Oil Transit Chokepoints* (Analysis Briefs, 2012) 5, available at http://www.eia.gov/countries/analysisbriefs/World_Oil_Transit_Chokepoints/wotc.pdf (last accessed 15 October 2013).

through regional waters, together with growing energy demand regionally and worldwide, sea lanes in Southeast Asia have become increasingly critical to international trade and energy security.

The increase in the volume and value of goods transported through regional waters, however, has been accompanied by rising concerns over maritime safety, e.g., accidents at sea caused by the operation of sub-standard vessels, unqualified crew or operator errors, and maritime security, e.g. incidents at sea caused by unlawful acts such as piracy, armed robbery against ships, and terrorist acts.[7] In particular, due to its long coastlines and its critical geographical location, Southeast Asia is highly susceptible to maritime security threats.[8] According to the 2013 Annual Report of the Regional Cooperation Agreement on Combating Piracy and Armed Robbery against Ships in Asia (ReCAAP) Information Sharing Centre (ISC), 133 incidents, including 124 actual and nine attempted incidents, mostly armed robbery against ships, were reported in 2013, a 20% increase from the total of 112 incidents reported in 2012 and the highest among the five year reporting period.[9] There were 11 incidents in the South China Sea and 12 incidents in the Straits of Malacca and Singapore involving ships while underway.[10] The Sulu and Celebes seas have also become a target for illegal maritime acts such as piracy and a base of operation for terrorist organizations, for instance, the Abu Sayyaf Group mainly based on the islands of Jojo and Basilan and the Moro Islamic Liberation Front based on the island of Mindanao.[11] While assessments indicate that terrorist groups currently operating do not have sufficient capacity to conduct complex and widespread maritime attacks, terrorists can still potentially employ a variety of acts that threaten maritime security, including using the sea to target land, attacking port facilities, and using remotely detonated explosives to target ships.[12]

---

[7] See Natalie Klein, Joanna Mossop and Donald R. Rothwell, "Australia, New Zealand and Maritime Security" in Natalie Klein, Joanna Mossop and Donald R. Rothwell (eds.), *Maritime Security* (Routledge, 2009) 1–21, at 6; Joshua Ho, "The Security of Regional Sea Lanes", *Working Paper Series* (Institute of Defence and Strategic Studies, Singapore, 2005) 10.

[8] ARF, "Report on Maritime Terrorism and Organized Crime Threats" (prepared by the ARF ISM on Counter-Terrorism and Transnational Organized Crime, April 2012) 2.

[9] ReCAAP ISC, "Annual Report: Situation of Piracy and Armed Robbery against Ships in Asia in 2013" (2013) 11.

[10] Id. at 3.

[11] Ian Storey, "Securing Southeast Asia's Sea Lanes: A Work in Progress", 6 *Asia Policy* (2008) 104.

[12] ARF, "Report on Maritime Terrorism and Organized Crime Threats" (prepared by the ARF ISM on Counter-Terrorism and Transnational Organized Crime, April 2012) 2.

Against this background, it is in the common interest of all concerned parties—flag States, coastal States, destination States and port States—to have secure sea lanes in Southeast Asia. Countries in Southeast Asia in particular have great incentives to ensure regional maritime security since potential threats or actual attacks may adversely affect the growth of their export-led economies and disrupt the stability of their commerce. As a matter of fact, the majority of seafarers traversing regional waters are from regional states.[13] In addition, regional countries have more control over maritime safety and security since ships transiting the area usually pass through waters that fall within some form of their jurisdiction, such as their territorial sea or archipelagic waters. Many attacks against ships actually take place in maritime zones subject to sovereignty of the coastal States (these attacks are termed "armed robbery against ships").[14] As maritime crimes tend to be transboundary in nature, Southeast Asian countries need to work together, especially through the Association of Southeast Asian Nations (ASEAN), the most important regional organization composed of Southeast Asian littoral States, to enhance regional maritime security. Cooperation may not only promote better understanding of maritime security, bolster political will to combat maritime crimes and create favorable conditions for information and experience exchange, but it could also help to strengthen legal frameworks, build capacity and increase the effectiveness of law enforcement activities to combat these crimes. Cooperation within ASEAN may be more readily welcomed by regional coastal States as it is regionally and locally initiated and led, rather than being driven by outside countries. Cooperation to combat maritime crimes is also in accordance with the 1982 United Nations Convention on the Law of the Sea, global counter-terrorism and counter-crimes treaties, as well as many counter-terrorism resolutions adopted by the United Nations Security Council.[15]

This paper highlights the significance of regional cooperation for ensuring maritime security and provides an overview of ASEAN maritime security cooperation. The next section traces the growing salience of maritime security on

---

13 Robert Beckman and J. Ashley Roach, "Introduction", in Robert Beckman and J. Ashley Roach (eds.) *Piracy and International Maritime Crimes in ASEAN: Prospect for Cooperation* (NUS Centre for International Law and Edward Elgar, 2012), 1–14 at 4.
14 Id. at 7.
15 For example, Resolution 1373 directs states to comprehensively address terrorism. Resolution 1540 deals with threats posed by non-state actors with weapons of mass destruction (WMD). Resolution 1822 focuses on sanction regimes against Al Qaida and Taliban. *See* the list and summary of 14 major counter-terrorism treaties at http://www.un.org/terrorism/instruments.shtml (last accessed 15 October 2013).

the ASEAN agenda. The third section then revisits different sectoral and functional bodies of ASEAN that are addressing regional maritime security issues. The fourth section provides a detailed account of recent cooperative efforts by ASEAN and its dialogue partners, especially under the ASEAN Regional Forum (ARF). In the concluding section, the paper makes several suggestions to increase the effectiveness of ASEAN cooperation on maritime security. It also lays out the case for a stronger legal framework and more institutionalized ASEAN mechanisms that, in addition to facilitating regional coordination, also monitor compliance and implementation of existing plans and programs on maritime security. The end result would be an ASEAN enabled to follow up on member States commitments, thereby contributing to enhancing maritime security in Southeast Asia.

At the outset, it should be noted that there is no single agreed definition of maritime security. While various approaches have been taken to define "maritime security," this paper approaches "maritime security" from the perspective of sea lanes security from maritime crimes such as piracy, armed robbery against ships, and terrorist acts. As such, the paper does not aim to address issues such as the South China Sea territorial and jurisdictional disputes. Furthermore, by focusing on ASEAN maritime security cooperation, the paper limits its scope of inquiry to cooperative activities under the ASEAN framework as opposed to bilateral and trilateral efforts among regional states.

2   ASEAN Instruments on Maritime Security

As in other areas of cooperation, ASEAN has chosen to deal with issues of maritime security on a step-by-step basis. Starting from 1997, the organization decided to include in the 1997 Declaration on Transnational Crime the transnational crime of piracy, together with terrorism, illicit drug trafficking, arms smuggling, money laundering and human trafficking.[16] The Declaration, which was the result of the first ASEAN Conference on Transnational Crime held in Manila in December 1997, proposed different cooperative measures for ASEAN to take to fight transnational crime. Some of these measures include convening the ASEAN Ministerial Meeting on Transnational Crime as the ASEAN coordinating body in countering transnational crime; holding discussions on drafting a mutual legal assistance agreement; creating a high-level *ad hoc*

---

16   1997 ASEAN Declaration on Transnational Crime, available at http://cil.nus.edu.sg/1997/1997-asean-declaration-on-transnational-crime-signed-on-20-december-1997-in-manila-philippines/ (last accessed 15 October 2013).

Experts Group to prepare the ASEAN Plan of Action on Transnational Crime and study the feasibility of establishing an ASEAN Centre on Transnational Crime (ACTC); and strengthening the ASEAN Secretariat's (ASEC) capacity to assist in initiating, planning, and coordinating activities, strategies, programs and projects to combat transnational crime.[17]

In the following year, to implement the 1997 Declaration, ASEAN established a high-level *ad hoc* Experts Group to draft the ASEAN Plan of Action on Transnational Crime, which was subsequently adopted in 1999. The Plan of Action encourages ASEAN member States to improve the ASEANAPOL regional database,[18] conduct studies to determine trends of "modus operandi" of transnational crime,[19] work towards criminalizing piracy in all member States,[20] harmonize relevant national policies among ASEAN member States,[21] ratify relevant international treaties,[22] conduct regular capacity-building activities and establish the ASEAN Centre for Combating Transnational Crime (ACTC).[23] The ASEAN Ministerial Meeting on Transnational Crime (AMMTC), assisted by the Senior Officials Meeting on Transnational Crime (SOMTC), is mentioned as the highest policy making body on ASEAN cooperation in combating transnational crime.[24] Like the 1997 Declaration, the 1998 Plan of Action does not have binding force. The use of terms such as "encourage" clearly indicate that the activities set out in the Plan of Action are not obligatory. Nor do the instruments provide any timeline for implementation, leaving such matters to be specified in the Work Programme to Implement the Plan of Action.

In 2002, ASEAN adopted the Work Programme to Implement the Plan of Action to Combat Transnational Crime, the first ASEAN instrument on countering transnational crime that includes a timeline for implementation. Under the Work Programme, a directory of focal points in ASEAN member States for combating transnational crime has been created and regularly updated

---

17 Id.
18 1999 ASEAN Plan of Action to Combat Transnational Crime, available at http://cil.nus.edu.sg/1999/1999-asean-plan-of-action-to-combat-transnational-crime-adopted-on-23-june-1999-in-yangon-myanmar-by-the-ministers-responsible-for-transnational-crime/ (last accessed 15 October 2013) C.1.
19 Id., C.3.
20 Id., C.6.
21 Id., C.7.
22 Id., C.12.
23 Id., C.20.
24 Id., D (a) & (b).

by ASEC.[25] ASEAN members were asked to enhance programs on anti-piracy coordinated patrols and submit to ASEC all relevant national laws and treaties on piracy and armed robbery against ships and existing cooperative programs and activities for anti-piracy to enable ASEC to establish a compilation of national laws and regulations of ASEAN member States on piracy and armed robbery against ships.[26] ASEC was then required to work with INTERPOL and other organizations such as think-tanks to produce a study of trends and "modus operandi" of piracy in Southeast Asia to be submitted to ASEAN member States to aid in promoting understanding regarding the threats of piracy in the region.[27] ASEC was also asked to explore the possibility of seeking technical and financial assistance for increased patrolling of particularly vulnerable sea areas and capacity-building assistance from ASEAN dialogue partners as well as from users of the waterways and other relevant specialized agencies of the United Nations and international organizations.[28] The Work Programme, in short, has managed to add much needed specifics to the 1997 Declaration on Transnational Crime and the 1999 Plan of Action. It should be noted, however, that some of the stronger measures provided for in the 1999 Plan of Action were not adopted in the 2002 Work Programme, including the criminalization of transnational crime and the harmonization of relevant national policies among ASEAN member States.

Prior to 2001, ASEAN cooperative efforts to address piracy were principally made within the framework of ASEAN cooperation to counter transnational crimes. The September 11 attacks in the United States may have had a catalyzing effect on heightening counter-terrorism and maritime security issues. In 2001, ASEAN adopted the Declaration on Joint Action to Counter Terrorism. In 2003 ASEAN began to put maritime security on its agenda at the highest level. The 2003 Bali Concord II identifies maritime security as a "matter of common concern" and provides that cooperation on maritime security shall contribute to the ASEAN Security Community.[29] It further states that ASEAN

---

25 2002 Work Programme to Implement ASEAN Plan of Action to Combat Transnational Crime, available at http://cil.nus.edu.sg/2002/2002-work-programme-to-implement-the-asean-plan-of-action-to-combat-transnational-crime-adopted-on-17-may-2002-in-kuala-lumpur-malaysia-by-the-ministers-responsible-for-transnational-crime/ (last accessed 15 October 2013), art. 3.1.a & b.
26 Id., art. 3.3.
27 Id., art. 3.1.c.
28 Id., arts. 3.4, 3.5, 3.6.
29 2003 Declaration of ASEAN Concord II, Available at http://cil.nus.edu.sg/2003/2003-declaration-of-asean-concord-ii-signed-on-7-october-2003-in-bali-indonesia-by-the-heads-of-stategovernment/ (last accessed 15 October 2013) A.4.

should share information to nurture its common values[30] and address maritime security issues at the regional level "in a holistic, integrated and comprehensive manner."[31] The Statement of the Chairperson of the 19th ASEAN Summit also emphasizes that maritime cooperation among ASEAN member States shall contribute to the establishment of the ASEAN Security Community.[32] In this regard, leaders of ASEAN member States agreed to consider the idea of establishing a maritime forum for ASEAN.[33] This could be considered an initial step to gradually institutionalizing cooperation efforts on maritime security issues in ASEAN.

To continue the momentum gathered at the 2003 ASEAN Summit, ASEAN leaders adopted the ASEAN Community Plan of Action and the Vientiane Action Programme in 2004, again embracing maritime security as part of the Association's Security Community. The Vientiane Action Programme specifically lists "promot[ing] ASEAN maritime security cooperation" as a strategy towards realizing the ASEAN Security Community and tasks ASEAN member States to continue to explore the establishment of the ASEAN maritime forum.[34]

The year 2004 saw a major step forward for ASEAN in terms of building the institutional infrastructure for the organization to combat transnational crime. It marked the first time that the region adopted a legally binding instrument on mutual legal assistance in combating crimes. The idea for a region-wide treaty on mutual legal assistance in criminal matters was proposed by

---

30   Press Statement by the Chairperson of the 9th ASEAN Summit and the 7th ASEAN Plus 3 Summit, Bali, Indonesia, 7 October 2003, available at http://www.asean.org/asean/asean-summit/item/press-statement-by-the-chairperson-of-the-9th-asean-summit-and-the-7th-asean-3-summit-bali-indonesia-7-october-2003 (last accessed 15 October 2013).

31   2003 Declaration of ASEAN Concord II, available at http://cil.nus.edu.sg/2003/2003-declaration-of-asean-concord-ii-signed-on-7-october-2003-in-bali-indonesia-by-the-heads-of-stategovernment/ (last accessed 15 October 2013), A.4.

32   Press Statement by the Chairperson of the 9th ASEAN Summit and the 7th ASEAN Plus 3 Summit, Bali, Indonesia, 7 October 2003, available at http://www.asean.org/asean/asean-summit/item/press-statement-by-the-chairperson-of-the-9th-asean-summit-and-the-7th-asean-3-summit-bali-indonesia-7-october-2003 (last accessed 15 October 2013).

33   Id.

34   2004 Vientiane Action Programme 2004–2010, available at http://cil.nus.edu.sg/2004/2004-vientiane-action-programme-2004-2010-signed-on-29-november-2004-in-vientiane-laos-by-the-heads-of-stategovernment-vap/ (last accessed 15 October 2013), Item II. 1, 1.3, vii.

Malaysia at a meeting of ASEAN Law Ministers (ALMM) in 2002.[35] It took ASEAN member States two years to draft the treaty and by 2004, the Treaty on Mutual Legal Assistance in Criminal Matters was signed. To date Brunei, Cambodia, Indonesia, Laos, Malaysia, Myanmar, the Philippines, Singapore and Vietnam have ratified the Treaty.[36] Thailand has signed but not ratified the Treaty. According to Article 31, the Treaty enters into force for parties who have ratified or acceded to it on the date of the deposit of the instrument of ratification or accession. The Treaty mandates an obligation upon its state parties to offer mutual legal assistance in investigations, prosecutions and resulting proceedings of criminal acts.[37] Mutual legal assistance includes, among others, executing search and seizure, examining objects and sites, locating suspects and witnesses, identifying and tracing properties derived from offences, temporarily transferring persons in custody for investigation purposes, making arrangements for persons to give evidence or to assist in criminal matters, taking evidence and obtaining statements from persons and effecting service of judicial documents.[38] The Treaty requires cooperation among law enforcement agencies in regional countries to the broadest extent possible[39] and helps expedite the procedure according to which law enforcement agencies provide mutual legal assistance to each other to combat crimes. Assistance requests and their execution can be made directly via a designated central authority instead of having to go through diplomatic channels.[40] Under the Treaty, the requirements in terms of the form and content of assistance requests, the grounds for the grant and refusal of requests and the certification and authentication of evidence have been standardized for all parties.[41]

However, a major limitation of the Treaty remains. If a request involves an act or omission that would not constitute an offence according to the laws

---

35 Office of the Attorney-General's Chamber of Malaysia, Secretariat For The Treaty On Mutual Legal Assistance In Criminal Matters Among Like-Minded ASEAN Member Countries, available at http://www.agc.gov.my/index.php?option=com_content&view=article&id=253&Itemid=212&lang=en (last accessed 15 October 2013).
36 See Robert Beckman and J. Ashley Roach "Appendix" in Robert Beckman and J. Ashley Roach (eds.), *Piracy and International Maritime Crimes in ASEAN: Prospect for Cooperation* (NUS Centre for International Law and Edward Elgar, 2012), 242.
37 2004 Treaty on Mutual Legal Assistance in Criminal Matters, available at http://cil.nus.edu.sg/2004/2004-treaty-on-mutual-legal-assistance-in-criminal-matters-signed-on-29-november-2004-in-kuala-lumpur-malaysia/ (last accessed 15 October 2013), art. 1(1).
38 Id., art. 1(2).
39 Id., art. 1(2).
40 Id., art. 4.
41 Id., arts. 5 & 6.

of the requested party, the requested party may refuse to render assistance, except when its domestic laws permit legal assistance in the absence of dual criminality (principles of double criminality).[42] The Treaty also contains additional grounds for refusal on the basis of concerns over sovereignty, security, public order, public interests or essential interests.[43] By implication, for the Treaty to be effective, all state parties need to have harmonized their respective legislation dealing with the crimes in question, including maritime crimes.

It was also in 2004 that ASEAN leaders agreed to work towards a regional treaty on counter-terrorism.[44] Negotiations on this treaty started in 2006 with a draft prepared by Indonesia. In 2007, the ASEAN Convention on Counter Terrorism was concluded. It entered into force in 2010 and has now been ratified by all ASEAN member States.[45] It aims to provide a legal framework for the region to work together to prevent and suppress terrorism in all forms and manifestations and to deepen cooperation among law enforcement agencies in all ASEAN states in countering terrorism.[46] Areas of cooperation include provision of early warning, suppression of terrorism financing and terrorist movement, exchange of intelligence information, public awareness, capacity building, development of regional database, study and research and cross-border cooperation.

The conclusion of the Counter Terrorism Convention was an important step forward in ASEAN's efforts to ensure maritime security as it is applicable to any offences within the scope of and as defined in major international treaties relevant to maritime security, including the 1979 International Convention Against the Taking of Hostages, the 1988 Convention for the Suppression of Unlawful Acts Against the Safety of Maritime Navigation, the 1988 Protocol for the Suppression of Unlawful Acts Against the Safety of Fixed Platforms Located on

---

42   Id., art. 3(1)(e).
43   Id., art. 3(1)(f).
44   2004 Vientiane Action Programme 2004–2010, available at http://cil.nus.edu.sg/2004/2004-vientiane-action-programme-2004-2010-signed-on-29-november-2004-in-vientiane-laos-by-the-heads-of-stategovernment-vap/ (last accessed 15 October 2013), Item II. 1, 2.v.
45   ASEAN Secretariat, *ASEAN Convention on Counter-Terrorism Completes Ratification Process*, available at http://www.asean.org/news/asean-secretariat-news/item/asean-convention-on-counter-terrorism-completes-ratification-process (last accessed 15 October 2013).
46   2007 ASEAN Convention on Counter Terrorism, available at http://cil.nus.edu.sg/2007/2007-asean-convention-on-counter-terrorism-signed-on-13-january-2007-in-cebu-philippines-by-the-heads-of-stategovernment/ (last accessed 15 October 2013), art. I.

the Continental Shelf, the 1999 International Convention for the Suppression of the Financing of Terrorism, the 2005 International Convention for the Suppression of Acts of Nuclear Terrorism, the 2005 Protocol to the Convention for the Suppression of Unlawful Acts against the Safety of Maritime Navigation and the 2005 Protocol to the 1988 Protocol for the Suppression of Unlawful Acts Against the Safety of Fixed Platforms Located on the Continental Shelf.[47] For example, the seizure or exercise of control over a vessel by force, threat or any other intimidation, violence that endangers maritime navigation is an offence under the 1988 Convention for the Suppression of Unlawful Acts against the Safety of Maritime Navigation; and the transport of nuclear weapons on board ships is an offence under the 2005 Protocol to the Convention for the Suppression of Unlawful Acts against the Safety of Maritime Navigation, therefore these activities are also considered offences under the 2007 ASEAN Convention on Counter Terrorism.

The 2007 ASEAN Convention on Counter Terrorism requires state parties to establish jurisdiction over these offences if the offences are committed in their territory, on board a vessel flying their flag or by their nationals.[48] A party "may" establish its jurisdiction over such offences when the offence is committed against its nationals or its facilities abroad, or the offence is committed by a stateless person with habitual residence in its territory.[49] A party is also obliged to establish jurisdiction over these offences if the offender is present in its territory and it chooses not to extradite to another state party.[50] In short, similar to most but not all global counter-terrorism treaties,[51] the 2007 ASEAN Convention on Counter Terrorism establishes very broad jurisdiction over the offences in question, including not only the traditional jurisdiction based on territoriality (territoriality principle), jurisdiction based on the nationality of the offender (nationality principle), jurisdiction based on the vessel's flag (flag State principle), jurisdiction based on the nationality of the victims (passive nationality principle) and jurisdiction based on the mere presence of a suspect in the territory of the state party (quasi-universal jurisdiction). In addition, to further ensure that an alleged offender must not find a safe haven in the territory of any party, whatever his nationality or wherever the offence was committed, state parties to the Convention also accept the *aut dedere*

---

47   Id., art. II.
48   Id., art. VII.
49   Id., art. VII.
50   Id., art. VII.
51   See the list and summary of 14 major counter-terrorism treaties at http://www.un.org/terrorism/instruments.shtml (last accessed 15 October 2013).

aut judicare (extradite or prosecute) obligation. The Convention may be considered a legal basis for extradition and applicable offences shall be deemed extraditable offences between parties.[52]

A major limitation of the Convention is that it allows a state party to make a declaration to opt out with regard to the offences provided for in international counter-terrorism treaties to which it is not a party.[53] This declaration will lapse when the treaties have been ratified by the state party and have entered into force.[54] This means that, for the Convention to be effective, all state parties need to ratify all major international counter-terrorism treaties, especially those relevant to maritime security as listed above. These limitations notwithstanding, the 2004 Treaty on Mutual Legal Assistance in Criminal Matters and the 2007 ASEAN Convention on Counter Terrorism have hitherto remained the strongest legal tools for ASEAN member States to work together in combating maritime crimes and transnational crimes in general.[55]

In 2009, the ASEAN Summit adopted the Blueprint on the ASEAN Political-Security Community (APSC). The Blueprint basically serves as both a roadmap and a timetable for establishing the ASEAN Political-Security Community by 2015.[56] Although it is not a treaty, the Blueprint does establish a mechanism to coordinate and review the Blueprint's implementation by all relevant ASEAN senior official bodies.[57] It assigns the Coordinating Conference for the APSC Plan of Action (ASCCO) and the APSC Council to assume the function of coordinating efforts of various sectoral bodies in implementing the Blueprint.[58] The Blueprint has a separate section on ASEAN maritime cooperation.[59] It sets out different measures to maintain and enhance maritime security, including regional collaboration to review and assess maritime security issues,

---

52   2007 ASEAN Convention on Counter Terrorism, available at http://cil.nus.edu.sg/2007/2007-asean-convention-on-counter-terrorism-signed-on-13-january-2007-in-cebu-philippines-by-the-heads-of-stategovernment/ (last accessed 15 October 2013), art. XIII.
53   Id., art. II.
54   Id.
55   ASEAN has been engaged in negotiations for the conclusion of a regional extradition treaty, and though formal bilateral extradition treaties have been concluded between its members, the regional organization has not yet been able to obtain sufficient consensus over the terms of a regional extradition treaty.
56   2009 Blueprint on the ASEAN Political-Security Community, available at http://cil.nus.edu.sg/2009/2009-blueprint-on-the-asean-political-security-community/ (last accessed 15 October 2013), para. 5.
57   Id., para. 29.
58   Id., para. 30.
59   Id., section A.2.5.

ratifying the Treaty on Mutual Legal Assistance in Criminal Matters and working towards elevating it to an ASEAN treaty,[60] continuing the work of the working group on extradition, identifying maritime cooperation among ASEAN member States and prioritizing capacity-building activities such as information sharing, technological cooperation and exchange of visits of authorities concerned.[61] It explicitly says that, in building a rules-based community of shared values and norms, a cohesive, peaceful, stable and resilient region with shared responsibility for comprehensive security,[62] ASEAN will have to apply a comprehensive approach to maritime cooperation that focuses on safety and security of navigation. Together with other instruments that have been adopted since 2003, the Blueprint once again underscores the importance of maritime security in ASEAN. In other words, it can now safely be said that, for ASEAN, maritime security has become an integral component in the Association's perception and understanding of common security.

3   ASEAN Sectoral Bodies and Maritime Security

Under the 2009 Blueprint on the ASEAN Political-Security Community, the ASEAN Maritime Forum (AMF) was no longer an abstract idea, but rather a specific measure that ASEAN committed to undertake.[63] It was materialized in 2010 when ASEAN officially launched the AMF to institutionalize its cooperation on maritime issues. Indonesia played host to the launch of the AMF and was also one of the ASEAN member States that actively contributed to its creation. Indonesia put forward the proposal on establishing the AMF, took the initiative to convene the 2007 Workshop on the AMF Establishment and participated in drafting the AMF concept paper. According to the concept paper, the AMF functions as a multi-dimensional dialogue forum that helps to foster maritime cooperation through constructive dialogues and consultations, promotes common understanding and views among ASEAN member States on regional and global maritime issues, carries out policy-oriented studies on specific regional maritime problems and enhances the ability of its member States to manage maritime issues of common interest and concern.[64] To date,

---

60   The Treaty was concluded outside an ASEAN framework.
61   Id., para. 16.
62   Id., para. 10.
63   Id., para. 16.
64   ASEAN, *Concept Paper for the Establishment of an ASEAN Maritime Forum* (AMF), para. 7. According to the Concept Paper, the AMF does not only address maritime security issues,

four AMF meetings have been organized, the latest of which took place in Kuala Lumpur, Malaysia in 2013 where ASEAN member States discussed and exchanged views on maintaining freedom and safety of navigation, addressing sea piracy and maritime security concerns, protecting the marine environment and promoting eco-tourism and fishery regimes.[65]

In addition to the AMF, ASEAN has also established the Expanded AMF (EAMF). The launch of the EAMF in 2012 was a significant development as it was the first regular specialized forum on maritime issues where government officials and experts from international organizations, maritime industries, academia and civil society from all major nations in the wider East Asia region, including Australia, China, India, Japan, New Zealand, South Korea, Russia, the United States, and ten ASEAN member States came together to discuss maritime issues. At the first EAMF meeting it was agreed that future meetings would be held back-to-back with meetings of the AMF so as to utilize opportunities and address current challenges on maritime issues by building upon the existing AMF.[66]

The AMF and the EAMF are just two ASEAN mechanisms that address maritime security issues. Another institutional body dealing with these issues is the ASEAN Ministerial Meeting on Transnational Crime (AMMTC). The AMMTC, assisted by the Senior Officials Meeting on Transnational Crime (SOMTC), is the highest policy-making body for ASEAN cooperation in combating transnational crime, including piracy and armed robbery against ships. Also, under the framework of the ASEAN Transport Ministers Meeting (ATM) and the ASEAN Maritime Transport Working Group (MTWG), ASEAN has organized the ASEAN Forum on the International Maritime Organization (IMO) conventions and regularly invites representatives from the private sector, such as the Federation of ASEAN Ship-owners Association (FASA) and the Federation of ASEAN Shippers Council (FASC), to its plenary sessions for input and exchanges of views on the latest developments on piracy and armed robbery against ships in the region.[67]

---

but also navigation, environment protection, search and rescue, and promotion of business through maritime cooperation.

65 "Closing Ranks and Enhancing Cooperation at Sea", 4th ASEAN Maritime Forum & 2nd Expanded ASEAN Maritime Forum. Available at http://www.mima.gov.my/mima/closing-ranks-and-enhancing-cooperation-at-sea/ (last accessed 14 April 2014).

66 ASEAN, *Chairman's Statement of 1st Expanded ASEAN Maritime Forum*, available at http://www.asean.org/news/asean-statement-communiques/item/chairman-s-statement-3rd-asean-maritime-forum (last accessed 15 October 2013).

67 ASEC Information Paper, *ASEAN and ARF Maritime Security Dialogue and Cooperation* (2007), available at http://www.un.org/depts/los/consultative_process/mar_sec_sub missions/asean.pdf (last accessed 15 October 2013) 8.

Joint efforts to address issues of maritime security also involve cooperation between military forces in regional countries. In fact, discussing and developing norms that facilitate ASEAN maritime security cooperation are among activities provided for in the 2006 Concept Paper for the Establishment of an ASEAN Defense Ministers' Meeting[68] and the Three-Year Work Programme (2008–2010) of the ASEAN Defense Ministers Meeting (ADMM).[69] Maritime security is also a priority area for cooperation in the ADMM Plus framework.[70] For that purpose, the ADMM has established an Experts' Working Group on Maritime Security (EWG on MS) and agreed to create a website to facilitate information sharing. The initial preparation for the website is still ongoing and is being coordinated by Malaysia. The EWG on MS is now preparing the scenario for a tabletop exercise, which focuses on practical assistance to encourage partnership to address maritime security issues.[71]

Another ASEAN mechanism that potentially has a great role to play in regional cooperation for maritime security is the ASEAN Law Ministers Meeting (ALAWMM). This institutional body is examining issues such as harmonization of national laws, ASEAN agreements on service abroad, harmonization of judicial and extra-judicial documents. It is also exploring the possibility of establishing legal frameworks for extradition and, in particular, creating a model law for ASEAN member States on maritime security.[72]

---

68   ASEAN, *2006 Concept Paper for the Establishment of an ASEAN Defense Ministers' Meeting*, available at http://cil.nus.edu.sg/2006/2006-concept-paper-for-the-establishment-of-the-asean-defence-ministers%E2%80%99-meeting-adopted-on-9-may-2006-in-kuala-lumpur-malaysia-by-the-defence-ministers/ (last accessed 15 October 2013).

69   2007 ASEAN Defence Ministers' Meeting Three-Year Work Programme, available at http://cil.nus.edu.sg/2007/2007-asean-defence-ministers'-meeting-three-year-work-programme-adopted-on-14-november-2007-in-singapore-by-the-defence-ministers/ (last accessed 15 October 2013), paras. 2.1.6 & 3.2.3.2.

70   Ron Huisken, "ADMM Plus cooperates on security and defence issues", East Asia Forum, available at http://www.eastasiaforum.org/2010/10/19/admm-plus-cooperates-on-security-and-defence-issues/ (last accessed 15 October 2013).

71   ARF, *Co-Chairs' Summary Report of the Fourth ARF Inter-Sessional Meeting on Maritime Security* (San Francisco, 14–15 June 2012), available at http://aseanregionalforum.asean.org/files/library/ARF%20Chairman's%20Statements%20and%20Reports/The%20Nineteenth%20ASEAN%20Regional%20Forum,%202011-2012/02%20-%20Co-Chairs%20Summary%20Report%20-%204th%20ARF%20ISM%20on%20MS,%20San%20Francisco.pdf, 3.

72   2005 Joint Communiqué of the 6th ASEAN Law Ministers Meeting, available at http://www.asean.org/communities/asean-political-security-community/item/joint-communique-of-the-6th-asean-law-ministers-meeting-alawmm-ha-noi-viet-nam-19-20-september-2005 (last accessed 15 October 2013).

In addition, ASEAN has also made use of its good relationships with major dialogue partners to promote cooperation on maritime issues in general and maritime security in particular. With China, from 2002 to 2010, ASEAN signed four instruments, namely the 2002 Declaration on the Conduct of the Parties in the South China Sea, the 2004 Memorandum of Understanding on Transport Cooperation, the 2007 Agreement on Maritime Transport, and the 2010 Memorandum of Understanding on Maritime Consultation to establish the ASEAN-China Maritime Consultation Mechanism. Under these instruments, ASEAN and China are encouraged to explore and undertake cooperative activities to combat transnational crime, including trafficking in illicit drugs, piracy and armed robbery against ships, and illegal traffic in arms[73] and promote the exchange of information and sharing of experiences on the implementation of the IMO International Ship and Port Facility Security (ISPS) Code.[74] There is now a mechanism for maritime consultation between ASEAN and China operating under the auspices of the ASEAN-China Senior Transport Officials Meeting which also discusses issues relating to maritime security.[75] Implementation of these instruments is, however, still a challenge.

---

[73] 2002 the Declaration on the Conduct of the Parties in the South China Sea, available at http://cil.nus.edu.sg/2002/2002-declaration-on-the-conduct-of-parties-in-the-south-china-sea-signed-on-4-november-2002-in-phnom-penh-cambodia-by-the-foreign-ministers/ (last accessed 15 October 2013) art. 6.

[74] 2004 Memorandum of Understanding between the Governments of ASEAN Member States and China on Transport Cooperation, available at http://cil.nus.edu.sg/2004/2004-memorandum-of-understanding-between-the-governments-of-the-member-countries-of-the-association-of-southeast-asian-nations-and-the-government-of-the-people's-republic-of-china-on-transport/ (last accessed 15 October 2013), art. II(3)(e); 2007 Agreement between the Governments of ASEAN Member States and China on Maritime Transport, available at http://cil.nus.edu.sg/2007/2007-agreement-on-maritime-transport-between-the-governments-of-the-member-countries-of-the-association-of-southeast-asian-nations-and-the-government-of-the-peoples-republic-of-china/ (last accessed 15 October 2013) art. 10(g); 2010 Memorandum of Understanding on Maritime Consultation to Establish the ASEAN-China Maritime Consultation Mechanism, available at http://cil.nus.edu.sg/2010/2010-memorandum-of-understanding-between-the-governments-of-the-member-states-of-the-association-of-southeast-asian-nations-and-the-government-of-the-people's-republic-of-china-on-maritime-con/ (last accessed 15 October 2013) art. II(3).

[75] 2010 Memorandum of Understanding on Maritime Consultation to Establish the ASEAN-China Maritime Consultation Mechanism, available at http://cil.nus.edu.sg/2010/2010-memorandum-of-understanding-between-the-governments-of-the-member-states-of-the-association-of-southeast-asian-nations-and-the-government-of-the-people's-republic-of-china-on-maritime-con/ (last accessed 15 October 2013) art. II(3).

Difficulties regarding implementation include the differences in the levels of interest and threat perception among member countries as well as sensitivities over issues of sovereignty and disputed maritime claims.

With Japan, ASEAN has organized the Maritime Transport Security Programme, the ASEAN–Japan Port Security Expert Meeting and the ASEAN–Japan Seminar on Maritime Security and Combating Piracy.[76] With respect to the United States, ASEAN has co-organized various workshops on maritime security, starting with the ASEAN–US Workshop on Enhancing Maritime Anti-piracy and Counter-terrorism Cooperation in the ASEAN region in 2004.[77] With India, ASEAN concluded in 2012 the India—ASEAN Special Commemorative Summit in which cooperation on maritime security was touted as a priority for future cooperation.[78] From as early as 2002, ASEAN has held the EU-ASEAN Experts' Meeting on Maritime Security.[79] Overall, these cooperative arrangements and mechanisms with external partners, especially those conducted under the framework of the ASEAN Regional Forum as described below, have provided ASEAN member States with further opportunities and resources to develop the infrastructure needed to ensure maritime security in the future.

4   ASEAN Regional Forum and Maritime Security

The ASEAN Regional Forum was established in 1993 and now has 27 participants, including every ASEAN member State as well as all major powers and countries that are using the sea lanes in the region such as China, Japan, South Korea, the United States and Australia. The ARF is an official framework intended to foster constructive dialogues and promote confidence building as well as preventive diplomacy on political and security issues. In 1994, one year after its establishment, ARF circulated a Concept Paper that features two lists of its proposed future cooperative activities. The first list provides measures to be implemented in the immediate future, including high-level exchanges and

---

76   ASEC Information Paper, *ASEAN and ARF Maritime Security Dialogue and Cooperation* (2007), available at http://www.un.org/depts/los/consultative_process/mar_sec_sub missions/asean.pdf (last accessed 15 October 2013) 10.
77   Id.
78   2012 India-ASEAN Special Commemorative Summit, available at http://www.asean .org/news/asean-statement-communiques/item/vision-statement-asean-india-commemorative-summit (last accessed 15 October 2013).
79   ASEC Information Paper, *ASEAN and ARF Maritime Security Dialogue and Cooperation* (2007), available at http://www.un.org/depts/los/consultative_process/mar_sec_sub missions/asean.pdf (last accessed 15 October 2013) 9.

dialogue on traditional security issues, publications of statements of defense policy and participation in multilateral treaties on arms register. The second list proposes activities to be explored and implemented over the medium and long term. Activities to ensure sea lines of communication and maritime information databases are included in the second list.[80] It took the ARF nearly ten years to formally translate the maritime security component in the second list into reality.[81] In the same year that ASEAN started to address maritime security issues at the Summit level, the ARF issued a ministerial statement on maritime security—the 2003 ARF Statement on Cooperation against Piracy and Other Threats to Maritime Security.

Through the 2003 ARF Statement on Cooperation against Piracy and Other Threats to Maritime Security, ARF participants commit to work together to protect ships that engage in international voyages. Their commitment takes the form of endorsing IMO instruments, recommendations and guidance for use in preventing and suppressing piracy and armed-robbery against ships, particularly the ISPS Code;[82] enhancing cooperation between ARF participants and the IMO and the Piracy Reporting Center of the International Maritime Bureau (IMB);[83] and ratifying early and effectively implementing the 1974 International Convention for the Safety of Life at Sea, the 1982 United Nations Convention on the Law of the Sea, the 1988 Convention for the Suppression of Unlawful Acts against the Safety of Maritime Navigation 1988 and its Protocol for the Suppression of Unlawful Acts against the Safety of Fixed Platforms Located on the Continental Shelf.[84] The 2003 ARF Statement recognizes that maritime security is an indispensable and fundamental condition for the welfare and economic security of the region and ensuring this security is in the direct interest of all countries, and regional countries in particular.[85] It encourages ARF discussion about the IMB proposals regarding prescribed traffic lanes for supertankers with coast guard or naval escorts whenever and wherever

---

80 ASEAN, Chairman's Statement of the Second ASEAN Regional Forum, Brunei, 1 August 1995, available at http://aseanregionalforum.asean.org/library/arf-chairmans-statements-and-reports/133.html (last accessed 15 October 2013).

81 A few workshops or seminars on maritime security were organized before 2003.

82 2003 ARF Statement on Cooperation against Piracy and Other Threats to Maritime Security, available at http://aseanregionalforum.asean.org/library/arf-chairmans-statements-and-reports/172.html (last accessed 15 October 2013) para. 3.

83 Id.

84 Id., para. 2.

85 Id., para. 1.

possible on the high seas upon the consent of all ARF countries concerned.[86] The ARF Statement urges transport industries and the shipping community to report security incidents to the relevant coastal States and to the ship's flag administrations for follow-up action by the proper authorities.[87] It also calls for more information sharing, capacity-building and technical assistance to countries that need help to enact necessary laws, extending training, and where and when possible, providing equipment.[88]

The ARF issued another ministerial statement in 2004, the Statement on Strengthening Transport Security against International Terrorism. This Statement focuses on regional efforts to step up cooperation to combat terrorism in all modes of transport, including transport at sea. The 2004 ARF Statement emphasizes the need for efforts by ARF participants to effectively implement their obligations under the IMO ISPS Code; strengthen practical cooperation between law-enforcement bodies and relevant security and intelligence services as well as state transportation agencies and organizations in counteracting terrorism in transport; explore possible measures to improve methods of identifying members of international terrorist groups active in international transport routes; hold simulation and joint exercises with a view to enhancing institutional capacity building of coastal States, especially with regard to piracy and maritime terrorism, to ensure effective modal coordination of maritime security measures; consider opportunities to plan and implement coordinated special operations and criminal investigations and set up joint operative teams to mitigate the effects of terrorist attacks on transport facilitates and bring the perpetrators to justice; and harmonize measures aimed at enhancing necessary security regimes for container shipping.[89]

Following the release of these two important ministerial documents, the ARF began conducting a series of activities on maritime security. In September 2004, it hosted a workshop in Malaysia on responses to threats to maritime security. The workshop identified problems that hindered regional cooperation in responding to threats to maritime security. These problems included the lack of a common definition of maritime crimes and shared understandings

---

86 Id., para. 4.
87 Id., para. 4.
88 Id., para. 4.
89 2004 ARF Statement on Strengthening Transport Security against International Terrorism, available at http://cil.nus.edu.sg/2004/2004-asean-regional-forum-arf-statement-on-strengthening-transport-security-against-international-terrorism-issued-on-2-july-2004-in-jakarta-indonesia/ (last accessed 15 October 2013) paras. 3–15.

of the threats to maritime security as well as a lack of resources and capacity to respond to threats.[90]

To build mutual trust and strengthen capacity to address threats to maritime security among its participants, the ARF conducted in 2005 a Confidence-Building Measure Meeting on Maritime Security in Singapore and two workshops on Training for Cooperative Maritime Security and Capacity Building of Maritime Security in Japan. These activities provided a forum for ARF participants to explore the idea of creating a regional maritime training center.[91] The workshops also discussed specific measures to follow up on the ARF's previous statements regarding maritime security. These measures included creation of a database, which could identify focal points of maritime agencies in ARF participants and existing bilateral and multilateral initiatives.[92] The ARF Directory of Contact Points on Maritime Security has been developed and coordinated by the ARF Unit at ASEC and is accessible from the ARFNet.[93]

In a further effort to push for concrete and practical measures rather than simply general exchanges of ideas, ARF participants also started to organize a large number of capacity building and training activities. English language training programs, for instance, have been conducted for border and maritime security officials from developing countries within the ARF such as Cambodia, Laos, Myanmar and Viet Nam.[94] In 2007, the ARF held the first Maritime Security Shore Exercise to facilitate exchange of operational experiences among ARF participants through tabletop and scenario-based maritime

---

90 ARF Unit Information Paper, *Highlights of Developments in ARF Cooperation on Maritime Security* (2012), available at http://aseanregionalforum.asean.org/files/References/Highlights%20of%20ARF%20Cooperation%20on%20Maritime%20Security%20(July%202012).pdf (last accessed 15 October 2013) 3.

91 ASEC Information Paper, *ASEAN and ARF Maritime Security Dialogue and Cooperation* (2007), available at http://www.un.org/depts/los/consultative_process/mar_sec_submissions/asean.pdf (last accessed 15 October 2013) 3.

92 ARF Unit Information Paper, *Highlights of Developments in ARF Cooperation on Maritime Security* (2012), available at http://aseanregionalforum.asean.org/files/References/Highlights%20of%20ARF%20Cooperation%20on%20Maritime%20Security%20(July%202012).pdf (last accessed 15 October 2013) 5.

93 Co-Chairs Summary Report of the Third ARF Inter-Sessional Meeting on Maritime Security, Tokyo, Japan, 14–15 February 2011, available at http://aseanregionalforum.asean.org/library/arf-chairmans-statements-and-reports.html (last accessed 15 October 2013) 6.

94 Co-Chairs' Summary Report of the Second ARF Inter-Sessional Meeting on Maritime Security, Auckland, New Zealand, 29–30 March 2010, available at http://aseanregionalforum.asean.org/library/arf-chairmans-statements-and-reports.html (last accessed 15 October 2013) 8.

security exercises. In the following year, the Indian Coast Guard hosted an ARF maritime security training workshop which covered topical issues such as search and rescue, smuggling, piracy, hijacking and armed robbery against ships, port security and ship security, the confiscation and repatriation of ships, fishing rights, drug trafficking and narco-terrorism. The training programme was modeled as a Basic Course and aimed at familiarizing young officers with various aspects of maritime security issues.[95] These exercises were important steps in the ARF's progress from merely conducting dialogue to forging concrete and practical cooperation in the area of maritime security. These activities have demonstrated that the key to addressing the transnational nature of maritime security threats is through multilateral and inter-agency information sharing and cooperation.[96]

In 2007, pursuant to the decision of the 14th ARF Ministerial Meeting, ARF conducted a Roundtable Discussion on Stocktaking Maritime Security Issues. The discussion once again highlighted the challenges that stem from a lack of a common understanding of maritime security and different national interests in ensuring maritime security.[97] To address these challenges, the ARF held the Belgium Seminar on Measures to Enhance Maritime Security in 2009. The Seminar underscored the lack of comprehensive legislative framework to combat maritime crimes and proposed that the issue of implementation of international conventions should be prioritized in future ARF activities.[98]

Based on the recommendations made by these activities, more recently ARF Ministers adopted the Hanoi Plan of Action to Implement the ARF Vision Statement at the 17th ARF Meeting in 2010. The Plan of Action sets out a series of specific measures to further improve the efficacy of the ARF in responding to maritime security challenges by 2020.[99] These measures include

---

95   ARF Unit Information Paper, ARF Maritime Security Training Workshop, available at http://aseanregionalforum.asean.org/files/library/ARF%20Chairman's%20Statements%20and%20Reports/The%20Fifteenth%20ASEAN%20Regional%20Forum,%202007-2008/Maritime%20Security%20Training%20Workshop%20Report.doc (last accessed 15 October 2013) 1.

96   ARF Unit Information Paper, *Highlights of Developments in ARF Cooperation on Maritime Security* (2012), available at http://aseanregionalforum.asean.org/files/References/Highlights%20of%20ARF%20Cooperation%20on%20Maritime%20Security%20(July%202012).pdf (last accessed 15 October 2013) 6.

97   Id.

98   Id., p. 7.

99   2010 Hanoi Plan of Action to Implement the ARF Vision Statement, available at http://aseanregionalforum.asean.org/files/library/ARF%20Chairman's%20Statements%20and%20Reports/The%20Seventeenth%20ASEAN%20Regional%20Forum,%202009-

complying with and adhering to relevant international legal instruments; implementing international standards and adopting best practices; sharing data for small vessel registration; enhancing transparency in regional maritime security; holding maritime security-related tabletop and joint training exercises; and promoting networking and coordination among maritime-related forums such as ARF, AMF, IMO and ReCAAP.[100] The adoption of the Hanoi Plan of Action was followed by the decision of ARF Ministers at their 18th Meeting to task ARF Senior Officials with working out the details of the ARF Work Plan on Maritime Security. This includes specific projects on (i) information/intelligence exchange and sharing of best practices, including on naval operations; (ii) confidence building activities; and (iii) capacity building of maritime law enforcement agencies, including table-top and field exercises. This list of projects is accompanied by a list of the lead countries or co-sponsors together with a timeline for implementation.[101] The ARF Unit at ASEC is responsible for frequently updating the implementation status of these projects.

Another ARF-established mechanism that reflects the ongoing institutional building to address maritime security issues is the ARF Inter-Sessional Meeting on Maritime Security. This was established by ARF Ministers at the 15th ARF in Singapore in 2008 as a regular forum focusing on assessing basic and common regional needs and developing practical forms of cooperation among concerned agencies of all ARF participants. Unlike the Expanded ASEAN Maritime Forum which covers all maritime issues and includes a large audience ranging from governments to international organizations to maritime industries to academia and civil society, the ARF Inter-Sessional Meeting mechanism mostly deals with maritime security and primarily involves government officials. It should be noted that, in addition to the ARF Inter-Sessional Meeting on Maritime Security, maritime security has also been discussed in the framework of ARF Inter-Sessional Meeting on Counter-Terrorism and Transnational Crime. While this mechanism of counter-terrorism does not specialize in maritime security, it has put maritime security on its agenda since 2004. It recognized very early on that terrorists might shift their attacks from land to sea and

---

2010/Annex21-ARF%20POA%20(endorsed%20by%20ARF%20SOM%2017[1].00%20 20%20May%202010).pdf (last accessed 15 October 2013) 3.

100   Id., p. 4.

101   ARF Unit Information Paper, *Highlights of Developments in ARF Cooperation on Maritime Security* (2012), available at http://aseanregionalforum.asean.org/files/References/Highlights%20of%20ARF%20Cooperation%20on%20Maritime%20Security%20 (July%202012).pdf (last accessed 15 October 2013) 7.

that sea transport infrastructure and services are among the most vulnerable targets of terrorist attacks.[102]

To date, five ARF Inter-Sessional Meetings on Maritime Security have been organized. The first meeting in 2009 underscored the need to facilitate common understanding and seek agreement on definitions of key maritime security concepts.[103] Also agreed at the meeting was to consider the possibility of developing a work plan of the ARF Inter-Sessional Meeting on Maritime Security based on the two updated and revised reports on "Stocktaking of ARF Decisions and Recommendations on Maritime Security Issues" and "Matrix of Progress ARF Discussion on Maritime Security Issues."[104]

At the second meeting in the following year, the United States made a proposal regarding the establishment of the ARF Transnational Threat Information Sharing Centre (ATTIC), which ARF States could join on a voluntary basis. The ATTIC would collaborate with the open-source Maritime Safety and Security Information System (MSSIS) to ensure members would have full access to information.[105] At the ARF Ministerial Meeting, the Ministers noted the United States' Concept Paper on the Establishment of the ARF Transnational Threat Information-sharing Centre, maintaining that the Concept Paper needed further examination and deliberation. In consequence, the United States has been consulting with ASEAN member States to organize a series of workshops to further develop the ATTIC concept.[106]

While the third ARF Inter-Sessional Meeting in 2011 was mostly devoted to drafting the ARF Work Plan on Maritime Security, the fourth meeting in 2012 focused on civil maritime law enforcement, including interagency and civil-military cooperation in maritime security and existing cooperation among the

---

102 ASEC Information Paper, *ASEAN and ARF Maritime Security Dialogue and Cooperation* (2007), available at http://www.un.org/depts/los/consultative_process/mar_sec_submissions/asean.pdf (last accessed 15 October 2013) 6.

103 Co-Chairs' Summary Report of the First ARF Inter-Sessional Meeting on Maritime Security, Surabaya, Indonesia, 5–6 March 2009, available at http://aseanregionalforum.asean.org/library/arf-chairmans-statements-and-reports.html (last accessed 15 October 2013) 9.

104 Id.

105 Co-Chairs' Summary Report of the Second ARF Inter-Sessional Meeting on Maritime Security, Auckland, New Zealand, 29–30 March 2010, available at http://aseanregionalforum.asean.org/library/arf-chairmans-statements-and-reports.html (last accessed 15 October 2013) 7.

106 ARF Unit Information Paper, Highlights of Developments in ARF Cooperation on Maritime Security, available at http://aseanregionalforum.asean.org/files/References/Highlights%20of%20ARF%20Cooperation%20on%20Maritime%20Security%20(July%202012).pdf (last accessed 15 October 2013) 3.

coast guards in the Asia—Pacific region.[107] Participants at the meeting also discussed the implementation of the ISPS Code including programs such as the International Port Security (IPS) Program being conducted by the United States Coast Guard.[108] As a result of these meetings, Japan has been collecting information on the ARF States' best practices on maritime enforcement activities and capacity building through questionnaires.[109] Information collected from ARF participants will be a basis for ARF to identify priorities for future work on maritime security.

5 Conclusion: The Way Forward

ASEAN has made substantial progress, particularly in the past ten years, in strengthening regional cooperation for addressing rising concerns of maritime security. Whereas in the past maritime security issues were nowhere to be found on the ASEAN agenda, they are now addressed at the highest levels of the Association. Whereas maritime security used to be considered an internal issue of state security, it is now perceived as part of ASEAN common security. ASEAN has gone from having no forum in which maritime security issues were discussed to establishing many sectoral bodies to deal with them, namely the ASEAN Ministerial Meeting on Transnational Crime, the ASEAN Transport Ministers Meeting, the ASEAN Defense Ministers Meeting, the ASEAN Law Ministers Meeting and the ASEAN Maritime Forum. Discussions, meetings, workshops and seminars on the subject have been organized. Many instruments on transnational crimes, terrorism, capacity building, training and information sharing have been adopted. Of particular significance are relevant treaties that have been concluded such as the 2004 Treaty on Mutual Legal Assistance in Criminal Matters and the 2007 ASEAN Convention on Counter Terrorism. External cooperation mechanisms between ASEAN and its dialogue

---

107   Id., p. 2.
108   Co-Chairs' Summary Report of the Third ARF Inter-Sessional Meeting on Maritime Security, Tokyo, Japan, 14–15 February 2011, available at http://aseanregionalforum.asean .org/library/arf-chairmans-statements-and-reports.html (last accessed 15 October 2013) 4 and Co-Chairs' Summary Report of the Fourth ARF Inter-Sessional Meeting on Maritime Security, San Francisco, 14–15 June 2012, available at http://aseanregionalforum.asean .org/library/arf-chairmans-statements-and-reports.html (last accessed 15 October 2013) 8.
109   ARF Unit Information Paper, *Status of Implementation of the ARF Hanoi Plan of Action* (2012), available at http://aseanregionalforum.asean.org/files/References/Matrix%20 Status%20of%20Implementation%20of%20ARF%20Hanoi%20PoA,%20as%20of %2006July2012%20(19th%20ARF).pdf (last accessed 15 October 2013) 5.

partners have also been established, notably under the ARF framework and the Expanded ASEAN Maritime Forum. ARF activities have now been institutionalized in the form of Inter-Sessional Meetings on Maritime Security. It was in the framework of the ASEAN Plus One that Japan proposed convening a governmental-level working group to formulate the Regional Cooperation Agreement on Combating Piracy and Armed Robbery against Ships in Asia. In sum, a regional framework on maritime security has been established. Throughout this process, ASEAN, at a minimum, has served as a multilateral forum for promoting shared understanding and common awareness of maritime security issues, building a recognizable degree of mutual confidence and sending a clear message to the international community about the region's willingness and efforts to ensure maritime security.

That being said, there remains a lot of work to be done for regional cooperation on maritime security to be effective. In terms of legal framework, to increase the efficacy of the Treaty on Mutual Legal Assistance on Criminal Matters, each of the ASEAN member States should adopt laws to criminalize acts of piracy by foreign nationals on foreign vessels outside of its territorial sea and other maritime offences in accordance with global counter-terrorism and counter-crime treaties. All ASEAN member States should harmonize their legislation on maritime crimes and develop working procedures to further facilitate mutual legal assistance arrangements. This can be achieved through the ASEAN Law Ministers Meeting mechanism in coordination with the ASEAN Ministerial Meeting on Transnational Crime and with the assistance of national and regional think-tanks and research centers. Similarly, to enhance the effects of the ASEAN Convention on Counter-Terrorism, ASEAN member States should ratify and implement all relevant global counter-terrorism treaties, particularly the 1979 International Convention Against the Taking of Hostages, the 1988 Convention for the Suppression of Unlawful Acts Against the Safety of Maritime Navigation, the 1988 Protocol for the Suppression of Unlawful Acts Against the Safety of Fixed Platforms Located on the Continental Shelf, the 1999 International Convention for the Suppression of the Financing of Terrorism, the 2005 International Convention for the Suppression of Acts of Nuclear Terrorism, the Protocol of 2005 to the Convention for the Suppression of Unlawful Acts against the Safety of Maritime Navigation and the Protocol of 2005 to the 1988 Protocol for the Suppression of Unlawful Acts Against the Safety of Fixed Platforms Located on the Continental Shelf.[110] Each

---

110 ASEAN Convention on Counter Terrorism, available at http://cil.nus.edu.sg/2007/2007-asean-convention-on-counter-terrorism-signed-on-13-january-2007-in-cebu-philippines-by-the-heads-of-stategovernment/ (last accessed 15 October 2013), art. II.

of these treaties deals with a different aspect of maritime crimes. Together, they represent a relatively holistic and comprehensive approach to combating maritime crimes. However, these treaties will only prove effective if all ASEAN member States become parties and implement their obligations by making the necessary changes in their national laws, possibly with technical assistance provided by ASEAN's dialogue partners.[111] As mandated by the Vientiane Action Programme, ASEAN should complete its work on an agreement on extradition. A proposal for ASEAN member States, especially those with similar legal systems, to assist each other in studying and drafting domestic legislation on maritime security is also worth considering because there remains a problem of defining and categorizing maritime issues within ASEAN.

In terms of institutional design, since there are many different sectoral bodies concurrently dealing with maritime security issues, cooperation activities should be well coordinated or an overarching mechanism needs to be established to avoid duplication of work and ensure the most efficient use of resources. Efforts should also be made to coordinate activities within ASEAN and those undertaken outside the ASEAN framework such as ReCAAP Information Sharing Centre. Ensuring the effective implementation of ASEAN instruments has always been a challenge for ASEAN. As provided by the ASEAN Charter, the implementation of ASEAN instruments and agreements shall now be monitored by the Secretary-General, with the assistance of ASEC.[112] In order for the Secretary-General to do his or her job and for ASEAN to increase the effectiveness of its cooperation, it would perhaps be better for ASEAN to establish rules of procedure whereby ASEAN member States are required to submit implementing reports to the relevant sectoral bodies and the Secretary-General. The Secretary-General, working closely with the relevant sectoral bodies, should then be required to prepare and submit monitoring reports to the relevant ASEAN Councils and the ASEAN Summit for consideration. Reporting frequency also needs to be clarified. All reports, except for those of sensitive political and security nature, should be published or made available

---

[111] All ASEAN member States, except Cambodia, are parties to UNCLOS. All ASEAN member States are parties to the 1999 Financing of Terrorism Convention; eight are parties to the 1979 Hostages Convention; and seven are parties to the 1988 SUA Convention. *See* Robert Beckman and J. Ashley Roach, "The Way Forward: Enhancing Legal Cooperation between ASEAN Member States", in Robert Beckman and J. Ashley Roach (eds.), *Piracy and International Maritime Crimes in ASEAN: Prospects for Cooperation* (NUS Centre for International Law and Edward Elgar, 2012), 233–242, at 234.

[112] ASEAN Charter, art. 11(2)(b).

online. This would place pressure on member States to implement their commitments so as to avoid critical scrutiny from interested stakeholders.

Finally, in terms of specific cooperative measures, ASEAN should consider increasing the range of its activities from exchanging views, sharing information, and building capacity to include conducting more coordinated or even joint enforcement measures. While in coordinated patrols, each country conducts patrols in its own territory, for joint patrols all concerned countries may operate under a common command and "hot pursuit" by one country may be allowed into the partner country's territorial sea.[113] Singapore, Indonesia and Malaysia have conducted coordinated patrols before[114] but these activities were undertaken outside an ASEAN framework and were confined to the Straits of Singapore and Malacca. The 2002 Work Programme to Implement ASEAN Plan of Action to Combat Transnational Crime does have a provision on the enhancement of programs for anti-piracy coordinated patrols. However it is not clear whether strategic plans on coordinated patrols have been worked out and how they have been implemented.[115] Given that the coordinated patrols conducted by Indonesia, Malaysia and Singapore have reportedly contributed to improving security in the Straits of Singapore and Malacca,[116] ASEAN member States should consider replicating these activities at the regional level on a regular basis. Organizing joint patrols may present a challenge in light of understandable concerns over sovereignty; however, as ASEAN moves closer to the goal of establishing an ASEAN Community by 2015 and maritime security is now viewed as being part of the region's common security rather than an internal issue for each state, there will come a time when joint patrols have to be considered by the Association. This is especially so if ASEAN genuinely wants to fulfill its goal of establishing a political and security community and taking responsibility for its own peace and security.

---

113   Rodolfo C. Severino, *The ASEAN Regional Forum* (Institute of Southeast Asian Studies, 2009), 95.
114   *See* Ian Storey, "Securing Southeast Asia's Sea Lanes: A Work in Progress", 6 *Asia Policy* (2008), 116.
115   2002 Work Programme to Implement ASEAN Plan of Action to Combat Transnational Crime, available at http://cil.nus.edu.sg/2002/2002-work-programme-to-implement-the-asean-plan-of-action-to-combat-transnational-crime-adopted-on-17-may-2002-in-kuala-lumpur-malaysia-by-the-ministers-responsible-for-transnational-crime/ (last accessed 15 October 2013), 3.4, 3.5, 3.6.
116   ReCAAP ISC, "Annual Report: Situation of Piracy and Armed Robbery against Ships in Asia in 2012" (2013), available at http://www.recaap.org/Portals/0/docs/Reports/ReCAAP%20ISC%20Annual%20Report%202012.pdf (last accessed 15 October 2013), 13.

CHAPTER 9

Freedom of Navigation and the Chinese Straight Baselines in the South China Sea

Kuen-chen FU

Recently, criticism has begun over the Chinese two- thousand-year-presence and its U-shaped historic water limits in the South China Sea. One of the reasons behind this criticism was that China had hindered freedom of navigation in the region.

Is Freedom of Navigation a Real Issue in the South China Sea?

The real answer to this question is clear: no. Though complicated, there has never been any such issue in the region. For decades, every year, more than 50,000 vessels sail through the water enclosed within the Chinese claimed U-shaped line in the South China Sea. Probably some Vietnamese fishing vessels would insist that they were blocked by the Chinese authorities to fish in the Spratly Island waters. Obviously, that was an issue of fishing rights, not of freedom of navigation.

Freedom of navigation is needed by everyone in the region. China, as the largest regional trading party, would need freedom of navigation the most. Thus there is no reason to believe that China would hinder freedom of navigation in the South China Sea, nor in any other parts of the world.

However, since the PRC has publicized its straight baselines in the Paracel Islands area,[1] theoretically speaking, innocent passage might be suspended

---

* Kuen-chen FU, SJD. State "One Thousand Elites Program" Expert; Dean, South China Sea Institute, Xiamen University; ZhiYuan Chair Professor of Law, Shanghai Jiao Tong University. The author's PowerPoint is available at http://www.virginia.edu/colp/pdf/Seoul-Fu.pdf.

1 *Statement of the People's Republic of China on the Territorial Sea Baselines of the PRC*, 15 May 1996. According to this Statement, the straight baselines around the Paracel Islands consists of the following base points:

    1. Lat. 16°40.5'N; Lon. 112°44.2'E.   2. Lat. 16°40.1'N; Lon. 112°44.5'E.
    3. Lat. 16°39.8'N; Lon. 112°44.7'E.   4. Lat. 16°04.4'N; Lon. 112°35.8'E.
    5. Lat. 16°01.9'N; Lon. 112°32.7'E.   6. Lat. 16°01.5'N; Lon. 112°31.8'E.
    7. Lat. 16°01.0'N; Lon. 112°29.8'E.   8. Lat. 15°46.5'N; Lon. 111°12.6'E.

sometime in the future by China within its internal waters encircled by the straight baselines of the Paracel Islands. This could cause some obstacles to the freedom of navigation in this small water area.

Chinese Straight Baselines of the Paracel Islands and Their Impacts on the Right of Navigation and Overflight

Article 2 of the 1992 PRC Law of Territorial Sea and Contiguous Zone provides that the South China Sea islands, including the Paracel Islands, the Prata Islands, the Macclasfield Banks and the Spratly Islands are Chinese territories.

Article 3 of the 1992 PRC Law of Territorial Sea and Contiguous Zone further provides that the delineation of the PRC territorial sea baselines applies [only] the "straight baselines method." This is the reason why even in some not-so-reasonable places, straight baselines are still delineated.

This law needs to be amended, because it is not reasonable, and does not even serve the interests of China itself. On the other side of the Taiwan Strait, Chinese Taiwan applies a more reasonable method to delineate its baselines—by applying the "mixed system method". In some places when a straight baseline is not suitable or hard to apply, e.g., at the turning corners of a small island, normal baselines are used instead of many short straight baselines.

According to Article 8(2) of UNCLOS, foreign vessels enjoy the right of innocent passage within internal waters encircled by newly demarcated straight baselines, such as the internal waters created by the PRC straight baselines in the Paracel Islands. But, for foreign aircraft, the right of free overflight across the internal waters area is not allowed. Notably, the right of innocent passage itself through the PRC internal waters of the Paracel Islands is subject to suspension, according to the UNCLOS. Thus, the PRC straight baselines could cause some theoretical obstacles for the freedom of navigation in this small

9. Lat. 15°46.4'N; Lon. 111°12.1'E.
10. Lat. 15°46.4'N; Lon. 111°11.8'E.
11. Lat. 15°46.5'N; Lon. 111°11.6'E.
12. Lat. 15°46.7'N; Lon. 111°11.4'E.
13. Lat. 15°46.9'N; Lon. 111°11.3'E.
14. Lat. 15°47.2'N; Lon. 111°11.4'E.
15. Lat. 17°04.9'N; Lon. 111°26.9'E.
16. Lat. 17°05.4'N; Lon. 111°26.9'E.
17. Lat. 17°05.7'N; Lon. 111°27.2'E.
18. Lat. 17°06.0'N; Lon. 111°27.8'
19. Lat. 17°06.5'N; Lon. 111°29.2'
20. Lat. 17°07.0'N; Lon. 111°31.0'
21. Lat. 17°07.1'N; Lon. 111°31.6'
22. Lat. 17°06.9'N; Lon. 111°32.0'
23. Lat. 16°59.9'N; Lon. 112°14.7'
24. Lat. 16°59.7'N; Lon. 112°15.6'
25. Lat. 16°59.4'N; Lon. 112°16.6'
26. Lat. 16°58.4'N.; Lon. 112°18.3'E.
27. Lat. 16°57.6'N.; Lon. 112°19.6'E.
28. Lat. 16°56.9'N; Lon. 112°20.5'E.

waters area of the Paracel Islands, which, navigators say, has always been a "dangerous zone" clearly marked on charts published by any map producers in the world. Practically speaking, no ordinary navigators would like to sail through it.

How to Resolve the Issue—If It Is an Issue?

To avoid the above mentioned theoretical obstacles to the freedom of navigation, this author would like to make two suggestions for China to consider:

- Suggestion 1: Move to amend UNCLOS and allow non-archipelagic States to delineate their own archipelagic waters baselines.
- Suggestion 2: Designate proper sea lanes unilaterally and allow foreign vessels and aircraft to sail through or to fly over the internal waters of its Paracel Islands.

For today's China, this might offer an opportunity to have a graceful turning around in the South China Sea region. And it may both benefit China itself and other members of the South China Sea semi-enclosed international community. Allow me to elaborate on this a bit more.

With the straight baselines proclaimed by it around the Paracel Islands, China, as a contracting party State of UNCLOS, should allow foreign vessels innocent passage, but may legally suspend it any time it deems necessary. China would not be able to allow freedom of overflight according to UNCLOS. And even if China wishes to do so, China would not have any legal basis to allow transit passages—unless the Paracel Islands internal waters are regarded as a strait used for international navigation (SUIN); and China will not have any legal basis to designate any sea lanes for foreign vessels and aircrafts to pass through the area—unless it is regarded as archipelagic waters.

In this case, if China could claim straight "archipelagic baselines," instead of "ordinary straight baselines" in the Paracel Islands area, then a better, safer and friendlier transportation environment will be created by China in the South China Sea. Innocent passage will be allowed. Free overflight will be allowed. And sea lanes passage will also be allowed, all legally according to UNCLOS.

Is it Possible to Amend UNCLOS 40 Years after the Big Debate (1974–2014)?

In 1974, various countries expressed their differing opinions in the 36th and the 37th meeting of the Second Committee, the Second Session of the UNCLOS III.[2] As shown in the official records, during that big debate, Indonesia described the concept of an archipelagic State as essential to the national unity, political stability, economic, social and cultural cohesiveness and territorial integrity. Its representative insisted that "without the concept of an archipelagic State, most of Indonesia's waters would have become pockets of so-called 'high seas', open to activities which might endanger the country's unity, security and territorial integrity."

Most countries, including China, sympathized with the difficulties faced by the archipelagic States. They demanded a strict definition of the "archipelagic State", and asked for a satisfactory regime of navigation and overflight through the archipelagic waters.

Australia, Japan, and some other States, supported a 5:1 (water: land) ratio, and a 48 nm length of baselines section limit. The United Kingdom, the Netherlands, Soviet Union, Malaysia and Thailand emphasized that equity demanded that due account be taken of the rights and interests of neighboring States affected by the archipelagic claims.

Some delegates argued that non-archipelagic State's archipelagic waters should be given equal status. Among them, India proclaimed that India had over 1280 islands and islets, of which approximately half constituted the archipelago of the Andaman and Nicobar islands and that of Lakshwadeep. The principle (of archipelagic waters) should apply to these archipelagos. It acknowledged the right of a coastal State having archipelagos which formed an integral part of its territory to apply the principles applicable to the archipelagic States, on the clear understanding that such principles would apply to those archipelagos only. Furthermore, such out-lying archipelagos could not be joined with the mainland of the coastal State by straight baselines.

---

2   The following paragraphs of various countries statements are selected from *The Third United Nations Conference on the Law of the Sea, Official Records*, Vol. II, pages 260–273. *Summary records of the Second Session—Second Committee, 36th and 37th meeting*, Monday, 12 August 1974.

As we could imagine, as India's neighbor, Burma strongly opposed India, for any extension of that concept (of archipelagic waters) to oceanic archipelagos or other groups or chains of islands belonging to a continental State.

Portugal argued that "the arguments in favor of the establishment of a special regime for archipelagic States were also valid for archipelagos forming part of the territory of a coastal State, particularly with regard to the security and economic interests of such States". 'Application of a different regime for the latter would mean that the archipelagic part of the territory of mixed States would be regarded as second class territory."

Ecuador and Spain were supportive of the arguments brought out by India and Portugal.

Argentina's representatives explained the issue by categorizing coastal States in three categories: (1) archipelagic States; (2) States which possessed archipelagos far from their coasts; and (3) States which possessed a fringe of islands in close proximity to their coast. It agreed with the delegations of Ecuador, Spain and India to the effect that the provisions relating to archipelagic States should apply *mutatis mutandis* to distant archipelagos which belonged to a continental State. Argentina also insisted that "it should be made clear that the coastal State could not draw baselines connecting the coasts of its continental territory with those of its distant archipelago."

At the end, the "77 Club" member States reached some agreement with the major sea powers. And the current archipelagic State regime was finalized without permitting the non-archipelagic States to apply the principle of archipelagic water to their distant archipelagos.

Are the non-archipelagic States' (distant) archipelagos better controlled and managed, where they are encircled within their "ordinary straight baselines" and become their "internal waters?" Is this legal arrangement a more reasonable one than allowing them to be encircled within their "straight archipelagic water baselines," and be regarded as "archipelagic waters"?

This is truly an unresolved issue.

One of the remaining unanswered questions is: For those out-lying or distant islands, how far is far enough to be regarded as "distant archipelagos," and be given their "archipelagic waters?" The answer should be clearer today: as long as they are beyond the reach of a reasonable coastal territorial sea straight baseline, reasonably the distance should be 100 nm or more.

Anyway, China's South China Sea islands, the Paracel Islands and the Spratly islands are definitely far enough away to be regarded as "distant archipelagos." And the water areas of these islands should be given the status of archipelagic waters, for the interests of everyone, including China itself.

Some Conclusions

Comparing the two suggested policies mentioned above, if China would unilaterally claim its South China Sea as "archipelagic waters" and allow the right of sea lanes passage through its South China Sea archipelagos, its "face" might be derogated, and some domestic criticism might occur.

On the other hand, if China could claim its South China Sea "archipelagic waters" according to an "amended" UNCLOS, then its "face" would be maintained, freedom of navigation and overflight would be better preserved, and a positive precedent would be made for other similar non-archipelagic States' archipelagos.

The reality is, however, amending UNCLOS would be like opening Pandora's Box, and cannot be expected by the international community today. If China really wants to apply the principle of archipelagic waters for its Paracel Islands, it has to do it unilaterally.

Applying the principle of archipelagic waters unilaterally, with some "loss of face" and some internal criticism, China would also gain something of real interest.

Other than practicing a graceful turning around leading to easier bilateral negotiations with its neighbors in the South China Sea region, China could use the wider drying reefs to delineate its territorial sea baselines in the region, according to the UNCLOS archipelagic waters principle. This might give China longer baselines, and (archipelagic) water areas larger than its internal waters.

Also, some other non-archipelagic States might follow the precedent created by China, and apply the same principle and allow Chinese vessels and aircrafts to sail through or overfly their own distant archipelagic waters in other parts of the world. This should be of interest for everyone in the world.

In summary, although there is actually no real issue of freedom of navigation in the South China Sea region today, Chinese distant archipelagos in the region could cause theoretical obstacles of freedom of navigation in the future. To avoid these theoretical obstacles, China could consider unilaterally applying the principle of archipelagic waters, and delineate sea lanes to allow foreign vessels and aircrafts to sail through and fly over the internal waters created by its straight territorial sea baselines in the region.

CHAPTER 10

The Cooperative Mechanism in the Straits of Malacca and Singapore

Leonardo Bernard

Abstract

Article 43 of the 1982 United Nations Convention on the Law of the Sea (UNCLOS) obliges littoral and user States to cooperate to ensure the safety of navigation and management of ship-source pollution in straits used for international navigation. This article has been consistently used by Indonesia, Malaysia and Singapore—the three littoral States bordering the Straits of Malacca and Singapore—to argue that user States should 'share the burden' in managing the navigational safety and environmental risks in the Straits of Malacca and Singapore. In 2007, the three littoral States, implementing Article 43 of UNCLOS, agreed to establish a Cooperative Mechanism that enables user States and other stakeholders to cooperate with the littoral States in enhancing navigational safety and environmental protection in the Straits of Malacca and Singapore.

The establishment of the cooperative mechanism was the first time that Article 43 of UNCLOS has been implemented. This paper highlights the significance of the cooperative mechanism in light of Article 43 of UNCLOS and its contribution in the development of the international law of the sea. The first section of the chapter traces the history of the conclusion of Article 43 of UNCLOS to provide an understanding of what the intentions of the State Parties to UNCLOS were when negotiating this article. The next section provides a general description of the Straits of Malacca and Singapore, as well as the history of cooperation amongst the littoral States with regard to the Straits. The following section provides an analysis of the results achieved by the littoral States through the cooperative mechanism. The concluding section offers several recommendations to enhance the effectiveness of the cooperative mechanism in the Straits of Malacca and Singapore.

Article 43 of the 1982 United Nations Convention on the Law of the Sea (UNCLOS)[1] obliges littoral and user States to cooperate to ensure the

---

* Leonardo Bernard, Research Fellow, Centre for International Law, National University of Singapore. cillb@nus.edu.sg. The author's PowerPoint is available at http://www.virginia.edu/colp/pdf/Seoul-Bernard.pdf.

safety of navigation and management of ship-source pollution in straits used for international navigation. This article has been repeatedly used by Indonesia, Malaysia and Singapore—the three littoral States bordering the Straits of Malacca and Singapore—to argue that user States should 'share the burden' in managing the navigational safety and environmental risks in the Straits of Malacca and Singapore. In 2007, the three littoral States, implementing Article 43 of UNCLOS, agreed to establish a Cooperative Mechanism that enables user States and other stakeholders to cooperate with the littoral States in enhancing navigational safety and environmental protection in the Straits of Malacca and Singapore.

The establishment of the Cooperative Mechanism was the first time that Article 43 of UNCLOS was implemented. This chapter highlights the significance of the Cooperative Mechanism in light of Article 43 of UNCLOS, and its contribution to the development of the international law of the sea. The first part of the section traces the development of the norms that regulated passage of ships through straits, as well as the history of Article 43, so as to provide an understanding of the intentions of the State Parties to UNCLOS during the negotiation of the provision. The next section provides a general description of the Straits of Malacca and Singapore, as well as the history of cooperation between the littoral States with regard to the Straits. The following section provides an analysis of the results achieved by the littoral States through the Cooperative Mechanism. The concluding section highlights several challenges in improving the effectiveness of the Cooperative Mechanism in the Straits of Malacca and Singapore.

1   History of Passage through Straits

The history of passage through straits is intricately linked with arguments on the breadth of territorial seas and freedom of navigation. Grotius in his work 'Mare Liberum', restricted his arguments for the free sea to the high seas, and not to bays or narrow straits or any part of the sea that can be seen from the shore, and he did not discuss the issue of straits.[2] In his subsequent work,

---

1 *United Nations Convention on the Law of the Sea*, 10 December 1982, UNTS 1833 at 3 (entered into force 16 November 1994), [UNCLOS] online: United Nations <http://www.un.org/Depts/los/convention_agreements/convention_overview_convention.htm>.
2 Hugo Grotius, *The Free Sea*, translated by Richard Hakluyt (Indianapolis: Liberty Fund, 2004), at 32–33; see also Scott Truver, *The Strait of Gibraltar and the Mediterranean* (The Netherlands: Sijthoff & Noordhoff, 1980), at 146.

De jure Belli ac Pacis, Grotius acknowledged the right of coastal States to appropriate gulfs, bays and straits enclosed by their land, but stressed that innocent passage cannot be forbidden in these parts of the ocean.[3] He also argued that a State that undertakes to protect and promote navigation in these parts of the ocean may make such passage conditional upon payment of a moderate due.[4]

Emmerich de Vattel was the first to distinguish between straits that serve for communication between two seas and straits that have no such function.[5] Regarding the latter, Vattel remarked that navigation through such straits is common to all nations and that the State possessing the strait cannot deny passage as long as such passage is innocent.[6] Like Grotius, Vattel also recognized that such passage may be made conditional upon payment of a moderate due for keeping the strait lit, marked off and free from pirates.[7]

1.1 First Half of the Twentieth Century

The International Court of Justice (ICJ) clarified the elements of a strait used for international navigation and laid down the rules regarding passage through such straits in the 1949 *Corfu Channel Case*.[8] In that case, Albania claimed that the United Kingdom had violated Albania's sovereignty by sending warships passing through the north Corfu Channel without Albania's authorization. The Court, however, ruled that there exists in international law a right of passage for warships through straits used for international navigation in times of peace, so long as the passage is innocent, and that no prior authorization from the coastal States is necessary for such passage.[9] Albania also argued that the north Corfu Channel was mostly used for local traffic, and that the criterion of number of foreign ships should be applied to determine whether the north Corfu Channel could be considered as a strait used for international navigation. The Court, however, disagreed with Albania's contention, and ruled that

---

3   Truver, ibid., at 148; see also Erik Brüel, *International Straits, A Treatise on International Law* (London: Sweet & Maxwell, 1947), at 48–49. Brüel argued that the degree of importance of a strait to international navigation depends on facts such as the number of ships passing through the strait, their total tonnage, the values of the cargoes, the average size of the ships and whether they are distributed among a greater number of nations, see Brüel, at 42–43.
4   Brüel, ibid., at 49.
5   Brüel, *supra* note 3, at 53; Truver, *supra* note 2, at 149.
6   Emmerich de Vattel, *The Law of Nations*, Book I, Chapter 23, Section 292, translated by Charles Fenwick, Vol. 3 (Washington: Carnegie Institution of Washington, 1916), at 109.
7   Brüel, *supra* note 3, at 54.
8   *Corfu Channel Case* (*United Kingdom of Great Britain and Northern Ireland v Albania*) (1949) Judgment, ICJ Rep 4 [Corfu Channel Case].
9   *Corfu Channel Case*, ibid., at 28.

the decisive criterion to determine whether a strait is used for international navigation is its geographical situation as connecting two parts of the high seas and the fact that it is used for international navigation.[10] The Court thus combined the functional and geographical aspects in determining whether a strait is used for international navigation, but put less weight on the actual frequency of use of the strait for international navigation.[11]

The decision of the Court in the *Corfu Channel Case* influenced the proceedings of the first United Nations Law of the Sea Conference at Geneva in April 1958. During the conference, the International Law Commission (ILC) submitted a draft that would restrict the regime of passage to straits 'normally' used for international navigation between two parts of the high seas.[12] This attempt, however, failed at the conference because the major maritime powers argued that limiting the passage regime would be contrary to the Court's decision in the *Corfu Channel Case*.[13] In the end, the Conference adopted the ILC's draft, while omitting the word 'normally' and adding a new category of straits through which innocent passage could not be suspended.[14] The result was Article 16 (4) of the 1958 Convention on the Territorial Sea and the Contiguous Zone, which provides for non-suspendable rights of passage in straits connecting one part of the high seas and the territorial sea of another State.[15]

1.2   UNCLOS 1982

When the Third United Nations Conference of the Law of the Sea convened its first session in New York in 1973,[16] it assigned the question of straits used for international navigation to the Second Committee of the Conference. The main conflict regarding straits used for international navigation in the third conference was the extent of the passage regime within such straits. Some

---

10   *Corfu Channel Case, supra* note 8, at 28–29.
11   Truver, *supra* note 2, at 150; see also José Antoni de Yturriaga, *Straits Used for International Navigation, A Spanish Perspective* (The Netherlands: Martinus Nijhoff Publishers, 1990), at 29–30.
12   *Yearbook of the International Law Commission*, Vol. 2 (1956), at 258, Art. 17(4) of the Draft Articles Concerning the Law of the Sea.
13   *Official Records of the United Nations Conference of the Law of the Sea*, Vol. 3 (1958) UN Doc A/CONF.13/39, at 220.
14   Yturriaga, *supra* note 11, at 31; see also Koh Kheng Lian, *Straits in International Navigation* (New York: Oceana Publications, 1982), at 36.
15   Yturriaga, *supra* note 11, at 32. This amendment was clearly added to address the situation of the Strait of Tiran, see Koh Kheng Lian, ibid., at 36–37.
16   The conference held its first session in 1973, and worked for several months each year until it finally adopted a convention in 1982.

States were of the view that the only passage through such straits is that of non-suspendable innocent passage.[17] Other States claimed that the regime of passage in these straits was wider than that provided for under the 1958 Convention, covering freedom of navigation that extends to foreign aircrafts.[18]

The issue of breadth of the territorial sea was central to reaching an agreement on the regime of passage through straits. When negotiations for the third Conference started, a number of States had already declared a 12 nautical miles (nm) territorial sea.[19] During the negotiations for the regime of passage through straits, major maritime powers like the United States and the United Kingdom stated that they were prepared to support the extension of the territorial sea to 12 nm if a satisfactory regime for the passage of straits used for international navigation could be agreed.[20] Indonesia suggested that a more precise definition was needed to balance the concerns of the coastal States and of the international maritime powers.[21] In the end, a compromise was reached and a new regime of 'transit passage' through straits used for international navigation was created. Article 38 (2) of UNCLOS defines transit passage as the "freedom of navigation and overflight for the purpose of expeditious transit of the strait between one part of the high seas or an Exclusive Economic Zone (EEZ) and another part of the high seas or an EEZ."[22]

This compromise allows passage of warships and overflight through straits used for international navigation, but falls short of granting freedom of navigation. Transit passage does not apply in straits that connect the high seas or an EEZ with the territorial sea of a third State, such as the Strait of Tiran which connects the Gulf of Aqaba with the Red Sea, but UNCLOS maintained the right of non-suspendable innocent passage through such straits,[23] as provided

---

17   Robin R. Churchill and Alan V. Lowe, *The Law of the Sea*, 2nd ed. (Manchester: Manchester University Press, 1988), at 88.
18   Churchill and Lowe, ibid., at 89.
19   Countries like China, Canada, Costa Rica, Egupt, France, India, Indonesia, and Malaysia had already claimed a 12 nm territorial sea prior to 1973. See Churchill and Lowe, ibid., Appendix 1, at 343–352.
20   UN Division for Ocean Affairs and the Law of the Sea, *Straits Used for International Navigation, Legislative History of Part III of the United Nations Convention on the Law of the Sea*, Vol. II (New York: United Nations Publishing, 1992), at 5 & 11.
21   UN Division for Ocean Affairs and the Law of the Sea, ibid., at 14.
22   This provision was adopted largely from the draft proposed by the United Kingdom. See UN Division for Ocean Affairs and the Law of the Sea, *supra* note 20, at 15.
23   UNCLOS, Art. 45.

in the 1958 Geneva Convention.[24] The text of UNCLOS was finally adopted in Jamaica on 10 December 1982 and entered into force on 16 November 1994. As of October 2013, 165 countries and the European Union are parties to UNCLOS.[25]

2 The Straits of Malacca and Singapore

The Strait of Malacca and the Singapore Strait (the Straits) have long played an important role in international navigation. They form one continuous channel that connects the Indian Ocean with the South China Sea and provide the shortest routes between the Middle East and Far East Asia. The channel spans approximately 520 nm, which makes it the longest strait used for international navigation. Three States border the Straits: Indonesia, Malaysia and Singapore. The narrowest part of the Strait of Malacca is 8.4 nm wide and only 3.2 nm wide in the Singapore Strait. More than 80% of crude oil supplies for Japan and Korea are transported through the Straits, with up to 60,000 vessels transiting through it per year, which in 2002 amounted to 10.3 million barrels of oil per day.[26] In 2020, it is estimated that 114,000 ships will traverse the Straits.[27] Oil carriage through the Straits is three times greater than that through the Suez Canal and fifteen times greater than that through the Panama Canal. The Straits are also rich fishing grounds and home to extensive mangrove ecosystems along their coasts.

---

24 UNCLOS also excludes straits that are subject to special treaties, such as the Montreux Convention that regulates the Straits of Dardanelles and Bosphorus, from the application of Part III, see UNCLOS, Art. 35(c).
25 Niger was the latest country to ratify UNCLOS on 7 August 2013; see *Chronological lists of ratifications of, accessions and successions to the Convention and the related Agreements as at 29 October 2013*, online: United Nations <http://www.un.org/depts/los/reference_files/chronological_lists_of_ratifications.htm#The United Nations Convention on the Law of the Sea>.
26 International Maritime Organization, 'Protection of Vital Shipping Lanes', Notes from the Secretary General, IMO Document C 93/15, 7 October 2004, Annex, Profile of the Straits of Malacca and Singapore, at 2.
27 Japan's Ministry of Land Infrastructure and Transport, as quoted in Sheldon W. Simon, 'Safety and Security in the Malacca Straits: The Limits of Collaboration' (2011) 7:1 *Asian Security* 27, at 27.

2.1 Maritime Boundaries

There are maritime boundary agreements covering most, but not all, parts of the Straits. In the Strait of Malacca, Malaysia and Indonesia agreed on a continental shelf boundary in 1969 and a territorial sea boundary in the southeast part of the Malacca Strait in 1990. In the Singapore Strait, Singapore and Indonesia have concluded agreements on several segments of maritime boundaries, most recently in 2009. Singapore and Malaysia are currently in talks to determine the maritime boundaries around Pedra Branca and Middle Rock.

2.1.1 Boundaries between Indonesia and Malaysia in the Strait of Malacca

Indonesia and Malaysia signed a continental shelf boundary agreement on 27 October 1969 (Continental Shelf Agreement), just a few months after the ICJ issued its judgment in the *North Sea Continental Shelf Cases*.[28] The Agreement claimed to be based on the equidistance principle between Indonesia's and Malaysia's baselines.[29] A look at the actual boundary on the map, however, suggests that the boundary is actually closer to the Indonesian coast than to the Malaysian coast.

States with sovereignty over land territory are permitted to claim maritime zones from such land territory. During the negotiation of the Continental Shelf Agreement, both Indonesia and Malaysia accepted that like all maritime zones, the boundary between them should be measured from their respective baselines. Under the 1958 Convention on the Territorial Sea and the Contiguous Zone, the normal baseline for measuring maritime zones is the low-water mark along the coast.[30] It is generally recognized that straight baselines may be employed if a coast is deeply indented or has a fringe of islands, provided that the baseline does not depart to an appreciable extent from the general

---

28 *Agreement between the Government of Malaysia and the Government of the Republic of Indonesia on the Delimitation of the Continental Shelf between the Two Countries*, 27 October 1969 (entered into force 7 November 1969), US Department of State, 'International Boundary Study, Series A, Limits in the Seas', No 1, 21 January 1970 [Continental Shelf Agreement].

29 Ibid., at 7.

30 *Convention on the Territorial Sea and the Contiguous Zone*, 29 April 1958, 15 UST 1606; 516 UNTS 205 (entered into force 10 September 1964) [Territorial Sea Convention], Article 3, online: Centre for International Law, National University of Singapore (CIL) <http://cil.nus.edu.sg/1958/1958-convention-on-the-territorial-sea-and-the-contiguous-zone/>.

direction of the coast.[31] If a State employs straight baselines, the waters landward of the baseline are considered to be internal waters. However, if the use of straight baselines has the effect of enclosing as internal waters areas which were not previously considered as such, the right of innocent passage still applies in the waters.[32]

Prior to the signing of the Continental Shelf Agreement, Indonesia had been promoting the regime of 'Archipelagic Waters'; and during negotiations for the 1958 Law of the Sea Conference, Indonesia had unsuccessfully argued the use of 'archipelagic baselines' to enclose mid-ocean archipelagos (which are States that consist entirely of island archipelagos, such as Indonesia and the Philippines). Indonesia argued that archipelagic States should be permitted to draw straight baselines connecting the outermost points of the outermost islands in their archipelago. During the negotiation of the Continental Shelf Agreement, Indonesia proposed the use of this archipelagic baseline system as the base points for measuring the boundary from their land territory.

Malaysia countered Indonesia's use of archipelagic baselines by applying the straight baselines system to enclose all of its islands off the coast of the western Malay Peninsula. This was Malaysia's way of achieving an equal footing in the division of the continental shelf with Indonesia, the latter having drawn straight baselines around its archipelago.[33] Malaysia drew straight baselines to join its coast with two of its outermost islands in the north Malacca Strait, these being Pulau Perak and Pulau Jarak. Pulau Perak is approximately 55 nm from the nearest point of Malaysian land (the island of Pulau Singa Besar), while Pulau Jarak lies approximately 25 nm from the nearest point of Malaysian land at Pulau Butuh.[34]

Indonesia agreed to Malaysia's use of straight baselines to delimit the continental shelf boundary between the two countries. The distance between Pulau Perak and Indonesia's nearest territory is 84 nm and the distance between Pulau Jarak and Indonesia's nearest 'archipelagic baseline' is 30 nm.[35] The two countries then agreed to delimit the continental shelf boundary by drawing a median line from the straight baselines of both countries, which was an

---

31 Ibid., Article 4.
32 1958 Territorial Sea Convention, *supra* note 30, Article 5.
33 Continental Shelf Agreement, *supra* note 28, at 4.
34 Maxx Herriman and Raja Petra Mohamed, 'A Malacca Straits EEZ Boundary: Factors for Consideration', in M Shariff, et al., eds., *Towards Sustainable Management of the Straits of Malacca* (Malacca Straits Research and Development Centre: 2000), at 758–759.
35 Continental Shelf Agreement, *supra* note 28, at 5.

approach that is in conformity with that set out in the 1958 Continental Shelf Convention.[36]

If baselines were ignored and equidistance was measured from the coast of both countries, Indonesia should have gained more continental shelf than what was agreed in the Continental Shelf Agreement.[37] Indonesia's acceptance of Malaysia's use of 'straight-baselines' as the basis for the Continental Shelf Agreement between the two States was seen as 'a gift' from Indonesia to Malaysia for the latter's support in pushing the regime of Archipelagic Waters during negotiations for the Third United Nations Law of the Sea Conference. Hence, Malaysia secured a larger continental shelf area in the north Malacca Strait than Indonesia.

This, however, posed a problem after the establishment of the EEZ regime following the conclusion of UNCLOS in 1982. In 1996, Malaysia unilaterally declared that it considered the continental shelf boundaries in the north Malacca Strait concluded between Indonesia and Malaysia to represent the boundary for the EEZ as well.[38] The fact remains, however, that the Continental Shelf Agreement signed in 1969 does not extend to the water column above the seabed, and it is unlikely that Indonesia will concede to Malaysia's claim.

2.1.2 Boundaries between Indonesia and Singapore in the Strait of Singapore

The maritime boundaries between Indonesia and Singapore in the Strait of Singapore consist of three segments: the western segment, the central segment and the eastern segment. All three segments concern the delimitation of territorial seas, as the distance between the two States at any point is less than 24 nm. The boundaries of the central segment were the first to be agreed upon in

---

36 *Convention on the Continental Shelf*, 29 April 1958, UNTS 499 at 311 (entered into force 10 June 1964), Art. 6 [Continental Shelf Convention], online: CIL <http://cil.nus.edu.sg/1958/1958-convention-on-the-continental-shelf/>.

37 Prescott claimed that if a strict line of equidistance was drawn in this sector, Indonesia would gain about 1,000 nm² of continental shelf; see Victor Prescott, *Indonesia's Maritime Claims and Outstanding Delimitation Problems*, in IBRU *Boundary and Security Bulletin*, Winter 1995–1996, at 94–95.

38 Upon its ratification of UNCLOS, Malaysia declared that if the maritime area is less than 200 nm from baselines, the boundary for the EEZ shall be the same line with the boundary of continental shelf; see *Malaysian Declaration Upon Ratification of the Convention of the Law of the Sea 1982*, 14 October 1996, online: United Nations <http://www.un.org/depts/los/convention_agreements/convention_declarations.htm#Malaysia%20Upon%20ratification>.

1973.[39] This boundary extends for a distance of 24.55 nm between the southwestern part and the southeastern part of the Strait of Singapore. The boundaries for the western segment were completed in 2009[40] and follow a median line between Indonesia's Nipah Island and Singapore's Sultan Shoal Island.[41]

The boundaries for the eastern segment are yet to be completed. The eastern segment is divided into parts, the first part is the Changi/Batam segment and the second part is the Pedra Branca/Bintan segment. Indonesia and Singapore are currently in talks to conclude the boundary for the Changi/Batam segment,[42] but the negotiation for the Pedra Branca/Bintan segment will need to involve Malaysia, as the presence of Malaysia's Middle Rock between Singapore's Pedra Branca and Indonesia's Bintan means that a tripartite agreement is required.

2.2   Security Issues in the Straits of Malacca and Singapore

The heavy traffic in the Straits and the high poverty level of the coastal communities have made the Straits of Malacca and Singapore a lucrative target for maritime crime. Coupled with the geographical condition of the Straits, with its narrow waterways, tiny islets around the coasts and outlets to many rivers, it is no surprise that the Straits are havens for so called 'local pirates'. The types of attacks typical in the region are basically theft and armed robbery,[43] which mostly occur within the territorial sea of a littoral State (many accounts inaccurately refer to these incidents as piracy, although the majority of them do not meet the legal definition of piracy contained in Article 101 of UNCLOS).

---

39   *Agreement Stipulating the Territorial Sea Boundary Lines Between Indonesia and the Republic of Singapore in the Strait of Singapore*, 25 May 1973 (entered into force 29 August 1974).

40   *The Treaty Between The Republic Of Indonesia and Republic of Singapore Relating to the Delimitation of the Territorial Seas of the Two Countries in the Western Part of the Strait of Singapore*, 10 March 2009 (entered into force 30 August 2010).

41   'Indonesia and Singapore agree new maritime boundary', IBRU Boundary News, 5 February 2009, online: <https://www.dur.ac.uk/ibru/news/boundary_news/?itemno=75 41&rehref=%2Fibru%2Fnews%2F&resubj=Boundary+news%20Headlines>.

42   *Joint Statement by the Ministry of Foreign Affairs, Republic of Indonesia and the Ministry of Foreign Affairs, Republic of Singapore on the Technical Discussions on Maritime Boundaries between the Republic of Indonesia and the Republic of Singapore in the Eastern Part of the Strait of Singapore*, Seventh Round, 2–3 July 2013, online: <http://www.mfa.gov.sg/content/mfa/media_centre/press_room/pr/2013/201307/press_20130703_01.html>.

43   Karsten von Hoesslin, 'Piracy and Armed Robbery against Ships in the ASEAN Region: Incidents and Trends', in Robert C. Beckman and J. Ashley Roach, eds., *Piracy and International Maritime Crimes in ASEAN* (Cheltenham: Edward Elgar, 2012), at 122.

Most of the waters that comprise the Straits of Malacca and Singapore are territorial seas of the littoral States—all of the southern part of the Strait of Malacca consists of territorial seas of Indonesia and Malaysia and the whole of the Singapore Strait falls within either Indonesia's or Singapore's territorial seas. This means that enforcement of maritime crime depends heavily on the domestic law of the littoral States. Therein lies the problem. The nature of most (if not all) of the maritime crimes that occur in the Straits are transboundary crimes. A crime might occur in Singapore's territorial seas conducted by perpetrators based in Indonesia who then sold the stolen goods in Malaysia. Moreover, under UNCLOS the right of hot pursuit stops at the outer limit of the territorial sea of another State, which greatly limits the capabilities of each of the littoral States to pursue and apprehend perpetrators who can easily cross territorial boundaries to escape.

Between 2000 and 2004, there was an increase in the number of incidents of maritime crimes that occurred in the Straits. The International Maritime Bureau (IMB) noted that there was a sharp increase in incidents in the aftermath of the 1998 Asian Financial Crisis,[44] which suggests that piracy and armed robbery are closely linked to the economic situation on land. Many of those who engaged in attacks were trying to compensate for their loss of income.[45] There were also suggestions that some of the attackers came from the Indonesian territory of Aceh in the northwest tip of Sumatra, which had been torn apart by a separatist struggle for three decades.[46]

The number of such incidents during this period was so high that in 2005 Lloyd's Market Association designated the Strait of Malacca as a war-risk zone for insurance purposes.[47] The inclusion of the Strait of Malacca on this list meant higher costs for shipping, which was bad for the businesses of the three littoral States. The littoral States took a series of collective measures to improve the security in the Strait, such as coordinated sea patrols, eyes in the sky and exchanges of information. These efforts were by no means perfect, as they were not a collective

---

44   There were 75 reported incidents in the Malacca Straits in 2000, up from only two in 1999. See ICC International Maritime Bureau, *Piracy and Armed Robbery against Ships, Annual Report, 1 January–31 December 2005*, at 5.
45   Karsten von Hoesslin, *supra* note 43, at 121.
46   Michael Schuman, 'How to Defeat Pirates: Success in the Strait', *Time* (22 April 2009).
47   Joint War Committee—Llyod's Market Association, *JWC Hull War, Strikes, Terrorism and Related Perils—Listed Areas 20th June 2005*, Bulletin, online: International Underwriting Association <http://www.iua.co.uk/IUA_Test/Communities_folder/marine/JWC_Risk_List_folder/JWLA001__Hull_War__Strikes__Terrorism_and_Related_Perils_Listed_Areas.aspx>.

security framework and merely "an exchange of scheduling activities."[48] Despite their shortcomings, these measures managed to reduce the number of incidents in the Strait to the extent that in 2006 Lloyd's Market Association decided to remove the Strait of Malacca from its war-risk zone listing.[49]

Other factors also contributed to the drop of incidents in the Strait of Malacca, such as the Boxing Day tsunami in 2004, which devastated many of the coastal communities around the Strait, the peace agreement between the Government of Indonesia and the Aceh rebels, as well as technical assistance provided to the governments of the littoral States by Japan and the United States. By 2013, the littoral States seemed to have been successful in suppressing the incidents in the Straits to a minimal level.[50]

3 Cooperation in the Straits of Malacca and Singapore

Cooperation in the management of the Straits did not come easy, since the three littoral States have a complex history of rivalry and distrust. The three littoral States did not see themselves as having the same interests in management of use and users in the Straits.[51] Relationships improved after the formation of the Association of South East Asian Nations (ASEAN) in 1967, but even then, throughout the 1970s and 80s, cooperation in the Straits was minimal.

3.1 *Cooperation between the Littoral States Prior to UNCLOS*

Although during the 1970s and 80s cooperation between the littoral States on the management of the Straits was minimal, it does not mean that there was no cooperation at all. The littoral States of the Straits of Malacca and Singapore have in fact been cooperating since the early 1970s through various trilateral consultations, which culminated in the formation of the Tripartite

---

48   Frederick Situmorang, 'The Need for Cooperation in the Malacca Strait', *The Jakarta Post* (19 July 2012).

49   Joint War Committee—Llyod's Market Association, *JWC Hull War, Strikes, Terrorism and Related Perils—Listed Areas* (7 August 2006), Bulletin, online: International Underwriting Association <http://www.iua.co.uk/IUA_Test/Communities_folder/marine/JWC_Risk_List_folder/JWLA005_Hull_War__Strikes__Terrorism_and_Related_Perils_Listed_Areas.aspx>.

50   There was only one reported incident in the Malacca Strait in 2011 and 2012 respectively. See ICC International Maritime Bureau, *Piracy and Armed Robbery against Ships, Annual Report, 1 January–31 December 2012*, at 5.

51   Abu Bakar Jaafar and Mark J. Valencia, *Management of the Malacca/Singapore Straits: Some Issues, Options and Probable Responses*, Akademika No. 26, January 1985, at 111.

Technical Experts Group (TTEG) in 1975. The TTEG was formed through the Joint Statement between the three littoral States and was formalized in 1977 through the signing of the Agreement on Safety of Navigation. The TTEG is comprised of experts from the maritime administrations of the three littoral States, who meet every year to discuss and collaborate on issues to enhance navigational safety and the protection of the marine environment, as well as other traffic management measures in the Straits.[52]

The TTEG has made small but significant strides in the enhancement of navigational safety in the Straits of Malacca and Singapore. In 1977, it proposed to the International Maritime Organization (IMO) a Routeing System that includes a Traffic Separation Scheme (TSS) as well as rules for vessels moving in the Straits. This proposal was approved by the IMO and implemented in 1981.[53] Another proposal submitted to the IMO by the TTEG was the mandatory ship reporting system (STRAITREP) in the Straits, which was introduced to enable the authorities to update transiting ships on the traffic situation and to contribute towards search and rescue response and operations in the Straits.[54] The STRAITREP was implemented in 1998. The TTEG also organized a *Four Nations Joint Re-survey of Critical Areas and Investigation of Dangerous/ Unconfirmed Shoals and Wrecks in the Straits of Malacca and Singapore*. The survey was jointly undertaken by the littoral States and Japan from October 1996 to February 1998, covering a total area of 780 km^2.[55]

The TTEG has continued to serve as an effective framework in which the littoral States and user States can discuss and cooperate to tackle issues in the Straits. The TTEG annual meetings are now attended not only by the three littoral States, but also by observers from Australia, China, India, Japan, Norway, Republic of Korea, the IMO, the Malacca Strait Council, the Nippon Maritime Center, as well as members of shipping industries, such as the International Association of Independent Tanker Owners (INTERTANKO), the International Chamber of Shipping (ICS), the Baltic and International Maritime Council (BIMCO), the Federation of ASEAN Shipowners' Association (FASA), and the Asian Shipowners Forum (ASF).

Japan has been very active in enhancing the safety of navigation in the Straits and has been cooperating with the littoral States since the 1960s. The Japanese Government and maritime community, through organizations such as the

---

52 Maritime Port Authority of Singapore, *Factsheet on the Tripartite Technical Experts Group (TTEG)*, online: <http://www.mpa.gov.sg/sites/images/pdf_capture/annexb_270510.pdf>.
53 Maritime Port Authority of Singapore, ibid.
54 Maritime Port Authority of Singapore, ibid.
55 Maritime Port Authority of Singapore, ibid.

Nippon Foundation, the Japan Maritime Foundation, the Japanese Shipowners' Association, the Petroleum Association of Japan, the General Insurance Association of Japan and the Shipbuilders' Association of Japan, have all been very active in contributing to efforts to enhance navigational safety in the Straits. They have been channeling their contribution through the Tokyo-based Malacca Strait Council (MSC). The MSC was established in 1969 for the purpose of route maintenance along the Straits of Malacca and Singapore. Since then, it has supported efforts to improve navigational safety and environmental protection in the Straits, such as conducting hydrographic surveys, providing buoy tenders and installing navigational aids.[56] More than three-fifths of the aids to navigation used by mariners in the Straits were installed by the Malacca Strait Council, at the cost of more than JPY 5.4 billion, with some 41 buoys, beacons and lighthouses being installed at 30 locations.[57]

The MSC also established the Revolving Fund scheme in 1981, from which the three littoral States can draw an advance to combat oil spills from ships. Japan has been the sole country contributing to this fund, which now amounts to JPY 450 million. The fund is managed by a committee, which regularly submits financial reports to the MSC. To date, the littoral States have drawn on the fund on several occasions: Indonesia and Malaysia in October 1992 to clean up the Nagasaki Spirit incident in the north Malacca Strait; Indonesia in October 2000 to clean up the *Natuna Sea* incident near Tanjung Pinang; and all three littoral States in May 2010 to deal with the *MT Bunga Kelana* 3 and the *MV Waily* collision.[58]

All of these cooperation arrangements continue to exist and have been incorporated into the Cooperative Mechanism established under Article 43 of UNCLOS.

3.2   *Article 43 of UNCLOS*

During the negotiation of Part III of UNCLOS, the littoral States were concerned with preserving their sovereignty and territorial integrity, but lacked the capabilities to protect their coasts and waters adequately from the effects

---

56   Nazery Khalid, *Yen and the Art of Malacca Strait Maintenance*, June 2007, online: <http://www.mima.gov.my/mima/wp-content/uploads/Japanese%20contribution%20in%20SOM%20_26June07_.pdf>.

57   Robert C. Beckman, 'International Cooperation to Enhance Environmental Protection in the Straits of Malacca and Singapore: Developments and Prospects' (Paper presented to the 8th Science Council of Asia Conference, Qingdao, China, May 2008) [unpublished].

58   Maritime Port Authority of Singapore, *Fact Sheet on the Revolving Fund*, online: <http://www.mpa.gov.sg/sites/pdf/060426c.pdf>.

of harm caused by traffic in the Straits. Malaysia in particular was concerned with the financial burden it would have to bear to ensure the safety of navigation and to protect the marine environment in the Strait of Malacca.[59] The littoral States could not pass the burden to those who use the Straits, as international practice does not allow the imposition of charges on ships by coastal States by reason only of their passage.

The States negotiating UNCLOS finally agreed to a compromise and to the wording of Article 43, which was drafted to encourage cooperation between States bordering straits and user States. The article reads as follows:

> User States and States bordering a strait should by agreement cooperate:
> (a.) in the establishment and maintenance in a strait of necessary navigational and safety aids or other improvements in aid of international navigation; and
> (b.) for the prevention, reduction and control of pollution from ships.

This article was negotiated 'with the case of shipping passing through straits such as Malacca particularly in mind'.[60] In light of Malaysia's concerns regarding financial costs, it unsuccessfully attempted to include a provision that authorized the coastal States to *require* the cooperation of user States and other relevant international organizations.[61] The article was thus drafted to address this concern without resolving into the imposition of tolls on ships by the coastal States by reason only of their transit passage,[62] while still allowing the user States to share the burden of improving navigational safety and preventing pollution. On the other hand, the article also ensures that

---

59 Satya N. Nandan, 'The Provisions on Straits Used for International Navigation in the 1982 United Nations Convention on the Law of the Sea', quoted in Robert Beckman, 'The Singapore Conference in the Straits of Malacca and Singapore—Issues, Perspectives and Post-Conference Developments' (1998) 2 *Singapore Journal of International & Comparative Law* 233, at 235.

60 Satya N. Nandan and David H. Anderson, 'Straits Used for International Navigation: A Commentary on Part III of the United Nations Convention on the Law of the Sea 1982', (1989) 60 BYIL 159 at 193.

61 Bernard H. Oxman, 'Observations on the Interpretation and Application of Art. 43 of UNCLOS with Particular Reference to the Straits of Malacca and Singapore' (1998) 2 *Singapore Journal of International & Comparative Law* 408, at 413.

62 David H. Anderson, 'The Imposition of Tolls on Ships: A Review of International Practice', quoted in Robert Beckman, *supra* note 59, at 236.

the interests of user States will be taken into account in any Cooperative Mechanism in straits used for international navigation.

Article 43 only provides authoritative guidance regarding goals, process and participation but leaves a lot of room for States to determine precise procedures and specific measures.[63] It is not an authorization for straits States and user States to establish cooperative agreements, but they are free to conclude such agreements, as long as they respect their duties to other States under the Convention.[64] Indeed, the institutional significance of Article 43 is "the guidance it provides to straits States, user States and international organizations about how certain problems in straits should be approached in the context of the Convention's overall system for promoting safety of navigation and protection of the marine environment."[65] This article thus serves as the basis, but not authority, for international cooperation to defray the costs of aids to navigation or other measures relating to navigational safety or marine pollution.

3.3 *The Current Cooperative Mechanism*

After the entry into force of UNCLOS in 1994, there were several discussions between the littoral States to try to implement Article 43. This was halted, however, in 1999 due to the repercussions of the Asian financial crisis and the political upheaval in Indonesia after the fall of Suharto. Maritime security became the focus after the September 11 incident in the United States in 2001, but talk of cooperation was again put on the back burner due to the 2003 Asian severe acute respiratory syndrome (SARS) crisis.[66] During this period, Japan remained the sole user State who volunteered to share the burden of managing the Straits with the coastal States.

The repercussions of the September 11 attack, however, were felt long after the incident. Following the attack, the United States initiated the Proliferation Security Initiative (PSI), which raised concerns regarding its implications for the sovereignty of the coastal States.[67] At the same time, the increase of piracy and armed robbery incidents in the Straits resulted in

---

63 Bernard H. Oxman, *supra* note 61, at 408.
64 Ibid., at 409.
65 Ibid., at 408.
66 Robert Beckman, 'The Establishment of Cooperative Mechanism', in Aldo Chircop, et al., eds., *The Future of Ocean Regime-Building* (Leiden: Martinus Nijhoff Publishers, 2009), at 243–244.
67 See US Department of State, *Proliferation Security Initiative*, online: <http://www.state.gov/t/isn/c10390.htm>.

the Malacca Strait being declared a war-risk zone by Lloyd's.[68] This development spurred countries like Japan to consider sending their coast guards to patrol the Straits.[69] In addition, Japan announced that it would no longer be able to solely bear all the costs for maintaining and replacing the aids for navigation in the Straits.[70]

In 2004, the Secretary General of the IMO led an initiative to enhance the safety, security and environmental protection in the Straits of Malacca and Singapore. After three years of negotiations, in 2007, the littoral States formally adopted the cooperative mechanism for the Straits of Malacca and Singapore. Despite being limited to safety of navigation and environmental protection, and not security, it set out the framework for cooperation between littoral States and user States to enhance navigation safety and environmental protection. Although this cooperative mechanism is the first scheme of its kind to implement Article 43 of UNCLOS, it built upon the already existing cooperative arrangements such as the TTEG and SMC.

The Cooperative Mechanism consists of three pillars: the Cooperation Forum; the Project Coordination Committee; and the Aids to Navigation Fund. The Cooperation Forum is a platform for dialogue between the littoral States, the user States, the shipping industry and other stakeholders in order to exchange views and facilitate more concrete and practical cooperation.[71] The Cooperation Forum's latest meeting was held on 7 October 2013 in Bali, Indonesia, and was attended not only by the littoral States and user States but also by other stakeholders from the shipping industry such as BIMCO and INTERTANKO.[72] In that meeting, the various stakeholders had the opportunity to discuss new projects such as raising awareness amongst seafarers transiting the Straits of local navigational considerations and the synergy between the Marine Electronic Highway and e-navigation.[73]

The Project Coordination Committee (PCC) decides on projects to enhance safety of navigation. This is an important part of the Cooperative Mechanism,

---

68   Joint War Committee—Lloyd's Market Association, *supra* note 47.
69   Ministry of Foreign Affairs of Japan, *Present State of the Piracy Problem and Japan's Efforts*, December 2001, online: <http://www.mofa.go.jp/policy/piracy/problem0112.html>.
70   Robert Beckman, *supra* note 66, at 246.
71   Cooperative Mechanism, *Cooperation Forum*, [Cooperative Mechanism], online: <http://www.cooperativemechanism.org.my/index.php?option=com_content&view=article&id=36&Itemid=33>.
72   BIMCO, *2013 Cooperative Mechanism Meetings Complete*, News Release, 14 October 2013, online: <https://www.bimco.org/news/2013/10/14_2013_cooperative_mechanism.aspx>.
73   BIMCO, ibid.

as this is the actual demonstration of effective cooperation and burden sharing between the littoral States and users of the Straits. The PCC is comprised of the littoral States and sponsors of projects who oversee the coordination of the implementation of the projects. The sponsors of a specific project and the littoral States may form a joint project implementation team, or other agreed mechanism, for the technical management and implementation of the project.[74]

The form of cooperation in the implementation of projects is not necessarily always in monetary terms, and includes the provision of expertise towards the implementation of more technical projects.[75] This allows user States, the shipping industry and other stakeholders to contribute either by financing a project or an individual component of a project, or by providing technical assistance and equipment for specific aspects of a project.[76] There are currently 51 aids to navigation installed within the Traffic Separation Scheme of the Straits, which were primarily installed by the littoral States and Japan. At their initial launch, six projects were identified as their focus:[77]

> Project 1: Removal of wrecks in the Traffic Separation Scheme (India and Germany);
> Project 2: Capability development on hazardous and noxious substance (HNS) preparedness and response in the Straits (Australia, China, European Commission, and the United States);
> Project 3: Development of automatic identification systems (AIS) transponder on small ships (Korea, Japan, and Australia);
> Project 4: Tide, current and wind measurement system (China and India);
> Project 5: Replacement and maintenance of existing Aids to Navigation in the Straits (Japan and Korea); and
> Project 6: Replacement of Aids to Navigation destroyed by the 2004 tsunami (China).

The first phase of Project 3 was completed in 2010, and implementation of Project 6, which is fully sponsored by China, is already in progress. The remaining projects are available for sponsorship, either in full or in part, through cooperation with user States or other stakeholders. At the 2nd Cooperation

---

74 Cooperative Mechanism, *Project Coordination Committee, supra* note 71.
75 Cooperative Mechanism, ibid.
76 Cooperative Mechanism, ibid.
77 Cooperative Mechanism, ibid.

Forum meeting in 2009, Singapore's proposal of a new Project 7, Emergency Towing Vessel (ETV) service in the Straits, was approved.[78] Each of the projects is supervised by a littoral State, with Malaysia supervising Projects 1 and 2; Singapore supervising Projects 3, 4 and 7; and Indonesia supervising Projects 5 and 6.[79]

The Aids to Navigation Fund was set up to ensure that there are long-term and sustainable means of financing the maintenance of critical aids to navigation in the Straits. The Aids to Navigation Fund (the Fund) is administered by the littoral States on a three-year rotation basis, and it serves as a forum where all users of the Straits can contribute financially towards the maintenance of the aids to navigation in the Straits.[80] Contributions to the Fund are voluntary and can be received from States, industry, private benefactors, non-governmental organizations and inter-governmental organizations, including the IMO.[81] To date, the Fund has received about USD15.2 million in both pledged and actual contributions.[82] The Aids to Navigation Fund Committee manages the Fund in accordance with the best international financial practices of transparency and accountability.[83] Aside from the three littoral States, other members of the Committee include China, India, Japan, Korea, Saudi Arabia, the UAE, the IMO, the MSC and Nippon Foundation.[84]

In addition to the Revolving Fund, the IMO also manages the Malacca and Singapore Straits Trust Fund, which now amounts to around USD1.86 million. This fund benefited from contributions made by China, Greece, Germany, Norway and the European Union, amongst others, to fund the navigational aid projects in the Straits.

4   Challenges

The establishment of the Cooperative Mechanism for the Straits of Malacca and Singapore was an unprecedented achievement and serves as an example

---

78   Cooperative Mechanism, ibid.
79   Cooperative Mechanism, ibid.
80   Cooperative Mechanism, *Aids to Navigation Fund, supra* note 71.
81   Cooperative Mechanism, ibid.
82   Maritime Port Authority of Singapore, *Factsheet on the Co-operative Mechanism*, Annex A online: <http://www.mpa.gov.sg/sites/pdf/annex_a_factsheet_on_co-operative_mechanism.pdf>.
83   Cooperative Mechanism, *Aids to Navigation Fund, supra* note 71.
84   Maritime Port Authority of Singapore, *Factsheet on the Co-operative Mechanism, supra* note 82.

of the implementation of Article 43 of UNCLOS. It established rules and regulations to enhance navigational safety and prevent pollution in the Straits. The success of this measure, however, still relies heavily on the support of the flag States. This is because the Cooperative Mechanism recognizes the jurisdiction of the flag States over vessels in cases of violation of the regulations in the Straits, unless the vessel in question enters any of the ports of the coastal States. But if a transiting ship violates the rules, the coastal States have no enforcement powers and can only request that the flag State deal with the violation. Thus, cooperation from flag States is crucial. Without adequate support from flag States, the coastal States can only rely on their port jurisdiction to enforce these rules.

Another issue arising from Article 43 of UNCLOS is identifying the 'user States' and whether other parties apart from the user and coastal States should be involved in the Cooperative Mechanism. It is reasonable to define user States to include not only the flag States, but also States whose nationals own the cargo, States whose nationals are the recipients of the cargo and States from which the cargo originates.[85] However, it is also important to encourage other stakeholders to participate in the Cooperative Mechanism, such as the shipping industry, the marine insurance industry and the oil and gas industry. Although Article 43 of UNCLOS only addresses States, it is implicit in the purpose of the article that the 'users' themselves should be engaged in the process.[86] So far, the Cooperative Mechanism has been quite successful in this regard, choosing to adopt an inclusive approach toward user States, shipping organizations and other stakeholders.[87] Their participation not only allows these private parties to have a voice in shaping the mechanism that has a huge impact on their businesses, but also provides a means for them to assist the coastal States by sharing their expertise or other resources.[88] The challenge is for the Cooperative Mechanism to broaden its reach beyond the shipping industry to include other industries that benefit from the use of the Straits, such as the oil and gas industry, the telecommunication industry, etc.

In order to attract interest from private parties to participate and contribute to the process, the Cooperative Mechanism should not shy away from talking to the public about its activities and the progress it has made. This transparency

---

[85] S. Tiwari, 'Legal Mechanism for Establishing a Fund' (1999) 3 *Singapore Journal of International & Comparative Law* 470, at 471.
[86] Bernard H. Oxman, *supra* note 61, at 417.
[87] Joshua H. Ho, 'Enhancing Safety, Security and Environmental Protection of the Straits of Malacca and Singapore: The Cooperative Mechanism' (2009) 40 *ODIL* 233, at 242.
[88] Bernard H. Oxman, *supra* note 61, at 417.

will not only stimulate interest and support from the public, such as from non-governmental organizations and other private groups that may have useful information and ideas, but it will also generate political support in user States to encourage stakeholders to commit their support.[89] By participating in the Cooperative Mechanism, the user States and other stakeholders are playing their part in implementing the spirit of UNCLOS.

Lack of clear maritime boundaries also posed a challenge for law enforcement in the Straits. The slight increase of maritime robbery incidents starting from 2008 was attributed in part to problematic maritime enforcement due to disputed maritime boundaries in two areas:[90] The first being the waters between Batam (Indonesia) and Changi (Singapore) along the eastbound traffic separation scheme;[91] the second area being the north Malacca Strait between Sumatra (Indonesia) and the west coast of Malaysia, where there are no EEZ boundaries between the two countries.[92] Clear maritime boundaries would definitely make enforcement easier, since most of the maritime crimes that occur in these waters are small-scale robberies that can be countered by more effective policing by local authorities.[93]

Cross-strait traffic is also increasingly becoming an issue. Most of the cross-strait ships are vessels of less than 300 Gross Registered Tonnage, making them not subject to the Straits' mandatory ship reporting system and the STRAITREP rule.[94] Despite predictions that cross-strait traffic will increase by 9% each year, the littoral States have yet to designate any cross-strait traffic lane in the Straits, although the issue has been discussed extensively in various meetings of the TTEG.[95] Although there has never been a major collision between cross-strait traffic and transiting traffic, this could present a hazard to traffic in the Straits in the future.[96]

---

89   Bernard H. Oxman, ibid., at 423.
90   Sheldon W. Simon, *supra* note 27, at 33.
91   Indonesia and Singapore allegedly have reached a provisional agreement on the boundaries in this segment, although technical negotiation continues; *supra* note 42; see also *S'pore and Indonesia meet for technical discussions on maritime boundaries*, Channel News Asia, 10 December 2013, online: <http://www.channelnewsasia.com/news/singapore/s-pore-and-indonesia-meet/917584.html>.
92   See the discussion on the maritime boundaries between Indonesia and Malaysia above, *supra* note 38.
93   Sheldon W. Simon, *supra* note 27, at 33.
94   Mohd Hazmi bin Mohd Rusli, 'The Cross-Strait Traffic in the Straits of Malacca and Singapore: An Impediment to Safe Navigation?', RSIS Commentaries, 1 August 2012.
95   Mohd Hazmi bin Mohd Rusli, ibid.
96   Mohd Hazmi bin Mohd Rusli, ibid.

Despite all its challenges, the Cooperative Mechanism is a historic breakthrough of great significance, and in some ways it goes beyond what is mandated by Article 43. The Mechanism expressly recognizes the role of the IMO and it also welcomes participation not only from user States, but also from private parties and other stakeholders.[97] It is deliberately simple, so that it can accommodate other forms of cooperative arrangements or consider the special circumstances of certain users.[98] Most importantly, it addresses the challenges in managing the Straits by involving user States and other stakeholders without infringing the sovereignty of the littoral States.

The latest meetings of the three pillars of the Cooperative Mechanism showed that the mechanism has been successful in addressing the financial concerns of the littoral States and in involving user States and other stakeholders in decision-making regarding passage through the Straits. The success of the mechanism can also be seen from the active participation of shipping companies and the initiatives they have taken to enhance the safety of navigation and to protect the environment in the Straits. The Cooperative Mechanism in the Straits of Malacca and Singapore can certainly be used as a model of cooperation for the management of other straits used for international navigation in the spirit of Article 43 of UNCLOS.

---

[97] Robert Beckman, *supra* note 66, at 252.
[98] 'The Co-operative Mechanism between the Littoral States and User States on Safety of Navigation and Environmental Protection in the Straits of Malacca and Singapore', Submission by Indonesia, Malaysia and Singapore to the IMO, IMO/SGP 2.1/1, 16 August 2007.

PART 5

*Balancing Marine Environment
and Freedom of Navigation*

∴

CHAPTER 11

European Law and Policy Review: Striking a Balance between Ecosystem Considerations and Navigation Rights under the Marine Strategy Framework Directive, the Law of the Sea Convention and the Draft Directive on Maritime Spatial Planning

Ronán Long

Introduction

The European Union (EU) is pressing ahead to give full effect to the provisions of the Marine Strategy Framework Directive (hereinafter, the "MSF Directive") with a view to achieving good environmental status of all European marine waters by 2020.[1] At the same time, Europe has a strong dependency on shipping

---

* Ronán Long, Jean Monnet Chair European Union Law and Personal Professorship, National University of Ireland Galway, and managing director, Marine Law and Ocean Policy Research Services Ltd. This research paper is undertaken as part of work package 7 of the ODEMM Project (Deliverable 14 and milestone 19), which examined various constraints and opportunities for implementing the ecosystem-based approach in the European marine environment. This includes a law and policy review. Supported by the European Commission's 7th Framework Research Programme, Theme ENV.2009.2.2.1.1, Project No 244273. Further information is available at: www.liv.ac.uk/odemm/. The author wishes to thank Margaret Armstrong MSc and Judith Ellis for their outstanding help as always. The author's PowerPoint is available at http://www.virginia.edu/colp/pdf/Seoul-Long.pdf.

1 Directive 2008/56/EC of the European Parliament and of the Council of 17 June 2008 establishing a framework for community action in the field of marine environmental policy (Marine Strategy Framework Directive) OJ L 164/19, 25.6.2008. See *inter alia*: R. Long, "The Marine Strategy Framework Directive: A new European approach to the regulation of the marine environment, marine natural resources and marine ecological services" (2011) *Journal of Energy and Natural Resources Law* 29 (1) pp. 1–44 L. Juda "The European Union and the Marine Strategy Framework Directive: Continuing the Development of Ocean Use Management", (2010) 41 *ODIL* 34–54; and by the same author, The European Union and Ocean Use Management: The Marine Strategy and the Maritime Policy," (2007) 38 *ODIL*

to ensure that it remains an economic powerhouse at a time when it faces intensive competition in global markets from China, India and the United States. Thus it comes as no surprise to see that the scholarship of Alfred Thayer Mahan continues to influence contemporary thinking on the strategic importance of international trade and freedom of navigation for the global community and for the EU most exceptionally. In light of the subject matter of this conference, perhaps it is pertinent to open this paper with a frequently cited quotation from Mahan's celebrated work *The Influence of Sea Power upon History, 1660–1783*, which reads as follows:

> The first and most obvious light in which the sea presents itself from the political and social point of view is that of a great highway; or better, perhaps, of a wide common, over which men may pass in all directions, but on which some well- worn paths show that controlling reasons have led them to choose certain lines of travel rather than others. These lines of travel are called trade routes; and the reasons which have determined them are to be sought in the history of the world.[2]

Captain Mahan was very perceptive in the manner in which he identified the influence of seaborne commerce on the wealth of many European countries, which he attributed to shipping interests at sea, as well as to the projection of power by maritime and naval means. In some respects, little has changed with the passage of time, as the commercial greatness of Europe remains very much contingent upon the free flow of maritime trade and the enduring existence of navigational rights and other freedoms, as since codified by the 1982 United Nations Convention on the Law of the Sea (hereinafter "the LOS Convention").[3]

The oceans bind humanity together and few will dispute that the problems associated with the use of maritime space continue to challenge the

---

259–282; Hans-Joachim Rätz et al., "Complementary roles of European and national institutions under the Common Fisheries Policy and the Marine Strategy Framework Directive", (2010) 34 *Marine Policy* 1028–1035; N. Westaway "The New European Marine Strategy Framework Directive" (2008) 10 *Env L Rev* 218–224.

2 Alfred Thayer Mahan, *The Influence of Sea Power upon History, 1660–1783* (London: Sampson Low, Marston and Company, Ltd., 1890), p. 25.

3 The inclusion of Annex IX in the Law of the Sea Convention enabled the predecessor to the EU, European Community (EC), to sign the treaty on 7 December 1984. The EC signed the Agreement on Part XI in 1994 and deposited its instrument of formal confirmation for both the Convention and the Part XI Agreement with the Secretary-General of the United Nations in 1998. The instrument which provides for EC participation is Council Decision 98/414/EC, OJ L 189/14, 3.07.1998.

international community to seek innovative solutions to complex regulatory questions.[4] In this quest, it is evident that the law of the sea is not immutable and that the intensive uses of the ocean and the regional seas around Europe requires further regulatory action, by means of the implementation of the LOS Convention and a broad swathe of related instruments, as well as by giving effect to more specific EU legislation concerning maritime safety and the protection of the marine environment. A brief perusal of current regulatory measures reveals that a wide range of factors including trade, international peace and security, as well as social and environmental considerations, are shaping EU policy in relation to maritime matters including shipping.

What is most noticeable is that in responding to the new challenges encountered in ocean governance, the regulatory rejoinder by the European institutions is increasingly informed by a new generation of normative principles that are based upon scientific knowledge about the marine environment, as well as the processes and phenomena that take place therein.[5] More thought provoking from a law of the sea perspective is that many of these tools, such as the ecosystem approach, are applied at a pan-European level on the basis of ecological regions and not on the basis of the maritime jurisdictional zones established by the Member States in accordance with the LOS Convention.[6] Indeed, as pointed out by a number of scholars in the specialist literature, the spatial extent of marine ecosystems is seldom coterminous with the maritime boundaries of the Member States and third countries.[7] As a result, the manner in which Europe is addressing concerns about the health of marine ecosystems is very much focused on tackling cumulative anthropogenic impacts on the marine environment in a holistic and integrated manner by means of cross-cutting and sophisticated regulatory instruments that aim to translate the ecosystem-based approach into coherent policy advice and legislative action. Equally, as noted previously in a number of my papers on this subject,

---

4 This is implicit as is evident from text of the Preamble, United Nations Convention on the Law of the Sea.
5 R. Long, "Principles and normative trends in European Union ocean governance" in C. Schofield, S. Lee, M. Kwon (eds.), *The Limits Of Maritime Jurisdiction* (Boston/Leiden, Brill/Nijhoff, Publishers, 2014), pp. 629–726.
6 R. Long, "Legal Aspects of Ecosystem-Based Marine Management in Europe" in A. Chircop, M.L. McConnell, S. Coffen-Smout (eds.), *Ocean Yearbook* Vol. 26, (Boston/Leiden, Brill Academic Publishers, 2012) pp. 417–484.
7 See *inter alia*: S.M. Garcia, M. Hayashi, "Division of the Oceans and Ecosystem: A contrastive spatial evolution of marine fisheries, 43 (6) 2000 *Ocean and Coastal Management*, pp. 445–474; Y. Tanaka, *A Dual Approach to Ocean Governance*, (Farnham, Ashgate, 2010) *passim*.

many of these instruments are transboundary in geographical and material scope.[8] Over the coming years, the implementation of these instruments will definitely test the structure and function of the regulatory framework, as well as the finely tuned equilibrium of rights and duties, codified in the LOS Convention and in related agreements.

A Finely Tuned Equilibrium of Rights and Duties

One of the enduring characteristics of the LOS Convention is the manner in which it skillfully balances rights and duties in an equitable manner and advances global interests for the benefit of the common good. This balance is very much evident in the key provisions of the Convention, that codify the traditional right of innocent passage through the territorial sea,[9] that provide for transit passage through straits that are used for international navigation,[10] and for archipelagic sea-lane passage in archipelagic waters,[11] as well as the many ambulatory references to the freedom of navigation in the Exclusive Economic Zone and on the high seas that permeate the entire text of the Convention (see Table 1 below).[12]

As is almost universally accepted, the provisions on navigation rights and other freedoms are the very backbone of the LOS Convention in that they facilitate international trade, communications, security and maritime transport. What is more, experience over the past three decades has revealed that they are fundamental to the effective working of the international legal order and the rule of law as it applies to the ocean. They are also finely poised with the many provisions in the LOS Convention that are aimed at the protection and preservation of the marine environment.[13] In this respect, it should also not be forgotten that the shipping industry is a major contributor to global greenhouse gas emissions and is a major polluter of the marine environment in its

---

8   See, for example, R. Long, "Stepping over Maritime Boundaries to Apply New Normative Tools in EU Law and Policy" in M. Nordquist, J. Norton Moore, (eds.), *Maritime Border Diplomacy* (Boston/Leiden, Martinus Nijhoff Publishers, 2012) pp. 213–264.
9   Arts 17–26, LOS Convention.
10 Arts 38, 39, 40, 41(7), 42(1), 42(2), 42(4), 44 and 45(1)(a), LOS Convention.
11 Arts 53(2), 53(5), 53(12), and 54, LOS Convention.
12 In the EEZ, Arts 38(2), 58(1) and 297(1)(a), LOS Convention. On the high seas, Arts 38(2), 87(1)(a) and 297(1)(a), LOS Convention.
13 Part XII: Arts 192, 194, 194(3), vessel source pollution, 210, 211, 219–221, and 234, LOS Convention.

own right.[14] More so because the term "pollution" is defined expansively by the LOS Convention to include:

> ... the introduction of substances or energy into the marine environment, including estuaries, which results or is likely to result in such deleterious effects as harm to living resources and marine life, hazards to human health, hindrance to marine activities, including fishing and other legitimate uses of the sea, impairment of quality for use of sea water and reduction of amenities.[15]

All forms of marine pollution come within the scope of this definition. Hence, the challenge faced by the EU is how best to abate pollution and achieve good environmental status of the European marine environment under the MSF Directive in sea areas under the sovereignty and jurisdiction of the EU Member States, and at the same time continue to show "due regard" to the other rights and duties that are codified by the LOS Convention, in particular as regards navigation and overflight.[16] As will be seen below, the stand-alone nature of EU policies on key sectors such as transport, environment, fisheries, trade, energy, together with the many other commercial activities that impinge upon maritime affairs, exacerbate this task and make it more difficult to bring about fundamental reform to the regulatory regimes applicable to individual maritime sectors.

One of the solutions tabled by the European Commission to address this conundrum comes in the form of a legislative proposal establishing a framework for maritime spatial planning and integrated coastal management (hereinafter the "Draft MSP Directive").[17] Briefly stated, this instrument requires all coastal Member States of the EU to adopt maritime spatial plans with respect to all offshore activities taking place in sea areas under their sovereignty or

---

14 See Second IMO GHG Study 2009 (London: IMO, 2010). Available at: http://www.imo.org/blast/blastDataHelper.asp?data_id=27795&filename=GHGStudyFINAL.pdf.
15 Preamble, LOS Convention.
16 Article 52(2), LOS Convention. In addition Articles 58, 59 and 60 deal with the relationship between the right and duties of other States and the coastal State in the Exclusive Economic Zone. See Nordquist (et al.) *United Nations Convention on the Law of the Sea 1982: A Commentary* (Dordrecht/Boston/Lancaster, Martinus Nijhoff Publishers, 1985) Vol. II, 491–817, especially at 553–565, 188–200 at 186.
17 Proposal for a Directive of the European Parliament and of the Council establishing a framework for maritime spatial planning and integrated coastal management. COM(2013) 133 final, SWD(2013) 65 final, Brussels, 12.3.2013. Available at: http://eur-lex.europa.eu/LexUriServ/LexUriServ.do?uri=COM:2013:0133:FIN:EN:PDF

jurisdiction, as well as strategies governing development in the coastal zone. As will be seen, an ancillary objective of this instrument is to develop maritime transport by providing "efficient and cost-effective shipping routes across Europe, including port accessibility and transport safety."[18] At the same time, it strives to ensure the prudent use of natural resources such as fisheries, the protection of the environment, the security of energy supply, as well as to improve coastal resilience to the effects of climate change.[19]

In light of these diffuse and somewhat competing objectives, the focus of this paper is to explore how, and if, the EU upholds international navigation rights and freedoms under the proposed framework set down by the Draft MSP Directive. The importance of this instrument should not be underestimated and we can anticipate considerable controversy over the coming years about the designation of maritime areas for different development activities. At this point in time in the initial stages of the EU law-making process, one can legitimately pose the question: What will designations of maritime space mean in practice for the shipping industry and its ability to exercise navigation rights and freedoms under the LOS Convention?

This paper does not attempt to provide a definitive answer to this question but reviews a number regulatory factors and other considerations that will have a bearing on the capacity of the EU to strike an appropriate balance between ecosystem considerations under the European MSF Directive, navigation rights and freedoms under the LOS Convention, and spatial management measures under the Draft MSP Directive. In doing so, it is hoped that the EU and the Member States remain true to the letter and spirit of the LOS Convention and maintain free and largely unimpeded navigation in European waters and set an important precedent to be followed by coastal States worldwide. Before turning to some of the key issues, we can elaborate a little more about the importance of shipping and maritime trade to the future economic prosperity of Europe in order to give greater context to the discussion further on below.[20]

---

18   Article 5(b) of Draft MSP & ICM Directive. COM(2013) 133 final, Brussels, 12.3.2013.
19   Article 5(a), (c), (d) and (e) of Draft MSP & ICM Directive.
20   Unusually, this is not mentioned in the European Commission's report on the first phase of implementation of the MSF Directive COM(2014) 97 final, Brussels, 20.02.2014. See discussion *infra*.

TABLE 1   *Navigation rights and freedoms under the LOS Convention*

Navigation Rights / Freedoms	Environment considerations /Sea lanes and traffic separation schemes
Innocent passage (Part II (Art 19))	**Laws and regulations of coastal States** • Preservation of the environment of the coastal State (Art 21(1)(f)) • Coastal State may designate or prescribe sea lanes or traffic separation schemes (Art 22)
Transit passage in straits used for international navigation (Part III)	**Laws and regulations of straits States** • Sea lanes and traffic separation schemes (Art 41) • Prevention, reduction and control of pollution by giving effect to the applicable international standards regarding the discharge of oily substances (Art 42 (1)(b)) • Strait States must not deny, hamper, or impair the right of transit passage. (Arts 42(2), 44)
Archipelagic sea lanes passage (Part IV)	**Laws and regulations of archipelagic States** • Designation of sea lanes, prescribe traffic separation schemes, refer proposals to competent international organisations, exercise of rights (Art 53) • Prevention, reduction and control of pollution by giving effect to the applicable international standards regarding the discharge of oily substances (Art 54 and Art 42 (1)(b) *mutatis mutandis*) • Archipelagic States must not deny, hamper, or impair the right of archipelagic sea lane passage. (Art 54 and Art 42 (2) *mutatis mutandis*)
Freedom of navigation in the EEZ and on the high seas/EEZ	In the EEZ, Arts 38(2), 58(1) and 297(1)(a), LOS Convention. On the high seas, Arts 38(2), 87(1)(a) and 297(1)(a), LOS Convention. Part XII: Arts 192, 194, 194(3), vessel source pollution, 210, 211, 219–221, 234

Importance of Shipping and Maritime Trade to the EU

The significance and relative importance of the shipping sector in Europe is best appreciated when one considers that the EU is made-up of 23 coastal Member States, which shares 70,000 km of coastline along two oceans (the Atlantic and the Arctic Oceans) and bordered by four regional seas: the Baltic, the North Sea, the Mediterranean, and the Black Sea. These are important areas for the movement of persons, goods and services. The European Maritime Safety Agency estimates that there are well over 17,000 ships on passage in EU waters on a daily basis and this figure is generally indicative of the intensity of maritime traffic.[21] Indeed, the European Commission has indicated that 90% of the EU's external trade in terms of volume and close to 40% of its internal trade is seaborne.[22] In addition, 400 million passengers embark and disembark in European ports annually.[23] Equally impressive and not well known, 25% of world tonnage is registered in the Member States, with 40% of global shipping in gross tonnage under the control of companies or natural persons that are incorporated or located in the European Economic Area.[24] Despite the fiscal austerity programme in many EU countries and the slow recovery from global recession, the European Environmental Agency forecasts that the transport of freight by shipping is expected to grow by between 3% and 4% per annum over the next decade.[25] What is more, it also forecasts that the shipbuilding industry will grow in response to increased demand for more fuel-efficient ships fit-

---

21   This figure relates only the vessels that are tracked by EMSA using AIS in accordance with the requirements of Directive 2002/59/EC, as since amended. See, European Maritime Safety Agency, Annual Report 2012, (Lisbon: ENSA, 2013) at 35.

22   Communication from the Commission to the European Parliament, the Council, the European Economic and Social Committee and the Committee of the Regions—Strategic goals and recommendations for the EU's maritime transport policy until 2018, COM(2009) 8 final, Brussels, 21.1.2009.

23   Ibid. at 2.

24   In addition to the 28 EU Member States, Iceland, Liechtenstein and Norway are part of the EEA. These countries have adopted the majority of the EU rules on the internal market apart from those on fisheries and agriculture. Information on the size of the shipping fleet controlled from EEA States is available from the ECSA Annual Report 2011–2012 (Brussels: ECSA, 2013) at p. 9. Available at: http://www.ecsa.eu/files/Annual_report_ECSA_2012.pdf.

25   European Environment agency, Marine messages, Our seas, our future—moving towards a new understanding (Copenhagen: EPA, 2014) at 18.

ted out with new technologies to reduce costs and the environmental footprint of the sector.[26]

The relative upbeat nature of these forecasts is not all pervasive and many industry representative bodies have voiced their concerns about the challenges faced by the industry in the years ahead. The European Community Shipowners' Association (ECSA), for example, has pointed out that high operational costs, over capacity and poor economic prospects, continue to make global and European markets extremely difficult for the provision of shipping services.[27] The industry also asserts that further impediments to growth arise from the ever-increasing regulatory burden imposed on shipping with a view to achieving IMO and European environmental and maritime safety standards.[28]

Such difficulties are sometimes exacerbated by the increasing scope for conflict between the shipping sector and other uses of the marine environment such as offshore wind energy development. The impact of offshore development such as wind farms in the vicinity of busy shipping lanes has been highlighted by the Baltic and International Maritime Council (BIMCO) in their correspondence with the European Commission regarding the proposed regulatory measures on spatial planning set down in the Draft MSP Directive.[29] Their concerns are not remarkable as European shipping interests have always defended robustly navigation rights and associated freedoms, as well as easy access to distance markets, which are central to the success of EU trade and competition policies. The ECSA has suggested that environmental measures ought to be adopted at a multilateral level under the auspices of the IMO and not at the level of a regional integration organization, such as the EU.[30] That said, the European institutions have adopted a comprehensive regulatory code that addresses sub-standard shipping, reducing the risk of maritime incidents, as well as mitigating the environmental footprint of the shipping sector.[31] In line with EU primary and secondary law, moreover, the EU has adopted extensive marine environmental measures that are applicable to maritime spaces both within and beyond the jurisdiction of the Member States. Periodically, the European institutions publish comprehensive reports on the effectiveness

---

26 Ibid.
27 ECSA Annual Report 2011–2012 (Brussels: ECSA, 2013) at 9–10.
28 Ibid.
29 See BIMCO contribution to the consultation on MSP and ICZM, sent on 19 May 2011, para. 55. BIMCO is the one of the world's leading international shipping associations and represents the interests of shipowners, operators, managers, brokers and agents.
30 ECSA Annual Report 2011–2012 (Brussels: ECSA, 2013) at p. 58.
31 Discussed *infra*.

of these measures and on the status of the marine environment, which more often than not make a pretty disheartening read.

Status of the European Marine Environment, the Ecosystem Approach and the MSF Directive

The European marine environment is diverse and subject to many pressures resulting from human interactions with the sea. In particular, the effects of climate change, over-fishing, land-based pollution of the coastal environment, litter, as well as the predominance of new alien and invasive species, continue to expose the ineffectiveness of EU policies and legislation in curbing the degradation of the marine environment. This trend is clearly evident if one takes a look at the European Commission's first assessment and guidance report on the implementation of the MSF Directive, which concludes that the European regional seas are not in a "good environmental status" due to catastrophic depletion of fish stocks in the Atlantic, Mediterranean and Black Seas.[32] This is compounded by high levels of eutrophication in the Baltic and Black Seas, widespread evidence of marine litter in the North Sea and Atlantic, as well as the loss or depletion of marine species, habitats and fragile ecosystems, that are all purportedly protected under nature conservation instruments.[33]

The reports of the European Environmental Agency are no better and describe the "worrying state" of European regional seas with sea surface temperature increasing 10 fold since 1870.[34] The EEA further report the disappearance of biodiversity including almost the entire population of European eel.[35] They note that the implementation of the MSF Directive and ecosystem-based approach are in their infancy and that much more political and legal effort is required on the part of the Member States to ensure that they discharge their regulatory obligations to protect and preserve the marine environment.[36]

Consequently, the Draft MSP Directive should not be viewed as a standalone instrument as it is intended clearly intended to supplement a whole range of EU legislative measures including the Birds and Habitats Directives,

---

[32] European Commission's report on the first phase of implementation of the MSF Directive COM(2014) 97 final, Brussels, 20.02.2014.
[33] Ibid. at 3–4.
[34] European Environmental Agency, "Marine messages, Our seas, our future—moving towards a new understanding" (Luxembourg: EEA, 2014).
[35] Ibid.
[36] Ibid.

which provide for the establishment of a coherent network of protected areas in the European marine environment.[37] Indeed, consolidating this crucial link is also one of the objectives of the MSF Directive, which provides expressly that the programmes of measures adopted by the Member States must include spatial protection measures under the Birds and Habitats Directives, as well as other marine protected areas designated by international or regional bodies.[38] In this regard, if shipping activity has a significant impact on the environment, Member States are compelled under the MSF Directive to work with the competent international body (i.e., the IMO) in taking appropriate measures to ensure the maintenance and restoration of the integrity, structure and functioning of ecosystems.[39] The MSP Directive will also supplement EU instruments on strategic environmental assessment and project based assessment.[40] Significantly, the EEA has noted the absence of a "correct spatial scale" at which an ecosystem-based approach should be implemented under the MSF Directive.[41] Moreover, it has suggested, "the appropriate scale should be determined by the connections between ecosystem features and human activities."[42]

According to this analysis, Member States have to consider pooling their efforts and to grasp the underlying premise that ecosystem-based management entails a number of trade-offs between policy objectives, sectors and spatial boundaries. Instructively, ecosystem-based management is defined by the EEA to mean "an integrated approach to management that considers the entire ecosystem including humans. The goal is to maintain ecosystems in a

---

37 Council Directive 92/43/EEC of 21 May 1992 on the conservation of natural habitats and of wild fauna and flora OJ L 2067, 22.7.1992; Council Directive 79/409/EEC of 2 April 1979 on the conservation of wild birds, O.J. L 103/1, 25.04.1979. Subsequently codified by Directive 2009/147/EC of the European Parliament and of the Council of 30 November 2009 on the conservation of wild birds OJ L 20/7, 26.1.2010. Council Directive 92/43/EEC of 21 May 1992 on the conservation of natural habitats and of wild fauna and flora OJ L 206/7, 22.7.1992. Consolidated version published on 1.01.2007. There is a substantial volume of case law in the European Court of Justice on both directives.
38 Article 13(4) of Directive 2008/56/EC.
39 Article 13(4) of Directive 2008/56/EC.
40 Council Directive 2001/42/EC of the European Parliament and of the Council of 27 June 2001 on the assessment of the effects of certain plans and programmes on the environment, OJ L 197/30, 21.7.2001; codified version of Directive 2011/92/EU of 13 December 2011 on the assessment of the effects of certain public and private projects on the environment, OJ L 26/1, 28.1.2012.
41 European Environmental Agency, "Marine messages, Our seas, our future—moving towards a new understanding" (Luxembourg: EEA, 2014) at 8.
42 Ibid.

healthy, clean, productive and resilient condition, so that they can provide humans with the services and benefits upon which we depend."[43] Furthermore, the EEA is of the view that this is very much the antithesis of the traditional EU regulatory approach, which addresses single concerns such as maritime sectors (fisheries or shipping), activities (renewable energy), or individual species or populations (cetaceans). Plainly, ecosystem-based management is best introduced or facilitated through a system of marine/maritime spatial planning, a prospect which may well open its own Pandora's box of legal issues pertaining to the implementation of the LOS Convention and the safeguarding of navigation rights and freedoms codified therein.

What is Marine/Maritime Spatial Planning?

There are many definitions of what constitutes maritime/marine spatial planning in the specialist literature.[44] There is no express reference to spatial planning in the LOS Convention but this does not appear to have deterred many coastal States worldwide including Belgium, the Netherlands, Germany, the United States and Canada,[45] as well as numerous international bodies including UNESCO and the OECD, from promoting and implementing maritime spatial planning in some shape or form.[46] In Europe, there have also been several MSP and integrated coastal zone management initiatives taken by the regional seas bodies, as can be seen from the information shown on Table 2

---

43   The EEA report cites K. McLeod, H. Leslie, (eds.), *Ecosystem-Based Management for the Oceans* (Washington: Islands Press, 2009).

44   On the policy literature, see, *inter alia*: F. Maes, "The international legal framework for Marine Spatial Planning" (2008) 32 *Marine Policy* 797–810; F. Douvere, "The importance of marine spatial planning in advancing ecosystem-based sea use management" (2008) 32(5) *Marine Policy* 762–771; J. Taussik, "The opportunities of spatial planning for integrated coastal zone management" (2007) 31(5) *Marine Policy* 611–618.

45   See *inter alia*: C. Ehler, Myths of Marine Spatial Planning, (2012) 13 *Marine Ecosystems and Management*, 5–7; F. Douvere, C. Ehler, "Marine Spatial Planning: identifying the critical elements for success" in E. Ciccotelli, C. Benigno, eds. *Spatial Planning: Strategies, Developments and Management* (Hauppauge: Nova Sciences Publishers, 2012) at 233–250; F. Douvere, C.N. Ehler, "New perspectives on sea use management: Initial findings from European experience with marine spatial planning" (2009) 90 *Journal of Environmental Management* 77–88; F. Douvere *Marine Spatial Planning: Concepts, current practice and linkages to other management approaches* (Ghent: Ghent University, 2010) 124 pp.

46   See D. Rothwell, T. Stephens, *The International Law of the Sea* (Oxford and Portland, Oregon: Hart Publishing, 2010) 465–467.

below.[47] The mandate of the latter bodies is however extremely limited and as a consequence there are legal constraints in establishing appropriate regional measures governing all aspects of spatial planning in the marine environment.

One can learn from practice in the United States, where Executive Order 13547, *Stewardship of the Ocean, Our Coasts, and the Great Lakes*, sheds considerable light on the subject matter of spatial planning in that it provides:

> ...for the development of coastal and marine spatial plans that build upon and improve existing Federal, State, tribal, local, and regional decision making and planning processes. These regional plans will enable a more integrated, comprehensive, ecosystem-based, flexible, and proactive approach to planning and managing sustainable multiple uses across sectors and improve the conservation of the ocean, our coasts, and the Great Lakes.[48]

Instructively, the Executive Order defines "coastal and marine spatial planning" to mean:

> ...a comprehensive, adaptive, integrated, ecosystem-based, and transparent spatial planning process, based on sound science, for analyzing current and anticipated uses of ocean, coastal, and Great Lakes areas. Coastal and marine spatial planning identifies areas most suitable for various types or classes of activities in order to reduce conflicts among uses, reduce environmental impacts, facilitate compatible uses, and preserve critical ecosystem services to meet economic, environmental, security, and social objectives. In practical terms, coastal and marine spatial planning provides a public policy process for society to better determine how the ocean, our coasts, and Great Lakes are sustainably used and protected—now and for future generations.[49]

The importance of biological diversity of the oceans is noted in the Executive Order, which also highlights the exercise of "rights and ... duties in accordance

---

47 Source: Impact Assessment, Accompanying the Proposal for a Directive of the European Parliament and of the Council establishing a framework for maritime spatial planning and integrated coastal management, COM(2013) 133 final, SWD(2013) 65 final, Brussels, 12.3.2013, at 30–31.

48 Executive Order 13547, *Stewardship of the Ocean, Our Coasts, and the Great Lakes*, 19 July 2010.

49 Ibid.

with applicable international law, including respect for and preservation of navigational rights and freedoms, which are essential for the global economy and international peace and security".[50] The latter statement is unequivocal and again it is interesting to note that the US policy on MSP is inextricably linked with the promotion of environmental sustainability, international trade, as well as with maritime security. Crucially, navigation freedoms are a central aspect of US policy and solidly embedded in the ocean management paradigm foreseen and advanced by means of the Executive Order.

Coastal State practice in the EU supports the view that that MSP is a process leading to the development and implementation of maritime spatial plan(s) by the Member States.[51] Such plans identify and determine the range of maritime activities that ought to take place in a given spatial area. They also take into consideration the outcomes of stakeholder consultation and reflect an integrated ecosystem-based approach to management decisions with a view to achieving the desired economic, ecological and social objectives. Put another way, first and foremost, MSP is a strategic planning tool to control development and other activities that take place in the marine environment.[52]

Controlling and influencing the land-sea interactions are of fundamental importance if ecosystem-based management is to be implemented successfully by reliance on spatial management measures. Although much of the scholarship on the legal analysis of this subject in its infancy and requires further elaboration, MSP can be distinguished from terrestrial planning of the land environment on a number of grounds: first, it has more complex spatial dimensions that encompass the seabed, the water column, the surface of the ocean, and the airspace in the territorial sea and archipelagic waters; second, ocean space is not subject to private ownership but remains in principle a public resource; third, the rights and jurisdictions of States vary considerably in different maritime jurisdictional zones in the form of the obligations and entitlements imposed on the flag State, coastal State and port State.[53]

---

50   Ibid.
51   Most notably, the practice of Belgium, Germany, Greece, France, Malta, the Netherlands, Portugal and Slovenia, and perhaps to a lesser extent the United Kingdom. See COM(2013) 133 final, SWD(2013) 65 final, Brussels, 12.3.2013, at 27–28.
52   Impact Assessment, Accompanying the Proposal for a Directive of the European Parliament and of the Council establishing a framework for maritime spatial planning and integrated coastal management, COM(2013) 133 final, SWD(2013) 65 final, Brussels, 12.3.2013.
53   For an incisive overview of some of the differences, see A. Slater, "What is marine planning?" (2012) 14(1) *Environmental Law Review* 1–6.

To this assessment, we should also add that the principal jurisdictional framework for regulating and controlling human interactions with the ocean is well established at a multilateral level in the form of the LOS Convention and related international and regional agreements. This has many implications for the rolling-out of maritime spatial plans at national levels in the EU and elsewhere. In marked contrast to town and county planning, for instance, EU Member States are required to give "due regard" to the rights and duties of other States in exercising their rights in the EEZ.[54] Similarly, the transnational nature of international trade and shipping is perhaps one of the best ways to distinguish the activities that are subject to marine spatial planning from the subject matter of its terrestrial equivalent. Another point of distinction is that MSP is very much science driven and the Draft MSP Directive places a clear emphasis on the collection of environmental, economic, and social data for planning purposes, with these requirements extending to the acquisition of oceanographic and geomorphological data.[55]

The marine environment is exceptionally dynamic and is likely to remain so as a result of the extreme weather events associated with the effects of climate change. Furthermore, regulatory practice and policy initiatives in both the United States and the EU indicates that MSP is very much informed by the ecosystem-approach to marine resource management with a view to ensuring that the natural environment is not compromised by the anthropogenic impacts of human activities. One should not take this distinction too far as circumstances will often necessitate the adoption of a coordinated approach to MSP and to terrestrial planning with a view to ensuring that the two systems are closely linked. In particular, the land sea-interface is crucial for the successful planning of port infrastructure and other physical developments in the coastal environment and this is going to be achieved at a pan-European level through the adoption of integrated coastal management strategies.

---

54 Article 56(2), LOS Convention.
55 Article 10 of the Draft MSP Directive.

TABLE 2   MSP and ICZM activities undertaken under European Regional Seas Conventions[56]

Regional Seas Convention	MSP and/or ICZM Guidance?	Regional MSP and/or ICZM forum?	Non-Binding MSP and/or ICZM legislation?	Binding MSP and or ICZM legislation?
OSPAR Convention for the Protection of the Marine Environment of the North-East Atlantic	No, but the need for OSPAR measures is under consideration	Yes, the Environmental Impacts of Human Activities Committee	No	No
Helsinki Convention on the Protection of the Marine Environment of the Baltic Sea Area	Principles, Guidance documents, on-going project (PlanBothnia)	Yes, a joint Working Group with VASAB on MSP, HELCOM-GIS webpage	Yes, Recommendations for both MSP and ICZM	No Yes, for ICZM applicable in national waters
Barcelona Convention for the Protection of the Mediterranean Sea Against Pollution	Yes	Yes, regional co-operation as a part of the protocol implementation	No	Yes, for ICZM applicable in national waters
Convention on the Protection of the Black Sea Against Pollution	Yes	Yes	No	No

56   Source European Commission, COM(2013) 133 final, SWD(2013) 65 final, Brussels, 12.3.2013.

Form and Legislative History of MSP in the EU

The EU has a sophisticated array of secondary legislation and other measures in the form of regulations, directives and decisions, as well as recommendations, to give effect to European policies pertaining to marine and oceanic matters.[57] For those that are unfamiliar with the European legal order, it is important to note that directives are unique legal instruments, which are legally binding in relation to the results to be achieved, but leave considerable discretion to the national authorities in the Member States in selecting the most appropriate form and methods on implementation.[58] This flexibility means, on the one hand, that directives are a particularly suitable instrument to harmonize policy or thematic areas such as those associated with maritime affairs, which are often inherently complex or legally multifaceted with different approaches evident in the national jurisdictions of the 28 EU Member States. On the other hand, the requirements set down in a directive must be transposed into national law and Member States have not always been fastidious in meeting their European obligations in this regard, particularly when it comes to meeting EU obligations to protect and preserve the marine environment. In view of the diverse practice of the Member States in relation to the licensing and planning of offshore activities, it comes as no surprise that the European institutions selected this means of regulatory intervention (a directive) to set out in rather general terms what needs to be done in relation to MSP and coastal zone management. This broad scheme set down in the Draft MSP Directive will have to be followed by more detailed measures, normally legislation, in the Member States.

The origins of the Draft MSP Directive may be traced back to the EU's Integrated Maritime Policy and a number of specialist publications by the European Commission including a so-called *Roadmap for Maritime Spatial Planning: Achieving Common Principles in the EU*.[59] The latter defined MSP as: "a process that consists of data collection, stakeholder consultation and the participatory development of a plan, the subsequent stages of implementation, enforcement, evaluation and revision."[60] Importantly the *Roadmap* notes the fundamental importance of the principle of freedom of navigation under the LOS Convention, which it points out is conditioned or balanced by rules and

---

57   Article 288, Treaty on the Functioning of the European Union.
58   Ibid.
59   COM(2008) 791 final, Brussels, 25.11.2008.
60   Ibid., at 3.

standards on maritime safety and the protection of the marine environment.[61] The role of the International Maritime Organisation (IMO) in adopting the appropriate rules and standards for shipping and maritime transport, such as traffic separation schemes, is fully acknowledged, as is the primacy of international agreements including the Protocol to the London Convention, which regulates dumping at sea.[62]

The *Roadmap* was followed by a second Communication mapping out the achievements and the scope for the future development of MSP in the EU.[63] Specifically, shipping is mentioned as one of the areas where EU Member States ought to have a joint vision based upon common interests. In many respects, the Communication sets out a far more coherent view of the relevance of maritime spatial planning to the future growth and development of the European shipping industry in that it acknowledges that maritime transport is regulated at a multilateral level, through various international agreements including the LOS Convention, as well as by IMO Conventions and Resolutions.[64] At the same time, the Communication notes that the EU had adopted Directive 2002/59/EC, which establishes a vessel traffic monitoring and information system in the Member States.[65] In the words of the European Commission, MSP can support the implementation of this Directive by ensuring the coordination of the related spatial measures.[66] Subsequently, the European Commission undertook extensive stakeholder consultation with the public and specialist interest groups, which revealed that these were largely supportive of the introduction of spatial planning to address trans-boundary activities such as shipping, fishing, seabed cables, offshore energy, and for the purpose of protecting and preserving the marine environment.[67] In 2011, the European Commission published a study on the economic effects of MSP, which identified a number of benefits that could be derived from its introduction including enhancing

---

61 Ibid., at 6.
62 Ibid., at 7.
63 COM(2010) 771 final, Brussels, 17.12.2010.
64 Ibid., at 8.
65 Directive 2002/59/EC of the European Parliament and of the Council of 27 June 2002 establishing a Community vessel traffic monitoring and information system and repealing Council Directive 93/75/EEC, OJ L 208/10, 05.08.2002.
66 COM(2010) 771 final, Brussels, 17.12.2010 at 8.
67 Summary report available at: http://ec.europa.eu/dgs/maritimeaffairs_fisheries/consultations/msp/summary-results-of-msp-questionnaire_en.pdf.

co-ordination of decision-making, legal certainty for stakeholders, and greater coherence with other planning systems including coastal zone management.[68]

Given the complexity of the issues to be addressed and in light of the diversity of Member State practice in relation to spatial planning matters on land and at sea, the European Commission published a proposal for a Directive of the European Parliament and the European Council establishing a framework for maritime spatial planning and integrated coastal management in March 2013.[69] The Commission expressed the view that the selection of this particular form of instrument, that is to say a directive, will allow Member States to shape the national transposition measures to reflect their economic, social and environmental policies, as well as their distinctive legal traditions.[70] The Draft MSP Directive is at the time of writing following the law-making procedures in the European institutions and will require the approval of both the Council and Parliament before it passes into law. This process may take-up to two years to complete and there are many opportunities for the introduction of amendments and revisions to the Commission's initial legislative proposal. Notably, the European Parliament put forward many amendments to the proposal at its first reading in December 2013 and referred the proposal back to the competent committee for re-consideration prior to voting, which was postponed to a later plenary session in 2014. Some of the proposed amendments tabled by the Parliament are discussed below.[71]

Objectives of the Draft MSP Directive

The Draft MSP Directive, similar to the United States Executive Order 13547, *Stewardship of the Ocean, Our Coasts, and the Great Lakes* as seen above, does not have a single purpose but is intended to address a whole range of concerns that impinge upon maritime transport, offshore development and the protection of the marine environment. Noticeably, the importance of avoiding conflicts between different commercial sectors regarding the use of maritime space is the principal purpose of the Draft MSP Directive. In this respect,

---

68   Study on the economic effects of Maritime Spatial Planning: Final Report, (Luxembourg: European Commission, 2011). Available at: http://ec.europa.eu/maritimeaffairs/documentation/studies/documents/economic_effects_maritime_spatial_planning_en.pdf.
69   COM(2013) 133 final. Brussels, 12.3.2013.
70   Ibid.
71   See, See European Parliament: Legislative Observatory. 013/0074(COD)—12/12/2013. Procedural file on maritime spatial planning and integrated coastal management.

the Directive aims to contribute to a number of specific objectives, which are extremely broad in ambit in so far as they include: promoting energy security; the development of alternative sources of marine energy; fostering the growth of fisheries and aquaculture; improving environmental protection in line with the objectives of various EU secondary legislation; and combating the effects of climate change.[72] At the heart of these objectives, as mentioned previously, is the goal of improving maritime transport safety, access to ports, and the provision of shipping routes.[73] On a similar note, the European Parliament highlighted the importance of establishing a framework that promotes the growth of maritime and coastal economies and the sustainable use of marine and coastal resources.[74] Moreover, the European Parliament expressed the view that MSP and ICM should contribute to the following objectives: "promoting multimodal links and sustainability; fostering the sustainable development of the fisheries sector and sustainable growth of the aquaculture sector; ensuring the preservation, protection and improvement of the environment through a representative and coherent network of protected areas and reduce and prevent marine and coastal areas pollution risks; and protect vulnerable coastal areas."[75]

An obvious and somewhat surprising omission in both the original proposal from the Commission and the amendments tabled by the Parliament in December 2013 is the absence of any specific reference of the importance of international law rights and duties in relation to shipping, including respect for and the preservation of navigational rights and freedoms under the LOS Convention. Indisputably, this ought to be one of the objectives of the Draft MSP Directive if one is to take into consideration the fundamental importance of the free flow of shipping for the future prosperity and growth of the European economy.

Rationale Underpinning the MSP Proposal

The Draft MSP Directive *raison d'être* can be gleaned from the above-mentioned objectives. Predictably, the regulatory impact assessment of the Draft MSP

---

72 Article 5, Draft MSP Directive.
73 Ibid.
74 See European Parliament: Legislative Observatory. 013/0074(COD)—12/12/2013 Text adopted by Parliament, partial vote at 1st reading/single reading.
75 See European Parliament: Legislative Observatory. 013/0074(COD)—12/12/2013 Text adopted by Parliament, partial vote at 1st reading/single reading.

Directive published by the European Commission identified several problems pertaining to the "inefficient and unbalanced use of maritime and coastal space", the "suboptimal exploitation of economic potentials", and insufficient adaptation to climate change, as some of the principal reasons underpinning the need for EU legislative intervention in the domain of MSP.[76] Indeed, the rationale underpinning the Draft MSP Directive is founded ostensibly upon the belief that competition and conflicts pertaining to the use of maritime space is undermining the commercial development of various activities that are undertaken in the coastal environment and further offshore. In particular, competition between various sectors such as shipping, offshore energy, ports development, fisheries and aquaculture, as well as environmental considerations, are perceived as necessitating a more efficient planning framework for the use of maritime space.[77] Moreover the Draft MSP Directive is intended to give effect to a number of discrete European policies and strategies including: the Europe 2020 Strategy for smart, sustainable and inclusive growth;[78] the policy on the growth of maritime industries (referred to as "Blue Growth");[79] the so-called "Motorways of the Sea"; the EU's integrated maritime policy; as well as the common fisheries policy. Also, the Draft MSP Directive when adopted will complement many EU regulatory instruments that are applicable to the marine environment including the Renewable Energy Directive, as well as the Habitats and Birds Directives. Within this context, the Draft MSP Directive is aimed at introducing practical mechanisms in the form of planning tools that will facilitate Member States in discharging their various duties under the LOS Convention.[80]

As mentioned above, there is no express statement in the Draft MSP Directive about the importance of preserving navigational rights and freedoms or how such rights are essential for preserving the EU's economic prosperity, as well as its interest in promoting global stability, peace and security. This omission is all the more surprising as the importance of such rights were highlighted indirectly in the regulatory impact assessment, which called for the coordination of planning activities to avoid conflicts between shipping and other uses of the marine environment.[81] The assessment noted that shipping companies often contest decisions and engage in expensive legal redress

---

76   COM(2013) 133 final, SWD(2013) 65 final, Brussels, 12.3.2013, at 14–30.
77   COM(2008) 791 final, Brussels, 25.11.2008, at 2.
78   COM(2010) 2020 final.
79   COM(2013) 133 final, p. 6.
80   Recital 7, Preamble, Draft MSP Directive.
81   COM(2013) 133 final, SWD(2013) 65 final, Brussels, 12.3.2013, at 15–16.

regarding the location or adjustment of shipping lanes and navigation routes, and related port and infrastructural developments.[82] The need to coordinate Member State actions in relation to transnational transport routes and to work through the good offices of the IMO are undoubtedly fundamental to avoiding conflict between maritime transport and other sectors. Apart from setting down a requirement that Member States must take maritime transport routes into consideration in their maritime spatial plans, there is little else of substance regarding navigation rights and freedoms in the Draft MSP Directive as currently presented.[83] An obligation is placed on Member States, however, to take "into account" issues of a transnational nature and to ensure that their plans and strategies are coherent and coordinated with other Member States (emphasis added).[84]

Normative Justification

Apart from conflict avoidance and resolution, the normative methodology advanced by the Draft MSP Directive is aimed at implementing an ecosystem-based approach to manage the cross-boundary activities that take place in the marine environment.[85] This accords fully with the scheme of environmental protection set down by the MSF Directive, which aims to achieve good environmental status of all European marine waters by 2020.[86] Indicatively in light of the EU's predilection for economic development, "sustainable growth", "sustainable use" and "sustainable management" of marine and coastal resources, as well as in relation to the maritime economies of the Member States, are three of the themes that permeate the Draft MSP Directive. The importance of "sustainability" is also evident from the financial statement attached to the draft instrument, which emphasizes a similar theme and points out that "the ultimate objective of the proposal is to secure... *sustainable* economic growth... by considering the economic, social and environmental pillars of *sustainability* in line with the eco-system approach (emphasis added)."[87] Significantly, the Draft MSP Directive does not mention any of the other environmental principles that are enumerated in the Treaty on the Functioning

---

82 Ibid.
83 Article 7(2)(c), Draft MSP Directive.
84 Article 12(1) of the Draft MSP Directive.
85 Recital 15 of the Preamble and Article 5 of the Draft MSP Directive.
86 Article 3(5) of Directive 2008/56/EC.
87 COM(2013) 133 final, p. 6.

of the EU such as the precautionary principle, pollution should be rectified at source and that the polluter should pay.[88]

That said, many of the substantive and procedural provisions of the Draft MSP Directive reflect the principle of integration under the Treaty, which requires the incorporation of environmental considerations into all EU sector policies such as energy, fisheries, transport and communications, with a view to achieving sustainable development.[89] Indeed, one of the *leitmotifs* of the Draft MSP Directive is to improve the integrated planning and management of maritime infrastructure and systems that run across national borders such as pipelines, seabed cables, petroleum related development, impact of wind farms, as well as shipping lanes in areas where there is high maritime traffic. This accords fully with the EU's integrated maritime policy, which identifies the integrated management of various sector activities as one of the main ways to promote growth of the maritime and coastal economies in the Member States.[90] One should not ignore the natural environment when considering the utility of this paradigm, indeed the Preamble of the Draft MSP Directive points out that marine ecosystems and the services derived therefrom, if integrated into planning and management decisions concerning the use of maritime space and the coastal zone, are capable of delivering "substantial benefits in terms of food production, recreation and tourism, climate change mitigation and adaptation, shoreline dynamics control and disaster prevention."[91] The integrated management approach is of course foursquare with recent developments in international law and the move away from the zonal management approach, which is clearly linked with the spatial distribution of the rights and duties of States under the LOS Convention.[92] As noted in one significant study, however, the purpose of integrated management is not to replace one system with another but to resolve issues that are essentially transboundary in geographical and material scope and to provide appropriate mechanisms and procedures to ensure that this done in an expedient and efficient manner.[93] Indeed, there is considerable scope for the adoption of such an approach under the LOS Convention.

---

88   Article 191(2), TFEU.
89   Article 11, TFEU.
90   COM(2007) 575 final.
91   Recital 14, Preamble, Draft MSP Directive.
92   See UN General Assembly Resolution 60/30, Distrib. 8 March 2006.
93   See Y. Tanaka, *A Dual Approach to Ocean Governance*, (Farnham, Ashgate, 2010) 16–25, especially 21–25.

Which Legal Actors Are Subject to the Draft MSP Directive?

There are many interested parties concerned with activities that take place in the marine environment including public and private bodies in the Member States, bodies with international legal personality, non-governmental organisations, economic operators, as well as various other categories of stakeholders. That said, the principal legal actors under the scheme advanced by the Directive are quite clearly EU coastal States, and to a lesser extent, third countries that border the European regional seas. Somewhat predictably and in line with the division of legal competence under the EU Treaties, Member States remain fully responsible for agreeing to the substance of the plans and strategies that appertain to land and sea areas under their sovereignty and jurisdiction. They also retain full discretion regarding the apportionment of maritime space for different purposes, subject of course to the constraints imposed by international law on matters such as navigation rights. Moreover, the Draft MSP Directive does not appear to intrude upon the competence of national bodies to determine oceans-related matters, such as the utilization of natural resources. Indeed, as expressly stated in the Preamble, national bodies are fully responsible for the "full cycle of problem identification, information collection, planning, decision-making, implementation," as well as ensuring compliance with the national plan and strategies.[94]

The Draft MSP Directive does not appear to place any great onus on Member States to take specific management measures, apart from preparing an inventory of the actions that are required to be taken to "prevent erosion and manage accretion, adapt to the effects of climate change, combat coastal and marine litter, develop green infrastructure and help prevent natural disasters".[95] Likewise it does not dwell on the important functions discharged by international bodies in relation to the marine environment such as the regional seas bodies under the OSPAR, HELCOM and Barcelona Conventions. On the other hand, there is some emphasis on the collection of information about the marine environment and this will necessitate the consolidation of the nexus between the role of national bodies such as the regional seas commissions as well as specialist scientific bodies such as ICES. The European Parliament has also advocated for engagement with the relevant stakeholders and public so that their views are taken into account regarding the making and varying of plans and strategies by the Member States.[96]

---

94   Recital 13, Preamble, Draft MSP Directive.
95   Articles 5 and 8, Draft MSP Directive.
96   Ibid.

In general, one can conclude that all sectors concerned with maritime affairs will come within the planning and management schemes that are adopted by the Member States pursuant to the Draft MSP Directive. In this respect, the instrument is intended to complement many other EU measures that are much more sector-specific such as those concerning the maritime transport sector. Conversely, we can see some noticeable differences between the Draft MSP Directive and the approach taken by the EU to address specific sector problems such as vessel source pollution.

A Different Approach under the EU Directive on Ship Source Pollution

Noticeably, there are a number of questions that catch the eye about the extent of EU legislative and enforcement jurisdiction under the Draft MSP Directive, particularly when it is compared to the EU Directive on Ship Source Pollution.[97] The latter was first adopted in 2005 and has since been amended on a number of occasions. Perhaps it is best to start by pointing out that the EU transposes many of the international agreements adopted by international bodies such as the IMO by means of secondary legislation that binds the Member States. EU law is often drafted with a view to bolstering international measures and in response to the threats posed by shipping to marine biodiversity and the European coastal environment. These difficulties were highlighted in a dramatic and catastrophic fashion by the loss of the *Erika* in 1999 and again by the *Prestige* 2001. Similar to the loss of *Torrey Canyon* on the south coast of the United Kingdom in 1967, these events had a profound and long-lasting influence on the maritime policies pursued by European coastal States at the IMO and within the framework of EU law.[98] In particular, the EU through its Member States has actively sought to push forward a tougher regulatory agenda addressing the contributory causes of vessel source pollution at the

---

97 Directive 2005/35/EC of the European Parliament and of the Council of 7 September 2005 on ship-source pollution and on the introduction of penalties for infringements, OJ L 255, 30.9.2005; Directive 2009/123/EC of the European Parliament and of the Council of 21 October 2009 amending Directive 2005/35/EC on ship-source pollution and on the introduction of penalties for infringements, OJ L 280/52, 27.10.2009.

98 On vessel source pollution and tankers, see, M. Nordquist, "International Law Governing Places of Refuge for Tankers threatening Pollution of the Coastal Environments" in T. Malick Ndiaye, R. Wolfrum (ed.) *Law of the Sea, Environmental Law and Settlement of Disputes: Liber Amicorum Judge Thomas A. Mensah* (Leiden/Boston, Martinus Nijhoff, 2007) 497–519.

IMO.[99] In parallel, the EU has adopted a comprehensive package of legislative that impinges upon navigation rights and freedoms as codified in the LOS Convention, including the application of the criminal code to vessels or persons responsible for vessel source pollution.[100]

In 2009, for instance, as a part of the Third Maritime Safety Package, the European Parliament and Council adopted the "New Inspection Regime" pursuant to the Paris MOU on Port State Control, which applies in all of the EU coastal States.[101] Specific legislative measures have also been adopted by the EU concerning: compliance with flag State requirements;[102] classification societies;[103] trafficking monitoring and double hull requirements (both discussed further below);[104] port reception facilities for ship-generated waste and cargo residues;[105] accident investigation, liability of carriers and insurance.[106] Clearly, it is well beyond the scope of this paper to examine any of these instruments in any detail. A few cursory remarks can however be made regarding the extent of EU legislative and enforcement jurisdiction under the EU Directive

---

99   See V. Frank, "Consequences of the Prestige Sinking for European and International Law" (2005) 2(1) *IJMCL* 1–64.
100 Directive 2009/123/EC on the definition of ship-source pollution offences committed by natural or legal persons, the scope of their liability and the criminal nature of penalties that can be imposed for such criminal offences by natural persons, amending Directive 2005/35/EC, OJ L 280/52, 27.10.2009.
101 Directive 2009/16/EC of 23 April 2009 on port State control, OJ L131/57, 28.05.2009.
102 Directive 2009/21/EC of the European Parliament and of the Council of 23 April 2009 on compliance with flag State requirements, OJ L 131/132, 28.05.2009.
103 Directive 2009/15/EC of the European Parliament and of the Council of 23 April 2009 on common rules and standards for ship inspection and survey organisations and for the relevant activities of maritime administrations, OJ L131/47, 28.05.2009; Regulation EC) No 391/2009 of 23 April 2009 on common rules and standards for ship inspection and survey organisations, OJ L131/11, 28.05.2009.
104 Directive 2009/17/EC of the European Parliament and the Council of 23 April 2009 amending Directive 2002/59/EC establishing a Community vessel traffic monitoring and information system, OJ L131/101, 28.05.2009.
105 Directive 2009/21/EC of the European Parliament and of the Council of 23 April 2009 on compliance with flag State requirements, OJ L131/132, 28.05.2009.
106 Directive 2009/18/EC of 23 April 2009 establishing the fundamental principles governing the investigation of accidents in the maritime transport sector and amending Council Directive 1999/35/EC and Directive 2002/59/EC of the European Parliament and of the Council, OJ L131/114, 28.05.2009; Regulation (EC) No 392/2009 of 23 April 2009 on the liability of carriers of passengers by sea in the event of accidents, OJ L131/14, 28.05.2009; Directive 2009/20/EC of 23 April 2009 on the insurance of shipowners for maritime claims, OJ L131/128, 28.05.2009.

on Ship Source Pollution that indicates that it is fundamentally different from the regulatory approach advanced by the MSP Directive.

First, the personal scope (*ratione personae*) of the EU Directive on Ship Source Pollution is much wider than the spatial management measures proposed under the Draft MSP Directive in so far as the former is targeted at flag States, ship owners and charterers, classification societies, port States and coastal States, with a view to ensuring that all of these entities comply their pollution obligations under national, EU and international law. In particular, it is aimed at ensuring that all persons responsible for discharges are subject to adequate penalties with a view to reducing and abating pollution by ships.[107] Moreover, this instrument applies to discharges of polluting substances "from any ship, irrespective of its flag, with the exception of any warship, naval auxiliary or other ship owned or operated by a State and used, for the time being, only on government non-commercial service."[108]

The material scope (*ratione materiae*) of the EU Directive on Ship Source Pollution is far-reaching in so far as the term "ship' is defined to mean a "seagoing vessel, irrespective of its flag, of any type whatsoever operating in the marine environment and shall include hydrofoil boats, air-cushion vehicles, submersibles and floating craft."[109] As noted above, however, naval ships are excluded from the scope of the Directive and it must be assumed by implication that this derogation extends to naval submarines or other underwater vehicles in government service in line with the definition of warships under the LOS Convention.[110] A similar approach is evident with respect to some aspects of the MSP Directive as it provides explicitly that it does "not apply to activities the sole purpose of which is defence or national security."[111] Each Member State shall, however, strive to ensure that such activities are conducted in a manner compatible with the objectives of the MSP Directive.

The geographical scope (*ratione loci*) of the EU Directive on Ship Source Pollution is also broader that the Draft MSP Directive in so far as it is applicable to discharges of polluting substances into the following maritime jurisdictional areas: "(a) the internal waters, including ports, of a Member State, in so far as the MARPOL 73/78 regime is applicable; (b) the territorial sea of a Member State; (c) straits used for international navigation subject to the regime of transit passage, as laid down in Part III, section 2, of the LOS Convention, to

---

107   Article 1 of Directive 2005/35/EC, OJ L 255/11, 30.09.2005.
108   Ibid.
109   Article 2(4) of Directive 2005/35/EC, OJ L 255/11, 30.09.2005.
110   Article 29 of the LOS Convention.
111   Article 2(2) of the Draft MSP Directive.

the extent that a Member State exercises jurisdiction over such straits; (d) the exclusive economic zone or equivalent zone of a Member State, established in accordance with international law; and (e) the high seas."[112] Within the overall scheme of protection afforded by the EU Directive on Ship Source Pollution, Member States are required to ensure that vessel source pollution is regarded as an infringement if committed with intent, recklessly or by serious negligence.[113] Again in line with the case law of the Court of Justice of the EU, offences must be subject to effective, proportionate and dissuasive penalties, which may include criminal or administrative sanctions.[114]

Most significantly, the Directive is enforceable on the basis of port State measures and only where there is clear and objective evidence in relation to offences in the territorial sea or the EEZ can coastal States institute enforcement proceedings that include detaining a ship.[115] Instructively, the EU Directive on Ship Source Pollution provides that Member States must apply its provisions without "any discrimination in form or in fact against foreign ships and in accordance with applicable international law, including Section 7 of Part XII of the LOS Convention, and that they shall promptly notify the flag State of the vessel and any other State concerned of any measures taken" under its terms.[116]

Regrettably, the case law of the Court of Justice of the EU sheds little additional light on the operation of the EU Directive on Ship Source Pollution from the point of view of international obligations, particularly regarding crucial issues such as the right of the EU to legislate for third country vessels navigating in the EEZ or on the high seas.[117] Most notably in a somewhat controversial judgment, the Court of Justice held that it could only review the validity of an EU measure such as the EU Directive on Ship Source Pollution in the light of the rules of international law, subject to two conditions: firstly, the EU must be bound by those rules; and secondly, the nature and the broad logic of the act of international law in question did not preclude such an examination. In relation to the case at hand, the Court noted that the EU was not party

---

112   Article 3 of Directive 2005/35/EC, OJ L 255/11, 30.09.2005.
113   Article 4 of Directive 2009/123/EC.
114   Case 68/88 *Commission v Greece* [1989] ECR 2965, paragraph 23.
115   Article 7(1) and 7(2) of Directive 2005/35/EC, OJ L 255/11, 30.09.2005.
116   Article 9 of Directive 2005/35/EC, OJ L 255/11, 30.09.2005.
117   See D. Konig, 'The EU Directive on Ship-Source Pollution and on the Introduction of Penalties for Infringements: Development or Breach of International Law?" in T. Malick Ndiaye, R. Wolfrum, eds., *Law of the Sea, Environmental Law and Settlement of Disputes* (Leiden/Boston: Martinus Nijhoff, 2007) at 767–785.

to the MARPOL 73/78 and therefore it was not willing to review the legality of EU measures in light of the provisions therein. More surprisingly, it concluded that the LOS Convention does not establish rules intended to apply directly and immediately to individuals and to confer upon them rights or freedoms capable of being relied upon against States. Accordingly, the Court did not review the contested provisions in light of the LOS Convention. A golden opportunity thus appears to have been missed by the Court to explore the scope for the EU to regulate environmental matters that impinge upon navigation rights and freedoms under the LOS Convention. This in turn would have clarified the latitude afforded to the EU and the Member States to encroach upon the navigation entitlements of international shipping in order to give effect to environmental objectives of the Draft MSP Directive, as well as the MSF Directive.

Reconciling Competing Values: EU Regulation on Double Hull Oil Tankers

The proposed EU measures on maritime spatial planning are intended to provide a framework for reconciling competing values concerning the use of the maritime space. The EU has traditionally been proactive in striving to balance environmental considerations with international navigation rights and this can be seen in the unilateral regulation adopted by the EU to address the safety of shipping and to reduce the risk of pollution from oil tankers, specifically by accelerating the phasing-in of double hull or equivalent design requirements for single hull oil tankers.[118] The IMO had introduced the double hull requirement in response to *Exxon Valdez* by the amendment of Annex I of MARPOL 73/78 in 1992. This Annex was amended again in response to the unilateral measures adopted by the EU with a view to meeting the new target dates for the introduction of double hulls for different categories of oil tankers.[119]

Although the EU regulation is principally directed at improving the safety of shipping, one of its ancillary objectives is to mitigate the risk of damage to fauna and flora and other marine resources from the maritime transport of

---

[118] Consolidated by Regulation (EU) No 530/2012 of 13 June 2012 on the accelerated phasing-in of double-hull or equivalent design requirements for single-hull oil tankers, OJ L172/3, 30.6.2012. See A. Boyle, "EU Unilateralism and the Law of the Sea" 21 (2006) *International Journal Marine and Coastal Law* 15.

[119] Regulations 20.5 and 20.8.2 of Annex I to MARPOL 73/78.

hydrocarbons.[120] In this context, it should be kept in mind that the European Commission has pointed out that older ships are more prone to accident and that further regulatory action was required by the IMO to improve the safety of shipping and to prevent marine pollution.[121] Since the late 1990s, EU policy on these matters has informed the debate at the IMO and accelerated the schedule for the phasing-out of single hull oil tankers at both global and regional levels. The EU regulation is unambiguous in this regard as it sets down an express prohibition on oil tankers operating under the flag of a Member State, or indeed on all tankers irrespective of their flag from entering into ports or offshore terminals under the jurisdiction of a Member State, unless such a vessel is a double-hull oil tanker.[122]

The EU has actively sought to work with its Member States through the IMO to improve international standards on the safety of merchant vessels. Instructively, in notifying the IMO of the adoption of the regulation on single hull tankers in 2002, the EU made specific reference to article 211(3) of UNCLOS and the notification requirements set out therein.[123] Article 211(3) of course operates "without prejudice to the continued exercise by a vessel of its right of innocent passage or to the application of Article 25(2) of the Convention". Again with the general scheme of EU secondary legislation pertaining to vessel source pollution, the EU measures do not apply to warships, naval auxiliary or other ships owned or operated by a State and used only for government non-commercial services.[124] Furthermore, there are specific provisions aimed at not endangering the safety of crew or oil tankers in search of a safe haven or a place of refuge, as well as measures that are aimed at facilitating shipyards in the Member States repairing single hull oil tankers.[125]

At first sight, the EU measures on single hull tankers cannot be said to be an ecosystem-based management measure, as these measures are limited to a specific sector (namely, maritime transport) and to a specific class of vessel (tankers). Nonetheless, they demonstrate the inherent tension and balancing-of-interests, as well a degree of symbiosis between the EU's transport and environmental policies. On the one hand, the former is aimed at facilitating trade including, it must be assumed, upholding navigation rights and freedoms. The environmental policy, on the other hand, is aimed at protecting and preserv-

---

120 Recital 3 of Regulation (EU) No 530/2012.
121 Communication on a common policy on safe seas, COM(93)66.
122 Article 4(1) of Regulation (EU) No 530/2012.
123 Article 9 of Regulation (EC) No 417/2002.
124 Article 2(2) of Regulation (EU) No 530/2012.
125 Article 8(a) of Regulation (EU) No 530/2012.

ing the marine environment and at ensuring an effective regulatory regime to combat vessel source pollution. Most noticeable, the above-mentioned measures on ship source pollution and on double hull tankers were adopted within the framework of the common transport policy. Furthermore, although no mention is made to the relevant legal basis in the EU treaties, they also reflect the requirement under the Treaty on the Functioning of the EU that environmental considerations are integrated into EU sector policies.[126] In effect, they provide the EU with a higher degree of protection at a regional level against accidental oil pollution in the event of collision or stranding of tankers. At a global level, they also resulted in the adoption of more stringent measures and tighter deadlines by the IMO. Despite the fact that the Third Maritime Safety Package (two Regulations and six Directives) is made-up of sector specific instruments,[127] they are nonetheless entirely complementary to the proposed scheme and objectives advanced by the Draft MSP Directive in so far as the ultimate goal is to reduce the risk and incidence of environmental pollution.

Will the Draft MSP Directive Impinge upon Navigation Rights and Freedoms?

International trade is a fundamental feature of the European single market and crucial to maintaining the EU's position as a global economic power. Shipping is the lifeblood of the Union and, as noted above, it is thus somewhat surprising that the Draft MSP Directive is silent on how it proposes to influence the exercise of navigation rights and other freedoms in sea areas under the sovereignty or jurisdiction of the Member States including the right of innocent passage, the right of transit passage in international straits, as well as the freedom of navigation in the EEZ and on the high seas. In the fullness of time, however, it may well impinge upon the practice and procedures followed by EU coastal States in relation to the establishment of traffic separation schemes and in the adoption of other routeing measures such as traffic lanes, separation zone, roundabouts, inshore traffic zones, recommended routes, deep-water routes, precautionary areas or areas to be avoided.

The scope for EU coastal States to set down specific measures applicable to shipping in their national maritime spatial plans is clearly constrained by what is permissible under international law. More precisely, the IMO is the only international body vested with the power to establish ships' routeing

---
126 Article 11 of the Treaty on the Functioning of the European Union.
127 See discussion *supra.*

systems under the SOLAS Convention,[128] and is universally accepted and acknowledged as the "competent international organization" under the LOS Convention for this purpose. Indeed, IMO Contracting Governments such as EU Member States bear the initial responsibility for bringing forward draft proposals to the IMO concerning routeing and reporting systems. Moreover, decisions about the adoption of such measures within territorial waters remain the prerogative of the coastal State that must take into account the recommendations of the IMO, as well as a number of other factors including any international navigation channels, the characteristics of particular ships and channels, as well as the density of traffic.[129] Nuclear powered ships or ships carrying hazardous cargoes may be obliged to confine their passage to designated sea lanes in accordance with the LOS Convention.[130]

There is little scope for the EU or the Member States to act unilaterally in this regard as the IMO provides considerable guidance on the technical aspects of preparing proposals on ships' routeing and reporting systems.[131] This process has served the interests of Member States well. Notably, the first traffic separation scheme was established in the Dover Strait in late 1960s and there are over 120 schemes in operation in the European regional seas at the time of writing. Many of these schemes do not set down mandatory requirements but are aimed at ensuring the safe and expeditious flow of shipping. Further details of the precise measures are published on navigation charts and described by the IMO in their annual publication, *Ships Routeing*.[132] In Europe, some of the most important traffic schemes are established for environmental purposes such as in approaches to the Scilly Isles, the Straits of Dover, and in the southern part of the North Sea.

This experience suggests that the tension that sometimes arises between navigation and environmental interests in the European regional seas can be resolved by means of practical measures entailing the establishment of traffic separation schemes and the adoption of other routeing measures. Indeed, as is evident from the IMO Guidelines, any proposal put forward by Contracting Governments for routing measures should contain information on environ-

---

128 Regulation 10 of Chapter V of the 1974, International Convention for the Safety of Life at Sea (SOLAS), as since amended.
129 Article 22(3) of the LOS Convention.
130 Ibid. Article 22(2).
131 IMO Resolution A.572(14)), as amended. Also see, MSC/Circ.1060 Guidance Note on the Preparation of Proposals on Ships' Routeing Systems and Ship Reporting Systems. Available at: http://www.imo.org/OurWork/Safety/Navigation/Documents/1060.pdf.
132 IMO, *Ships Routeing 2013*, (London: IMO, 2014).

mental factors including the "prevailing weather conditions, tidal streams, and currents, and the possibility of ice concentrations."[133] What is more, proposals intended to protect the marine environment should have specific information as to how they will contribute to the prevention or reduction of pollution from shipping or the risk of environmental damage.[134]

Although there is no mandatory requirement that coastal States designate sea lanes for the purpose of enhancing the safety of navigation, the Draft MSP Directive may in the fullness of time have a major influence on the whole future process of establishing ship routeing measures in Europe in order to give effect to EU legislation on nature conservation and marine environmental protection. When considering the veracity of this contention, it should not be forgotten that one of the principal aims of the Draft MSP Directive is to improve the effectiveness of shipping routes across Europe, including port accessibility and transport safety. Similarly, it is anticipated that the Draft MSP Directive will complement more specific instruments that have been adopted by the EU to protect the offshore environment from vessel source pollution, including Directive 2002/59/EC, which requires the establishment of a vessel traffic monitoring and information system to improve the safety of maritime traffic and to prevent and detect pollution by ships.[135] The latter Directive provides for the establishment of mandatory ship reporting systems in the European coastal environment in accordance with the relevant IMO rules and thereby preventing maritime accidents and pollution incidents at sea. Furthermore, in line with the obligations set down by Commission Directive 2011/15/EU, certain categories of ships must comply with requirements of the automatic identification system (AIS), as well as the voyage data recorder (VDR) system.[136]

In line with the general scheme of the LOS Convention, the freedom of navigation in the EEZ is constrained by the sovereign rights and jurisdictions vested in coastal States regarding the exploration and exploitation of natural resources in seas areas under their sovereignty or jurisdiction.[137] Coastal States have extensive jurisdiction under the LOS Convention regarding the

---

133   Para 3.4(1) of the MSC/Circ. 1060 Guidance Note, op cit. note 131.
134   Ibid.
135   Directive 2002/59/EC of the European Parliament and of the Council of 27 June 2002 establishing a Community vessel traffic monitoring and information system and repealing Council Directive 93/75/EEC, OJ L 208, 5.8.2002, 10–27.
136   Commission Directive 2011/15/EU of 23 February 2011 amending Directive 2002/59/EC of the European Parliament and of the Council establishing a Community vessel traffic monitoring and information system Text with EEA relevance, OJ L 49, 24.2.2011, 33–36.
137   Article 56, LOS Convention.

establishment and use of artificial islands, installations and structures for this purpose such as wind farms and oil rigs, as well as jurisdiction to take measures to protect and preserve the marine environment.[138] As seen above, such rights and jurisdictions are of course qualified by the obligation to "have due regard" to the rights and duties of other States such as freedom of navigation, overflight and of the laying of submarine cables and pipelines, as well as other internationally lawful uses of the sea relating to such freedoms.[139] Moreover, it is important to point out that the spatial planning of offshore development that entails the construction of artificial islands, installations and structures and the safety zones around them must not interfere with the "use of recognized sea lanes essential to international navigation" by virtue of the obligations set down in the LOS Convention.[140]

At an operational level, we can expect to see that the plans adopted by Member States pursuant to the Draft MSP Directive will also have a major bearing on the management of shipping incidents in the future. Specifically, they may incorporate a number of operational requirements that allow Member States to discharge their obligations under Commission Directive 2011/15/EU, which provides a legal basis for the emergency services to do any or all of the following: "(a) restrict the movement of the ship or direct it to follow a specific course; (b) give official notice to the master of the ship to put an end to the threat to the environment or maritime safety; (c) send an evaluation team aboard the ship to assess the degree of risk and to help the master to remedy the situation; and (d) instruct the master to put in at a place of refuge in the event of imminent peril, or cause the ship to be piloted or towed."[141]

The fire on board the very large German flagged container ship of 85,823 tons, *MSC Flaminia*, in the mid-Atlantic in 2012 revealed the difficulties encountered by EU Member States in dealing with shipping emergencies.[142] This particular incident resulted in the deaths of three crewmembers, the abandoning of the ship, before the derelict hull was taken in tow by salvage vessels. Subsequently, it was reported in the media that Ireland, the United Kingdom, France, Belgium, the Netherlands, Spain and Portugal denied the

---

138   Article 56(1)(b), LOS Convention.
139   Articles 56(2) and 58 of the LOS Convention.
140   Article 60(7) of the LOS Convention.
141   Article 19(1) and Annex IV of Directive 2002/59/EC as inserted by Annex II of Commission Directive 2011/15/EU.
142   UK Maritime and Coastguard Agency Press Office, 14 July 2012. Available at: http://hmcoastguard.blogspot.co.uk/2012/07/container-vessel-abandoned-mid-atlantic.html.

salvage vessel and its consort a place or port of refuge.[143] Germany in its capacity as the flag State ultimately arranged for the ship and its escort to enter the port of Willemhaven. This incident suggests that the identification of places of refuge ought to be addressed specifically as a matter or priority in national maritime spatial plans. As it stands, however, the Draft MSP Directive is silent on this subject matter and makes little reference to the risk of vessel source pollution or the adoption of appropriate management measures to deal with maritime emergencies.

As seen previously, maritime spatial planning is also relevant to the implementation of two EU initiatives "Motorways of the Sea" and the "European Maritime Transport Space without Barriers".[144] The former is aimed at moving the transport of freight from road to sea, thus reducing congestion on the roads and improving the environmental footprint of the transport sector.[145] This entails the designation of four motorways of the sea as part of the trans-European transport networks, and thus linking a number of distinctive European regions including: the Baltic Sea with the North Sea and the Baltic Sea canal; western Europe from the North Sea through to Portugal; south-east Europe, from the Adriatic Sea to the Ionian Sea and the Eastern Mediterranean; and the western Mediterranean through to south-east Europe and the Black Sea. Patently, the designation of such routes will form an important component of the national spatial plans adopted by the Member States under the MSP directive as soon as it enters force.

Conclusions

The EU is endeavoring to take a leadership role in implementing the Rio+20 conference chapter on the oceans. The application of the ecosystem approach through the medium of EU secondary legislation such as the MSF Directive is informed by developments in international and regional law, as well as by state practice worldwide. Similarly, the EU's integrated maritime policy and the Draft MSP Directive give effect to this approach and are both aimed at achieving

---

143   Lloyd's List, 30 August 2012.
144   Decision No 884/2004/EC of the European Parliament and of the Council of 29 April 2004 amending Decision No 1692/96/EC on Community guidelines for the development of the trans-European transport network, OJ L 167, 30.04.2004. Also see, Communication from the Commission providing guidance on State aid complementary to Community funding for the launching of the motorways of the sea, OJ 2008 C 317, 12.12.2008.
145   Ibid.

environmental, economic and social objectives. All of these instruments acknowledge in both form and content the interdependency of activities undertaken in the marine environment. In this respect, the new generation of EU instruments such as the legislative proposal on maritime spatial planning is very much focused on delivering sophisticated regulatory solutions that incorporate integrated and holistic management of competing uses of the marine environment. In light of the innovative nature of EU legislation, one must return to the question posed at the start of this paper: will the application of the ecosystem approach and the rolling out of maritime spatial plans by the Member States in due course undermine navigation rights and freedoms under the LOS Convention? The answer is not yet apparent but we can deduce important elements that ought to inform EU and Member State practice in this regard. First and foremost, the EU is a major trading entity and freedom of navigation is fundamental to the prosperity of the Union. Secondly, all EU secondary legislation has to be interpreted in accordance with the LOS Convention. Thirdly, the ecosystems-based approach itself requires a "balancing of interests" between economic and environmental pillars of EU policies. Hence, it is easy to conclude that this balance must respect the carefully crafted provisions of the Convention on navigation rights and other freedoms.

Ultimately, in order to give full effect to these vital interests, the author of this paper proposes that the European Parliament Committee should give serious consideration to amending the Draft MSP Directive at its second reading by inserting an express provision that provides that the EU and Member States in implementing maritime spatial planning and coastal management strategies are obliged to uphold and preserve navigational rights and freedoms in accordance with applicable international law. Such an amendment will send out a clear signal to the global community about the leadership role of the EU as an international actor that is committed to implementing both the letter and the spirit of the LOS Convention in relation to what many consider its most important provisions, which relate to navigation freedoms and a stable legal order in the world's oceans.

CHAPTER 12

Responsibility of Flag States for Pollution of the Marine Environment: The Relevance of the UNCLOS Dispute Settlement Regime

Robert C. Beckman

Abstract

This paper addresses the issue of whether the dispute settlement regime in the 1982 United Nations Convention on the Law of the Sea (UNCLOS) and the 2001 Articles on the Responsibility of States for Internationally Wrongful Acts (2001 ILC Articles) can be utilized to hold flag States internationally responsible for breaches of their obligations under UNCLOS to prevent pollution of the marine environment by ships flying their flag. It argues that UNCLOS establishes clear obligations on flag States to adopt laws and regulations to prevent, reduce and control pollution of the marine environment by ships flying their flag, including dumping. It also imposes clear obligations on flag States to effectively enforce such laws and regulations.

This paper further argues that the 2001 ILC Articles set out rules whereby a flag State can be held to be internationally responsible if it fails to fulfill its obligations under UNCLOS to adopt and effectively enforce national laws to prevent pollution of the marine environment by ships flying its flag. The 2001 ILC Articles give a State Party to UNCLOS the right as an injured State to invoke the responsibility of a flag State if a maritime zone under its jurisdiction is polluted by a ship of the flag State. The 2001 ILC Articles also give any State Party to UNCLOS the right to invoke the responsibility of the flag State for acts of pollution on the high seas.

---

* Robert Beckman is Director of the Centre for International Law, National University of Singapore (NUS) and an Associate Professor, Faculty of Law, NUS. The author would like to thank Sun Zhen and Monique Page of the Centre for International Law for their assistance in preparing this article. The author's PowerPoint is available at http://www.virginia.edu/colp/pdf/Seoul-Beckman.pdf.

Introduction

This chapter addresses the issue of whether the dispute settlement regime in the 1982 *United Nations Convention on the Law of the Sea* (UNCLOS)[1] and the 2001 *Articles on the Responsibility of States for Internationally Wrongful Acts*[2] (2001 ILC Articles) can be utilized to hold flag States internationally responsible for breaches of their obligations under UNCLOS to prevent pollution of the marine environment by ships flying their flag.

It will first examine the obligations of States under UNCLOS with respect to ship-source pollution and dumping by ships flying their flag. It will then examine whether the acts and omissions of flag States could be internationally wrongful acts which give rise to the responsibility of the flag State under international law as set out in the 2001 ILC Articles. It will then consider the extent to which the dispute settlement regime in UNCLOS could be used as a tool to seek legal remedies against States that fail to fulfill their obligations under UNCLOS to prevent, reduce and control pollution by ships flying their flag.

Flag State jurisdiction has long been the system used to regulate high seas activities. The general principle is that ships on the high seas are subject to the exclusive jurisdiction of the flag State.[3] Ship owners have a right to choose which flag their ship will sail under. For a variety of reasons, principally economic, many ship owners opt to register their ships with low-cost open registries or flags of convenience rather than with their national flag. Alongside the rise of these registries, there has developed a lack of national attachment or a lack of genuine link between ships and their administrating State.[4]

Whilst some open registry States exercise their regulatory and supervisory responsibilities diligently, others have eschewed their duties and use the open registration system primarily as a means to raise revenue. Such States may become parties to the relevant international instruments governing maritime safety and ship-source pollution, but they take few steps to ensure that

---

1 United Nations Convention on the Law of the Sea, adopted in Montego Bay, Jamaica, 10 December 1982, 1833 UNTS 3 (entered into force 16 November 1994). <http://cil.nus.edu.sg/rp/il/pdf/1982%20United%20Nations%20Convention%20on%20the%20Law%20of%20the%20Sea-pdf.pdf> (All website addresses in this paper were accurate as at 21 October 2013 except where otherwise noted.)
2 Articles on Responsibility of States for International Wrongful Acts, adopted by the International Law Commission on 3 August 2001, <http://legal.un.org/ilc/texts/instruments/english/draft%20articles/9_6_2001.pdf>.
3 R.R. Churchill and A.V. Lowe, *The Law of the Sea* (3rd ed., Manchester 1999), p. 203.
4 A.K.J. Tan, *Vessel-Source Marine Pollution—The Law and Politics of International Regulation* (Cambridge, 2006), pp. 47–50.

ships flying their flag comply with the standards established in the instruments. Furthermore, some of these flag States do not have the capacity to implement and enforce their obligations under the international instruments. Consequently, ships flagged to their registries are able to operate in a largely unregulated manner with irresponsible ship owners finding few incentives to reduce and control pollution from their ships.[5] In a summary of factual information of 106 flag States' performance produced by five cooperating international institutions of shipping, the open registry States dominated the top 10 worst ranking flag States in global performance.[6]

The issue of flag State jurisdiction is being addressed by the international community in various ways, including the use of port State control measures and efforts of the International Maritime Organization (IMO) through its Sub-Committee on Flag State Implementation, its Voluntary IMO Member State Audit Scheme and its Technical Co-operation Programme.[7]

The thesis of this chapter is that the provisions in UNCLOS establish clear obligations on flag States with respect to pollution of the marine environment, and the 2001 ILC Articles and the UNCLOS dispute settlement provisions create effective mechanisms for holding errant States responsible for breaches of their international obligations.

The Framework Established in the UN Convention on the Law of the Sea

UNCLOS establishes a framework to prevent, reduce and control pollution of the marine environment from ship-source pollution and from ocean dumping. It contains general provisions on the rights and obligations of flag States, general obligations on all States with respect to the protection and preservation of the marine environment, and obligations on flag States to prevent, reduce and control pollution from the marine environment from ships and from dumping. The obligations with respect to pollution from ships and from dumping are linked to the more detailed obligations set out in the conventions administered by the IMO.

Disputes between States Parties concerning the interpretation or application of the provisions in UNCLOS are subject to the dispute settlement regime

---

5 Ibid., pp. 49–50.
6 A.J.E. Corres and A.A. Pallis, 'Flag State Performance: An Empirical Analysis' (2008) *WMU Journal of Maritime Affairs* 248.
7 International Maritime Organization <www.imo.org>.

in Part XV of that Convention. The regime provides a right for States Parties to a dispute to unilaterally invoke the compulsory procedures entailing binding decisions before an international court or arbitral tribunal.

General Duties of Flag States under UNCLOS

Under UNCLOS, every State has the right to sail ships flying its flag on the high seas.[8] Ships have the nationality of the State whose flag they are entitled to fly.[9] States have a duty to fix the conditions for the grant of its nationality to ships and for the right to fly its flag.[10] Ships shall sail under the flag of one State only and, save in exceptional cases expressly provided for in international treaties or in UNCLOS, they are subject to the exclusive jurisdiction of the flag State on the high seas.[11]

States have a duty to effectively exercise jurisdiction and control in administrative, technical and social matters over ships flying their flag.[12] Flag States have an obligation to take such measures for ships flying their flag as are necessary to ensure safety at sea with regard, *inter alia*, to the construction, equipment and seaworthiness of ships. Such measures include those necessary to ensure that the master, officers and, to the extent appropriate, the crew are fully conversant with and required to observe the applicable international regulations concerning the prevention, reduction and control of marine pollution. In taking these measures, each State is required to conform to generally accepted international regulations, procedures and practices and to take any steps which may be necessary to secure their observance.[13]

Upon receiving a report from another State that proper jurisdiction and control has not been exercised by a ship flying its flag, the flag State has a duty to investigate the matter and, if appropriate, take any action necessary to remedy the situation.[14] A flag State must hold an inquiry into every marine casualty or incident of navigation on the high seas involving a ship flying its flag and causing serious damage to the marine environment.[15] In addition, the

---

8   UNCLOS, Article 90, *supra* note 1.
9   Ibid., Article 91(1).
10 Ibid., Article 91(1).
11 Ibid., Article 92(1).
12 Ibid., Article 94(1).
13 Ibid., Article 94(5).
14 Ibid., Article 94(6).
15 Ibid., Article 94(7).

flag State must cooperate in the conduct of any inquiry held by that other State into any such marine casualty or incident of navigation.[16]

General Obligations of States to Protect and Preserve the Marine Environment

Part XII of UNCLOS sets out general obligations on States to protect and preserve the marine environment.[17] Article 194 imposes a duty on States to take measures to prevent, reduce and control pollution of the marine environment from any source, using for this purpose the best practicable means at their disposal and in accordance with their capabilities. It also provides that the measures to be taken by States include, *inter alia*, those designed to minimize to the fullest possible extent pollution from ships, in particular measures for preventing accidents and dealing with emergencies, ensuring the safety of operations at sea, preventing intentional and unintentional discharges, and regulating the design, construction, equipment, operation and manning of ships.[18]

Obligations of Flag States with Respect to Ship-source Pollution

Part XII of UNCLOS sets out a fairly detailed framework to prevent, reduce and control pollution of the marine environment from ships.

First, it provides that States, acting through the competent international organization or general diplomatic conference, shall establish international rules and standards to prevent, reduce and control pollution of the marine environment from ships.[19] States have established such international rules and standards through the IMO, this being the UN specialized agency responsible for the safety and security of shipping and the prevention of marine pollution by ships.[20] The main IMO convention establishing international rules and standards for the prevention, reduction and control of ship-source pollution is the *International Convention for the Prevention of Pollution from Ships*, 1973,[21] which

---

16 Ibid., Article 94(7).
17 Ibid., Article 192.
18 Ibid., Article 194(3)(b).
19 Ibid., Article 211(1).
20 Introduction to the IMO <http://www.imo.org/About/Pages/Default.aspx>.
21 1978 Protocol Relating to the 1973 International Convention for the Prevention of Pollution from Ships (including Annexes, Final Act and 1973 International Convention), adopted in London, United Kingdom, 17 February 1978, 1340 UNTS 61 (entered into force 2 October 1983) <treaties.un.org/doc/Publication/UNTS/Volume%201340/volume-1340-A-22484-English.pdf>.

has been amended by the Protocols of 1978 and 1997 and thereafter updated through amendments to the Convention and its Annexes.[22] This Convention is generally known as MARPOL 73/78. The detailed regulations on particular sources of pollution from ships are set out in the Annexes. States Parties to MARPOL 73/78 are automatically bound by Annexes I and II. States Parties must expressly consent to the other Annexes. The Annexes are as follows:

> Annex I. Prevention of pollution by oil;
> Annex II. Control of pollution by noxious liquid substances;
> Annex III. Prevention of pollution by harmful substances in packaged form;
> Annex IV. Prevention of pollution by sewage from ships;
> Annex V. Prevention of pollution by garbage from ships; and
> Annex VI. Prevention of air pollution from ships.

Second, UNCLOS sets out the obligations of flag States, coastal States and port States to adopt national laws and regulations. Under Article 211(2), States have an obligation to adopt laws and regulations for the prevention, reduction and control of pollution of the marine environment from ships flying their flag. It further provides that such laws and regulations shall *at least have the same effect* as that of the 'generally accepted international rules and standards'.[23]

The question which arises is how many of the other Annexes to MARPOL 73/78 can be considered to be the 'generally accepted international rules and standards'. This is an important issue because once the rules and standards in an Annex are considered to be the 'generally accepted international rules and standards', flag States are under an obligation to adopt laws and regulations which are *at least as effective* as those Annexes in preventing, reducing and controlling pollution. The current status of the six Annexes to MAROL 73/78 is as follows:[24]

---

22 IMO, overview of MARPOL and its Annexes <http://www.imo.org/About/Conventions/ListOfConventions/Pages/International-Convention-for-the-Prevention-of-Pollution-from-Ships-(MARPOL).aspx>.

23 UNCLOS, Article 211(2), *supra* note 1. On the phrase "generally accepted", see G.K. Walker (ed.), *Definitions for the Law of the Sea—Terms Not Defined by the 1982 Convention* (Martinus Nijhoff Publishers, 2012), p. 93.

24 IMO, Status of Multilateral Conventions and Instruments in respect of which the IMO or Its Secretary-General Performs Depositary or other Functions, as at 30 September 2013 <http://www.imo.org/About/Conventions/StatusOfConventions/Pages/Default.aspx>.

Annex Number	Date of Entry into Force	Number of States Parties	% World Tonnage of Shipping
MARPOL 73/78 (Annex I/II)	2-Oct-83	152	99.20
MARPOL 73/78 (Annex III)	1-Jul-92	138	97.59
MARPOL 73/78 (Annex IV)	27-Sep-03	131	89.65
MARPOL 73/78 (Annex V)	31-Dec-88	145	98.47
MARPOL Protocol 1997 (Annex VI)	19-May-05	73	94.12

Some scholars argue that once a MARPOL Annex receives the requisite number of ratifications for it to enter into force, it should be considered to be the 'generally accepted international rules and standards'.[25] Others take a more cautious approach.[26] However, once 90 percent or more of the world's shipping tonnage is a party to the relevant Annex, there would be a very good argument that the Annex should be considered as the best evidence of the 'generally accepted international rules and standards'. As all of the Annexes of MARPOL 73/78 have surpassed the 90 percent tonnage mark, it can be argued that they represent the generally accepted international rules and standards with respect to each of the individual sources of marine pollution they seek to regulate.

Other IMO conventions governing pollution of the marine environment by ships address anti-fouling systems used on ships and the transfer of alien species by ships' ballast water. The 2001 *International Convention on the Control of Harmful Anti-fouling Systems on Ships*[27] prohibits the use of harmful

---

25 G.K. Walker (2012), pp. 93–96, *supra* note 23. IMO, LEG/MISC.7, 19 January 2012, *Implications of the United Nations Convention on the Law of the Sea for the International Maritime Organization*, p. 11, <http://www.imo.org/OurWork/Legal/Pages/UnitedNations ConventionOnTheLawOfTheSea.aspx>.

26 W. van Reenen, 'Rules of Reference in the New Convention on the Law of the Sea in Particular in Connection with the Pollution of the Sea by Oil from Tankers', 12 *Netherlands Yearbook of International Law*, December 1981, pp. 3–44 for a general discussion of applicable standards and pp. 27–29 with respect to a specific discussion regarding MARPOL.

27 2001 International Convention on the Control of Harmful Anti-fouling Systems on Ships, adopted in London, United Kingdom, 5 October 2001, [2008] ATS 15/AFS/CONF/26 (entered into force 17 September 2008) <http://cil.nus.edu.sg/rp/il/pdf/2001%20International%20Convention%20on%20the%20Control%20of%20Harmful%20Anti-fouling%20Systems%20on%20Ships-pdf.pdf>.

organotins in anti-fouling paints used on ships and establishes a mechanism to prevent the potential future use of other harmful substances in anti-fouling systems. The Convention entered into force on 17 September 2008 and has 66 parties, representing 82 percent of the world tonnage of shipping.[28] After more than 14 years of complex negotiations between IMO Member States, the *International Convention for the Control and Management of Ships' Ballast Water and Sediments*[29] (BWM Convention) was adopted on 13 February 2004. The Convention is not yet in force. It has 38 contracting States, representing 30 percent of the world tonnage of shipping.[30] Since it is not yet in force, it seems clear that the BWM Convention cannot be considered as part of the 'generally accepted international rules and standards' on ship-source pollution. The Anti-fouling Convention might be considered as falling within this phrase, although there could be doubts because it only has 65 States Parties.

Third, UNCLOS establishes rights and imposes obligations on flag States, coastal States and port States to enforce the international rules and standards. Article 217 of UNCLOS provides that States shall ensure compliance by ships flying their flag with applicable international rules and standards and shall accordingly adopt laws and regulations and take other measures necessary for their implementation.[31] Article 217 further provides that States shall, at the written request of any State, investigate any violation alleged to have been committed by ships flying their flag and, if they are satisfied that sufficient evidence is available to enable proceedings to be brought in respect of the alleged violation, flag States shall without delay institute such proceedings in accordance with their laws.[32]

The jurisdiction of the flag State has primacy if a ship flying its flag commits a violation of the international rules and standards concerning ship-source pollution in the EEZ of another State. In certain circumstances, the coastal State may institute proceedings against the foreign ship.[33] However, the coastal State is required to suspend its proceedings if the flag State institutes proceedings within six months from the date the coastal State instituted proceedings.[34]

---

28 IMO, Status of Multilateral Conventions, as at 30 September 2013, p. 494, *supra* note 24.
29 2004 International Convention for the Control and Management of Ships' Ballast Water and Sediments, adopted London, United Kingdom 13 February 2004, not yet in force <www.ecolex.org/server2.php/libcat/docs/TRE/Multilateral/En/TRE001412.pdf>.
30 IMO, Status of Multilateral Conventions, as at 30 September 2013, p. 499, *supra* note 24.
31 UNCLOS, Article 217(1), *supra* note 1.
32 Ibid., Article 217(6).
33 Ibid., Article 220(3), (5)–(6).
34 Ibid., Article 228(1).

Whenever the flag State has requested the suspension of proceedings, it is required in due course to make available to the coastal State a full dossier of the case and the records of the proceedings. When proceedings instituted by the flag State have been brought to a conclusion, the suspended proceedings of the coastal State shall be terminated.[35] There are two exceptions to the rule that the coastal State must suspend its proceedings at the request of the flag State. The first is when the proceedings of the coastal State relate to a case of major damage to the coastal State. The second is when the flag State in question has repeatedly disregarded its obligation to enforce effectively the applicable international rules and standards in respect of violations committed by its ships.[36]

Obligations of Flag States with Respect to Pollution from Dumping

Article 1 of UNCLOS provides that 'dumping' means any deliberate disposal of wastes or other matter from ships, aircraft, platforms or other man-made structures at sea.

Article 210 of UNCLOS provides that States shall endeavor to establish global and regional rules, standards and recommended practices and procedures to prevent, reduce and control pollution from dumping. Article 210 also imposes an obligation on States to adopt laws and regulations to prevent, reduce and control pollution of the marine environment by dumping, and to take other measures as may be necessary to prevent, reduce and control such pollution. Further, UNCLOS provides that national laws, regulations and measures shall be no less effective in preventing, reducing and controlling pollution from dumping than the 'global rules and standards'.[37]

With respect to enforcement of the laws and regulations on dumping, Article 216 of UNCLOS provides that laws and regulations adopted in accordance with this Convention and applicable international rules and standards shall be enforced by the flag State with regard to ships flying its flag.

At the time of the drafting of UNCLOS, there was an international convention on ocean dumping, the 1972 *Convention on the Prevention of Marine Pollution by Dumping of Wastes and Other Matter* (the 1972 London Convention).[38]

---

35 Ibid., Article 228(1).
36 Ibid., Article 228(1).
37 Ibid., Article 210(6).
38 1972 Convention on the Prevention of Marine Pollution by Dumping of Wastes and Other Matter, adopted 29 December 1972, Washington, Moscow, London, Mexico City, 1046 UNTS 120 (entered into force 30 August 1975) <treaties.un.org/doc/Publication/UNTS/Volume%201046/volume-1046-I-15749-English.pdf>.

The 1972 London Convention entered into force on 30 August 1975. It regulates the deliberate disposal at sea of wastes or other matter from ships, aircraft, and platforms. It does not cover discharges from land-based sources such as pipes and outfalls, wastes generated incidental to normal operation of ships, or placement of materials for purposes other than mere disposal, providing such disposal is not contrary to the aims of the Convention. The London Convention takes a 'black list-grey list' approach to regulation, whereby dumping is generally permitted, but some items are black-listed and others require special permits.[39]

The London Convention has been updated by the 1996 *Protocol to the 1972 Convention on the Prevention of Marine Pollution by Dumping of Wastes and Other Matter* (1996 Protocol).[40] The 1996 Protocol updates the 1972 London Convention to incorporate principles of modern environmental law, including the precautionary approach.[41] The 1996 Protocol contains a so-called 'reverse list' approach. The Parties are obligated to prohibit the dumping of any waste or other matter that is not listed in Annex 1 ('the reverse list'). Dumping of wastes or other matter on this reverse list requires a permit.[42] Parties to the 1996 Protocol are further obligated to adopt measures to ensure that the issuance of permits and permit conditions for the dumping of reverse list substances comply with Annex 2 (the Waste Assessment Annex) of the Protocol.[43] The substances on the reverse list include dredged material; sewage sludge; industrial fish processing waste; ships and offshore platforms or other man-made structures at sea; inert, inorganic geological material; organic material of natural origin; and bulky items including iron, steel, concrete and similar materials for which the concern is physical impact, and limited to those circumstances where such wastes are generated at locations with no land-disposal alternatives.[44] In addition, the 1996 Protocol prohibits altogether the practice of incineration at sea, except for emergencies, and prohibits the export of wastes or other matter to non-parties for the purpose of dumping or incineration at sea.[45]

---

39   Ibid., Article IV(1), Annexes I and II.
40   1996 Protocol to the 1972 Convention on the Prevention of Marine Pollution by Dumping of Wastes and Other Matter, adopted 7 November 1996, London, United Kingdom, 2006 ATS 11 (entered into force 24 March 2006) <http://www.admiraltylawguide.com/conven/protodumping1996.html>.
41   Ibid., Preamble and Article 3(1).
42   Ibid., Article 4(1) and Annex 1.
43   Ibid., Article 4(1.2) and Annex 2.
44   Ibid., Article 1 and Annex 1.
45   Ibid., Articles 5 and 6.

An important question is whether either the 1972 London Convention or its 1996 Protocol is the set of 'global rules and standards' referred to in Article 210 of UNCLOS. This is important because States Parties to UNCLOS must adopt national laws and regulations 'at least as effective' as the global rules and standards in order to prevent pollution of the marine environment by dumping.

As of 30 September 2013, there are 87 States Parties to the 1972 London Convention, representing 67 percent of the world tonnage of shipping.[46] The 1996 Protocol entered into force on 24 March 2006, and as of 30 September 2013 it has 43 States Parties, representing 36 percent of the world tonnage of shipping.[47] Given the fact that the 1972 London Convention has 87 States Parties representing 67 percent of the world tonnage of shipping, it can be argued that it represents the 'global rules and standards' referred to in Article 210. By contrast, given the relatively low number of parties to the 1996 Protocol, it would be difficult to argue that it represents the global rules and standards.

Therefore, it seems reasonable to conclude that flag States that are parties to UNCLOS must adopt national laws and regulations and take other measures to regulate dumping from ships flying their flag. Flag States have discretion as to exactly what measures they take, but such measures must be 'at least as effective' as those set out in the 1972 London Convention. In addition, flag States are under an obligation to enforce their national rules and standards on dumping with regard to ships flying their flag.

Responsibility and Liability of Flag States under UNCLOS

Article 235 of UNCLOS provides that States are responsible for the fulfillment of their international obligations concerning the protection and preservation of the marine environment, and that they shall be liable in accordance with international law.[48] This would include flag States that fail to fulfill their obligations to take measures to prevent, reduce and control pollution of the marine environment by ships flying their flag, including dumping by such ships.

Article 235 also requires that States ensure that recourse is available in accordance with their legal systems for prompt and adequate compensation or other relief in respect of damage caused by pollution of the marine environment by natural or juridical persons under their jurisdiction.[49] This provision is applicable to flag States because they have jurisdiction over ships flying their flag.

---

46   IMO, Status of Multilateral Conventions, as at 30 September 2013, p. 511, *supra* note 24.
47   Ibid., p. 522.
48   UNCLOS, Article 235(1), *supra* note 1.
49   Ibid., Article 235(2).

For more clarification on the responsibility of States for the fulfillment of their international obligations concerning the protection and preservation of the marine environment, guidance can be sought from the rules of general international law on the responsibility of States that have been articulated by the International Law Commission (ILC) in the 2001 ILC Articles.

2001 ILC Articles on Responsibility of States for Internationally Wrongful Acts

The General Principles

The principles of general international law on 'state responsibility' are set out in the 2001 ILC Articles, which were adopted by the ILC at its 53rd Session on 3 August 2001.[50] Several of the provisions in the 2001 ILC Articles have been cited by international courts and tribunals as evidence of general international law, and they have therefore become the starting point for analyzing the general international law on the responsibility of States.[51]

Like the provisions of the 1969 *Vienna Convention on the Law of Treaties*, the 2001 ILC Articles are 'secondary rules'. The 2001 ILC Articles set out the general conditions under international law for a State to be considered responsible for wrongful actions or omissions in breach of its primary obligations, and the legal consequences which flow therefrom. The 'primary rules' of international law are the obligations imposed on States in treaties and in rules of customary international law governing particular areas of law.[52] For example, the primary rules governing the law of the sea are set out in UNCLOS. Secondary rules in the 1969 Vienna Convention and in the 2001 ILC Articles set out general rules on matters such as the legal consequences which result if a State Party breaches the primary rules set out in UNCLOS.

The fundamental principle in the 2001 ILC Articles is set out in Article 1, which provides that every 'internationally wrongful act' of a State entails the international responsibility of that State. Article 2 provides that there is an internationally wrongful act of a State when conduct consisting of an act or omission (a) is attributable to the State under international law, and

---

[50] 2001 ILC Articles, *supra* note 2.
[51] J.R. Crawford, *Brownlie's Principles of Public International Law* (8th ed., Oxford, 2012), p. 540.
[52] 'ILC Draft Articles on Responsibility of States for Internationally Wrongful Acts, with Commentaries, General Commentary', *Yearbook of the International Law Commission*, 2001, Vol. II, Part Two, para 1, p. 31, <http://www.un.org/law/ilc/>.

(b) constitutes a breach of an international obligation of the State. In other words, for there to be an internationally wrongful act, two conditions must be satisfied. First, the State must owe a legal obligation to another State under a treaty or under general international law. Second, the State must breach that obligation by conduct (either an act or an omission) which is attributable to the State under international law. The general principle on attribution is that the conduct of a government official is attributable to the State, but the conduct of a private individual or company is not (even though they may be nationals of that State).[53]

Nature of the International Obligation

Earlier drafts of the 2001 ILC Articles distinguished between obligations of conduct and obligations of result. However, these distinctions were opposed by some States and consequently they were not included in the 2001 ILC Articles.[54]

The obligation to adopt nationals laws and regulations and take other measures to prevent pollution of the marine environment which are at least as effective as the generally accepted international rules and standards can be characterized as an obligation of due diligence which gives States wide discretion on exactly what measures they are required to take.[55] If a flag State has adopted national laws and regulations and has procedures in place to investigate incidents involving its ships, it would be difficult to prove that it is in breach of its international obligations. However, if it has not adopted any laws or regulations governing ships flying its flag, and it has no procedures to investigate incidents concerning its ships, a complaining State would be able to establish a *prima facie* case that the flag State breached its international obligations. In such case, the responsibility would arise from conduct consisting partly of acts and partly of omissions.

Invocation of the Responsibility of a State

An important contribution of the 2001 ILC Articles is that they set out when a State can invoke the responsibility of another State that breaches its obligations under international law. These provisions are especially important when considering the obligations undertaken by States when they become parties to

---

53 J.R. Crawford, *The International Law Commission's Articles on State Responsibility—Introduction, Text and Commentaries* (Cambridge University Press, 2001), p. 91.
54 J.R. Crawford, *State Responsibility: The General Part* (Cambridge University Press, 2013), pp. 220–226.
55 Ibid., p. 227.

an international treaty that contains provisions obligating States to take measures to protect the marine environment.

The general principle that an 'injured State' can invoke the responsibility of another State is set out in Article 42 of the 2001 ILC Articles, which reads as follows:

> A State is entitled as an injured State to invoke the responsibility of another State if the obligation breached is owed to:
>
> a) that State individually; or
> b) a group of States including that State, or the international community as a whole, and the breach of the obligation:
>   i) specially affects that State; or
>   ii) is of such a character as radically to change the position of all the other States to which the obligation is owed with respect to the further performance of the obligation.

A flag State has an obligation under UNCLOS to investigate a violation alleged to have been committed by a ship flying its flag in a maritime zone subject to the jurisdiction of a coastal State and to institute proceedings against its ship if the available evidence warrants it.[56] The flag State owes this obligation to that particular coastal State individually and, if it breaches its obligation, that coastal State is entitled as an injured State to invoke the responsibility of the flag State.

The obligations of a flag State under UNCLOS to adopt and effectively enforce laws and regulations to prevent, reduce and control pollution of the marine environment by ships flying its flag are obligations owed to a group of States, that is, to all States Parties to the Convention. If a breach of those obligations results in the pollution of the marine environment in a maritime zone subject to the jurisdiction of a coastal State, that coastal State would be specially affected. Therefore, it would be an injured State under Article 42 of the 2001 ILC Articles. The requirement is that a State is an injured State only if it is 'specially affected', that is, it must be affected by the breach in a way which distinguishes it from the generality of other States to which the obligation is owed.[57]

---

56   UNCLOS, Article 94(6), *supra* note 1.
57   2001 ILC Articles with Commentaries, Commentary to Article 42, para (1), p. 117, *supra* note 52.

Article 48 of the 2001 ILC Articles sets out the circumstances under which a State *other than an injured State* can invoke the responsibility of a State. The relevant language reads as follows:

1. Any State other than an injured State is entitled to invoke the responsibility of another State in accordance with paragraph 2 if:
    a. The obligation breached is owed to a group of States including that State, and is established for the protection of a collective interest of the group.

The official commentary to Article 48 states that obligations coming within the scope of this Article must be 'collective obligations', that is, they must apply between a group of States and they must have been established in some collective interest, such as protection and preservation of the environment.[58] A State entitled to invoke responsibility under Article 48(1) is 'acting not in its individual capacity by reason of having suffered injury, but in its capacity as a member of the group of States to which the obligation is owed'.[59]

Article 48 would enable any State Party to UNCLOS to invoke the responsibility of a flag State if it breaches its obligations to adopt and effectively enforce laws and regulations to protect the marine environment of the high seas, as these obligations are established for the collective interest of all States Parties. The State invoking the responsibility of the flag State would be acting in its capacity as a member of the group of States to which the obligation is owed, that is, as one of the States Parties to the Convention.

Consequences of an Internationally Wrongful Act

If there is an internationally wrongful act, the 2001 ILC Articles establish that two consequences follow for the responsible State. First, it must cease the unlawful conduct, and offer assurances and guarantees of non-repetition. Second, it is under an obligation to make full 'reparation' for the injury caused by the internationally wrongful act.[60]

If an injured State has the right to invoke the responsibility of another State, it can seek remedies such as assurances and guarantees of non-repetition or an order that the conduct of the State is a breach of its international obligations

---

58 2001 ILC Articles with Commentaries, Commentary to Article 48, para (6), p. 126, *supra* note 52.
59 2001 ILC Articles with Commentaries, Commentary to Article 48, para (1), p. 126, *supra* note 52.
60 2001 ILC Articles, Articles 30 and 31, *supra* note 2.

without having to prove that the internationally wrongful act caused injury to it. However, if an injured State is seeking reparation for injury or damage caused to it, it must show that the injury was caused by the internationally wrongful act.[61]

Relevance of UNCLOS Dispute Settlement Regime

Overview of the Dispute Settlement Regime in Part XV of UNCLOS
As a general principle, all disputes concerning the interpretation or application of any provision in UNCLOS are subject to the system of compulsory procedures entailing binding decisions.[62] In other words, when States become parties to UNCLOS, they consent in advance to the system of compulsory binding dispute settlement in the Convention.

The 'default' rule in UNCLOS is that if there is a dispute between two States concerning the interpretation or application of any provision in the Convention, it is subject to the system of compulsory procedures entailing binding decisions in Section 2 of Part XV. States are obligated to first exchange views to try to resolve the dispute by following the procedures set out in Section 1 of Part XV.[63] However, where no settlement has been reached by recourse to Section 1, the dispute may be unilaterally submitted *at the request of any party to the dispute* to the court or tribunal having jurisdiction under Section 2.[64]

The court or tribunal which has jurisdiction to hear a dispute depends on whether the parties to the dispute have exercised their right to select a procedure for resolving disputes to which they are parties.[65] Under Article 287, a State is free to choose, by means of a written declaration, one or more of four procedures for the settlement of disputes concerning the interpretation or application of the Convention: (1) adjudication before the International Court of Justice (ICJ); (2) adjudication before the International Tribunal for the Law of the Sea (ITLOS); (3) arbitration under Annex VII of UNCLOS; or

---

61 2001 ILC Articles with Commentaries, Commentary to Article 31, para (9), p. 92, *supra* note 52.
62 Tommy Koh and S. Jayakumar, 'Negotiating Process of the Third United Nations Conference on the Law of the Sea', in M.H. Nordquist (ed.), *United Nations Convention on the Law of the Sea 1982: A Commentary* (Martinus Nijhoff, Volume I, 1985), pp. 29–134.
63 UNCLOS, Article 283, *supra* note 1.
64 Ibid., Article 286.
65 Ibid., Article 288.

(4) special arbitration under Annex VIII of UNCLOS.[66] A State may indicate its choice of procedure when signing, ratifying or acceding to UNCLOS, or at any time thereafter.[67] If two States Parties to a dispute have elected the same procedure, the dispute may only be referred to that procedure, unless the parties otherwise agree.[68] If the States Parties to the dispute have not elected the same procedure, or if one of them has not made a choice of procedure, the dispute may be submitted only to arbitration under Annex VII, unless the parties otherwise agree.[69]

A State Party to a dispute which is referred to dispute settlement under Section 2 of Part XV may also request provisional measures to prevent serious harm to the marine environment.[70] The only prerequisite is that the court or tribunal to which the dispute has been duly submitted must first determine that *prima facie* it has jurisdiction under Part XV or Part XI.[71] Such provisional measures are legally binding.[72] Even if a dispute is being referred to an arbitration tribunal, a State Party may request provisional measures from ITLOS pending the establishment of the arbitral tribunal if ITLOS 'considers that *prima facie* the tribunal which is to be constituted would have jurisdiction and that the urgency of the situation so requires'.[73]

Part XV and Disputes on the Responsibility of Flag States with Respect to the Marine Environment

Disputes between a flag State and another State on whether the flag State is in breach of its obligations under UNCLOS to prevent pollution of the marine environment by ships flying its flag could arise on several provisions. First, a legal dispute could arise on whether a flag State has breached its obligation to adopt laws and regulations at least as effective as the generally accepted international rules and standards in MARPOL 73/78 to prevent, reduce and control ship-source pollution by ships flying its flag.[74] Second, a dispute could arise on whether a flag State is in breach of its obligations under UNCLOS to effectively enforce its laws and regulations on ship-source pollution in a particular

---

66 Ibid., Article 287(1).
67 Ibid., Article 287(1).
68 Ibid., Article 287(4).
69 Ibid., Article 287(5).
70 Ibid., Article 290(1).
71 Ibid., Article 290(1).
72 Ibid., Article 290(6).
73 Ibid., Article 290(5).
74 Ibid., Article 211(2).

case, including its obligations to investigate incidents and institute proceedings.[75] Third, a dispute could arise as to whether a flag State has adopted laws and regulations at least as effective as those in the 1972 London Convention to prevent, reduce and control pollution of the marine environment by dumping from its ships, and on whether it has breached its obligation to enforce those laws and regulations when there is an incident involving dumping by a ship flying its flag.[76]

Such disputes would be subject to the procedures in Part XV. If they cannot be settled by negotiation in accordance with Section 1 of Part XV, either party to the dispute can invoke the compulsory procedures entailing binding decisions in Section 2 of Part XV. The State bringing the action against the flag State could seek the remedies available under the 2001 ILC Articles.

Responsibility of Flag State for Failing to Effectively Implement and Enforce Its International Obligations under UNCLOS

As explained earlier, a State Party to UNCLOS has an obligation to adopt laws and regulations to prevent pollution of the marine environment by ships flying its flag.[77] This includes both pollution from the operation of ships and pollution by dumping. Such laws and regulations must be at least as effective as the international rules and standards set out in MARPOL 73/78 and its Annexes and in the 1972 London Convention. Flag States have an obligation to ensure that ships flying their flag comply with these laws and regulations, in particular to take measures to enforce these laws and regulations by requiring certificates and inspections, conducting investigations and instituting proceedings.[78]

Disputes between two States Parties to UNCLOS on the interpretation and application of any provision in UNCLOS are subject to the dispute settlement regime in Part XV of the Convention. In order to use the dispute settlement regime, the complaining State would need to show that a dispute has arisen between it and the errant flag State.

A dispute could arise between a coastal State and a flag State if the flag State fails to fulfill its obligations to investigate and institute proceedings as required in Article 217 of UNCLOS when a ship flying its flag commits a violation of the rules and standards established in the applicable IMO conventions. A dispute

---

75 Ibid., Articles 220 and 228.
76 Ibid., Articles 210(1)–(3) and 216(1)(b).
77 UNCLOS, Article 211(2), *supra* note 1.
78 Ibid., Article 217.

could also arise on the interpretation of Article 228 if the flag State requests a coastal State suspend proceedings against a ship flying its flag and the coastal State refuses to do so because the flag State has continually disregarded its obligations to enforce effectively the applicable international rules and standards.

A dispute could also arise as to whether a flag State has adopted and effectively enforced laws and regulations at least as effective as the international regulations, practices and procedures set out in MARPOL 73/78 and its Annexes to prevent pollution of the marine environment by ships flying its flag. Issues could arise as to whether the flag State has fulfilled its specific obligations under Articles 211 and 217, as well as its general obligations in Articles 94, 192 and 194. If a flag State has no laws and regulations in place or few, if any, officials in its maritime administration who have the technical expertise to implement the rules and standards in MARPOL 73/78, then arguably it is in breach of its obligations under UNCLOS.

The majority of flag States that are parties to UNCLOS are also likely to be parties to MARPOL and its Annexes.[79] The issue that would arise would be whether the flag State has adopted laws and regulations and taken other measures which enable it to effectively prevent ships flying its flag from polluting the marine environment. If an international court or arbitral tribunal examined whether the measures taken by a given flag were adequate to fulfill its obligations under UNCLOS, its ruling would provide an authoritative precedent that would provide guidance for other flag States.

A dispute could also arise on whether a flag State has fulfilled its obligations with respect to pollution by dumping from ships flying its flag. Article 210 imposes an obligation on States to adopt laws and regulations to prevent pollution from dumping. This would include provisions requiring ships flying their flag to seek a permit from a coastal State before disposing of waste in a maritime zone of the coastal State.[80] Further, Article 216 requires flag States to enforce such laws against ships flying their flag.

If an act of pollution took place in a maritime zone under the jurisdiction of the coastal State, and the flag State was unable or unwilling to investigate and prosecute, the coastal State could invoke the responsibility of the flag State

---

[79] IMO, Status of Conventions, as at 30 September 2012, <http://www.imo.org/About/Conventions/StatusOfConventions/Pages/Default.aspx>; UN DOALOS, Chronological Lists of Ratifications of, Accessions and Successions to the Convention and the Related Agreements as at 20 September 2013, <http://www.un.org/depts/los/reference_files/chronological_lists_of_ratifications.htm#The%20United%20Nations%20Convention%20on%20the%20Law%20of%20the%20Sea>.

[80] Ibid., Article 210(5).

because the obligation is owed to all States and it is specially affected.[81] If the act of pollution took place on the high seas, and the flag State was unable or unwilling to investigate and prosecute, any State could invoke its responsibility because the obligation is established for the collective interest of the group and it is a member of that group.[82]

The State invoking the responsibility of the flag State may not be able to seek reparations for the damage caused to its marine environment, because the pollution of the marine environment was not caused by the failure of the flag State to adopt and effectively enforce its obligations to protect the marine environment from acts of ships flying its flag, but rather by the intentional act of the master of the ship. However, the coastal State could seek a declaration that the flag State had breached its obligations by failing to adopt or to adequately enforce laws and regulations as required by UNCLOS. It could also seek an order requiring the flag State to fulfill its obligations by adopting laws and regulations and establishing procedures to enforce them. Such a ruling would send a clear signal to other flag States.

Conclusions

The legal framework in UNCLOS establishes clear obligations on flag States to adopt laws and regulations to prevent, reduce and control pollution of the marine environment by ships flying their flag, including dumping. It also imposes clear obligations on flag States to effectively enforce such laws and regulations.

The 2001 ILC Articles set out rules whereby a flag State can be held to be internationally responsible if it fails to fulfill its obligations under UNCLOS to adopt and effectively enforce national laws to prevent pollution of the marine environment by ships flying its flag. The 2001 ILC Articles give a State Party to UNCLOS the right as an injured State to invoke the responsibility of a flag State if a maritime zone under its jurisdiction is polluted by a ship of the flag State. The 2001 ILC Articles give any State Party to UNCLOS the right to invoke the responsibility of the flag State for acts of pollution on the high seas. The 2001 ILC Articles also set out what remedies or relief may be requested from the flag State whose responsibility is engaged.

The dispute settlement regime in UNCLOS applies to any dispute concerning the breach by a flag State of its obligations under UNCLOS to prevent,

---

81   2001 ILC Articles, Article 42, *supra* note 2.
82   Ibid., Article 48.

reduce and control pollution of the marine environment by ships flying its flag. If the dispute cannot be resolved through negotiation, the State concerned can unilaterally invoke the compulsory procedures entailing binding decisions in Section 2 of Part XV and bring the case to an international court or arbitral tribunal in order to seek the remedies permitted under the 2001 ILC Articles.

The high costs of bringing a case to an international court or tribunal may mean coastal States will be reluctant to bring an action under the UNCLOS dispute settlement system against errant flag States. However, if the marine environment of a coastal State was seriously polluted by a ship flying the flag of a State that has blatantly failed to fulfill its obligations under UNCLOS, the coastal State may be willing to bear the costs of bringing an action under UNCLOS in order to send a message to the flag State. If the flag State were required to incur the costs of the case, and if it was ordered by an international court or arbitral tribunal to take steps to ensure that it has adequate laws in place and a system for effectively enforcing such laws, the case would send a very serious message to other flag States who are not taking their international obligations under UNCLOS seriously. In effect, the benefits of allowing questionable ships to fly its flag would be far outweighed by the costs of a potential legal action before an international court or tribunal. The result could be that some flags of convenience would no longer find it profitable to allow substandard ships to fly their flag, and as a result the threat to the marine environment from substandard ships would be reduced.

CHAPTER 13

Cooperative Environmental Mechanisms for the South China Sea

Shichun Wu

This chapter is composed of four sections. First, it briefly discusses the current situation for the marine environment of the South China Sea (SCS). It then elaborates on a few existing marine environment cooperation projects in the SCS. It goes on to discuss the relationship between state interests and international cooperation on the marine environment, upon which the author argues that environment security could serve as a driving force for cooperation in the SCS. In the last part, the author addresses the relationship between the marine environment and freedom of navigation. Two observations are made in this paper. First, that regional cooperation on the marine environment is difficult to achieve due to the existing territorial and maritime disputes in the South China Sea. Second, that despite the disputes, freedom of navigation has never been jeopardized in the SCS.

1 The Current Situation for the SCS Marine Environment

The South China Sea, which has long been a flashpoint for regional rivalries and tensions, is rich in a plethora of living and non-living resources, serving as a source of livelihood for one of the most populous regions in the world. However, this region has become increasingly besieged by environmental pollution, which is attributable to rapid economic growth, excessive consumption of natural resources and intensified maritime conflicts. In recent years, the marine environment there has shown a trend of uncontrollable degradation, which can be seen in the shrinkage of mangroves, the increase in land-based pollution and the erosion of coastal strips. This degradation is partly due to the absence of a cooperative mechanism for marine environment protection. The catastrophic scenario caused by the oil leakage at the Gulf of Mexico should

* Shichun Wu, President, National Institute for South China Sea Studies (China). Email: wsc9961@hotmail.com. The author's PowerPoint is available at http://www.virginia.edu/colp/pdf/Seoul-Wu.pdf.

have put all the countries bordering the SCS on high alert. It is imperative to put environmental conservation on the agenda. As far as I am concerned, it would be better for them to put more effort into environmental conservation, rather than to rack their brains trying to maximize their respective energy supplies for the biggest share of economic gains. Without a cooperative mechanism, the end result may be horrible disasters.

2 The Current Cooperative Mechanism for the Conservation of the Marine Environment in the SCS Region

Countries surrounding the SCS should take a comprehensive approach to the conservation of the marine environment. A regional cooperative mechanism is vital for dealing with the severe problem of degradation of the marine environment. There have been some successful attempts to put in place such a cooperative mechanism. As early as September 1994, China, Japan, Russia and the Republic of Korea, under the guidance of the United Nations Environment Programme (UNEP) and the International Maritime Organization (IMO), passed the North West Pacific Action Plan (NOWPAP) in response to oil spill incidents. In November 2004, these four nations signed the Memorandum of Understanding on Regional Cooperation in Marine Pollution Preparedness and Response and the NOWPAP Regional Oil Spill Contingency Plan, marking the establishment of an emergency mechanism to combat oil spills.

In order to ensure a cleaner environment and regional marine environmental cooperation amid the highly complex situation in the SCS, several programs have been put in place and have taken leading roles, just as UNEP has done. Other examples of cooperation programs include the South China Sea Large Marine Ecosystem (LME), the UNEP/GEF Project and the UNEP/Action Plan. Let me discuss these projects in more detail.

The SCS Large Marine Ecosystem (LME) is characterized by its tropical climate. Different sub-systems within the ecosystem have been identified. Intensive fishing is the primary force driving the SCS LME, while climate is secondary. The Global Environment Facility (GEF) is supporting this LME project in order to address critical threats to the marine environment in the SCS and to promote ecosystem-based management of coastal and marine resources.

Another example is the UNEP/GEF South China Sea project. It is the first of its kind to develop a regionally coordinated program of actions in order to reverse environmental degradation in the South China Sea, particularly in the areas of coastal habitat degradation and loss, land-based pollution, and fisheries. It was initiated in 1996 and is the first inter-governmental project involving all the major countries bordering the SCS. It is funded by the GEF and carried out by the UNEP together with seven countries bordering the SCS, including Cambodia, China, Indonesia, Malaysia, the Philippines, Thailand and Vietnam. Thanks to the trust and confidence gained through the Informal SCS Working Group, the UNEP/GEF SCS Project has made remarkable progress in promoting regional cooperation toward conserving the marine environment of the SCS.

However, there is much more to be done in order to establish a cooperative environment conservation mechanism in the South China Sea. Territorial and maritime disputes may be an obstacle to such efforts.

3 Territorial and Maritime Disputes Serve as an Obstacle to Environmental Cooperation

Given the complexity and inter-connectedness of the marine environment, the countries bordering the SCS must attempt to reverse the trend of environmental degradation. However, relentless territorial and maritime disputes may prove an obstacle to environmental cooperation. It takes political will and wisdom for the statesmen of multiple nations to cooperate in resolving the contradictions between international environmental cooperation and their respective national rights.

Besides, they need to understand the concept of environmental security and that it is consistent with their common interests. There is no contradiction between an international environmental conservation mechanism and vital national interests. Rather, international cooperation is the only way to secure a nation's sustainable access to vital resources for the long-term. Dealing with environmental problems will often require some pooling of state sovereignty on behalf of common ecological security. Political/military security and environmental security are interlinked because we live in an interdependent world.

4 Balancing Freedom of Navigation and the Marine Environment

We must acknowledge the key connection between two concepts, freedom of navigation and the marine environment. The importance of the South China Sea as a strategic passageway is unquestioned. It contains critical sea lanes through which oil and many other commercial resources flow from the Middle East and Southeast Asia to Japan, Korea, and China. More than 80 percent of crude oil supplies for Japan, South Korea and Taiwan flow through the SCS from the Middle East, Africa and SCS nations such as Indonesia and Malaysia. Almost all shipping that passes through the Malacca and Sunda Straits must pass near the contested Spratly Islands. Therefore, stabilized transportation through these waters is a prerequisite for the continuation of world trade.

The South China Sea issues could be analyzed from two perspectives, the territorial and maritime disputes between claimant states and the increasing interests of user States. The users' interest in the South China Sea stems from their concern over freedom of navigation in this region. Part 12 of UNCLOS reflects the tension between the protection of coastal State interests and the protection of the freedom of navigation, which is prevalent throughout UNCLOS.

Freedom of navigation is in the common interest of all states, be it coastal States or user States. We have to admit that there are different interpretations of the legitimacy of military activities in foreign countries' EEZs. While some user States argue that military activities concern freedom of navigation, whether it is conducted on the high seas or in an EEZ, some coastal States will raise questions about whether some types of military activities may harm the marine environment of coastal States, thus requiring permission from or prior notification to said States. This question remains open to debate.

Freedom of navigation is not only in the interest of user States, but it is also in the interest of coastal States. Despite the pending territorial and maritime disputes, freedom of navigation has never been jeopardized in the South China Sea. By the same token, the marine environment is vital not only for the coastal States, but also for all user States, which means that a cooperative mechanism is needed to address this common concern. We certainly need a balance between the freedom of navigation and the preservation of the marine environment in the South China Sea.

PART 6

Marine Data Collection

CHAPTER 14

Marine Data Collection: US Perspectives

Captain J. Ashley Roach JAGC, USN (retired)

Abstract

This paper discusses what is marine scientific research, identifies marine scientific research that is subject to Part XIII of the LOS Convention, discusses marine scientific research that is not subject to Part XIII, and identifies other forms of marine data collection that are not subject to Part XIII.

Marine Data Collection

Coastal State jurisdiction over foreign marine data collection activities depends on which type of activity is involved and on the maritime zone in which it is conducted. The 1982 Law of the Sea Convention[1] (LOS Convention) does not use the term "marine data collection" which is used in this paper as a generic term without legal content, as the umbrella under which to consider the various collection activities.[2]

---

* The author was an attorney advisor in the Office of the Legal Advisor, US Department of State, from 1988 until he retired at the end of January 2009, responsible for law of the sea matters. This paper is presented in his personal capacity but draws heavily on US Government public sources. He has taught, advised and published extensively on a wide range of law of the sea issues. This paper is based upon the chapter (15) on marine data collection in J.A. Roach and R.W. Smith, *Excessive Maritime Claims* (Leiden/Boston, Nijhoff, 2012). The author's PowerPoint is available at <http://www.virginia.edu/colp/pdf/seoul-roach.pdf>.

1 UN Convention on the Law of the Sea, Montego Bay, Dec. 10, 1982, entered into force Nov. 10, 1994, 1833 UNTS 397.
2 The term is also used by the US Navy: "Marine data collection is a general term used when referring to all types of survey or marine scientific activity (e.g., military surveys, hydrographic surveys, and marine scientific research)." US Chief of Naval Operations, OPNAV Instruction 3128.9E, *Diplomatic Clearance for US Navy Marine Data Collection Activities in Foreign Jurisdictions*, September 27, 2007, para. 3.d(1), *available at* http://doni.daps.dla.mil/Directives/03000%20Naval%20Operations%20and%20Readiness/03-100%20Naval%20Operations%20Support/3128.9E.pdf.

Under "marine data collection" the following four categories, with seven subcategories, are considered:

- Marine scientific research (MSR);
- Surveys;
    - Hydrographic surveys; and
    - Military surveys;
- Operational oceanography;
    - Ocean state estimation;
    - Weather forecasting; and
    - Climate prediction;
- Exploration and exploitation[3] of
    - Natural resources; and
    - Underwater cultural heritage (shipwrecks).

The LOS Convention uses, but does not define, the terms "marine scientific research," "hydrographic survey," "survey activities," "exploitation" and "exploration." It does not mention "military surveys," "operational oceanography" or their subcategories. Nevertheless, the concepts are distinct, and this paper seeks to clarify those differences.

The relevant maritime zones where these activities take place are the territorial sea, the contiguous zone, the Exclusive Economic Zone (EEZ), the continental shelf, the deep seabed beyond the limits of national jurisdiction (the Area), straits used for international navigation, and archipelagic sea lanes.

This paper will examine what is involved in each of these activities, review the applicable legal regimes, and demonstrates that surveys, operational oceanography, and exploration and exploitation are not marine scientific research regulated by Part XIII of the LOS Convention; rather they are subject to separate legal regimes.

Even though none of these four categories and seven subcategories is defined in the law of the sea, including the LOS Convention, it is necessary to understand what they each factually entail to appreciate the legal regime applicable to each.

US Views: What is MSR?

Although not defined in the Convention, "marine scientific research" is the general term most often used to describe those activities undertaken in the ocean

---

3   The term "exploitation" is used in the sense of resource development and management.

and coastal waters to expand scientific knowledge of the marine environment and its processes.[4] The United States accepts this definition. MSR includes physical oceanography, marine chemistry, marine biology, scientific ocean drilling and coring, geological/geophysical research, as well as other activities with a scientific purpose.

MSR Subject to Part XIII, LOS Convention

The LOS Convention devotes a whole part, Part XIII, containing 28 articles in six sections, to the subject of MSR. MSR is the most data-intensive form of marine data collection regulated by the LOS Convention.

While MSR is not defined in the LOS Convention, its scope can be deduced from how MSR and other forms of research are treated in the Convention.

- "Research or survey activities" in the territorial sea are subject to express consent of the coastal State (Article 19(2)(j));
- Coastal State may legislate regarding innocent passage in the territorial sea regarding MSR and hydrographic surveys (Article 21(1)(g));
- MSR in the territorial sea is subject to coastal State consent (Article 245);
- During transit passage of straits used for international navigation, foreign ships, "including marine scientific research and hydrographic survey ships" may not carry out "any research or survey activities" without prior authorization of States bordering the strait (Article 40);
- The same rule applies to archipelagic sea lane passage (Article 54); and
- MSR in the EEZ and on the continental shelf is subject to coastal State consent, which is to be exercised subject to certain standards and qualifications (Article 246).

---

4 *Accord*, G.K. Walker, General Editor, *Definitions for the Law of the Sea: Terms Not Defined by the 1982 Convention* 241 (Leiden/Boston, Nijhoff, 2012) (recounting the unsuccessful attempts to define MSR during the Third UN Conference on the Law of the Sea (UNCLOS III)). *Compare* LOS Convention, Articles 243 ("scientists ... studying the essence of phenomena and processes occurring in the marine environment and the interrelations between them" and 246(3) "to increase scientific knowledge of the marine environment for the benefit of all mankind"). *Accord*, A.H.A. Soons, *Marine Scientific Research and the Law of the Sea* (Deventer, Kluwer, 1982), p. 124 [hereinafter, Soons]. *See generally* M. Gorina-Ysern, *An International Regime for Marine Scientific Research* (Ardsley NY, Transnational Publishers, 2003). Japanese law does not define MSR. *See* Takada, 'Marine Scientific Research in the Exclusive Economic Zone and Japan-China Agreement for Prior Notification (1995–2001),' *Japanese Digest of International Law JD (III) 3*, 44 *Japanese Annual of International Law 2001* (Tokyo, International Law Association of Japan, 2002), p. 134.

Part XIII EEZ MSR Controls

Unlike other forms of marine data collection in the EEZ or on the continental shelf, Part XIII imposes the following requirements on MSR conducted in the EEZ or on the shelf:

- A minimum of six months prior notice to the coastal State with a full description of the MSR project in the EEZ or on the continental shelf (Article 248);
- The right of the coastal State to participate in the project (Article 249(1)(a));
- The researcher's duty to provide preliminary and final reports and provide access to the data collected (Article 249(1)(b)-(c));
- The research results are to be internationally available as soon as practicable (Article 249(1)(e)); and
- However, prior agreement from the coastal State is needed if the results are of direct significance for the exploration and exploitation of natural resources (Article 249(2)).

MSR Not Subject to Part XIII Controls

- MSR on the high seas is a freedom of the seas (Articles 87 and 257); and
- MSR in the Area may be conducted by all States and competent international organizations (Article 256) exclusively for peaceful purposes (Article 143).

US Marine Scientific Research Policy

The LOS Convention solidifies coastal States' control over MSR in waters subject to their jurisdiction, waters which now encompass considerably more of the globe than in 1958.[5] Nevertheless, US policy is to encourage freedom

---

5   Accompanying Germany's instrument of accession to the LOS Convention was a declaration concerning MSR, which reads as follows:

> Although the traditional freedom of research suffered a considerable erosion by the Convention, this freedom will remain in force for States, international organizations and private entities in some maritime areas, e.g., the sea-bed beyond the continental shelf and the high seas. However, the exclusive economic zone and the continental shelf, which are of particular interest to marine scientific research, will be subject to a consent regime, a basic element of which is the obligation of the coastal State under article 246, para-

of MSR. That policy was fostered by the US decision not to claim jurisdiction over MSR in its EEZ, first stated in the President's Oceans Policy Statement of March 10, 1983,[6] and reaffirmed in October 1994 in the documents transmitting the LOS Convention to the Senate.[7] The United States declined to assert jurisdiction in its EEZ over MSR because of its interest in encouraging MSR and promoting its maximum freedom while avoiding unnecessary burdens. The Department of State is charged with facilitating access by US scientists to foreign EEZs under reasonable conditions. Consequently, since 1983 the US requests permission through diplomatic channels for US research vessels to conduct MSR within 200 miles of a State asserting such jurisdiction.[8]

The United States does not require its permission to conduct MSR in US waters unless any portion of the MSR is conducted within the US territorial

---

graph 3, to grant its consent in normal circumstances. In this regard, promotion and creation of favourable conditions for scientific research, as postulated in the Convention, are general principles governing the application and interpretation of all relevant provisions of the Convention.

The marine scientific research regime on the continental shelf beyond 200 nautical miles denies the coastal State the discretion to withhold consent under article 246, paragraph 5(a), outside areas it has publicly designated in accordance with the prerequisites stipulated in paragraph 6. Relating to the obligation to disclose information about exploitation or exploratory operations in the process of designation is taken into account in article 246, paragraph 6, which explicitly excluded details from the information to be provided.

UN, Multilateral Treaties Deposited with the Secretary-General: Status, *available at* http://treaties.un.org/pages/Participation/Status.aspx.

6 When claiming its EEZ in 1983, the United States chose not to assert the right of jurisdiction over MSR within the zone. President Reagan explained the rationale for not doing so, as follows:

While international law provides for a right of jurisdiction over marine scientific research within such a zone, the proclamation does not assert this right. I have elected not to do so because of the United States interest in encouraging marine scientific research and avoiding any unnecessary burdens. The United States will nevertheless recognize the right of other coastal states to exercise jurisdiction over marine scientific research within 200 nautical miles of their coasts, if that jurisdiction is exercised in a manner consistent with international law.

President's Ocean Policy Statement, March 10, 1983, *available at* http://www.un.org/Depts/los/LEGISLATIONANDTREATIES/PDFFILES/USA_1983_Statement.pdf.

7 Commentary on LOS Convention, Sen. Treaty Doc. 103-39, at 80, *available at* http://www.jag.navy.mil/organization/documents/Senate_Transmittal.pdf.

8 The United Kingdom similarly acts on behalf of British scientists seeking authorization to conduct MSR in foreign waters. 56 *Brit. Y.B. Int'l L. 1985* (Oxford, 1986), p. 500. The United States would similarly request permission to conduct MSR on a continental shelf seaward of the 200-mile limit.

sea, any portion of the MSR within the US EEZ is conducted within a national marine sanctuary or other marine protected area (16 US Code § 1436), any portion of the MSR within the US EEZ involves the study of marine mammals or endangered species (16 US Code §§ 1371(a)(1), 1374(c), 1538), any portion of the MSR within the US EEZ requires taking commercial quantities of living marine resources (16 US Code § 1857(2) & (4)), any portion of the MSR within the US EEZ involves contact with the US continental shelf (43 US Code § 1340), or any portion of the MSR involves ocean dumping research (33 US Code § 1443).[9]

Role of the US State Department in Marine Scientific Research

Within the Bureau of Oceans and International Environmental and Scientific Affairs (OES) is the Office of Ocean and Polar Affairs (OPA), a division of which is the Marine Science and Technology Affairs Division (OPA/MST). The Marine Science Division is responsible for assuring that US MSR policy is adhered to in acquiring permission from a coastal State, when required for such research, and for coordinating and processing of the requests, as well as in processing requests from foreign researchers to conduct MSR in the US territorial sea or other situations described above.

Other Forms of Marine Data Collection

The Senate Foreign Relations Committee's (SFRC) proposed resolution of advice and consent to the LOS Convention contains an understanding that:

> "marine scientific research" does not include, inter alia—
> (A) prospecting and exploration of natural resources;
> (B) hydrographic surveys;
> (C) military activities, including military surveys;
> (D) environmental monitoring and assessment pursuant to section 4 of Part XII [Articles 204–206]; or

---

9 US Dept. of State Office of Oceans and Polar Affairs, 'Marine Science Research Authorizations,' *available at* http://www.state.gov/e/oes/ocns/opa/rvc/index.htm. The requirements of other countries may be viewed *at* http://www.state.gov/www/global/oes/oceans/notices.html (notices to research vessel operators 1976–1999). *See also* http://www.unols.org/publications/index.html#foreign.

(E) activities related to submerged wrecks or objects of an archaeological and historical nature.[10]

In its report, the SFRC explained:

> The fifth understanding concerns marine scientific research. Part XIII of the Convention addresses the rights of coastal States to require consent for marine scientific research undertaken in marine areas under their jurisdiction. The understanding indicates that the term "marine scientific research" does not include certain activities, such as military activities, including military surveys. It is an illustrative list; therefore, there are other activities, such as operational oceanography, that are also not considered marine scientific research.[11]

Surveys

For the purposes of this analysis, there are two forms of *surveys*, hydrographic surveys and military surveys.

Hydrographic Surveys

"Hydrographic surveys" are activities undertaken to obtain information for the making of navigational charts and for the safety of navigation. Hydrographic surveys include the determination of the depth of water, the configuration and nature of the sea floor, the direction and force of currents, heights and times of tides and water stages, and hazards for navigation. This information is used for the production of nautical charts and similar products to support safety of navigation, such as Sailing Directions, Light Lists and Tide Manuals for both civil and military use.[12] Coastal, harbor and harbor approach charts of

---

10   Senate Executive Reports 108–10, 2004 and 110–9, 2007, Understanding no. 5, reprinted in Roach and Smith, *Excessive Maritime Claims, supra* n. 1, p. 809.
11   Roach and Smith, *Excessive Maritime Claims, supra* n. 1, p. 798.
12   Cf. Definition 46, *in* International Hydrographic Bureau, *A Manual on Technical Aspects of the United Nations Convention on the Law of the Sea - 1982*, Special Pub. No. 51, (Monaco, 4th ed., 2006), Appendix 1, pp. Appendix 1–16, *available at* http://www.iho.shom.fr/publicat/free/files/S-51_Ed4-EN.pdf, and in OPNAVINST 3128.9E, para. 3.d(3), *supra* n. 3 ("Hydrographic survey refers to marine data collection activities undertaken in the territorial seas, archipelagic waters, straits for navigation, the EEZ, high seas, and on the continental shelf for the production of nautical charts and similar products to support safety of navigation. Hydrographic surveys can include one or more of several classes of data, such as depth of water, configuration and nature of the natural bottom, direction and force of currents, heights and times of tides and water stages, and hazards to navigation.").

non-US waters and other products are published by the US National Geospatial-Intelligence Agency and made available to mariners of all countries.[13]

In many areas of the world, the production of up-to-date charts has had a positive impact on economic development in coastal areas, stimulating trade and commerce and the construction or modernization of harbor and port facilities. By helping safety of navigation for ships in transit, up-to-date charts also play a role in protecting coastal areas from the environmental pollution which results from wrecks of tankers carrying hazardous cargoes and freighters. Data collected during hydrographic surveys may also be of value in coastal zone management and coastal science engineering.

The UN General Assembly in its annual resolutions on oceans and the law of the sea has recognized the importance of hydrographic surveys and nautical charting:

> Recognizing further that hydrographic surveys and nautical charting are critical to the safety of navigation and life at sea, environmental protection, including the protection of vulnerable marine ecosystems, and the economics of the global shipping industry, and encouraging further efforts towards electronic charting, which not only provides significantly increased benefits for safe navigation and management of ship movement, but also provides data and information that can be used for sustainable fisheries activities and other sectoral uses of the marine environment, the delimitation of maritime boundaries and environmental protection...
>
> 14. Encourages intensified efforts to build capacity for developing countries, in particular for the least developed countries and small island

---

The definition of "hydrographic survey" in *Definitions for the Law of the Sea, supra* n. 5, is different:
> the science of measuring and depicting those parameters necessary to describe the precise nature and configuration of the seabed and coastal strip, its geographical relationship to the land mass, and the characteristics and dynamics of the sea.... Hydrographic surveys may be necessary to determine the features that constitute baselines or basepoints and their geographical position.

Id. p. 227.

13 10 USC § 451 *et seq.* "Nautical chart" or "chart" is defined in *Definitions for the Law of the Sea* as
> a map specially designed to meet the needs of marine navigation. A chart depicts such information as depth of water, nature of the sea-bed, configuration and nature of the coast, and dangers and aids to navigation, in a standardized format....

Id. p. 126.

developing States, as well as coastal African States, to improve hydrographic services and the production of nautical charts, including electronic charts....[14]

Survey activities are not MSR. The LOS Convention distinguishes clearly between the concepts of "research" and "MSR" on the one hand, and "hydrographic surveys" and "survey activities" on the other hand. Article 19(2)(j) of the LOS Convention includes "research or survey activities" as inconsistent with innocent passage in the territorial sea. Article 21(1)(g) authorizes the coastal State to adopt laws and regulations, in conformity with the provisions of the Convention and other rules of international law, relating to innocent passage through the territorial sea in respect of "marine scientific research and hydrographic surveys". Article 40, entitled "research and survey activities," provides that in transit passage through straits used for international navigation, foreign ships, including "marine scientific research and hydrographic survey ships", may not carry out "any research or survey activities" without the prior authorization of the States bordering the straits. The same rule applies to ships engaged in archipelagic sea lanes passage (Article 54). While Part XIII of the LOS Convention fully regulates MSR, it does not refer to survey activities at all.

This conclusion, that MSR is distinct from survey activities, is supported by other respected publications on this subject.[15]

---

14   UNGA resolution A/RES/67/78, Dec. 11, 2012. Similar paragraphs appear in earlier resolutions A/RES/66/231, A/RES/65/37A, A/RES/64/71, A/RES/63/111, A/RES/62/215, A/RES/61/222, A/RES/60/30, A/RES/59/24 and A/RES/58/240, *available through links at* http://www.un.org/Depts/los/general_assembly/general_assembly_resolutions.htm.

15   For example, the UN MSR Guide notes that "'survey activities'... are primarily dealt with in other parts... of the Convention rather than in Part XIII. UN, *Marine Scientific Research: A Guide to the Implementation of the Relevant Provisions of the United Nations Convention on the Law of the Sea* (New York, UN, 1991), p. 1. This could indicate that these activities do not fall under the regime of Part XIII." The MSR Revised Guide states that "[t]he freedom [of scientific research] envisioned in art. 87 is not limited to marine scientific research but also extends to such activities as hydrographic surveys." UN, *Marine Scientific Research: A revised guide to the implementation of the relevant provisions of the United Nations Convention on the Law of the Sea* (New York, UN, 2010), p. 16, para. 56. Professor Soons has written: "From articles 19, 21 and 40, which use the term 'hydrographic surveying' separately from 'research', it follows that the term 'marine scientific research', for the purposes of the Draft Convention, does not cover hydrographic surveying activities." (Soons, *supra* n. 5, p. 125) Later in the same book, Professor Soons wrote: "With respect to hydrographic surveying (an activity which is not to be considered marine scientific research, although it is somewhat similar to it...), it is submitted that this activity, when it is conducted for the purpose of enhancing the safety of navigation..., must

The Convention therefore limits survey activities during passage in the territorial sea, straits used for international navigation and archipelagic sea lanes, but does not limit the activities of survey ships in the EEZ.

Like MSR, survey activities in the territorial sea are expressly subject to coastal State consent.[16]

Again, like MSR, survey activities while in transit passage or archipelagic sea lanes passage with its concomitant rights are expressly subject to prior authorization of the States bordering straits or the archipelagic State.[17]

Seaward of the territorial sea, all States remain able to conduct surveys free of coastal State regulation or control.[18]

International law, as reflected in the LOS Convention, authorizes coastal States to claim limited rights and jurisdiction in an EEZ. The jurisdictional rights relate primarily to the exploration, exploitation, and conservation of natural resources, MSR, and the marine environment. Beyond the territorial sea, all States enjoy the freedoms of navigation and overflight and other related uses of the sea within the EEZ, provided that they do so with due regard to the rights of the coastal State and other States.[19] The conduct of surveys in the EEZ is thus an exercise of the freedoms of navigation and other internationally lawful uses of the sea related to those freedoms, such as those associated with the operations of ships, which Article 58 of the LOS Convention guarantees to all States.

Military Activities, Including Military Surveys

The LOS Convention recognizes that all States have, within the EEZ, in contrast to the territorial sea, the right to conduct military activities, provided that they do so with due regard to the rights of the coastal State and other States (Article 58(3)). Appropriate activities include normal ship operations, task force maneuvering, launching and landing of aircraft, operating military devices, military exercises, intelligence collection, weapons exercises, ordnance testing, and military surveys. There is no general competence of the coastal State over military activities in the EEZ. Therefore, military activities,

---

       be regarded as an internationally lawful use of the sea associated with the operations of ships... in accordance with article 58, and can therefore be conducted freely in the exclusive economic zone...." (Soons, p. 157) The United Kingdom agrees. 68 *Brit. Y.B. Int'l L. 1997* (Oxford, 1998), p. 609.

16   LOS Convention, Arts. 19(2)(j) and 21(1)(g).
17   Id. Arts. 40 and 54.
18   Id. Arts. 56(1)(b)(ii), 78 and 87(1)(f).
19   Id. Art. 58.

including military surveys, conducted outside foreign territorial seas are not subject to coastal State regulation.[20]

Military surveys refer to activities undertaken in territorial seas, archipelagic waters, straits used for international navigation, the EEZ, high seas, and on the continental shelf involving marine data collection (whether or not classified) for military purposes (e.g., not shared with the general public). Military surveys can include oceanographic, hydrographic, marine geological, geophysical, chemical, biological, acoustic, and related data.[21]

Military surveys are not specifically addressed in the LOS Convention and there is no language stating or implying that military surveys may be regulated in any manner by coastal States outside their territorial sea or archipelagic waters. The United States therefore considers it to be fully consistent with the LOS Convention that the conduct of such surveys is a high seas freedom and the United States reserves the right to engage in military surveys anywhere outside foreign territorial seas and archipelagic waters. To provide prior notice or request permission would create an adverse precedent for restrictions on mobility and flexibility of military survey operations.

These definitions thus clearly distinguish between MSR, which the coastal State can regulate, and hydrographic survey and military survey activities, which are freedoms the coastal State cannot regulate outside its territorial sea.

A few States have questioned the activities of military survey and hydrographic vessels in their EEZs.[22] The United States has explained along the foregoing lines why such survey activities are not subject to coastal State regulation.[23]

---

20 See LOS Convention, art. 56, and Oxman, 'The Regime of Warships Under the United Nations Convention on the Law of the Sea,' 24 *Va. J. Int'l L.*, 1984, 847. *See further* Roach and Smith, *Excessive Maritime Claims, supra* n. 1, Chapter 14, section 14.2.1.

21 OPNAV Instruction 3128.9E, para. 3.d(2), *supra* n. 3 ("Military survey refers to activities undertaken in territorial seas, archipelagic waters, straits for navigation, the EEZ, high seas, and on the continental shelf involving marine data collection (whether or not classified) for military purposes (e.g., not shared with the general public). Military surveys can include oceanographic, hydrographic, marine geological, geophysical, chemical, biological, acoustic, and related data.").

22 For example, China claims the right to approve all mapping and surveying activities in "sea areas under the jurisdiction of the People's Republic of China." Surveying and Mapping Law of the People's Republic of China, Presidential Order No. 75, Aug. 29, 2002, effective Dec. 1, 2002, Art. 2, *available at* http://www.asianlii.org/cn/legis/cen/laws/samlotproc506/.

23 State Dep't telegram 092114, Apr. 8, 1994, para. 6; *Digest of United States Practice in International Law 2001* (Oxford, 2002), pp. 698–699; id. *2003* (Oxford, 2004), pp. 728, 738;

Marine Meteorological Data

It should be recalled that the Third UN Conference on the Law of the Sea decided that the collection of marine meteorological data is not marine scientific research regulated by Part XIII of the Law of the Sea Convention.

In 1979 the Eighth WMO Congress noted that the Members of the WMO engaged in operational activities, such as the collection of meteorological information from voluntary observing ships, buoys, other ocean platforms, aircraft and meteorological satellites, as well as meteorological and oceanographic research activities, considered that "adequate marine meteorological data coverage from ocean areas, in particular from those areas in the so-called 'exclusive economic zone', is indispensable for the issue of timely and accurate storm warnings for the safety of life at sea and for the protection of life and property in coastal and off-shore areas," and that SOLAS required States to issue warnings of gales, storms and tropical storms and to arrange for selected ships to take meteorological observations,[24] expressed the hope that the provisions on marine scientific research then being negotiated by the Third UN Conference on the Law of the Sea "would not result in restrictions on operational meteorological and related oceanographic observational activities carried out in accordance with international programmes such as WWW and IGOSS" and appealed to its Members to ensure that the Conference was "made aware of the vital need for observational data from sea areas for the timely issue of weather forecasts and storm warnings."[25]

On August 20, 1980, after the completion of the negotiations on the MSR articles at the Resumed Ninth Session of the Conference, the Chairman of the Third Committee announced that he was now in a position to reply to the letter from the WMO forwarding this Resolution. The Chairman stated he agreed with the content of the Resolution and that

---

id. *2007* (Oxford, 2008), pp. 647–650; id. *2009* (Oxford, 2010), pp. 468–469; Roach and Smith, *Excessive Maritime Claims, supra* n. 1, pp. 383–387. The *Digests* are *available at* http://www.state.gov/s/l/c8183.htm.

[24] SOLAS 1960, regulation V/4, 536 UNTS 325–328. The current version is SOLAS 1974, regulation V/5 (rev. 2002), *quoted in* attachment 3 to J.A. Roach, 'Marine Data Collection: Methods and Law,' M. Nordquist, T. Koh and J.N. Moore (eds.), *Freedom of the Seas, Passage Rights and the 1982 Law of the Sea Convention* (Leiden/Boston, Nijhoff, 2009), pp. 205–208.

[25] WMO Res. 16 (Cg-VIII), United Nations Conference on the Law of the Sea, March 1979, Doc. A/CONF.62/80, Aug. 9, 1979, XII *Official Records of the Third United Nations Conference on the Law of the Sea*, 1979, p. 56, *available at* http://unreaty.un.org/cod/diplomatic conferences/lawofthesea-1982/lawofthesea-1982.html (hereinafter, *Official Records*).

in his opinion, the provisions on marine scientific research would not create any difficulties and obstacles hindering adequate meteorological coverage from ocean areas, including areas within the exclusive economic zone, carried out both within the framework of existing international programs and by all vessels, since such activities had already been recognized as routine observations and data collecting which were not covered by Part XIII of the negotiating text. Furthermore, they were in the common interest of all countries and had undoubted universal significance.[26]

Chairman Yankov repeated these comments in his Report of the Third Committee to the Plenary, without objection,[27] and so wrote to the WMO on August 25, 1980.

The WMO continues to be committed to the free and unrestricted international exchange of basic meteorological data and products which are necessary for the provision of services in support of the protection of life and property and the well-being of all nations, particularly those basic data and products required to describe and forecast accurately weather and climate. Members of the WMO are obligated under Article 2 of the WMO Convention, *inter alia*, to facilitate worldwide cooperation in the establishment of observing networks.[28]

Operational Oceanography

Clearly analogous to the collection and distribution of marine meteorological data described above is the routine collection of ocean observations that are distributed freely and openly, and are used for the monitoring and forecasting of ocean state, weather (meteorology), and climate, a process known as *operational oceanography*, a term also not mentioned in the LOS Convention.

Operational oceanography is the routine collection of ocean observations, such as temperature, pressure, current, salinity and wind, in all maritime zones. It may be conducted in the oceans, at the air-sea interface, and in the atmosphere. This data is used for the monitoring and forecasting of weather (meteorology), climate, and ocean state (e.g., surface currents and waves). The

---

26 Statement of Mr. Yankov, XIV *Official Records*, p. 103, para. 5.
27 Report of the Chairman of the Third Committee, Doc. A/CONF.62/L.61, Aug. 25, 1980, para. 8, XIV *Official Records*, pp. 133–134; XIV *Official Records*, p. 15, para. 43.
28 WMO 12th Congress resolution 40 (Cg-XII) (1995), *available at* www.wmo.int/pages/about/resolution40_en.html.

data is transmitted from sensor to shore in near real time and is made available to the public in near real time.

The various operational oceanography programs and data collection instruments are described elsewhere to facilitate a better understanding why they are, for the most part, conducted in the exercise of the high sea freedoms of navigation and overflight, and are not MSR governed by Part XIII of the LOS Convention.[29] Nevertheless, some coastal States remain concerned that some or all of this data collected within their EEZs may be of direct significance for the exploration and exploitation of natural resources, whether living or non-living, within their EEZs[30] and thus wish to have some say as to the collection and use of that data.

The world's oceans exhibit wide variability on both spatial and temporal scales. While designated by basins (e.g., Atlantic, Pacific, Indian, Southern), boundaries used to delineate them are geographical and somewhat artificial as the oceans interact on global as well as regional scales. For example, changes in overturning circulations (North Atlantic, Southern Ocean) eventually will impact all of the ocean basins thereby manifesting changes regionally. Like the atmosphere, the oceans do not recognize geopolitical boundaries. Similarly, the oceans' interactions with the atmosphere often manifested through changes in weather and storm patterns are global processes, reflected regionally.

Understanding of the global ocean provides the context for understanding and predicting regional and coastal variability. The key to understanding is observations, observations of the oceans globally, regionally and locally. The operational ocean observing system allows nations to:

- monitor, understand and predict weather and climate;
- describe and forecast the state of the ocean, including living resources;
- improve management of marine and coastal ecosystems and resources;
- mitigate damage from natural hazards and pollution;
- protect life and property on coasts and at sea; and
- enable scientific research.[31]

---

29   Roach and Smith, *Excessive Maritime Claims, supra* n. 1, pp. 439–447.
30   Cf. LOS Convention, Arts. 56(1)(a) and 246(5)(a). *See* Roach and Smith, *Excessive Maritime Claims, supra* n. 1, pp. 439 & 448.
31   These six bullets are what GOOS is designed to do. *See* http://www.ioc-goos.org/index.php?option=com_content&view=article&id=12&Itemid=26&lang=en. "Enable" means observe from which hypotheses are developed and tested, not conduct scientific research.

In view of the United States, operational oceanography is not MSR.[32] The large-scale programs of oceanographic data collection, described elsewhere,[33] that operate independently from the users of the data distinguish operational oceanography from MSR. The Intergovernmental Oceanographic Commission's Advisory Body of Experts on the Law of the Sea (IOC/ABE-LOS) has considered the implications for the conduct of this form of marine data collection in the EEZ, and in 2008 the IOC Executive Council approved the "Argo Guidelines" adopted by ABE-LOS.[34]

Exploration and Exploitation
The Law of the Sea Convention contains separate regimes for exploration and exploitation of natural resources and of underwater cultural heritage.

Of Natural Resources
Exploration and exploitation of *natural resources* involves the searching for and removal of living or non-living natural resources found in the oceans or beneath the seabed. The term *"natural resources"* has four separate meanings in the law of the sea, depending on the maritime zone where they are located.[35] The natural resources governed by the EEZ regime are the living and

---

[32] Text of Senate Ex. Rep. 110–9, 2007, accompanying *supra* n. 12, p. 798 ("there are other activities, such as operational oceanography, that are also not considered marine scientific research"). F.H. Th. Wegelein, *Marine Scientific Research: The Operation and Status of Research Vessels and other Platforms in International Law* (Leiden/Boston, Nijhoff, 2005), p. 116, notes that the procedures for advance access request to a coastal State is "impracticable" and the "scientific value of their measurements would be significantly impaired if drifters had to be retrieved before they enter foreign waters and not be re-released before permission is obtained; conversely, the exact date of entry can usually not be predicted…, neither which foreign waters it may stray into."

[33] See e.g., Roach and Smith, *Excessive Maritime Claims, supra* n. 1, pp. 437–447.

[34] UNESCO doc. 'Guidelines for the implementation of resolution XX-6 of the IOC Assembly regarding the deployment of profiling floats in the high seas within the framework of the Argo Programme,' IOC EC-XLI.4 doc. IOC/EC-XLI/3/prov., annex II, pp. 7–10, *available at* http://ioc3.unesco.org/iocaribe/files/Iocaribe_X/IOC-XLI%20Adopted_Res-e.pdf. See A. Mateos and M. Gorina-Ysern, 'Climate Change and Guidelines for Argo Profiling Float Deployment on the High Seas,' 14 *ASIL Insight*, 2010, 8, *available at* http://www.asil.org/insights/volume/14/issue/8/climate-change-and-guidelines-argo-profiling-float-deployment-high-seas

[35] In *Definitions for the Law of the Sea, supra* n. 5, the term "natural resources" is generally defined as "the living organisms and nonliving matter in a given ocean area of space." Id. pp. 254. The appended comments describe the various contexts in which the term is used. Id. pp. 255–257.

non-living natural resources located within the EEZ.[36] The natural resources governed by the continental shelf regime are the mineral and other non-living resources of the seabed and subsoil, together with the living organisms belonging to sedentary species.[37] The natural resources of the deep seabed beyond the limits of national jurisdiction (the Area) are all solid, liquid or gaseous mineral resources *in situ* in the Area at or beneath the seabed, including polymetallic nodules;[38] this definition does not include living marine resources. The natural resources of the high seas regime are referred to as "the living resources of the high seas" and include fish and marine mammals.[39]

Part V of the LOS Convention regulates exploration for and exploitation of the living and non-living natural resources located within the EEZ separately from the conduct of MSR within the EEZ.[40] Part VI of the Convention governs exploration for and exploitation of the mineral and other non-living resources of the seabed and subsoil, i.e., the continental shelf, together with living organisms belonging to sedentary species.[41] Part VI does not address MSR at all.[42] Thus it follows that, even though exploration and exploitation in both maritime zones are subject to exclusive coastal State control, those activities are not MSR.[43]

Part XIII of the Convention and its Implementing Agreement regulate exploration for and exploitation of all solid, liquid or gaseous mineral resources *in situ* in the deep seabed beyond the limits of national jurisdiction at or beneath the seabed, including polymetallic nodules. Exploration and exploitation in the Area are subject to regulation by the International Seabed Authority.

---

36   LOS Convention, Art. 56(1)(a).
37   Id. Art. 77(4). Sedentary species are those organisms which, at the harvestable stage, either are immobile on or under the seabed or are unable to move except in constant contact with the seabed or subsoil. Ibid.
38   Id. Art. 133. When recovered from the Area, these resources are referred to in the Convention as "minerals".
39   Id. Part VII, section 2, Arts. 116–120.
40   *Compare* LOS Convention, Arts. 56(1)(a) & 56(1)(b)(ii).
41   Id. Art. 77.
42   MSR in the EEZ and on the continental shelf is regulated by Part XIII, Article 246 of the Convention.
43   Because they directly implicate exploration or exploitation of the natural resources of the continental shelf, Article 246(5) permits a coastal State to withhold its consent to the conduct of a MSR project on its continental shelf, *inter alia*, if (a) it is of direct significance for the exploration and exploitation of natural resources, whether living or non-living, (b) involves drilling into the continental shelf, or (c) involves the construction, operation or use of artificial islands, installations and structures.

Article 256 provides that MSR in the Area is to be conducted in conformity with Part XI, particularly Article 143. Hence, exploration and exploitation of mineral resources in the Area is not MSR.

Part VII, Section 2, governs the conservation and management of the living resources of the high seas. Article 119 refers to "scientific evidence" and "scientific information" to be used in determining the conservation measures for these resources.

Exploration for and exploitation of all forms of natural resources is therefore not MSR.

Of Underwater Cultural Heritage (UCH)

Exploration and exploitation of *underwater cultural heritage* involves the search for, recording of, and removal of items of cultural heritage, such as artifacts from shipwrecks. These items are, of course, not natural resources as that term is variously used in the LOS Convention but are man-made resources.

UCH is addressed in only two articles of the LOS Convention, Article 303 with regard to the contiguous zone, and Article 149 with regard to archaeological and historical objects found in the Area. UNESCO has developed a regulatory scheme for UCH found at sea that seeks to provide coastal States authority to regulate the search for and recovery of UCH located landward of the outer limit of a declared contiguous zone, and seaward of such a zone contrary to the allocation of rights and duties in the LOS Convention.[44]

Exploration for and exploitation of UCH is also not MSR.[45]

Summary

This chapter has demonstrated that not all methods of collection of data about the oceans is marine scientific research regulated by Part XIII of the Law of the Sea Convention. The means of data collection are often the same, and may appear indistinguishable from MSR. The data collected may be the same or different. The *parameters* collected, their *intended* use, and the detailed *controls* on foreign MSR in the EEZ distinguish MSR from surveys, operational

---

44 Convention on the Protection of Underwater Cultural Heritage, Paris, 2001. For details see Roach and Smith, *Excessive Maritime Claims, supra* n. 1, section 21.3, and http://www.unesco.org/new/en/culture/themes/underwater-cultural-heritage/2001-convention/.

45 *Accord*, Wegelein, *supra* n. 33, pp. 218–219.

oceanography, and exploration and exploitation of resources, which are dealt with in other Parts of the Law of the Sea Convention.[46]

The chapter has also demonstrated that proposals that all forms of marine data collection should be under coastal State control[47] would deprive the people of all nations of the benefits of free and open access to data that enhance safety and environmental protection.

While the lack of agreed definitions of the various methods for marine data collection has resulted in differences of views on the legal regimes governing them, this paper has sought to provide clarification and further understanding.

---

46 *See* the discussion in id. pp. 82–83 and the text following note 5 *supra*.
47 *See*, e.g., J. Xue, 'Marine Scientific Research and Hydrographic Surveys in the EEZs: Closing up the Legal Loopholes?,' *Freedom of the Seas, supra* n. 25, pp. 209–225; and S. Bateman, 'Hydrographic Surveying in the Exclusive Economic Zones—Is it Marine Scientific Research?,' id. pp. 105–131.

CHAPTER 15

Global Ocean Challenges

Stephen A. Macko

Abstract

The ocean influences nearly all activities on the planet, serving as a source of nutrition, energy and pathway for transport of resources while buffering the scale of variations in climate. It is also the portion of the planet that is perhaps in greatest need of data to address issues of the dramatic changes that are happening globally. Some of the changes are clearly the result of human inaction and lack of foresight. Fisheries, on which one sixth of human protein nutrition is derived, are in a state of near collapse for some species in the near term, owing to overfishing and mismanagement of a sustainable infrastructure. Lack of cautious application of new technologies and oversight has led to increasing levels of pollutants, sometimes catastrophically, as was evidenced in the recent Deepwater Horizon oil spill in the Gulf of Mexico. Global warming is influencing many aspects of the ocean system and will have collateral impacts beyond simply raising the temperature of the planet. Navigation and influence on transport are chief in our envisioning eventual impacts, and need to be anticipated, based on the best of models and data. Sea level rise and the associated coastal erosion, modifying waterways and ports, call for adaptive planning. Climate change could easily be seen to affect ocean circulation, wind dynamics, storm production and associated storm surges. Loss of sea ice in the Arctic will open new avenues which are economically and energetically more efficient for transport. With warming, and heightened destruction of ice sheets will likely come increased hazards from sea ice in shipping lanes. The rate of loss of the ice sheets such as that of Greenland is only beginning to be understood, and appears to be increasing. Sea ice coverage in the Arctic was the lowest on record in the summer of 2012, and the area of surface melt on the Greenland Ice Sheet was recorded at the highest, at 97%, since satellite images have documented its status. Diminishing ice cover will also influence an increase of fishing efforts and exploration for fossil fuels in the high Arctic. Without precise data on the sizes of fish stocks, the effects on commercial fisheries are complex, and beg for fundamental knowledge. Additionally, with the loss of sea ice, diminishing ice-based productivity may lead to a loss of diversity and

---

* Stephen A. Macko, Professor, Department of Environmental Sciences, University of Virginia (sam8f@virginia.edu). The author's PowerPoint is available at http://www.virginia.edu/colp/pdf/seoul-macko.pdf.

modification of sustainable trophic structure in Arctic food webs. As a consequence of increased fossil fuel exploration, extraction and transport, the risk of contamination is heightened and at present only minimal preparation for impact and cleanup exists for this eventuality in fragile Arctic environments. The addition of massive amounts of carbon dioxide to the atmosphere and oceans, has changed the ocean chemistry, increasing the acidity or lowering the pH. Sound propagation in a more acid ocean may affect navigation as well as migration patterns of marine mammals and fish. Acidification influence on calcareous organisms at primary production levels could lead to catastrophic effects on the higher organisms of the food chains. The collateral impacts of the changing ocean in a period of global warming urgently require further study in order to enable adaptation and reduce vulnerability. Only through an appreciation for the past and a comprehensive understanding of the present, can we anticipate the future. The potential for that vision of the ocean lies with the cooperation among all nations.

Introduction

The Ocean covers 70% of the Earth's surface. It plays an especially important role in buffering the temperature of the Earth, and variations in the long term climate. Some of the expected variations in changes to the ocean that present challenges to navigation and human utilization of the resources of the sea are obvious and can be directly linked to the perturbations. Warming of the planet is causing the sea to thermally expand, and sea level is rising steadily. Other collateral effects of challenges to human use of the resource are not so clear: heightened levels of plastics, with compounds that may influence endocrine system disruption and low level toxicity from increased levels of petroleum hydrocarbons resulting from exploration for oil, or accidental spills are harder to quantify at this time. Still others are highly predictable, such as a diminishing pH of the Ocean (increasing acidity) as more carbon dioxide accumulates in the atmosphere, yet the speed of their impact is not well established, but hold potential for catastrophic changes in whole ecosystems. Climatic conditions in some locations like the Arctic are changing faster than at any time in the past 10,000 years. Some of the changes influenced by rising sea levels and warming temperatures are obvious. Globally, with increases in sea levels, potentially hundreds of millions of people will be affected and displaced from their homes; coastal cities will be flooded. Whereas the Arctic has fewer people directly affected by the impacts of global change, it receives less recognition for urgency to address issues on global change. However, such recognition is critical, because the Arctic generates unique perspectives, owing to the more rapid nature and magnitude of the change that is presently occurring. Significant loss of Arctic coastal zones is already occurring as sea level rises and once permanent ice cover disappears; temperatures have already risen far more than the World average fraction of a degree (NAS, 2008).

With increases in global temperatures and loss of sea ice, certain modifications in the Arctic can be predicted along with their expected influences. Clearly, a potential exists for benefits in certain economic sectors. For example, less ice cover will certainly increase access to regions that have yet to be explored for hydrocarbons or other minerals. Once ownership in offshore regions is delineated, exploitation of these resources will occur. Lessening of sea ice will also allow increased avenues for maritime transport between the Atlantic and Pacific through the Northwest Passage saving time and expense for international trade, although many issues involved with such passage presently remain to be resolved. Additionally, with increases in open water, the prospects for economic gain through enhanced tourism are clear. Other impacts involving the Ocean ecosystem itself and the scope of feedbacks of change in one location to the global environment need to be delineated. The Polar regions are especially vulnerable and understudied, owing to the great effort, expense and difficulty of obtaining a sufficient data set on any process or problems in this location. The impacts of global change on coastal mammals, birds and fish populations are far from understood. Some of the expected climatic changes clearly indicate a potential for significant negative effects, especially on animal populations already threatened by natural or human modifications of the environment.

Global Warming, Rising Sea Level and the Changing Ice Cover of the Polar Regions

The effects of global warming and climate change are of concern both for the environment and human life. Evidence of observed climate change includes the instrumental temperature record, rising sea levels, and decreased snow cover in the Northern Hemisphere. According to the IPCC Fifth Assessment Report (IPCC, 2013), most "of the observed increase in global average temperatures since the mid-20th century is *very likely* due to the observed increase in human greenhouse gas concentrations." Even if this is not the case, with much of the increase being natural instead, warming in the Arctic remains an issue that must be addressed owing to associated global implications. It is estimated that future climate changes will include further increased global temperatures, sea level rise, and a probable increase in the frequency of some extreme weather events. Ecosystems are seen as being particularly vulnerable

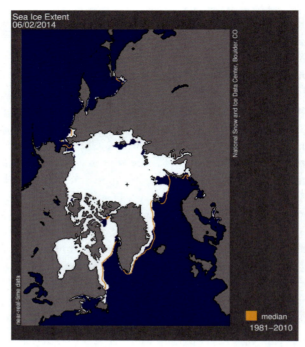

FIGURE 1A Arctic sea ice extent in the spring of 2014 was 12.78 million square kilometers. The line shows the 1981 to 2010 median coverage.

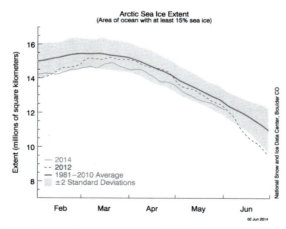

FIGURE 1B The sea ice variation over the year with 2012 showing the record minimum during late summer. Broad shaded area and dark line is the 30 year average with 2 standard deviation range. Images courtesy of the National Snow and Ice Data Center, University of Colorado, Boulder.

to climate change. With diminishing snow and ice cover, the albedo of the Arctic diminishes, and accelerates the impact of solar radiation, which goes into warming rather than being removed through reflection or evaporation. Warming is accelerated in the surface lands and waters which also accelerates the loss of sea ice cover. Sea ice cover in 2012 was the lowest on record at less than half of the typical minimum 6 to 7 million square kilometers to nearly 3.5 million square kilometers (Pew Charitable Trusts, 2013).

Under climate warming scenarios, the extent of current ice cover is expected to diminish further. Warming will continue even with conservation efforts and attempts to reduce or capture green house gases. On the timescales for present change, most human systems will have to adapt to future impacts of climate change. Changes seen in locations like the Arctic today are not unprecedented in Earth history, nor are they outside the natural variability on long timescales (million of years). The present rate of this change is, however, unprecedented and may in fact preclude natural environments from keeping pace with the change. In a worst case scenario, some locations may be faced with erasure of many ecosystems and a significant extinction of species.

Over the last hundred years or so, the instrumental temperature record has shown a trend in the climate for an increased global mean temperature. Other observed changes include Arctic ice cover shrinkage, Arctic methane release from permafrost regions and coastal sediments, and sea level rise. Global average temperature is predicted to increase over this century. The rise in temperatures of the Arctic will be greater than the global average, perhaps increasing 7–8°C. Sea level is expected to rise at least 18 to 59 cm by the end of the 21st century. Owing to a lack of full scientific understanding, this estimate does not include all contributions from the melting of glaciers and ice sheets. For a global warming of 1–4°C over the next 50 to 100 years, there is a moderate chance that partial deglaciation of the Greenland and West Antarctic ice sheets would occur with an eventual rise in sea level by 4–6 meters or more. For the first time in thousands of years, in the summer of 2012, the surface of Greenland was essentially covered by meltwater.

Increased meltwater, along with decreasing glacier ice will have potential to have great impact first by increasing the numbers of icebergs (already observed) generated by the ice sheets thereby influencing navigation in the most heavily utilized shipping lanes of the World in the North Atlantic. Second, increased meltwater from these icebergs has the potential to disrupt surface currents like the Gulf Stream. Currents dissipate perhaps about 50% of excess heat in equatorial regions to the poles. That heat, carried to the poles by currents, helps moderate the climate of land masses on the eastern side of ocean basins (the west coast of the US and Canada; Europe). Disruption of surface

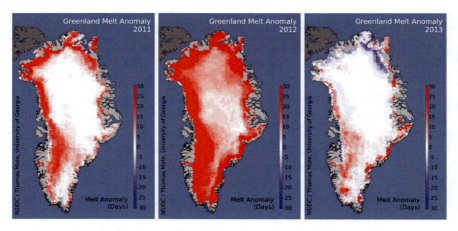

FIGURE 2 *Greenland melt anomalies which are the number of melt days in each year compared to an average as recorded by satellite observations from 1981 to 2010. The year 2012 set a record for melt extent, while 2011 showed some strong melt anomalies and 2013 melt days were more typical of the average. Image courtesy of Thomas Mote, University of Georgia, and the National Snow and Ice Data Center, University of Colorado, Boulder.*

currents and deepwater currents by thick lenses of fresher waters could even influence the formation of storms, perhaps causing increases in frequency and strength.

Loss of Coastal Zones and Decomposition of Methane Hydrates

Gas hydrates are naturally-occurring ice-like crystals that form at high pressure and low temperature in marine sediments at water depths greater than 300m whenever there is sufficient methane and pore water. Gas hydrates are now known to be widespread around the world and are often underlain by potentially vast fields of free gas. Together the gas hydrate and underlying free gas reservoirs comprise perhaps one third of the Earth's stores of fossil organic carbon. In the Arctic, gas hydrate is widespread, trapped within marine sediments and permafrost. The polar regions of the Earth being highly sensitive to the effects of global change, and climatic warming in particular, could cause widespread dissociation of gas hydrate and subsequent release of methane, a greenhouse gas, into the atmosphere.

Globally, clathrates have been found to occur naturally in large quantities (Kvenvolden 1995). Around 2500 gigatons (GT) of carbon in the form of methane lies trapped in deposits in the ocean. The Arctic alone is estimated to have greater than 400GT. Such deposits are commonly found on the continental shelf, and likely exist in large reservoirs on the Arctic Ocean continental shelf. Clathrates can also exist as permafrost, as at the Mallik gas hydrate field in the Mackenzie Delta of the northwestern Canadian Arctic. These natural gas hydrates are seen as a potentially vast energy resource, but an economical extraction method has so far proven elusive. At the present time, however, knowledge about the distribution and stability of Arctic gas hydrates is sparse. Methane is a significant greenhouse gas and is many times more effective than carbon dioxide in causing climate warming, despite its short half-life of approximately seven years in the atmosphere. Methane has a global warming potential perhaps 20 times that of carbon dioxide (IPCC, 2013). Methane bound in hydrates amounts to approximately 3,000 times the volume of methane in the atmosphere. There is only emerging information regarding the processes that affect the stability of hydrates in sediments or peat, and the possible release of that methane into the atmosphere. Methane would be released from gas hydrates in Arctic sediments as they become warmer during a sea-level rise and would contribute to the greenhouse gas budget. Atmospheric concentrations of methane are currently increasing at rates of about one percent per year, leading to a concern that methane will become an increasingly significant factor in global warming. Gas hydrates are stable only within a limited range of temperatures and pressures; outside these ranges, the structure breaks down and the gas molecules escape. The size of the oceanic methane clathrate reservoir is poorly known, and estimates of its size decreased since it was recognized that great abundances of clathrates could exist in the oceans during the late 1900s. The highest estimates were based on the assumption clathrates could exist over the entire floor of the deep ocean (Buffet and Archer, 2004). However, improvements in the understanding of clathrate chemistry and sedimentology have revealed that hydrates only form in a narrow range of depths on continental shelves and only at some locations. In the range of depths where they could occur they typically are found at low concentrations. This current estimate, corresponding up to 2500GT of carbon is smaller than the 5000GT of carbon estimated for all other fossil fuel reserves but substantially larger than the slightly more than 200GT of carbon estimated for other natural gas resources. The permafrost reservoir estimate at about 700GT of carbon is in fact an under representation of the hydrate carbon of the Arctic, since additional hydrate is stored offshore on the shelf. As a side note, such estimates have not been made of possible Antarctic reservoirs. For comparison the total carbon in the atmosphere is around 6000GT of carbon.

    The Arctic is particularly rich with gas hydrates because conditions for their occurrence are found in the offshore sediments of the continental shelf margin having water depths between 500 meters and 3000 meters in a zone of hydrate stability as well as onshore in areas of continuous permafrost or near shore on the shallow continental shelf in relict permafrost from times of lower sea levels. Changes in pressure and temperature modify the physical nature of these environments and the gas hydrates destabilize to become sources of water column or atmospheric methane. Recent research carried out in 2008 in the East Siberian Arctic Shelf has shown millions of tons of methane already being released to the water column with concentrations in some regions reaching up to 100 times above normal (Shakhova et al. 2008). A region better studied for methane releases from sediments, Svalbard Island, is a location with large amounts of gas sequestered in the coastal sediments; a one degree Centigrade increase in those waters has been suggested to be sufficient to increase methane releases to the water column by 20MT per year. Much of the Arctic remains unsurveyed for methane deposits but the impact of even a small temperature increase on likely methane-rich coasts and sea beds across the entire Arctic could result in enormous quantities of methane being released to the water column and eventually to the atmosphere. There would be potential for global feedbacks and forcings which may dramatically influence climate change by methane that would be far greater than the suggested impact of carbon dioxide. A release of large amounts of natural gas from methane clathrate deposits has been hypothesized as a cause of past and possibly future climate changes. Events thought to be possibly linked to large methane releases are the Permian-Triassic extinction event and the Paleocene-Eocene Thermal Maximum (PETM). The PETM is sometimes seen to be a geological equivalent of the present rise in carbon dioxide in the atmosphere and associated effects, some of which are addressed in this chapter.

Ecosystem Change, Habitat Loss, Fisheries and Diminishing Species Diversity

Climate change will likely result in reduced diversity of ecosystems and the extinction of many species. Adaptation potential for many natural biological ecosystems is estimated to be lower than that for human systems. With the diminishment of Arctic sea ice, which could disappear during summer months within 70 years, ice dependent animals will be affected. Some marine mammals such as polar bears that require the ice cover for hunting or some fish species that depend on ice for laying eggs or nurseries will be threatened The Western Arctic Ocean is a unique part of the World's Oceans, and is an area undergoing significant climate changes. The effects and possible climate feedbacks of these changes are not yet fully understood. Decreased sea ice cover could lead to increased productivity in the water column, or a reduction in total productivity through the loss of sea ice algal contributions. Climate change could also alter the patterns of terrestrial inputs from rivers and coastal erosion.

Primary production by algae under coastal ice diminishes as ice cover moves to deeper waters or falls off too early for nutrition by herbivores. Massive sea ice algal production supports the coastal community of the benthic environment. Diminished sea ice suggests significant loss of this production to coastal food webs. Perhaps 25% of Arctic primary production is associated with ice (Gradinger, 2009).

Global warming is expected to result in an acceleration of current rates of sea level rise, inundating many low-lying coastal and intertidal areas. This could have important implications for organisms that depend on these sites, including migratory shorebirds that rely on them for feeding habitat during their migrations and in winter. At present, hundreds of species of shorebirds, involving millions of birds, use the Arctic coastal zone for breeding. If one assumes a global warming of 2°C influencing sea level, over the next half century major coastal habitat loss will likely occur in these oversummering areas of the Arctic which serve as nesting and nursery areas. Receding sea ice along with potential earlier migration of coastal fisheries would add nutritional stress. Many of these already declining or threatened migratory populations will face severe consequences with further modification or loss of their Arctic habitat.

Total landings from global fisheries have remained nearly constant since about 1990 with the only significant increase to World Fishery production being from aquaculture/mariculture. In 2013, in fact, the total aquaculture production was approximately the same as that derived from wild capture of fish. The overall decline in essentially all of the major fisheries is generally attributed to mismanagement and overfishing (Myers and Worm 2003; Myers et al. 2007). With much of the Arctic now ice free seasonally, a new fishery zone is now becoming available. In the absence of consequential data on the sizes of stocks in the Arctic, in 2009 the North Pacific Fishery Management Council (NPFMC) voted to ban commercial fishing within the territorial/EEZ limits (3 to 200 nautical miles) of the U.S, north of the Alaskan coast. This area is 100% open water during the summer. Within the maritime boundary of Russia (78% ice free), Canada (30% ice free) and Norway (22% ice free) are large areas that are also open to fisheries, and regulated by those nations, although with similar lack of consequential stock assessments. Of great importance however is the ice free and potentially future ice free zones beyond the UNCLOS

370 kilometer Exclusive Economic Zone (EEZ) territorial limits of the five nations bordering the Arctic Ocean.

This region, approximately 2.8 million square kilometers, is especially attractive for fisheries, albeit essentially unregulated. For nations that normally go to Antarctica for fish capture, this zone would save perhaps 10,000 kilometers of transit, to utilize this newly opened ice free zone that previously was guarded by the extensive ice cover. This area is effectively a "donut hole" for fisheries management. Fish are likely there in abundances sufficient to maintain stocks of ringed seals, polar bears, and beluga whales. A cautious approach is clearly required. A similar overexploitation of a "donut hole" as discussed below has already occurred with devastating results.

In the 1980s, fishing fleets converged on the international waters in the central Bering Sea to catch pollock. These fleets, originating from many countries, including China, Japan. Poland, and South Korea, overfished this area to a level that the pollock stocks have never recovered. A clear lack of scientific assessment along with the fact that the territory was outside of the UNCLOS sovereign rights limits and regulations were the cornerstones for this collapse. The two nations bordering the zone, the United States and Russia succeeded in an international response, although too late for significant impact on the pollock of the "donut hole" with the Central Bering Sea Pollock Agreement, the agreement was signed by the China, Japan, the United States, Russia, South Korea, and Poland, closing the area until recovery. Notably, this area remains closed today.

Could such an overexploitation of the Arctic "donut hole" happen today? Absolutely. An international fisheries agreement for these waters of the Central Arctic Ocean is needed before fishing is allowed to start. In April, 2013, the five nations bordering the Central Arctic "donut hole" and international waters agreed in principle that with significant melting of the Arctic ice each summer, an understanding focused minimally at regulating commercial fishing and management (note this is not conservation) in the zone was warranted. Also note this is not a formal agreement binding on all, with enforcement like the Central Bering Sea Agreement.

The "Other Carbon Dioxide Problem": Ocean Acidification Arising from Increased Carbon Dioxide Emissions

Carbon dioxide levels in the atmosphere have now reached 400ppm. These levels are a direct consequence of the increased levels of carbon dioxide

GLOBAL OCEAN CHALLENGES 313

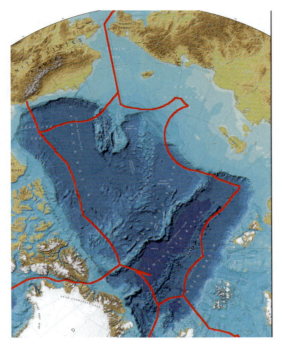

FIGURE 3A *Exclusive Economic Zone limits for Arctic Ocean, emphasizing the "donut hole" beyond the EEZ.*

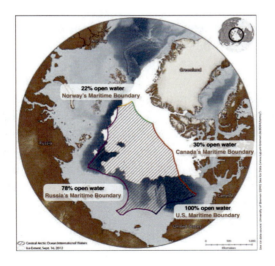

FIGURE 3B *EEZ overlap of ice, ice-free and shallower water regions available for fisheries. Image courtesy of the Pew Ocean Science Division of the Pew Charitable Trusts. URL: www. PewEnvironment.org/research-programs.*

emissions by human activities including the burning of fossil fuels. With the increased atmospheric concentration of carbon dioxide have come increased levels of dissolved carbon dioxide in the ocean as marine waters scavenge the gas out of the atmosphere thus increasing the amount dissolved in the ocean (Caldeira and Wickett, 2003). Over the past 100 years, the oceans have absorbed about one third of the carbon dioxide emitted by anthropogenic sources. This scavenging of the gaseous carbon dioxide can have great and predictable responses in the ocean water chemistry, affecting carbonate ion concentrations, calcite and aragonite mineral saturation levels and eventually influencing the pH of the ocean water. The ocean carbon cycle involves two forms of carbon: organic carbon and the inorganic carbon. The inorganic carbon cycle is particularly relevant when discussing ocean acidification for it includes the many forms of dissolved CO_2. When CO_2 dissolves, it reacts with water to form ions from the dissolved carbon dioxide: carbonic acid (H_2CO_3), bicarbonate (HCO_3^-) and carbonate (CO_3^{2-}). The relative abundance of these species depends on factors such as seawater temperature and alkalinity (Tyrrell, 2008).

Although the natural absorption of CO_2 by the World's oceans has helped mitigate the atmospheric climatic effects of anthropogenic emissions of CO_2, it is believed that increased levels in the ocean have caused a decrease in pH of approximately 0.15 units on the pH scale (Doney, 2006), or a 30% increase in acidity since this scale is logarithmic. This increase will likely have negative consequences, primarily for oceanic calcifying organisms. These span the food chain from autotrophs to heterotrophs and include organisms such as coccolithophores, corals, foraminifera, echinoderms, crustaceans and molluscs. The "skeletons" of these organisms are composed of calcite and aragonite (mineral forms of calcium carbonate) and are stable in surface waters since the carbonate ion is at supersaturating concentrations. However, as ocean pH falls further, so does the concentration of this ion, and when carbonate becomes undersaturated, structures made of calcium carbonate are vulnerable to dissolution (Feely et al. 2004). The ocean is approaching pH levels not seen in millions of years. Increasing ocean acidity will affect a vast majority of marine life (either directly or indirectly), but some of the first to feel the effects are shellfish, such as oysters. The slightest decrease of 0.1 units of pH has adverse repercussions on calcifiers. Acidification results in the water becoming unstable for calcium carbonate minerals that shellfish produce to make their shells. Without their protective shells, oysters are vulnerable and simply cannot live. Although the corrosion of their defensive shell seems enough to rapidly increase their death rate, the devastation of oysters from acidification goes even further (Waldbusser et al. 2010).

An important aspect of this "other carbon dioxide problem" is that, unlike models of climatic warming which are based on complex models of many forcings and feedbacks, heightened acidity, or lower pH of the ocean, is fairly predictable. The mechanisms for increasing acidity are well-established, physical chemical processes: increasing of carbon dioxide in the atmosphere will increase the amount dissolved in the ocean. The pH of the ocean is dependent on the amount of the dissolved CO_2. The "unknowns" are simply the levels that atmospheric carbon dioxide will reach, and the rate at which the surface ocean attains equilibrium with that level. As fossil fuels continue to contribute carbon dioxide to the atmosphere, the pH of the ocean will continue to decline.

Most studies have found that coccolithophores, a type of planktonic algae, coralline algae, corals, shellfish, foraminifera, and pteropods all experience reduced calcification or increased dissolution under lower pH or elevated CO_2 (Raven et al. 2005). However, a few studies have suggested that with ocean acidification, the direction of the response, enhanced or declining, varies between species. While the full ecological consequences of these changes in calcification are still uncertain, it appears likely that many calcifying species will be adversely affected. Lower pH also appears to negatively impact non-calcifying larvae during planktonic stages, affecting hardening of chitin and resulting in increased mortality.

Aside from calcification stress, organisms may suffer other adverse effects, either directly as reproductive or physiological effects, including CO_2-induced acidification of body fluids, or indirectly through negative impacts on food resources. With diminished calcifying planktonic organisms, the entire food resource may be disrupted, with a cascading effect up the food chain, should no other primary food source be readily available (Kleypas et al. 2006). A change in any part of the food web may have consequences on the rest of the food web, ocean biogeochemistry and the whole ecosystem. Such a modification has already been observed in the Antarctic: in the Southern Ocean GLOBEC study with diminishing krill, predators of krill have turned to alternate foods, with associated potential loss of energy from longer food chains or foods not supplying appropriate levels of essential biochemical nutrients. These more acidic conditions would hinder growth of calcium carbonate shells and skeletons by many other marine plants and animals.

Ocean acidification may also force some organisms to reallocate metabolic energy away from feeding and reproduction in order to maintain internal cell pH. It has even been suggested that ocean acidification will alter the acoustic properties of seawater, allowing sound to propagate farther, increasing ocean noise and impacting animals that use sound for echolocation or communication.

However, as with calcification, as yet there is not a full understanding of these processes in marine organisms or ecosystems. Leaving aside direct biological effects, it is expected that ocean acidification in the future will lead to a significant decrease in the burial of carbonate sediments for several centuries, and even the dissolution of existing carbonate sediments (Ridgewell et al. 2007; Turley, 2008). Inclusion of biological effects suggests that the ecosystem we know as the World's ocean, an environment that provides one sixth of the protein consumed by human, is dramatically changing. Millions of species of marine organisms will be affected directly by acidity, others by modification of the food chains on which they depend. At the extreme, large numbers of those species could be lost.

Ocean acidification has been seen to destroy ecosystems for marine life and the detrimental impacts are evident when looking at oysters; however, it is still not clear how capable other carbonate organisms will be in responding to the heightened acidity. Some organisms may have a higher resilience against a drop in pH, and therefore may still thrive at least for a while. A coral reef in the Western Pacific suggests that some calcifiers may be able to adapt. On Palau in the Western Pacific there exists high acidification, low aragonite saturation and yet from all appearances, a stable coral reef.

Despite low pH, carbonate, and aragonite, coral reefs at Palau show high coral calcification, diversity, and cover. Calcification in different areas of this reef are shown to be comparable to reefs with both high and low calcification rates, demonstrating that even under the stress induced by these conditions, calcification can occur for at least one of the reef building species (Shamberger et al. 2014).

Similar studies on the resilience of other reefs around the globe are also being conducted, including studies in the Eastern Tropical Pacific, Hawaii and near volcanic vents. Studies in Eastern Tropical Pacific reefs confirmed a general consensus that there would be reduced resilience of coral reefs in response to increasing carbon dioxide concentration. The Eastern Tropical Pacific reefs are in zones of upwelling with high CO_2 and nutrient concentrations. However, research found that there was an abnormally low saturation of carbonate in this ecosystem, and as a result, these reefs would be more susceptible to bio-erosion (Manzello et al. 2008).

A further consequence of ocean acidification will be an impact on humans through declining fish harvests resulting in diminishing captures for nutrition and also lower revenues from those captures of shellfish or finfish as well as associated habitat loss including that which results in ecotourism benefits in areas like coral reefs. A study of US commercial fisheries (Cooley and Doney, 2009) attempted to constrain the economic effects of ocean acidification using anticipated increases in atmospheric carbon dioxide. The annual domestic commercial harvest of molluscs alone could ultimately be impacted sufficiently to lower revenues by billions of dollars.

Assessment and Cooperation

As the Ocean warms, and is exposed to increasing modifications of ocean chemistry, a need for cooperation and better information has arisen unlike any since the beginning of human exploration and exploitation (Berkman and Young, 2009). Coastal erosion caused by sea level rise and warming is leading to significant sea level rise and to loss of ice cover and habitat. Erosion of peat filled coasts, along with their warming, and that of coastal waters is leading to the release of methane from gas hydrates either found on the seabed, or stored in the coastal permafrost. Diminishing ice-based productivity may lead to a loss of diversity and modification of sustainable trophic structure and food webs in shallow water coastal pelagic and benthic zones. Without precise data on the sizes of fish stocks, the effects on commercial fisheries are less obvious, more complex, and lacking fundamental knowledge. As a consequence of increased fossil fuel combustion and the addition of massive amounts of carbon dioxide to the atmosphere and oceans, changes to the ocean chemistry itself, in the acidity or pH, are occurring that will impact the calcareous organisms at primary production levels, and could lead to catastrophic effects on the higher organisms of the food chains. The collateral impacts of the addition of fossil fuel carbon dioxide to the atmosphere on fisheries desperately need further study. The Arctic is a detached portion of that Ocean, an area bounded by five "rim" states, with strong scientific and economic interests from a number of states outside the rim. The potential for a seasonally ice free Arctic in the near future dramatically calls for international efforts to understand the impact of the expected changes on the ecosystem, and a need to establish polar codes for, among other topics, navigation, investigative science, resources and fisheries management and shipping. The Antarctic Treaty is such a code. The initial Arctic Climate Impact Assessment (ACIA, 2004), recently expanded by the NPFMC banning commercial fisheries in one portion o the Arctic Ocean, are the beginnings of such an international program. Together, these place the emphasis on the evaluation of the present state of knowledge of climate variability and global warming in the Arctic. An extension to include effects on the Arctic region ecosystems by all interested parties is now required. The need for new and better knowledge is clear.

In the Southern Ocean, Antarctica represents a similar dilemma with multinational interests, yet Antarctica is distinct from the Arctic due to the lack of clearly defined "rim" states. Efforts are needed to gain knowledge on an international basis to understand how global change will affect the abundance, diversity and productivity of marine populations, through a better appreciation for the structure of a complex ecosystem. While strong parallels exist between the food webs of the Antarctic and the Arctic, major distinctions may make the Arctic more challenging. The potential for that vision of the Arctic lies with the cooperation among the nations of the Arctic Ocean. For the Ocean in general, and especially in polar areas, however, the goals are similar: understanding the perturbations of global change and how it affects all of the components of the ecosystem. The scientific knowledge base on which predictions of the expected changes from modification of climate, ocean chemistry and ecosystem population rely is too limited to do otherwise. This is a time of unprecedented change globally. This is also a time of unprecedented opportunity for international environmental cooperation in order to evaluate an ocean in transition. Only through an appreciation for the past and an understanding of the present, can we anticipate the future.

References

Bailey, K.M. (2011). An empty donut hole: the great collapse of a North American fishery. Ecology and Society 16: 28.

Berkman, P.A. and Young, O.R. (2009). Governance and environmental change in the Arctic Ocean. Science 324: 339–340.

Boetius, A. and the RV Polarstern ARK27-3 Shipboard Party (2013). Export of Algal Biomass from Melting Arctic Sea Ice. Science 339: 1430–1432.

Buffett, B. and Archer, D. (2004). Global inventory of methane clathrate: sensitivity to changes in the deep ocean. Earth Planet. Sci. Lett. 227: 185–199.

Caldeira, K.and Wickett, M.E. (2003). Anthropogenic carbon and ocean pH. Nature 425 (6956): 365–365.

Cooley, S.R. and S. Doney (2009). Anticipating ocean acidification's economic consequences for commercial fisheries. Environmental Research Letters 4 DOI 10.1088/1748-9326/4/2/024007/

Doney, S.C. (2006). The dangers of ocean acidification. Scientific American 294: 58–65.

Feely, R.A., Sabine, C.L., Lee, K., Berelson, W.L., Kleypas, J., Fabry, Victoria J., and Millero, F.J. (2004). Impact of anthropogenic CO_2 on the $CaCO_3$ system in the oceans, Science 305 (5682): 362–366.

Future Ocean. World Ocean Review 1 (2013). Living with the Ocean Mare, gGmbH.144p.

Future Ocean. World Ocean Review 2 (2013). The Future of Fish- the Fisheries of the Future. Mare, gGmbH.144p.

Gradinger, R. (2009). Sea-ice algae: Major contributors to primary production and algal biomass in the Chukchi and Beaufort Seas during May/June 2002. Deep-Sea Research II 56: 1201–1212.

Intergovernmental Panel on Climate Change (2013). Fifth Assessment Report: Climate Change. Cambridge University Press, Cambridge, United Kingdom and New York, NY, USA.

Kleypas, J.A., Feely, R.A., Fabry, V.J., Langdon, C., Sabine, C.L. and Robbins, L.L (2006). Impacts of ocean acidification on coral reefs and other marine calcifiers: A guide for future research. Report of a workshop held 18–20 April 2005, St. Petersburg, FL, sponsored by NSF, NOAA, and the U.S. Geological Survey, 88 pp.

Manzello, D.P., J.A. Kleypas, D.A. Budd, C.M. Eakin, P.W. Glynn and C. Langdon (2008). Poorly cemented coral reefs of the eastern tropical Pacific: Possible insights into reef development in a high-CO_2 world, Proc. Natl. Acad. Sci. U.S.A., 105: 450–510.

Myers R.A., Baum, J.K., Shepherd, T.D., Powers, S.P., Peterson C.H. (2007). Cascading effects of the loss of apex predatory sharks from a coastal ocean. Science 315: 1846–1850.

Myers R.A., Worm, B. (2003). Rapid worldwide depletion of predatory fish communities. Nature 423: 280–283.

National Academy of Sciences (2008a). The ecological impacts of climate change. NAS, Washington, DC, 28 pp.

——— (2008b). Understanding climate change. Washington, DC, 26 p.

Pew Charitable Trusts (2013a). The International Waters of the Central Arctic Ocean: Life in an Emerging Ocean.

——— (2013b). The International Waters of the Central Arctic Ocean: Protecting Fisheries in an Emerging Ocean.

PIANC (2013). Waterborne transport, ports and waterways: A review of climate change drivers, impacts, responses and mitigation.

Raven, J.A. et al. (2005). Ocean acidification due to increasing atmospheric carbon dioxide. Royal Society, London, UK. The Clyvedon Press Ltd.

Ridgwell, A., Zondervan, I., Hargreaves, J.C., Bijma, J. and Lenton, T.M. (2007). Assessing the potential long-term increase of oceanic fossil fuel CO_2 uptake due to CO_2-calcification feedback. Biogeosciences 4: 481–492.

Shakhova, N., I. Semiletov, A. Salyuk and D. Kosmach (2008). Anomalies of methane in the atmosphere over the East Siberian shelf: Is there any sign of methane leakage from shallow shelf hydrates? EGU General Assembly 2008, Geophysical Research Abstracts, 10, EGU2008-A-01526

Schubert, R., H.J. Schellnhuber, N. Buchmann, R. Griebhammer, M. Kulessa, D. Messner, S. Rahmstorf and J. Schmid (2006). The future Oceans—Warming up, rising high, turning sour. German Advisory Council on Global Change. 110 pp.

Turley, C. (2008). Impacts of changing ocean chemistry in a high-CO_2 world. Mineralogical Magazine 72(1): 359–362.

Tyrrell, T. (2008). Calcium carbonate cycling in future oceans and its influence on future climates. J. Plankton Res. 30: 141–156.

Waldbusser, G.G., H. Bergschneider, R. Newell, E.P. Voigt and M.A. Green (2010). Biocalcification in the Eastern Oyster (*Crassostrea virginica*) in relation to long-term trends in Chesapeake Bay pH.

Printed in the United States
By Bookmasters